AMERICAN
GOVERNMENT

AMERICAN GOVERNMENT
POLICY AND PROCESS

THIRD EDITION

ROBERT L. MORLAN
University of Redlands

Houghton Mifflin Company
BOSTON
Dallas   Geneva, Illinois   Hopewell, New Jersey
Palo Alto   London

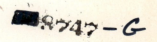

Library of Congress Catalog Card Number: 78-69574
ISBN: 0-395-26631-9

Cover art   Edith Allard

CONTENTS

5

6

7

THE MODERN PRESIDENCY   *176*

8

ADMINISTRATIVE POLITICS: THE
MANAGEMENT OF MONEY AND
PEOPLE   *217*

11

THE NATIONAL GOVERNMENT AND DOMESTIC POLICY   310

12

THE NATIONAL GOVERNMENT AND INTERNATIONAL POLICY   366

13

PREFACE

The study of politics and government has always held a special fascination. It is as alive as today's headlines, and it deals with the issues that dominate our lives. Both politics and its investigation thrive in an atmosphere of controversy. This is a book concerned with the realities of the political and governmental process in the United States: the way in which that process actually works in practice, its strengths and shortcomings, the needs and possibilities for change and reform, and the significant issues of public policy, both domestic and international. The book's aim is to convey to the reader a meaningful *understanding* of political processes and policies, rather than to provide a mere nodding acquaintance with them or a tedious compilation of facts and data.

The excellent reception accorded the first two editions has led to the preparation of this thoroughly revised third edition, a revision made quite extensive by the almost incredibly rapid pace of political events and change in America in recent years. Many of those events not only were dramatic but carried vast significance for the future of the entire political system. While a considerable amount of new material appears in every chapter, particular emphasis has been focused on such topics as the initiatives and problems of the Carter administration, congressional reform, trends in party affiliation and in campaigns, critical public policy dilemmas like the energy-environment issue, new directions in the protection of civil liberties, and the question of whether the nation has become overdependent on the courts for attempted solutions to social problems. The addition of six new case studies is designed to contribute to a more realistic feel for politics and the complexities of public decision making.

In this book I have sought to write a very readable and relatively concise treatment of the subject, yet one that offers a sound coverage of those aspects of American government and politics of which the well-informed citizen should have some knowledge. This study is contemporary and in no sense avoids the divisive issues of the present day. On the contrary, it places primary emphasis on those matters about which crucial decisions must be made, whether the problem be the energy crisis, the future of the political parties, or the search for peace. For the sake of readability, technical jargon has been avoided. Although I have shunned any partisan slant, my concern for values and social responsibility is undoubtedly evident throughout the book.

Authors are always indebted to a host of colleagues who have in some way contributed to their understanding of the subject, and naming them is a manifest impossibility. My special thanks are expressed to Richard L. Wilson (University of Tennessee at Chattanooga) and Dale Krane (Mississippi State University), who read the manuscript and provided many helpful suggestions. Responsibility for the accuracy of both fact and interpretation rests, of course, with me alone.

                                                          R.L.M.

AMERICAN GOVERNMENT

means better and that technological progress inevitably improves life were knocked to a shambles by belated recognition of the magnitude of the environmental crisis. The authority of virtually all institutions that help glue together a diverse society—not government alone but church, school, and family—was battered.

For some people this situation justified an ever increasing alienation from the political process. They lost faith in its ability to achieve social goals and serve the common good, although these had long been fundamental assumptions of twentieth-century liberalism. To some extent this was the result of an unrealistic belief in politics as some sort of panacea rather than as an instrument of human beings. But there was no shortage of grounds for disillusionment. Seemingly limitless amounts of money were expended for war and war-related activities while crucial social ills in the most affluent society the world has known were dealt with half-heartedly: environmental pollution, poverty, unequal educational opportunity, race and sex discrimination, crime, inadequate health care, unemployment, inequitable tax structures. Alienation was complicated further by increased awareness of the power of special interest groups, of high officials not completely honest with the public and press, of elaborate professional image building as a substitute for campaigning on public issues, of talk about morality, law, and order among officeholders engaged in illegal acts on the assumption that they were above the law, of a weakened concern of the government and the public for personal freedoms.

Extremists leaped to the simplistic conclusion that everything was bad and America always wrong, as irrational an attitude as the one that America was always right, common in an earlier era. But most critics were concerned for the apparent gap between what they believed America could and should be and what it was, between America's ideals and traditions and its present performance. The dilemma was evident abroad, too. In the later stages of the Vietnam War, or when the nature of United States involvement in Chile was revealed, friends of America throughout the world were confused by the seeming discrepancy between actions and the political ideals that had long been a beacon of hope to other people. The poignant question encountered daily by Americans in other countries was: This is not the America we have known—how can these things be?

The appropriate questions now are: Has America in reality been cut loose from its moorings and set adrift from its ideals and traditions? Have Americans become the new Huns, as some have charged? There is obviously vast disagreement on the answers to such questions, but all agree on the magnitude of the problems. Who is responsible, and what are the solutions? The customary course is to blame government as though it were some remote entity and to sink into a mild stupor before the television set. But democratic government cannot be separated from the people. They are its source and reason for existence. Even so, a great percentage of Americans, economically well-off beyond the wildest dreams of their ancestors, recognize the troubles that exist yet are notably fearful of rocking the boat. "The American people," James Reston has commented, "seem to have become largely incapable of rousing themselves out of their debilitating self-satisfaction. The result is a paralysis of the spirit, entirely uncharacteristic of Americans during the previous stages of their history." If there is hope for resuscitation, it will require recollection of what the American spirit of activist optimism has accomplished and can accomplish, when motivated by worthy shared ideals. John Gardner suggests that "we shall not get through our troubles safely until a considerable number of Americans acknowledge that they themselves are part of the process by which the society will be made whole."

Despite the rending of the fabric of American society in recent years, there still exist a broad remnant of fundamental ideals and a very considerable seam of good will. Moveover, in the governmental crisis brought on by Watergate, with investigations conducted by Congress and the special prosecutor, court decisions, impeachment proceedings, and a presidential resignation unprecedented in history, it was evident that the nation's political system did indeed work, that the rule of law remained pre-eminent, and that the transition of power could occur in a peaceful and orderly fashion even under such circumstances. In addition, there is evidence that Americans *are* bestirring themselves and moving to cope with national problems. The crisis gave impetus to reform, and serious efforts to correct many of the aforementioned shortcomings, in such areas as congressional ethics and procedures, campaign finance, and environmental pollution control, have shown significant accomplishments.

The need now is hardly for withdrawal from politics but for reassessment, for attempts to agree on broad common goals not based on the naive oversimplifications of the past, for development of the best qualities of a basically open, generous, and fair-minded people, and for reinvigoration of institutions that may be imperfect but are commended more than most throughout the world. Alistair Cooke, the distinguished British observer of this country, concluded his BBC television series on America by expressing what must be a wide-spread concern coupled with admiration:

> I think I recognize several of the symptoms that Edward Gibbon saw so acutely in the decline of Rome. . . . A love of show and luxury; a widening gap between the very rich and the very poor; the exercise of military might in places remote from the centers of power; an obsession with sex; freakishness in the arts masquerading as originality. . . . Yet I have tried

to show that the original institutions of this country still have great vitality; and much of America's turmoil springs from the energy of people who are trying to apply these institutions to forgotten minorities. . . . In this country, a land of the most persistent idealism and the blandest cynicism, the race is on between its decadence and its vitality.

One evident and crucial need is for the public's more realistic comprehension of the strengths and shortcomings of the political system. They must be aware of how it actually works rather than content with the myths that seem so abundant. The ability should thus be improved to strengthen that which has merit and to reform constructively that which is weak. Indeed, a central characteristic of any successful political system is its capacity to adapt to constantly changing societal needs while maintaining traditions that have proved their worth. One most persistent myth is the notion that political decisions are merely choices between good and bad policies. The truly important issues of politics are never simple; they are never neat questions of right against wrong that anyone of integrity could promptly decide. On the contrary, they are exasperating mixtures of advantage and disadvantage, social benefit and danger, and they are frequently complicated by the need to make difficult and uncertain ethical choices. This is the case even with minor day-to-day decisions of every public official.

Take a few moments to think how you would act in each of the following situations. A reflex response is of little value; try to judge honestly how you would make responsible decisions and justify them in a public meeting or a press conference. Problems such as these are by no means unusual; they are typical examples of the complex difficulties in making public policy decisions, a process that takes place often under considerable pressure of time and popular emotion. Realistic comprehension of the nature of such decision making is vital to the ability of the electorate to hold public officials accountable in a fair, rational, and effective manner.

Case Studies
PUBLIC DECISION MAKING

1   You are a city council member, deeply concerned with the increasingly serious environmental problems of your community. The strict new rules that you have proposed for air-pollution control will force the manufacturing enterprise that is currently the community's largest employer to close, causing significant unemployment, economic hardship for many families, and a great increase in welfare costs. Should the rules be weakened?

2 You are a state legislator who firmly believes capital punishment to be both immoral and ineffective as a deterrent to crime. Your state has been without a death penalty for several years, but polls show strong public support for it. Proponents in the legislature have advanced to final vote a bill reinstituting the death penalty for two specific offenses: the killing of a police officer or prison guard and the murder of a victim during a kidnapping or rape. They have announced that if the bill fails to pass, they will lead an initiative campaign that will bring to a popular vote an act establishing the death penalty for a wide range of major offenses. You know that such an initiative would probably pass, creating what you consider a much worse situation than would the legislative act. Yet you feel strongly about the entire matter of principle, and as a legislator it is the bill that is before you. The division is close, and your vote might be the deciding one. Should you vote for this bill that you oppose, in the name of avoiding what you perceive to be a greater evil?

3 You are the campaign manager for a candidate for Congress running against an opponent who you are convinced is incompetent and will prove to be a positive danger if elected. Your candidate fits almost perfectly your criteria for what a member of Congress ought to be, but your funds have been exhausted, and there are still two crucial weeks before election day. Money that can probably make the difference between defeat and victory has been offered, with no evident strings attached, but you know that the donors will expect favors in the form of government contracts once your candidate is in office. Should you accept the campaign contribution?

4 You are the president of the United States. Although there is no immediate, direct threat to American security, country A is a key geographic element in the defense arrangements of the United States and its allies, and its pro-western attitude is important to an effort to thwart the expansionist moves of country B. Country B is a major power seeking greater influence in the region; if successful, its actions will probably cause two small nations to become unwilling satellites and also threaten the independence of others. The current regime in country A is notoriously undemocratic, has stifled freedom of speech and press, and is reported to be imprisoning large numbers of political opponents without trial. Intelligence reports indicate that the regime can continue in power only if military aid from the United States is maintained. If it fails, power will almost certainly shift to an element favorable to and financed by country B. Should American aid be continued?

5 As a member of Congress you believe that comprehensive gun-control legislation is an absolute necessity. The only bill cleared by committee for congressional action is one to control the ownership and sale of handguns, which you concede to be at least a first step.

However, the bill is inseparably tied to a proposed constitutional amendment guaranteeing unrestricted public ownership of rifles, shotguns, and ammunition. The companion bills are not subject to amendment. How should you vote?

6   You campaigned successfully for the governorship of your state by pledging that there would be no increases in taxes even though state services in education, mental health, and care of the aged would be improved. During your second year in office it has become clear that these improvements are impossible without additional tax revenue. Which pledge should you violate, or what other course of action can you follow, given that most other state expenditures are essentially unalterable?

7   As a senator with a strong commitment to civil rights and adequate housing for the poor, you have coauthored a major bill to stimulate construction of low-income housing. The bill has come up on the floor for a vote, but opponents propose an amendment specifying that no funds will be made available to communities where full racial equality does not exist. You know that if the amendment is approved, the bill will subsequently be filibustered to death and a principle of nonsegregation will be established for housing that will never be built. Racial minorities look to you as one of their champions and are pressing for a yes vote on the amendment. The amendment must be voted on before the bill. How should you vote?

8   You have been appointed to a White House staff position in the service of a newly elected president for whom you have great respect and to whose program you are devoted. You agree that a certain economic policy proposal is of the utmost importance to the nation in the years to come. Because they believe that premature disclosure will totally wreck the proposal, your superiors have asked you to give inaccurate and misleading answers about it in a press conference. Under these circumstances is it justifiable for you to do so?

THE STUFF OF POLITICS

"It is truly a fantastic system," a contemporary journalist has remarked, "under which we treat our politicians as unsavory characters while at the same time we charge them with preserving our very civilization." This paradox has indeed been characteristic of much of American culture. Yet politics is the cement that holds a society together and makes it possible for people of diverse attitudes and goals to live together. It is a fascinating reflection of every aspect of human motivation. Politics is life writ large, with all its crassness and nobility, pettiness and high aspiration, selfishness and dedication, tragedy and glory. Politics is not machinery but people. To study it is to look into an enterprise that encompasses all human emotions, including love and hate, ambition and revenge, commitment and self-interest.

The politics of every nation and every community develops distinctive attitudes and customs, organizational structures, and institutions designed to accomplish social objectives. Serving a nation vast, varied, and complex, the government of the United States is vast in scope, varied, and complex. Its size and complexity raise certain problems in description and analysis, but they also contribute to the endless fascination of American politics and government. The goal of our study is not the mere acquisition of data but rather an understanding of the dynamics of our political system: how it works as a human institution. We shall savor the style of the politics of American democracy. We shall acquire a sense of the intricacies of the political behavior of citizens and the humanness of people in high places, of the infinite variety of all these individuals and their motives, most claiming devotion to the good of their country. We shall also appreciate the great differences of opinion as to what constitutes that good. We shall learn something of the importance of disagreement and dissent as long as personal friendship and respect are preserved, of the necessity for leaders to lead, and of the inevitability of the conflicts of national and local interests. We shall come to realize the degree to which great decisions of history rest on fallible human beings and on minute matters of chance and timing. In the political process there are often peaks of high drama rising above the plains of necessary routine.

Politics has been defined in many ways, but there is general agreement that it means the struggle for power and leadership and dominance in human relations and the resolution of conflicting values and interests. These words can have a harsh sound, but they need not. It is obvious, too, that defined in this way politics exists in all human organizations—churches, clubs, labor unions, business associations, schools, and colleges—though it may take different forms. In practice we use the term primarily to refer to activities in the governmental arena. Human cooperation is usually not spontaneous and undirected. Definite patterns normally develop that indicate the methods of choosing leaders and their responsibilities. Politics is concerned with society's allocation of values and the establishment of priorities, matters that continually change and are re-adapted over time and under different leaders. The fundamental business of politics is the welding of policy, power, and influence. It is the effective use of power and influence to accomplish desired goals. The noblest objectives are of limited consequence unless people have the ability and the will to bring them about in the real world. Power and influence are not evils; they are necessities. Our critical questions concern how and to what ends power and influence are used.

Opinion: S. I. Hayakawa
POLITICS IS THE ESSENCE
OF CIVILIZATION

Society is a network of agreements about future conduct. Here, let us say, are two tribes, the Blues and the Reds. Both tribes want exclusive access to the fish in Clearwater Bay. If the two tribes are equally strong, they will fight and fight and kill each other—until someone has the good sense to say, "Since we can't lick them and they can't lick us, let's call a conference and see what we can work out."

So, what Benjamin Lee Whorf calls "linguistic processes" are initiated. Delegates from the two tribes argue, shout and scream, but ultimately they come to an agreement. The Reds will fish the bay Mondays, Wednesdays and Fridays; the Blues on Tuesdays, Thursdays and Saturdays; no fishing on Sundays.

People who work out agreements of this kind are known as politicians. Politicians are people who resolve through linguistic processes conflicts that would otherwise have to be solved by force.

But politicians are rarely thanked for their efforts. Many of the Blues are disappointed. "Look at what the politicians gave away to the Reds," they say. "What a sellout! They must have been bribed."

The Reds are equally critical of their delegates. "Everyone knows," they say, "that God intended the bay for the exclusive use of us Reds, but now the Blues act as if they had equal rights to it. What we need are delegates who are men of principle, not compromisers."

The results of a political process are never satisfactory to all concerned. Give the Arabs what they want, and the Israelis are enraged. Give the employers what they want, and the unions are furious. Introduce a measure of gun control, and the National Rifle Association is apoplectic.

So, if the political process is successful, all get only part of what they want, and none get all they want. And everyone blames the politicians for their disappointments. . . .

Disgusted with politicians, people from time to time yearn for government without politics. Sometimes, to their dismay, they get it, as in Soviet Russia, Poland and North Korea, where the political process has been abolished, or as in Northern Ireland, where the political process has failed.

The *Redlands Daily Facts* (September 1975). Reprinted by permission of Senator Hayakawa.

As Americans we need more than ever today to understand and cherish the political process. It is admittedly untidy. It is confusing. But it is the very essence of civilization.

WHAT MAKES A GOVERNMENT DEMOCRATIC

"Man's capacity for justice makes democracy possible, but man's inclination to injustice makes democracy necessary," wrote Reinhold Niebuhr. Perhaps democracy does reflect both sides of human nature. People who have grown up within a society generally assume that theirs is the most normal, natural, and easy way of doing things, but democracy is surely not the easiest form of government to operate. It is the hardest and makes the greatest demands on its citizens.

No pattern of government has been more widely praised than democracy, yet it has meant different things to different people. Some years ago, at an international conference, a delegate from the Soviet Union demanded that the western delegates tell him precisely what they meant by this term, *democracy*, that they continually tossed about. The western powers found it necessary to call a recess so that they could agree on what they meant. It is not that the representatives of the democratic nations did not know what they were talking about but that a variety of connotations surround the term. On reflection, however, it is not difficult to reach a fair agreement on fundamental meanings.

Leaving aside the qualities that simply define any good society, we can derive the following characteristics that a society must have to call itself democratic, even if none achieves each one to perfection:

1   Acceptance of the principle of majority rule. The only alternative possibilities are rule by a majority and rule by a minority, either an individual or an elite group. Some theorists, absolute majoritarians, insist that democracy means majority decision making and nothing more; by their account, a decision to abolish democracy, if arrived at openly by a majority through free debate, would be a democratic decision. But in practice, for most people democracy is majority decision making played according to the rules of the game. It is assumed not that the majority is necessarily always right but rather that over time it is safer to trust the majority than any given individual or elite. If there are advantages to government by consent, majority rule provides the most acceptable means of gaining and preserving that consent. It is worth noting that decision by a minority can result whenever we require more than a simple majority for some action, as in the

case of a two-thirds vote. That is, the decision as to what course to take can be made by one-third of the voters plus one. It is important to realize in this context that a negative decision on a proposal, reflecting a desire to keep things as they are, is as much a political policy decision as a positive decision that indicates a desire to change things.

2 Protection of the political rights of the minority as one of the basic rules of the game. The rights of the minority do not include the right to rule—although this is occasionally claimed—but embrace freedoms implied by the following characteristics of a healthy democratic society.

3 The free exchange of information and opinion. That people vote is no criterion of democracy; they may be merely rubber-stamping decisions made elsewhere. Free decisions are made only when adequate information is available and communicated and when all points of view may be examined. This means that the people must enjoy liberties such as freedom of speech, press, and assembly and that they will not tolerate government interference in the exercise of these freedoms. Such a political atmosphere is not only desirable for the individual but vital to the democratic process.

4 The availability of realistic alternative choices or actions. Meaningful change can thus be achieved through active participation in the political process by a wide range of individuals lending their unique perspectives and concerns to the generation of policy proposals. The presence of a competitive political party system materially aids the availability of such choices.

5 Freedom to act on one's beliefs, including the opportunity to seek to persuade others and to participate at will in the electoral process. This freedom implies a willingness to accept and abide by the results of democratically made decisions, while reserving the right to continue to disagree and to work toward achieving a different result at the next opportunity.

6 Acceptance of government by law: namely, the principle that people are to be governed by stable and consistent rules, determined and changed through the processes previously mentioned and applicable to all citizens in the same manner rather than by undependable individual whim.

7 Equality of every citizen before the law and in the opportunity to participate in the political process. The political weight of the vote of each adult citizen is the same as that of every other, and there is no concept of second-class citizenship.

8 Belief that government exists to serve human beings, not the other way around, as some totalitarian doctrines boldly assert. The individual is to be treated as an end and not as a means.

Many believe that democracy implies economic and social equality as well; others respond that such equality, even if feasible and desirable, is more a product than a definition of democracy or is irrelevant to political democracy. Americans often stress the importance of the principle of the separation of powers to the preservation of democracy, but it is certainly not properly considered a fundamental element. Most of the world's great democracies, in fact, do not incorporate this separation.

Democracy is frequently criticized for slowness and inefficiency, and both charges are partially true. Policy making through free debate does not have speed as its primary goal. We pay a price for almost everything. The question is whether the advantages are worth the price. Most people who compare democracy with the alternatives would probably agree with Sir Winston Churchill's judgment that democracy is the "worst form of government except all those other forms that have been tried from time to time."

Democracy is made up of certain game rules, but it also expresses a spirit. It expects openness of mind and ability to see through the tactics of the demagogue. It avoids absolute positions and rigid ideological postures and recognizes the necessity of compromise. It requires a tolerance for different ideas, which is no less than attempting to understand the beliefs and practices of others without necessarily accepting or sharing them. It recognizes, as T. V. Smith wrote in *The Democratic Way of Life*, that "not all good men in any generation have agreed on goodness, nor all just men on justice, nor all holy men on holiness." Democracy is nurtured by and flourishes with practice; it is not preserved in documents or rituals. It is not something finished, complete, and possessed but is something that each person must continually live.

CONSTITUTIONAL FOUNDATIONS
OF AMERICAN POLITICS

The uniqueness of each nation's political system derives from a variety of factors, of which a major one is its constitutional framework. The Constitution of the United States was written for a republic, a representative type of democracy in contrast to direct democracy, typified by the town meeting of American colonial days. Written in the aftermath of a revolution and at a time when people were strongly inclined to keep governments strictly controlled, the document clearly reflects the common fear of too great concentrations of power in political decision making. Yet the Constitution was set up to replace the Articles of Confederation, which had established a government found unsatisfactory precisely because it was too weak and decentralized. The framers thus sought a balance: the creation of a central government that would be strong and effective but not too strong. They provided it with extensive powers while weaving into the system important limitations and restraints.

The division of government powers between the national government and the states is the organizing principle of the Constitution, and it established a system of federalism (the nature and problems of which will be discussed in the following chapter). To the central government were assigned powers appropriate to a nation, such as defense, regulation of a monetary system, and control of interstate and foreign commerce, plus those necessary to any government, such as the powers to tax and borrow money. Other powers were reserved for the states or for the people themselves. Ultimate sovereignty over both levels of government lay with the people.

SEPARATION OF POWERS

In a representative government periodic elections provide fundamental protection against possible abuse of power by public officials. The framers, however, feared that the people would not always be dependable and that an unchecked government might subvert the electoral process, so they introduced additional mechanisms of restraint. The doctrine of the separation of powers among the three branches of government was familiar in both colonial practice and the writings of political theorists, and it was thus logical to adopt it. The legislative, executive, and judicial arms of government were each to have independent spheres of authority and a different political base from the others: Members of one house of the legislature would be chosen by popular election and those of the other by state legislatures; the president would be selected by a group of electors chosen in the states; and the judges would be appointed for life by the president with Senate approval.

CHECKS AND BALANCES

To insure that officials of the different branches would not exceed their powers or merge powers to rule tyrannically, the elaborate system of checks and balances was established, somewhat counteracting the separation doctrine. The result was a system of interdependent branches with shared powers, each one having a hand in the performance of responsibilities by the others. The framers desired to implement in each branch not only the means but also the motivation to resist improper expansion or abuse of power by another branch; James Madison, primary architect of the Constitution, wisely perceived that "ambition must be made to counteract ambition." Thus, whereas Congress enacts the laws, the president

The Jefferson Memorial in Washington, D.C. "I know no safe depository of the ultimate powers of the society but the people themselves; and if we think them not enlightened enough to exercise their control with a wholesome discretion, the remedy is not to take it from them, but to inform their discretion." Thomas Jefferson in a letter to William Charles Jarvis, September 28, 1820.

may exercise a veto, and by extraordinary vote Congress may override that veto. Neither house of Congress can pass laws without the concurrence of the other. The Supreme Court may invalidate acts of Congress or the president, but its members are appointed by the president with the consent of the Senate and may be removed by a process of impeachment by the House and trial by the Senate. The president and his administrative agencies carry out the laws and provide day-to-day services to the public, but they depend on Congress for money.

The system was nicely calculated to make highly unlikely the possibility that any popular majority could gain control of the entire government at one time. Such a majority could win the presidency but still not have a majority in the Senate, or it could take over the House in an off-year election without controlling either the Senate or the presidency. Control of the judiciary would change even more slowly, after fairly prolonged possession of the presidency. If a popular majority prevailed for long enough, of course, it would inevitably have its way. Although today the system of checks and balances remains a fundamental feature of American government, such developments as the growth of national political parties and changing methods of election have clearly modified it. Parties help counteract the tendency toward paralysis inherent in a check-and-balance system, by making possible in an organized way cooperation between the presidency and Congress and by enabling groups of senators or representatives to mobilize on different issues.

Separation of powers and check-and-balance arrangements are by no means matters merely of historical interest; they are part of everyday governance, as contemporary struggles over the scope of the president's war powers, the meaning of executive privilege, the impoundment of funds appropriated by Congress, and the impeachment of the president bear witness. Their modern significance was the subject of thoughtful comment by Supreme Court Justice Felix Frankfurter in the case of the seizure of the steel industry during the Korean War. His words are still relevant in the aftermath of Watergate:

> Not so long ago it was fashionable to find our system of checks and balances . . . outmoded—too easy. The experience through which the world has passed in our own day has made vivid the realization that the framers of our Constitution were not inexperienced doctrinaires.
>
> These long-headed statesmen had no illusion that our people enjoyed biological or psychological or sociological immunities from the hazards of concentrated power. . . . The accretion of dangerous power does not come in a day. It does come, however slowly, from the generative force of unchecked disregard of the restrictions that fence in even the most disinterested assertion of authority.

This constitutional arrangement of divided powers has strongly influenced the complexion and activity of the nation's politics. Since a political party seeks to win control of both elected branches simultaneously, the focus of political activity is a major campaign every four years, at once nationwide, statewide (in at least a third of the states), and districtwide (in each of the 435 congressional districts, where of course the elections occur every two years.) In addition, many state and local government elections are held at the same time. This Herculean enterprise requires large parties that can raise sizable funds and accommodate a broad spectrum of political belief. The system of divided but interdependent powers contributes to the very limited degree of party responsibility that prevails in the United States. It is, in other words, difficult to elect a party to office and hold it responsible for carrying out a definite political program.

As one of the world's oldest functioning constitutions the United States Constitution has become not only an instrument of government, allocating and limiting powers, but also a symbol of national unity and the broad popular consensus that makes effective government possible. Indeed, it has been so idealized that some foreign observers have dubbed ours a nation of "constitution worshipers." Perhaps it has come to fill the role of a king in the constitutional monarchies, and thus it is all the more dangerous when people lose faith in its processes.

METHODS OF CONSTITUTIONAL CHANGE

The United States Constitution is not simply an honored but inflexible set of rules. A notable characteristic is its adaptability throughout the many radical changes the nation has experienced. This is partly a result of important compromises that were made at the constitutional convention and the generality of language that was found necessary. The framers, happily, did not try to spell out every detail.

It is natural to think that most constitutional change has been effected through amendments, but these have in fact played a secondary role. Most change has occurred through the gradual alteration of customs and through interpretation of the various constitutional provisions, as powers are re-evaluated to fit the needs of each new era. This continuous process of reappraisal is pre-eminently a function of the courts, but the legislative and executive branches necessarily also make interpretations that often remain unchallenged.

The formal amending process is extremely cumbersome and is weighted toward preserving the status quo, principally by requiring extraordinary majorities and action by a large number of separate bodies. The public never votes on amendments directly. Amendments may be proposed by a two-thirds vote of both houses of Congress, or the legislatures of two-thirds of the states may propose

FIGURE 1.1   Constitutional Amendment

an amendment or amendments to be considered by a convention called by Congress following this state initiative (see Figure 1.1). To date, the latter approach has never been used successfully, although several attempts have been made. Ratification must then come from either the legislatures in three-fourths of the states or special conventions called for this purpose in three-fourths of the states.

To be successful, proponents of an amendment must build a tremendous head of steam behind their proposal. Unless a measure is noncontroversial, great efforts are required to gain support from two-thirds of both the House and the Senate and then approval by both houses of thirty-eight state legislatures meeting at different periods and usually in time-limited sessions. To defeat an amendment, opponents need only to get a third of the votes in one house of Congress or to block the measure in one house of thirteen different state legislatures, and the people responsible for such action might obviously represent a very small minority of the United States population.

There have been only twenty-six amendments to the Constitution, and ten of those, the Bill of Rights, came in a block at the beginning as a condition for approval of the Constitution by some states. Until lately, most amendments have appeared in small clusters during periods of crisis or reform. Congress has been cautious in recommending amendments, and most that it has proposed have been ratified. When sentiment is strongly favorable, as in the case of the Twenty-fifth Amendment, dealing with presidential disability and succession, or the Twenty-sixth, dealing with lowering the voting age, approval may be gained quickly, but this has happened rarely. Where the issue is emotionally controversial, like the proposed Equal Rights Amendment, progress is likely to be frustratingly slow.

Proposal of amendments by the states is obviously far more complicated than action by Congress, and if there is sufficient public backing to make the proposal a realistic possibility, Congress can probably be persuaded to advance it. The route of state initiation is followed only when proponents are convinced that Congress will not touch their amendment or when the proposal is assumed to be particularly attractive to the states, as was the case several years ago with one that would have removed all constitutional restraints on the way states apportion their legislatures.

It is uncertain what would happen if thirty-four states were to petition Congress to call a constitutional convention, there being no precedents. Could Congress refuse, or could it delay action for long periods of time? Would the proposals from the states have to be identical in form? How would the convention be elected, and what procedures would it follow? Many people fear that, once established, a convention might take the bit in its teeth; after all, the convention of 1787 was assembled to amend the Articles of Confederation but ended by writing an entirely new constitution. Every group has its special concerns and interests to protect. What might be done about civil rights, the power of the courts, freedom of speech, and separation of church and state? Although advocates express confidence that delegates would act with restraint and recall that three-fourths of the states would have to ratify, the combined uncertainties make a convention unlikely.

THE POLITICAL ENVIRONMENT

AMBIVALENCE TOWARD POLITICS

Factors other than the constitutional framework also influence the distinctive character of any nation's politics. It is often remarked that Americans have a strong anti-authoritarian bias, but it is also true that our political behavior reflects heavily antipolitical and especially antipartisan attitudes. Although we delight in praising our democratic governmental processes to the world, a large number of Americans tend to ignore them by not participating in them. And while there is much legitimately to criticize in "the establishment" and its ways, the "alienation" from the political system so fervently expressed by members of certain movements is also partly a figure of these antipolitical stereotypes.

This suspicion of and antagonism to politics is basically the effect of a traditional culture pattern, although specific events at some point in history, like Watergate, may make it more apparent at some times than at others. Americans have been brought up on a belief in independence and hostility to authority, to some extent good qualities, but in an exaggerated form they offend some of the democratic principles discussed above. Rendering *politics* and *politician* as terms

"Frankly, I don't care one way or the other about voter apathy"

of abuse depreciates the process of democratic decision making with which those words are properly associated. Some politicians may bring discredit upon the profession, but questionable behavior is a personal matter and can occur in any vocation. It appears that Americans uphold a double standard. There is a ready tendency to cry, "That's politics," when a public official errs, but when a business employee embezzles funds, for example, we rarely hear the pejorative comment, "That's business." Throughout much of its history this nation has evidenced a predominantly business psychology, with the business executive as its hero. The criteria of success, for both the individual and the nation, have been largely materialistic: numbers of things produced and amounts of money acquired. It is not surprising that politics has been relegated to second rank and sometimes treated with contempt.

The ambivalence reflected in this coupling of patriotic rhetoric about democratic institutions with antipolitical practice is a significant aspect of American political life. Most of the great accomplishments in the nation's history were achieved by politicians using effective politics, yet America is hard on its political leaders. It honors them belatedly, in a manner aptly expressed by the phrase "a statesman is a dead politician." Few serve the nation better or under greater stress than the politician, who must always seek the grounds on which people can live and work together, to smooth strife and heal wounds, to be the broker among conflicting ideas and methods, to find ways to achieve reasonable social progress benefiting the many while disadvantaging as few as possible. This spirit was caught well in the words of a member of the clergy speaking at a memorial service following the death of President Harry S Truman:

"He was a man who was proud to be called a politician, for he knew that in the arena of politics the fate of all mankind is determined."

COMPROMISE

The politics of American democracy is a politics of compromise and limited objectives. This is the case in all true democracies. "Politics," it is often said, "is the art of the possible." Although there are exceptions, our major parties and most of our political leaders are not dogmatic about their objectives. They work vigorously for their goals but, recognizing that others who see things differently are doing likewise, are normally prepared to accept the most that can be achieved at the moment, reserving the right to continue to work for the total objective in the future. Examples of this attitude will be frequently evident throughout the discussions in subsequent chapters.

Compromise seems to be a bad word to some people. They automatically identify it with compromise of principle, but it is perfectly possible to compromise methods without compromising principle. The spirit of compromise is vital to the democratic process and essential to the resolution of conflicts among social values and over allocation of resources. If both sides to a controversy take absolute and unyielding positions, the result must be either violence or stalemate, rule by the most powerful or stagnation. To make and respect compromise is to recognize that no human being possesses a monopoly on wisdom.

PARTICIPATION

Government has a major role in the lives of all citizens, yet to a remarkable extent its services are taken for granted in the United States. Although feelings run high on some issues, we rarely think of the multitude of tasks performed on our behalf or of the many regulations that control aspects of our behavior to the advantage of the whole community. We react mainly when a regulation becomes a temporary annoyance or when a crisis arouses our hostility or suspicion. By definition a democratic society is predicated on popular participation and control, but the effectiveness of participation depends on its being based on sound information and reason. Not everyone need be a political activist, but unfortunate consequences are likely to appear if a large percentage of the people do not participate in politics. The citizen and the organized group cannot govern, but it is their function to seek out and to choose leaders, to attempt to influence policies, and periodically to judge the job being done.

Despite a too commonly weak and unrealistic understanding of government at all levels, most people think themselves experts in politics and government or at least well qualified to advise and criticize. Freedom to criticize is of great value to a free people, but there is a difference between its value to the individual and its value to society. The social value of criticism is intimately related to the accuracy of the information on which it is based and the intelligence with which it is exercised. Differences of opinion naturally exist; they are one criterion of a free society. But another criterion is the recognition that no one of us possesses all truth, that free discussion

The Population Estimate Board at the Census Bureau in Washington, D.C.

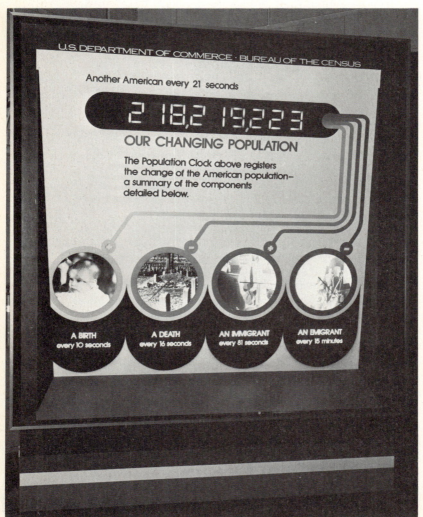

of different approaches should be possible without the imputation of evil motives or traitorous intent. One of the most serious aspects of the Watergate affair was the apparent rejection by some who held power of the valuable democratic concept of a "loyal opposition" and the assumption that political opponents are somehow enemies.

The United States has been favored in history by a high degree of security and stability, but serious problems arise as our population expands, resources are depleted, social frictions intensify, and the role of world leadership makes almost impossible demands. We cannot escape the obligation of dealing effectively with domestic and world problems, and demands of constructive and responsible citizenship therefore continue to increase.

The obligation of concerned citizens who wish to see their democratic society survive does not begin or end with casting a ballot. It involves service and cooperation in meeting the needs of one's community, participation in interest groups, and activity within a political party. Interestingly, involvement usually results in excitement and fascination with politics and not merely in hard or tedious work. Frequent reference to the "game" of politics suggests that while it is a very serious business, it also "gets in one's blood." Few who go into politics can ever really leave it. Like any worthwhile human endeavor, it has its share of frustration and disappointment, but it also carries a sense of accomplishment, of being on the inside, and of never ending challenge.

It is within the political parties, after all, that many of the decisions of a democratic government are made and much of its work is done. There is nothing inherently evil about politics or inherently good. It can be ennobling or corrupt or indifferent, just as can organized religion or a business organization or a labor union or any other human activity. Whether a people gets in its government competence, honesty, and genuine social concern or whether it gets corruption, incompetence, and abdication of responsibility depends to a much greater extent than most of us realize on the caliber of those individuals who have a hand in local political party activity, however vital the role of leadership may be.

THE DIVERSITY OF THE UNITED STATES

There are, finally, significant physical and structural features that influence American politics, not the least of which is sheer size. The political system must serve a nation of over 220 million people, spread across a huge continent and beyond. It is a population reflecting almost infinite variety of background, regional tradition, economic status, attitude, religion, race, and national origin. It is, moreover, the most mobile society in history. Rapid growth and constant change have been its keynotes in population, economic activity, and physical environment. A nation that began as a small and essentially agricultural society has been transformed into an overwhelmingly urban giant dominated by advanced technology. Today approximately 80 per cent of the population is urban, of which about two-thirds are concentrated in the great metropolitan areas.

The United States is a single political entity, yet it is much more than that. There are fifty states and more than seventy-eight thousand local governments, each with its own distinctive political system. The result is a staggering number of campaigns and elections and a great number of public officials and other political leaders. Each of these smaller political systems has its own interests and concerns. Some conflict is inevitable, and substantial cooperation is required if the system as a whole is to survive.

BASIC CONCEPTS AND TERMS

politics

democracy

majority rule

minority rights

government by law

equality before the law

republic

federalism

separation of powers

system of checks and balances

constitutional change by
  interpretation

amendment process

politics of compromise and
  limited objectives

antipolitical culture

A NATION
OF
STATES

2

Federalism was adopted in the United States not because it was thought to be the perfect model but for the purely practical reason that it was the only plan that had a chance of being adopted. The representatives of the independent and often quarrelsome new states were in no mood to submerge their identities in a unitary government. Most of the theoretical arguments for federalism appeared later, although that does not make them the less persuasive.

A federal system is one in which power is divided between a central government and regional governments of some kind, each having some degree of independence of action. Both exercise direct authority over individual citizens. The basic formal division of powers cannot be changed except by mutual consent. In contrast to this arrangement is a unitary system, in which a central government has complete authority throughout a country. Britain and France are examples. Usually local governments exist, but they are subordinate to the national government. Most governments in the world are unitary. The principal examples of the federal system are Australia, Canada, Switzerland, and the United States; Austria and West Germany may perhaps be properly included although their pattern of

Drawing by Ed Fisher, from the December 21, 1969 issue of the Saturday Review.

"One at a time, you guys!"

relations is a bit different from that of the other four. Some other governments are federal in name but not in practice, as found in several Latin American countries.

THE PROS AND CONS OF FEDERALISM

A federal system is undoubtedly complicated, somewhat unwieldy, and expensive to operate, since there is duplication and overlap; there are two complete sets of courts in the United States, for example (or more realistically, fifty-one—fifty belonging to the states and one to the federal government). There is likely to be lack of uniformity in the quality and quantity of public services, in the way citizens are treated in different areas, and in the manner that costs of government are distributed. Because each level has independent authority, federalism normally results in some spirit of contentiousness and considerable litigation among governments.

Where there are both a desire for regional independence and a recognition of the need for national unity, federalism furnishes a workable compromise. This mixture of diversity and unity is often highly prized. The states are supposedly in closer touch with popular wishes. This arrangement provides a counterbalance for excessive concentration of power in the central government. The availability of multiple levels of government and cooperation among any combinations of them makes possible greater administrative flexibility in complex and politically delicate questions. Some areas may have distinctive problems that can best be dealt with by local initiative and local understanding. The states can also serve as training grounds for those who may later hold national responsibility and as social laboratories for new governmental forms or solutions to public problems. Federalism is especially appropriate for a nation like the United States, of vast size, heterogeneous population, and distinctive regional histories and characteristics.

DIVIDING POWERS
AND POLICING BOUNDARIES

American federalism is no more static than the Constitution. It is in constant process of gradual adaptation to changing circumstances. The United States is now a powerful and solidly established nation facing social and political problems far different from those of 1789. The formal division of powers between the nation and the states has remained essentially unchanged, but the constitutional language is general and vague, so that change has come principally through slowly developing interpretations, primarily but not exclusively judicial, of the meaning of that language. Even though the powers have been little altered, governmental functions have increased greatly. The national or international scope of the critical problems of modern history has resulted in pre-eminence of the national government, but the flexibility of constitutional language clearly allowed for this development.

The simplest approach to understanding the distribution of powers in the United States is to identify the specific powers of the national government and remember that all remaining powers lie with the states or with the people. The national government and the states are in opposite constitutional positions. To act the national government must always have constitutional authorization, whereas a state can do what it chooses unless it is prohibited by the United States Constitution or its own constitution. In other words, a state need not show a specific grant of power; it has all power unless the matter has been granted exclusively to the nation or there is a clear national or state constitutional restriction on it, as in the protection of civil liberties.

NATIONAL AND STATE POWERS

The three kinds of power possessed by the national government are commonly termed delegated or enumerated powers, implied powers, and inherent powers. It is a familiar proposition that in Article I, Section 8, of the Constitution the people delegated a series of powers to the national government and left everything else to the states; for this reason the state powers are termed residual.* But the listing of powers concludes with the famous necessary-and-proper clause (or elastic clause) that has been the primary basis for expansion of national power. That clause does not say that Congress may do anything that it deems necessary and proper; this would be unlimited authorization. It states rather that Congress may make all laws necessary and proper "for carrying into execution the foregoing powers" and other powers granted to the government of the United States.

Early in the history of the country the Supreme Court elaborated this, in the landmark case of *McCulloch* v. *Maryland* (1819), by stating that if the end is legitimate and within the scope of the Constitution, all means appropriate and plainly adapted to that end, which are consistent with the Constitution, are constitutional. Thus appeared via the necessary-and-proper clause the broad doctrine of implied powers, those that may be reasonably implied from the delegated powers. The ability of the national government to control certain types of industrial pollution, for example, derives from its power to regulate interstate commerce.

In the middle years of the 1930s a United States corporation shipped some machine guns to Bolivia, then at war with Paraguay, despite a government embargo that had been placed on the shipment of arms to the belligerent countries. The company claimed that the national government had no power to impose such an embargo, and the Supreme Court had to decide whether such a power could be found. Its conclusion established another landmark, in *United States* v. *Curtiss-Wright Export Corporation* (1936), when it held that there are certain powers, specifically those involving the conduct of relations with other countries, that belong to the government of any nation simply because it is a nation. There is no need for a constitutional grant; such a power is inherent in nationhood and is assumed by all nations. Although there have been occasional attempts to persuade the court to expand the definition of inherent powers, it has so far left it restricted narrowly to foreign affairs.

This process of continually determining the boundary between

---

*The practice of placing the enumerated powers in the central government and leaving the residual powers to the states is not essential to federalism. In Canada, also a federation, certain powers are delegated to the provincial governments, with all others reserved to the national government.

national and state powers is a major function of the United States courts, especially the Supreme Court. A federal system obviously requires some official and ultimate mechanism for making such determination, though it need not be the judiciary. In Switzerland, for example, decisions of this sort are made by the national parliament (subject to popular referendum), but American practice has been to place this burden on the courts. The Constitution states specifically that the Constitution itself and valid national laws and treaties "shall be the supreme law of the land . . . anything in the Constitution or laws of any state to the contrary notwithstanding" (Article VI).

WHOSE POWER IS GREATER?

Over the years the courts have sought various formulas for guiding these determinations, but the doctrine of national supremacy has long been the established rule. This principle does not state that the national action is always supreme in case of jurisdictional conflict between the nation and a state or states. It means, rather, that in such conflicts the national action will be held to be supreme over a state's action if the national government is judged to be acting within the scope of its constitutional authority. It assumes further that the determination as to whether an authority exists is to be made by the national government, primarily by the Supreme Court. The alternative would be a hodgepodge of separate and often conflicting determinations by fifty different states. Through its courts the national government can keep the states in line, but it alone is the judge of its own actions. This nationwide uniformity of interpretation is important, but the fact that decisions are made by an agency of the national government has not meant in practice that they are always in favor of the nation and against the states. A national viewpoint has generally been predominant, nevertheless.

Some powers belong exclusively to the nation and others belong exclusively to the states, but there are a number that are concurrent, possessed by both levels at the same time. Familiar examples include the powers to tax, borrow money, and create a system of courts.

A different view of the nature of the federal union created by the United States Constitution is found in the argument that the national government was created by the states, which delegated certain powers to it, and that it thus properly serves only as their agent. This concept was the fundamental issue of the Civil War and still enjoys some popularity. It has been sanctified by much oratory but finds no foundation in the Constitution or in the circumstances of its adoption. The Supreme Court laid the concept to rest shortly after the Civil War, but it is exhumed with surprising frequency.

The entire federal system is based on the principle of popular sovereignty. The people, not one government or another, are sovereign. The people created a central government to serve them in certain ways and regional governments to serve in other ways. It was the people, not the states, who granted powers to the national government.* It is significant that the Constitution begins with the phrase "We the people of the United States . . . do ordain and establish."

NATIONAL AND STATE RELATIONS

OBLIGATIONS BOTH WAYS

The national government has a variety of formal obligations and specific limitations with regard to the states, but only a few require elaboration. The national government is obliged to aid in the control of domestic violence on the request of a state, for example. The president must decide whether and when to intervene but will do so ordinarily only when a state legislature or governor requests it or when there is a violation of national law or serious threat to national personnel or property.

In such cases, which are infrequent, there may be bitter dispute over whether national forces are in fact needed, as when President Eisenhower sent United States troops into Arkansas to enforce court orders on school desegregation and to try to prevent further violence or as when President Kennedy used United States marshals and other forces for the same purpose at the universities of Alabama and Mississippi. In the aftermath of the Detroit riots in the summer of 1967 there was sharp disagreement between President Johnson and Governor Romney, then a prospective presidential candidate, over such questions as whether United States forces were sent in quickly enough and whether the governor had been willing to take personal responsibility by making a proper request on which the president could act. Such situations are highly delicate.

The requirement that the United States guarantee to every state "a republican form of government" has had little practical effect, but it remains a basis for possible national intervention. The precise meaning of the phrase has been in doubt, though it is generally assumed that the intent was to preserve essentially democratic rather than totalitarian institutions. The courts have held that interpretation and enforcement of this clause are a "political question" and thus belong in the hands of the executive and legislative branches rather than of the courts.

---

*It is worth noticing also that thirty-seven of the states have been subsequently admitted to the Union by action of the national government.

The states are obliged to conduct elections for national offices because there is no national machinery for this purpose. Specific restrictions prohibit the states from conducting relations with foreign governments, maintaining armies, levying tariffs, interfering with interstate commerce, and entering into compacts with other states without congressional approval.

Throughout this country's history there has been great argument, more vehement during some periods than others, over what is loosely termed states' rights. Originally a doctrine of constitutional interpretation maintaining the opposite of national supremacy, the phrase has had many and varied connotations. In the past few decades it has been widely used, despite a cloaking of constitutional theory, to defend against national intervention in the practices of racial segregation in certain states and against national regulation of business. The scope of the argument varies with the user of the language, and often the drive behind states' rights assertions is a contemporary reaction to the growing size and complexity of national bureaucracy. But that the argument is perennial indicates the continuing tension between nation and states that is characteristic of federal systems. This tension has some desirable effects in that governments at each level watch and criticize each other, a form of protection lacking in unitary systems.

THE SPECIAL ROLE OF GRANTS-IN-AID

Financial grants from the central government to the states have become, largely in this century, one of the most important and controversial aspects of intergovernmental relations. (State grants to local governments have also mushroomed.) National aids now reaching a total of approximately $85 billion annually constitute cooperative financing of a variety of public services, including highway construction, education, welfare, health, housing and community development, employment security, agriculture, and conservation (see Figure 2.1).

Reasons for the use of the grant-in-aid are also varied. A common purpose is "equalization," not literally an equalizing of service levels among the states but the establishing of a minimum floor beneath which no state's services should fall. If a state is able and willing to go beyond the minimum, it is free to do so. Use of the generally more progressive tax structure of the national government, it is argued, spreads the burden of support more equitably. The rationale behind this kind of grant is expressed, for instance, in the position that no child should be denied at least satisfactory educational opportunities simply because of the accident of birth in an economically poor state.

Grants may be used at times to stimulate the provision of new or expanded services by the state or local units. This is the process of

FIGURE 2.1   Federal Grants to State and Local Governments for Fiscal Years 1969–1979

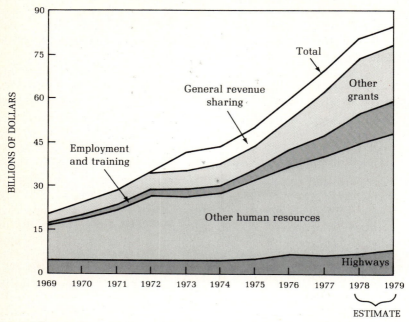

Source: Office of Management and Budget, *Special Analyses: Budget of the United States Government, Fiscal Year 1979*, Government Printing Office, Washington, D.C., 1978, p. 175.

dangling the carrot: a certain amount of money is promised if a particular service is provided. Though no state is required to accept a grant, all are strongly motivated to get their "share." Several years ago a state legislature passed a flowery resolution denouncing the "encroachment" of the national government, particularly through its grant programs, and praising the virtues of state self-reliance. But the same session of that legislature not only funded its share of existing grant programs but also appropriated a special discretionary fund that enabled the governor to match any national grants that might be created before the legislature met again.

Many grants simply reflect strong national interest as well as state and local interest in specific programs. There is a national stake in interstate highway transportation, for example. The national government is interested in assuring generally equal educational opportunities to all: a child educated in Montana may live as an adult in Ohio. The grant system is essentially a cooperation of the various levels of government to accomplish a job. Critics complain that national grants encourage an undesirable trend toward greater centralization, but it is as easily argued that they contribute to continued decentralization. They make possible continued state and local administration of services that might otherwise be taken over by the national government to insure reasonable uniformity nationwide.

Grants made for fairly specific purposes are often referred to as categorical grants; that is, the funds are provided for only certain categories of service. Moreover, the national government wants to be sure that the states are genuinely interested in providing the particular service and will use the money wisely and carefully. Thus it is customarily required that a state match the grant with its own funds, usually on a fifty-fifty basis, although other patterns occur. This procedure results in two other labels, such grants being called matching or conditional grants. Since the national government commonly requires reports and audits, it can set conditions that specify minimum standards for service and qualifications of the personnel administering the program. The intent is to guarantee responsibility without undue dictation from above.

Because of criticisms that categorical grants impose too many requirements, there have been frequent proposals for shifting to block grants—simply allocating sums of money to the states to use for whatever purposes they wish. The assumption is that state and local units are best able to determine their needs and that, since the national government has pre-empted the most lucrative tax sources, they should be entitled to a share. The argument seems reasonable, but it can also be contended that the states are not necessarily able or willing to make better decisions than the national government as to the needs of citizens. The nation may have at least an equal or even greater concern for its citizens than some states manifest. In the face of disturbing reports a few years ago suggesting the prevalence of hunger in the United States, some state and local officials in the most severely depressed areas flatly refused to distribute surplus food, insisting that there were no needy people within their jurisdictions.

There have also been proposals that the national government abandon certain taxes and turn them over to the states. The states rarely show equal interest in assuming in return some of the functions now performed by the central government, however. The real problem is that taxes do not simply migrate. Although the national government might abandon some taxes, state administrations and legislatures would then have to bear the political liability of enacting new taxes, which they are naturally loath to do.

One remaining argument sounds seductive. The gist of it is that the rich industrial states are grossly maltreated because they pay in taxes to the national government far more than they receive in grants. On reflection it is evident that this reasoning is invalid. No state pays taxes to the national government; neither government may tax the other. Rather, citizens of the United States pay taxes, but they pay national taxes at exactly the same rate wherever they happen to live. More people live in Michigan, for example, than in New Mexico, and thus a larger total amount of money flows into the United States treasury from the people living in Michigan; but they are in no way subject to tax discrimination.

It is also true that there is a greater industrial and commercial concentration in a state such as Michigan than in New Mexico. This means that greater revenue is collected from corporations in Michigan, but this is merely a chance matter of location. The national tax rates are the same throughout the country. Furthermore, the products of corporations are sold throughout the United States, and there is no reason why one state should be the sole beneficiary of taxation on profits. Each government spreads its taxes generally and uniformly and spends the revenues where it deems the greatest needs exist. No one is surprised that taxes paid to a city government are used to surface the streets in a part of town other than that in front of one's house. Clearly the national government spends more money on services in some areas of the country than in others, and more is likely to be spent in the poorer areas, which naturally do not produce large amounts of revenue. The relation under discussion is directly between a citizen and the national government; the same citizen has a similar relation to state government. To speak of a state's paying out more than it gets back injects the state inaccurately into nation-to-citizen contact and is both confusing and misleading.

Another controversy revolves around the legitimacy of control over grants-in-aid as a means of enforcing national social policy. The threat of withholding grants for established programs is powerful. For several years, for example, this tactic has been used with educational grants in an effort to accelerate school desegregation. Since the courts had long ruled that all United States citizens must be treated equally by state and local governments and that school segregation is a denial of equal protection, school districts were required to show that they were abiding by the spirit of the law if they were to continue to receive grants, on which they often depend. The national government defended this policy as one of simply protecting the rights of its citizens. Nevertheless, through its control of appropriations, Congress repeatedly sought to restrict the ability of the Department of Health, Education, and Welfare to withhold grants in order to compel busing programs, and there has been continuous heated controversy and turmoil.

REVENUE SHARING

The expressed desire of the Johnson and Nixon administrations to relinquish a larger share of government responsibility to the state and local governments led to steadily more numerous proposals from within both parties for some form of revenue sharing, by which a

The proof of the pudding . . .

given percentage of national revenues is automatically distributed to state and local governments to use as they wish without detailed reports and audits. It was assumed that such a system might help relieve the financial bind afflicting most of the state and local governments, provide greater freedom of policy judgment in local communities, and reduce national administrative expense. In 1972 Congress accepted a proposal to undertake a five-year trial program and to authorize appropriations of $30 billion in that period. It was extended for four years at the end of that time, at a slight increase in annual amount. The program had continuing support from President Carter.

The competition for relative advantage between state and local governments was resolved by providing that one-third of each state's share go directly to the state while the other two-thirds pass through to local governments. Allocations are calculated from a complex formula for population, relative income, and tax effort, or the extent to which state and local units tax themselves. A few national controls remain. In addition to antidiscrimination clauses there is, for example, a stipulation that local governments use the funds only for "priority expenditures," basic public services rather than "frills," and the broad categories of possible use are enumerated. These restrictions reflected widespread fears that the system might end in financial irresponsibility in some states or that taxes collected nationally might be used locally to perpetuate practices of which the rest of the nation disapproves.

As long as revenue-sharing allocations equal the value of previous grants or supplement—but not replace—such funds, they provide for state and local governments almost the best of all possible worlds.

They receive money, and the national government absorbs the public blame for the requisite taxes. State and local groups lobbied actively and successfully for passage of the act, but some of their officials, as well as some members of Congress, spoke of a suspicion that the Nixon administration was at least as eager to cut national government expenditures as it was to strengthen federalism by transferring greater discretion to the other levels. The financially hard-pressed major cities, facing problems of ever more staggering immensity, needed more assistance, not less. With the publication of the first budget proposals after enactment of revenue sharing, many mayors felt their suspicions confirmed and the immediate outcry was that the real effort was to eliminate grants. The cities are "worse off financially than before general revenue sharing was enacted," claimed the mayor of Milwaukee, while Seattle's mayor bitterly termed the new federalism "a Trojan horse for America's cities, a gift left behind by an administration retreating from its basic responsibilities to its citizens."

Flatly denying such charges, the Nixon administration sought to achieve a quite fundamental restructuring of the federal system. As the next step beyond general revenue sharing, the president proposed four "special revenue sharing" programs whereby broad category block grants would be substituted for a variety of grants in education, urban community development, manpower training and utilization, and law enforcement. Experiments in some of these directions have been undertaken.

The basic revenue-sharing law had not been long on the books when criticisms began to arise, and the intensity steadily increased. Most vocal were liberals who had been among the original proponents, with the following allegations being the principal complaints:

1 The distribution formulas did not insure that funds went where needs were greatest; big cities with crucial problems were short-changed, while some communities used revenue-sharing funds to build bridle paths and golf courses, viewed as relatively frivolous projects.

2 The funds were often used to reduce state and local taxes rather than to deal with social problems; and even if that were a legitimate use, it appeared to have little impact on making the tax structures more progressive or efficient.

3 There was frequently an overemphasis on capital projects compared to an attack on immediate social problems.

4 Funds were allocated in some communities on a racially discriminatory basis.

5 Although this had been heralded as "new money" for the states and local governments, the administration had immediately

sought to eliminate many categorical grants and to slash budgets supporting needed programs operated at the state and local levels.

6 The hopes of some proponents that revenue sharing could help promote the modernization of state and local units had been frustrated.

Some critics, in fact, suggested that perhaps the only way for Congress to insure that important national goals were met was to return to full reliance on conditional categorical grants. However, state and local officials, adding their weight to that of ideological proponents, provided a potent force for retention of the system. Occasional voices warning that state and local governments were becoming too dependent on the national government were lost in the clamor for extension. The final renewal bill did include further restraints on racially discriminatory use and did attempt to foster a larger degree of public participation in setting priorities for use of the funds at the community level.

Revenue-sharing and grant-in-aid distribution formulas have also become the focus of an increasing struggle between the "frost belt" and the "sun belt" states. The former—states of the East and North, containing the older cities with decaying areas and declining tax resources—contend that these needs are being ignored as disproportionate amounts are allocated to the growing states of the South and Southwest. The latter group also contains still impoverished areas, however, and claims with equal vehemence that problems follow increases of population and funds must go where the population is moving.

One muddle in our thinking about grants-in-aid, revenue sharing, and other aspects of national-state relations is our tendency to view all states as equal to each other. The demand that agencies of the national government deal with every state in like manner is understandable, but the agencies regularly find that some states are unreliable. Equal legal status is recognized, but beyond that no one seriously suggests that they are totally comparable. The differences among states are not only of size and population but also of capacity to provide public services, quality of the political system, stage of administrative development, and the like.

A long-standing controversy in national-state relations has centered on the complaint, common in some revenue-sharing arguments, for example, that the functions of the state and local governments are gradually disappearing as the role of the national government expands. On the contrary, the functions of all governments have been increasing, those of the state and local units at a generally more rapid rate. It may be argued with some justice that the degree of state discretion is lessened if more conflicts with the national government arise. Oddly enough, the assumption of state and local decline prevails, despite the obvious fact that the scope of state and local actions is broader, their budgets are bigger, and the number of their employees is greater than ever before.

INTERSTATE RELATIONS

Another battery of problems unique to federalism arises from the relations among the states themselves. These involve elements of both cooperation and friction. The framers of the Constitution, recognizing the potential for conflict and seeking to create a true union, attempted to arrange several procedures to guarantee reasonable harmony. Vagueness of language was a mixed blessing: Much interpretation of the pertinent constitutional clauses has been necessary, yet considerable uncertainty and disputed meaning remain.

FULL FAITH AND CREDIT

So many cases involving the full-faith-and-credit clause have been fought that one former justice of the Supreme Court termed it "the lawyer's clause of the Constitution." The constitutional requirement is simply that each state must give full faith and credit "to the public acts, records, and judicial proceedings" of all the other states. No state is expected to enforce the laws of another state, but each must recognize the validity of those laws. Without such a rule, person A could secure a judgment against B in the courts of Pennsylvania, say, whereupon B could move to Indiana and take with him all his movable property. Person A would then have to start from the beginning in the courts of Indiana, and then if A were ultimately successful, B could move again to Kentucky. Such a situation would be intolerable. Under full faith and credit, although the Indiana court would not enforce the Pennsylvania judgment, it would without holding another trial issue its own judgment based on the Pennsylvania court record.

A great deal of litigation issues from the migratory divorce—a divorce obtained from a state other than that in which the married couple lives. The divorce laws of the states are extremely different; a few are quite permissive whereas others grant divorces on very limited grounds and with long waiting periods. Nevada has long been famous for granting divorces on such grounds as mental cruelty and for requiring only six weeks' residence in Nevada for the purpose. As more states move toward a policy of no-fault dissolutions of marriages when irreconcilable differences exist, conflicts among the states on this matter will decline.

Case Study
THE MIGRATORY DIVORCE

A Mr. Williams and a Mrs. Hendrix left their respective spouses in their home state of North Carolina and went to Reno, Nevada, taking up residence in a trailer court for six weeks. At the end of that time they secured divorces and were then married to each other; shortly thereafter they returned to North Carolina. They were jailed in North Carolina, however, for "bigamous cohabitation," as that state refused to accept the validity of the Nevada divorces. Ultimately the Supreme Court of the United States had to decide the effect of the full-faith-and-credit clause under such circumstances.

The case turned on the question of jurisdiction. If Williams and Hendrix had established a bona fide domicile in Nevada, then that state would have jurisdiction to act concerning them and no other state could question the action. But the Court was willing to accept North Carolina's contention that they obviously had no intent to establish Nevada residence in good faith and therefore were not legally domiciled there. How does one prove intent, which is, after all, something within people's minds? In essence, the rule established by the majority of the Court as to the contemporary meaning of the full-faith-and-credit clause is that each state must recognize the validity of another state's actions *provided* that that state demonstrably has jurisdiction over the persons or things in question. Further, any state is entitled to question a claim of jurisdiction.

In dissent, Justice Black expressed a sharply divergent view that the clause contemplated no exceptions: "These petitioners . . . have been convicted under a statute so uncertain in its application that not even the most learned member of the bar could have advised them in advance as to whether their conduct would violate the law. . . . Without charge or proof of fraud in obtaining these decrees, and without holding the decrees invalid under Nevada law, this Court affirms a conviction. . . . A proper respect for the Constitution and the Congress would seem to me to require that we leave this problem where the Constitution did. . . ."

FUGITIVES FROM JUSTICE

The Constitution also stipulates that a fugitive from the justice of one state, apprehended in another, shall on proper request be returned to the state from which he or she is a fugitive—a process commonly called rendition or extradition. This involves a formal request from one governor to another and ordinarily proceeds with few complications. Governors may, however, at their discretion refuse rendition, and the courts have ruled, despite the definite language of this clause, that there is no way to compel rendition. Refusals are rare; and when they do occur, they often have resulted in retaliatory refusals by the other state when the opportunity arose. The usual grounds for refusal are a governor's feeling that the fugitive cannot receive a fair trial in the other state or that, during a period of many years, the fugitive has lived an exemplary life or that the prosecution is politically motivated. Yet substituting one governor's opinion for the regular judicial process is a risky business.*

PRIVILEGES AND IMMUNITIES

A third aspect of interstate relations stems from the cryptic statement in the Constitution that citizens of each state are entitled in every state to the "privileges and immunities of citizens in the several states." The framers did not indicate just what these privileges and immunities are, although the intent was clearly to prevent discrimination by one state against citizens of others.

In interpreting this clause the courts have drawn a distinction between the ordinary services of a state, such as police protection or access to the courts, and the rights or privileges that are called the "use of the common property of the people of the state." In the instance of the latter category, defined only by a succession of cases, nonresidents of a state may be treated differently from residents. At state universities nonresidents are commonly charged higher fees than residents, for example, and there are often differential fees for hunting and fishing licenses and for the use of libraries. (One southern state university until rather recently had two sets of nonresident fees, a modest one of general application and another, much higher, applying to residents of states of the Union during the Civil War.) Subject to these few limitations, citizens may move freely among the states, take up residence, hold property, or engage in business without discriminatory treatment. Free movement has been enhanced by recent court decisions prohibiting states from requiring certain periods of residence within a state before an individual may collect welfare benefits. Such decisions have, however, created critical problems for the states whose higher welfare-benefit levels encourage relief clients to migrate from other states.

---

*The enormity of potential complexities of rendition is illustrated by an unusual case that arose in the days of feuding in the Appalachians. A mountaineer named Hall shot and killed a man named Bryson, the unique circumstance being that he shot across a state line. Hall was brought to trial for murder in his home state of North Carolina, but the courts ultimately decided that they had no jurisdiction because the murder had occurred in Tennessee, where the bullet entered the body. Tennessee promptly requested rendition, but Hall sought the protection of the North Carolina courts, which finally concluded that he could not be extradited because the requirement is that *fugitives* must be returned and obviously a man "cannot be a fugitive from a state in which he has never been." Such matters today could involve national government action if necessary, but happily it is a case not likely to be frequently repeated.

COOPERATION

Although states are forbidden to enter into treaties, they may engage with each other in formal agreements known as interstate compacts, provided Congress consents. Congressional approval is not necessary for the many informal administrative agreements and understandings among the states, but compacts must be used in situations in which the powers or boundaries of states are altered. Compacts have not been common, even though Congress has been quite permissive and has encouraged such agreements. These devices are difficult to enforce when they require multiple appropriations; the best known are used for major and complex matters, such as operation of the Port of New York.

In some areas, as in the regulation of commercial transactions, uniformity of legal requirements among the various states is imperative. If by-passing the national government is desired, or if national action would be unconstitutional, efforts may be made to persuade all the states to pass identical laws. Success has been minimal, although a few uniform laws have been passed by most states. Even the allegedly uniform acts are usually much amended and subject to varying court interpretations in the different states, so that little uniformity is actually achieved.

Often one state will pass an act that is contingent upon reciprocal action by another. Kansas, for example, could indicate its intent to accept Oklahoma certification of teachers if Oklahoma would accept Kansas certification. By the same token, retaliatory legislation occasionally appears. When California insisted on an "agricultural inspection" of vehicles at its borders, Arizona did likewise for vehicles entering it from California, though it did not regularly inspect at either of its two other interstate boundaries. But emphasis on the few friction points in interstate relations is misleading. The problem areas must be understood if improvements are to be made; but although those problems are real, most relationships remain friendly and cooperative. One mechanism contributing toward this atmosphere is the Council of State Governments, an association of all the states, and the associations of officials—governors, legislators, attorneys general, and others—that it has fostered.

FEDERALISM VIEWED CONSTRUCTIVELY

A federal system of government, as noted earlier, is in its nature somewhat contentious. Officials at different levels naturally see issues from different perspectives, and the member states are far from alike. While welcoming national financial aid, many state officials do continue to protest what they consider excessive requirements and paperwork imposed by Washington. Yet the contentious spirit is less evident today than it was in the early history of the republic, and the contests that exist tend to be more political than legal or judicial.

In recent years there has been much talk of creative federalism, meaning essentially a cooperative effort on the part of national, state, and local governments to find the best ways to serve the public effectively, often with all three levels participating, rather than devotion of endless energy to arguments over the question of who has jurisdiction over an activity. National pre-eminence has long been accepted, but the atmosphere in recent years has been one of encouraging maximum possible responsibility on the part of state and local units. Federalism is highly regarded in the United States, and the effort to strengthen its workability seems to be considered a civic virtue.

BASIC CONCEPTS AND TERMS

federal system
division of powers
unitary government
delegated or enumerated powers
implied powers
inherent powers
residual powers
necessary-and-proper or elastic
  clause
doctrine of national supremacy
concurrent powers
popular sovereignty
states' rights

grant-in-aid
categorical grant
matching or conditional grant
block grant
revenue sharing
full-faith-and-credit clause
rendition or extradition
privileges-and-immunities
  clause
interstate compact
uniform state laws
reciprocal laws
creative federalism

CIVIL LIBERTIES:
THE FUSION
OF HOPES
AND
FEARS

3

Few things better illustrate the politically split personality of many American citizens than their attitude toward civil liberties. On the one hand, they respond enthusiastically to Fourth of July oratory praising the Bill of Rights and cherish their personal freedom to speak and worship as they please. Such freedoms, most would argue, are close to the essence of America. Yet faced with the expression of ideas that they disapprove of or consider dangerous, they often react with fear and antagonism, insisting that there is "no place for that kind of talk." How can these conflicting views—that every man and woman is free to say what he or she believes but that some kinds of utterance are forbidden—be reconciled?

Part of the problem is people's natural desire for a risk-free society and their assumption that something close to this is possible. It is not. The real question is what kind of risk we consider the more serious. There are risks inherent in permitting free expression, but are they more or less dangerous than the risks of allowing an individual or an elite group or even a majority to decide for the rest of us what we may say, hear, and see? And if we were to accept the latter alternative, to whom should we grant this authority? True freedom does not consist merely in allowing the airing of safe ideas. Every society permits the expression of orthodoxy. Just so was there freedom of speech in Nazi Germany for people who said what the government approved. The test of a free society is its willingness to permit the expression of unpopular ideas. It would be naive to assume that this carries no dangers; the question is whether the danger is worth the price.

LIBERTY VERSUS AUTHORITY

Throughout history a central problem of political theory has focused on the resolution of the conflict between liberty and authority. Both are necessary. How can they most reasonably be harmonized? Democratic societies seek to maximize personal liberty, but they also recognize that when people live together (not alone on a desert island), absence of social controls results in chaos. The individual good and the social good must be balanced.

It is a fallacy to assume that liberty results from an absence of government—the less government the more freedom, some people claim. All sorts of institutions other than governments, including economic, religious, and educational ones, may restrict freedom. And although the power and influence of government may be used to oppress, they may also be used to liberate. Inevitably the question becomes, Whose freedom is to be preserved when the rights of different individuals and groups conflict? Is freedom reduced or increased by using the power of government to prohibit child labor or by making it illegal to discriminate by race in employment? Are we unduly restricted, or is our freedom of movement made more meaningful, when we are required to stop for a traffic light?

EFFECT OF THE BILL OF RIGHTS

The framers of the Constitution introduced into it certain guarantees of personal liberties, assumed others, and recognized certain protections afforded by state constitutions, but the insistence of many people that additional rights be specified was responsible for the first ten amendments. These guarantees, known as the Bill of Rights, apply as protections only against government actions or actions taken with governmental approval. If a private person or group attempts to restrict one's freedom of worship, for example, the normal recourse is a damage suit. Only when the action involves public officers or agencies or laws does a constitutional issue arise. Moreover, the Bill of Rights taken by itself operates as a restraint only on actions by the national government. Protection against action by

"Maybe it'll go away if we put out the light."

state or local governments derives in part from state constitutions. Further, the courts have interpreted the due process clause of the Fourteenth Amendment to incorporate within the word *liberty* virtually all elements of the Bill of Rights. In this fashion such rights as freedom of speech and press are also protected by the national government against possible state or local infringements.

The Fourteenth Amendment has become the key in contemporary civil liberties issues, since most cases involve the actions of state and local governments. The important sections are the well-known due process and equal protection clauses, which provide that no state may "deprive any person of life, liberty, or property, without due process of law; nor deny to any person within its jurisdiction the equal protection of the laws." The meaning, intent, and significance of these clauses require special attention as a foundation for examination of the contemporary meaning of each of the specific freedoms given constitutional guarantee.

DUE PROCESS OF LAW

Because the Constitution specifically states that one may not be deprived of life, liberty, or property without due process of law, it presumably was assumed that one may be so deprived with due process. Life and property are relatively easy to define; liberty is more ambiguous and controversial. As noted, the courts have indicated that at least the term includes most of those freedoms enumerated in the Bill of Rights.

As a starting point for examination of this matter, three basic and broad principles of due process can be identified as familiar concepts of justice. First, for an action to be a punishable offense it must be clearly defined. One is not to be punished on the basis of a statute that is vague. Some years ago, for instance, a court invalidated an act that made it a misdemeanor to operate overcrowded streetcars in the District of Columbia. The fatal flaw, according to the judge, was that there was no standard by which the drivers or conductors could know whether or not they were violating the law. Was a car to be judged overcrowded when people were standing in the aisles or only when ribs began to crack? A statute prohibiting the operation of cars with more than a given number of standing persons would have been quite acceptable.

Second, guilt is personal. One would scarcely argue that if a man is convicted of burglary, his fraternity brothers are also guilty of burglary, unless they were actual accomplices. Every individual is to be judged by his or her own actions. There is a corollary to this rule: It is only acts for which one may be punished, not ideas. One may be punished for committing or attempting burglary but not for thinking about doing so. This proposition, phrased in such stark terms, seems perfectly acceptable, but matters become confusing when ideological questions are at issue and emotions cloud reason. One may, incidentally, be prosecuted for conspiring to commit a crime even if there is no evidence that one actually carried out the planned offense. Conspiracy itself is an act. While conspiracy is often difficult to prove and is susceptible of injustice in application, elimination of laws against conspiracy might mean that only low-level perpetrators of crimes would be punished while their superiors who planned the operations went free. Actions with intent to harm, even if unsuccessful, may be punishable. The question of intention is present in many legal problems, but since intention lies within a person's mind it is often difficult to prove that an individual intended to do x or had intended to do one thing rather than another.

Third, one is presumed innocent until proved guilty. The burden of proof is always on the prosecution. To realize the significance of this rule one need only conceive of what it would be like if the reverse were true. You could be arrested today and charged with a crime on impressive circumstantial evidence. Imagine the problem (and expense) of proving yourself innocent. Could you prove conclusively exactly where you were and what you were doing on a given evening of the week eight months ago? Could you prove easily that you did not conspire to commit a crime?

There are two aspects of due process, usually labeled *procedural* and *substantive*. Procedural due process is the more obvious kind and refers to the fairness of methods or procedures. A legislative body must follow certain prescribed procedures in passing an act, for example, for the act to be valid. In a court trial one's right to present witnesses in one's behalf and to confront hostile witnesses are procedural rights. Substantive due process is more complex and more important in civil liberties cases. The courts have held that even when all proper procedures have been meticulously followed, defendants still may not have had due process if the actions against them are arbitrary or unreasonable. Substantive due process is thus defined as protection against arbitrary and unreasonable actions by government. But what is arbitrary or unreasonable? This is clearly a matter of judgment; the phrase hardly provides a neat standard by which every action may be evaluated. The courts do not make these judgments by whim, however, and over the years many precedents have been established as guidelines. Yet it remains true that substantive due process involves the substitution of judicial opinion for legislative and executive judgments about the reasonableness and, thus, the merits of a law.

The protections involved in the concept of due process of law are of no small consequence. Equal protection will be dealt with later, but it is appropriate now to investigate the meaning and application of the major civil liberties as the courts today interpret them.

THE FIRST AMENDMENT LIBERTIES: CONTEMPORARY MEANINGS

Should there be no restrictions whatsoever on the exercise of the First Amendment freedoms, as the language of the Constitution seems to say? It states clearly that Congress "shall make no law" abridging the freedoms of speech, press, assembly, and religion; there is no qualification, such as Congress shall make no such laws except when danger is imminent. Some people believe that these rights should be absolute, but the Supreme Court has consistently held that there are practical limits beyond which the exercise of this freedom should not go. The justices have spent much time and effort trying to define such boundaries.

FREEDOM OF SPEECH

The conviction that there are limits to the exercise of First Amendment freedoms is epitomized in a remark by Justice Holmes: few would argue that under the guise of free speech a person has the right falsely to shout "Fire!" in a crowded theater. If one accepts that sort of restraint, then one has accepted the principle that restraint is legitimate, and it remains only to determine the point at which limitations can be invoked. Furthermore, society has traditionally assumed that there are certain contemporary standards of decency in public speech and that false and malicious defamation of character should not be permitted.

Speech is more likely to have inflammatory results than the exercise of the other First Amendment liberties, and it has been the subject of some of the most heated controversies, although each individual freedom has produced its share. The classic statement defining permissible free speech (although the Court did not appear to follow its own rule in making the decision) occurred in the case of a pacifist named Schenck, charged with "discouraging enlistments" during World War I. In this case Justice Holmes wrote that the point at which speech could be restrained is that point at which the words spoken constitute "a clear and present danger that they will bring about the substantive evils that Congress has a right to prevent." It is not enough for the speech to occur in a time of danger; it must create the danger. The danger must be clear and readily identifiable, not vague and uncertain, and fairly immediate, not simply conceivable at some future time.

This doctrine of clear and present danger has been at times abandoned and then again embraced by the Supreme Court. Other tests have been used, such as "the seriousness of the danger discounted by its improbability," but in all instances the courts have determined the seriousness and imminence of socially destructive action, and the old language remains as good an approximation as any of what they will enforce. Opinions of what is "clear and present" differ with judges and times; and to some extent what is being measured is the boiling point of judges and, one may add, of the people and their elected representatives. Society understandably believes it has a right to protect and preserve the institutions and practices that it values, and there is inevitably tension between this right and the right to express what are felt to be radical ideas. The task of the court, whenever it considers a problem about free speech, is that of balancing these two interests, the outspoken individual and the society at large.

Recently, strong voices advocating the concept of absolute freedoms have been heard, notably—though not exclusively—from the late Justice Black. In his view, the First Amendment liberties are something more than just desirable freedoms for the individual; they are so vital to the existence of democracy that they deserve a "preferred position" compared with other aspects of the Constitution, and the risk of abuses is simply a necessary price. Under this doctrine, these rights should be subject to no qualifications whatsoever.

The meaning of free speech is unlikely ever to be settled; it is under lively, constantly changing, ongoing debate. There are certain issues about free speech, however, that recur frequently, and the courts have difficulty resolving them. Typical is the case of some years ago of a university student named Feiner who aroused the indignation of some of his listeners while he was speaking in a public park. A couple of men approached police officers standing on the fringes of the small crowd and said: "If you don't get that guy down from there, we will." Subsequently the police arrested Feiner, and he was soon after convicted. But from where did the threat of violence come? Although the police action was simple and easy, should not the police have protected Feiner? If people there disliked what he was saying, they had the recourse of simply walking away. The common distinction is that the expression of philosophic ideas is permissible but that restraint can be applied when the expression constitutes an incitement to violent action. How can it be decided when a speech "incites" a breach of the peace? Does it depend on the intent of the speaker, or can it occur as a crowd reaction without his intent?

Such a question arose in a famous case in Chicago involving a former priest named Arthur Terminiello, at the time a lecturer for Gerald L. K. Smith's extremist organization, the Christian Nationalist Crusade. The hall in which Terminiello was to speak was picketed, and the pickets were noisy and provocative. The speech, vehemently anti-Semitic, was likewise provocative, and at the conclusion his followers swarmed outside, where a sizable riot ensued. Terminiello was subsequently charged with inciting a breach of the peace, but his initial conviction was ultimately reversed by the Supreme Court on technical grounds. The Court noted that however repulsive it might find the content of the speech, there was insufficient evidence that the speech had caused the riot.

These questions are always vexing. When the late George Lincoln Rockwell, head of the American Nazi party, advocated reinstituting the use of gas ovens to eliminate the Jews in order to solve the world's problems, should such speech have been stopped or should Rockwell merely have been dismissed as a crackpot? When speakers for the National States Rights party advocate stockpiling guns and talk of getting out the scythes to eliminate once and for all "the tares in the field" (identified in their language as "the niggers and kikes"), is this properly protected by freedom of speech? When a representative of a so-called new left organization exhorts his audience to bring "death to the establishment pigs" and suggests that everyone should "experience the sweet sensation of killing," is this merely flamboyant rhetoric? Even if it is, what if someone believes it to be true and acts on it? Where is the boundary at which speech can be halted before violence erupts, and how can direct cause and effect be proved? Do some individuals have to pay the price, perhaps by sacrificing their lives, for the exercise of free speech by others? Probably most people would agree with drawing the line at direct incitement to violence, but the line is not easy to draw.

In recent years the Supreme Court has added significantly to the understanding of the constitutional protection of free speech. Until lately it had been assumed that much commercial speech was outside the First Amendment protections, but a series of decisions has sharply altered that conept. In 1975 the Court (in *Bigelow* v. *Virginia*) ruled invalid a Virginia law allowing punishment of a newspaper editor for publishing an advertisement for an abortion referral service. The following year it struck down another Virginia law that prohibited the advertising of prescription drug prices (*Virginia State Board of Pharmacy* v. *Virginia Citizens Consumer Council*) and went on a year later (*Bates* v. *State Bar of Arizona*, 1977) to hold that lawyers could not be prevented from advertising fees for certain types of services. Yet another 1977 decision (*Linmark Associates* v. *Willingboro*) voided a municipal ordinance prohibiting the posting of "Sold" or "For Sale" signs on real estate (the city fearing they would stimulate "white flight"). Still a different angle appeared in a decision concluding that New Hampshire could not compel citizens to carry on their license plates a message to which they had religious or ideological objections (the state motto, "Live free or die"), on the grounds that their right to remain silent took precedence over state interest in such a matter (*Wooley* v. *Maynard*, 1977).

FREEDOM OF ASSEMBLY

Freedom of assembly has generated fewer cases than freedom of speech, but these rights are often closely related. One purpose of public assembly is speechmaking, and speeches are likely to create excitement. Assembly must of course be peaceable, and public authorities may establish reasonable regulations as to time, place, and manner, though they may not engage in prior censorship.* Freedom of assembly also has come to embrace freedom of voluntary association, which is a somewhat broader concept.

---

*Such regulations are presumably meant not as restraints on speech but as protections of other public interests (such as free movement of traffic or recreational uses of parks).

Both freedom of speech and freedom of association are at the heart of the periodic "loyalty" and "security" controversies that have arisen in modern history. In the name of national security the government on occasion has engaged in extensive secret surveillance of private citizens and public employees. At various times, laws have been enacted to control so-called subversive activities, and persons charged with disloyalty have been dismissed from public employment on suspicion but without significant evidence. Such actions invariably raise questions of free speech and association. The courts have tended to protect these freedoms against such onslaughts and have construed as narrowly as possible most statutes restricting the rights of speech and association. (An exception to this trend has been the courts' very broad interpretations of conspiracy, which have been seen by many as a threat to civil liberties.) Judge Learned Hand cogently expressed the civil libertarian position: "Risk for risk, for myself I had rather take my chance that some traitors will escape detection than spread abroad a spirit of general suspicion and distrust, which accepts rumor and gossip in place of undismayed and unintimidated inquiry."

Whether national loyalty can be forced is an interesting question. Loyalty may be defined as commitment to the best interests of one's country; it is obvious that there will be honest differences of opinion about where the best interest lies. If there are to be fixed standards indicating what constitutes loyal attitudes and behavior, who is to prescribe orthodoxy? A persistent problem is the tendency to define loyalty in terms of one's own views on issues of contemporary public policy. One need not believe in a given aspect of American foreign policy or be opposed to a social security system to be loyal. Citizens can hold earnest and sincere yet wholly contrary views on these or any policy matters, but such differences of belief have nothing to do with loyalty.

FREEDOM OF THE PRESS

The central meaning of freedom of the press in the United States is that there shall be no prior censorship. Presumably anyone may publish, and no government official can prescribe what can and cannot be published. Once material has been published, however, the writer or publisher takes responsibility for it, and it is possible to punish for publication of libelous or obscene matter. Both categories are extremely difficult to define. Most official efforts at limitation are likely to be in vain, since the press and other communications media cooperate in protesting vigorously any threatened actions that would restrict freedom of the press, and together they form a powerful interest group.

Early in the 1970s a rash of controversies erupted over such questions as the right of reporters to protect the confidentiality of their sources and the scope of the government's ability to withhold information from the public on the grounds of national security. On June 13, 1971, the *New York Times* (followed almost immediately by the *Washington Post,* the *Boston Globe,* and other papers) began publishing excerpts from what came to be called the "Pentagon Papers," a lengthy historical study of United States involvement in Vietnam that had been classified as secret by the Defense Department. The *Times* thus precipitated a confrontation on this classic issue. The Pentagon Papers had been copied and provided to the press by Daniel Ellsberg, an employee of a research organization under Defense Department contract. Ellsberg believed that the public was being misled about the war, and the *Times* concluded that the public's right to information takes precedence over what it deemed an arbitrary and improper Pentagon classification of papers that it believed could in no way threaten the security of the country.

Should such decisions be made by the press or by military authorities? The government went promptly to court and secured a temporary order restraining further publication. This is the first time that the national government had ever proposed prior restraint of a newspaper. Four days later the judge refused a permanent order. After complicated maneuvering, the Supreme Court considered an appeal with extraordinary haste and ruled 6 to 3 that the government had failed to justify its request. The urgent and emotional quality of the case was further evidenced by the unusual spectacle of the nine justices submitting nine separate written opinions. The broad questions of the legitimacy of classification systems and the procedures by which they are made remained unanswered, however.

Restraints on the press   Journalists have traditionally insisted on their ability to maintain the confidentiality of their sources, not only for personal advantage in securing information, but also on the much broader grounds that without it the flow of information to the public would be seriously endangered. Sources would simply dry up, they argue, and significant investigative reporting would die. Because reporters operating under confidentiality do often uncover information the sources of which might be important to prosecutors or defense attorneys, conflicts are frequent. When *New York Times* reporter Earl Caldwell refused to divulge what he knew about the Black Panthers even though he had been subpoenaed to give information to a grand jury, another landmark case was set in motion. Caldwell argued that he had established a relation of mutual trust and that his information was pledged to be confidential, but the district court cited him for contempt. Although the appeals court thought otherwise, the Supreme Court ultimately ruled in a 5 to 4 decision (*U.S.* v. *Caldwell,* 1972) that freedom of the press does not encompass the right to protect confidential news sources. Justice

White stated: "We cannot accept the argument that the public interest in possible future news about crime from undisclosed, unverified
sources must take precedence over the public interest in pursuing
and prosecuting those crimes reported to the press." Caldwell maintained his position and subsequently spent time in jail.

This aspect of freedom of the press has been heatedly debated in
editorials and rejoinders. Representatives of the press have been
adamant that journalists not be made agents of the law enforcement
agencies, and they have received considerable support in Congress,
where a flurry of bills specifically granting press immunity was
introduced following the *Caldwell* decision. Legislating proved complicated, however, and enthusiasm waned as a number of journalists
came to feel that the cure might be as bad as the disease. The status of
investigative reporting received a tremendous boost from the Watergate affair, which many people believed might never have come to
light had it not been for the dogged persistence of the staff of the
Washington Post.

Another relevant issue of increasing magnitude is that of efforts by
trial courts to prevent prejudicial publicity in sensational cases by
the issuance of what the press terms *gag orders.* The practice came
before the Supreme Court in a case from the small community of
Sutherland, Nebraska, where six members of a family were mur-
dered in the course of a sexual assault. Because of the nature of the
crime and the fact that it was an area of small population and a
limited number of potential jurors, the judge prohibited publication
of any testimony given in the preliminary hearing, any admissions
or confessions that might be made by the defendant except to the
media, and any other information strongly implicating him. Once
the jury had been chosen and sequestered, the prohibition would
expire. Conceding the aim of the trial judge to guarantee a fair trial,
the Supreme Court upheld the news media's contention that such a
prior restriction violated the First Amendment; it did not rule, however, that limited gag orders could never be permissible. In earlier
cases a number of convictions had been reversed where extensive
prejudicial publicity had been held to make a fair trial impossible,
but the Court now stated: "Pre-trial publicity—even pervasive,
adverse publicity—does not inevitably lead to an unfair trial"
(*Nebraska Press Association* v. *Stuart, 1976*). Trial judges are left to
walk a fine line.

Journalists were even more seriously perturbed by a further
Supreme Court decision in 1978 (*Zurcher* v. *Stanford Daily*), which
held that the First Amendment does not protect newspaper offices
from being searched by police with a proper warrant, seeking evidence that might be in the possession of the newspaper or its staff
members. Again there was concern that the ruling might have
a chilling effect upon the entire newsgathering and publishing

process. The trend of the Court's decisions in this area seem to indicate an intent to protect free expression by the press but not to provide special protections unavailable to citizens generally.

Libel   A few cases will illustrate the difficulties in drawing the boundary between what is and is not presumably permissible to publish. These are borderline or marginal situations, but it is among them that the lines must be drawn. Libel is defined as written defamation of character that is false and of malicious intent. The usual recourse is a damage suit. In 1964 the *New York Times* published a large advertisement that claimed that public officials in Montgomery, Alabama, were violating the rights of demonstrators seeking to improve the lot of blacks in the state. The police commissioner of that city thereupon sued the *Times* for damages in the amount of half a million dollars, correctly alleging that some of the claimed facts in the advertisement were untrue. In this instance the Supreme Court reversed the Alabama courts, holding that actual malice must be proved and that there was no evidence that the newspaper published factual inaccuracies with intent or foreknowledge (*New York Times Co.* v. *Sullivan,* 1964). Generally speaking, public officials, as servants in a democratic system, have no recourse to libel laws against vigorous public criticism of their actions unless there is malicious disregard for the truth, and the principle has been extended in a slightly narrower fashion to other "public figures." When *Time* magazine reported the Firestone divorce case with extensive comments on extramarital affairs that were said to be the basis for the decision, Mrs. Firestone successfully sued for damages, demonstrating that those were not the grounds on which the divorce was granted. The Supreme Court upheld her victory, rejecting *Time*'s claim that she was a public figure; thus there was no need to prove malice, although it was necessary to show some fault on the part of the publication, such as its failing to check the accuracy of statements. Controversies are now numerous over who is and is not a public figure.

The obscenity issue   It has been generally though not universally agreed that governments may act to suppress obscenity, which is deemed to be outside the protection of the First and Fourteenth Amendments. The difficulty of definition has at times seemed almost insurmountable. Movies, books, and other publications come under the umbrella of freedom of the press, and court cases have dealt with every medium and virtually every conceivable kind of circumstance. Do standards of decency remain unchanged or are they subject to revision over time? Should national or local standards be followed? Who should set the standards? In the *Esquire* case some years ago Justice Douglas spoke with feeling about this problem:

What is good literature, what has educational value, what is refined public information, what is good art, varies with individuals as it does from one generation to another. There doubtless would be a contrariety of views concerning Cervantes' *Don Quixote,* Shakespeare's *Venus* and *Adonis,* or Zola's *Nana.* But a requirement that literature or art conform to some norm prescribed by an official smacks of an ideology foreign to our system.

In the *Roth* case in 1957 (*Roth* v. *U.S.*) the Court struggled over a workable definition of obscenity. "All ideas," the Court stated, "having even the slightest redeeming social importance—unorthodox ideas, controversial ideas, even ideas hateful to the prevailing climate of opinion—have the full protection of the [constitutional] guaranties." Obscenity is denied those guaranties because it is "utterly without redeeming social importance." The definition of obscenity was then offered: "Whether to the average person applying contemporary community standards, the dominant theme of the material taken as a whole appeals to prurient interests." "Prurient" was defined in a footnote as applicable to "material having a tendency to excite lustful thoughts," but the Court clearly indicated that "sex and obscenity are not synonymous." How much help do such guidelines furnish? Do they merely set off another round of definitions? How are we to characterize the average person and determine contemporary community standards?

Nine years after the *Roth* decision, the guidelines were significantly modified in the case of *Memoirs* v. *Massachusetts.* Where it had been assumed in *Roth* that obscenity is without redeeming social value, *Memoirs* required that for a work to be regarded as obscene it would be necessary to establish that "the material is utterly without redeeming social value." Prosecutors complained that they were required to prove a negative, a virtually impossible task. The Supreme Court has until lately been permissive because of the obvious difficulties of definition and its strong concern for the preservation of First Amendment liberties. It struck down the attempted ban in some communities on such books as *Fanny Hill* and *Tropic of Cancer,* just as it voided censorship of a series of films. In a short time, books and movies using language and describing activities that were formerly considered unfit for publication became commonplace, and rapidly multiplying X-rated movies were frequently advertised with tongue-in-cheek suggestions about "redeeming social importance."

Having sought to stop somewhat short of banning all state and local government controls, the Court had to decide each case on its individual merits, and it found itself inundated. At times it indicated that there could be no protection for "hard-core pornography," but this is not appreciably easier to define. Justice Stewart was driven to remark, "I can't define it, but I know it when I see it"; this also is a

difficult standard to apply. Movie advertising soon openly claimed "the best hard-core in the city," and self-styled pornographic magazines became readily available.

The Court has customarily recognized that governments, in the interest of protecting children, may go further than would be permissible for adults, but this too is beset with difficulties. In the same year as the *Roth* decision, the Court considered a Michigan statute prohibiting the publication or sale of printed materials containing "obscene, immoral, lewd or lascivious language . . . tending to incite minors to violent or depraved or immoral acts." Alfred Butler, a bookseller, sold to a plainclothes police officer a book that the trial court found to have "a potentially deleterious influence upon youth." The Supreme Court held, however, that the Michigan legislation was "not reasonably restricted to the evil with which it is said to deal." Its effect was to limit adults to "reading only what is fit for children." Quarantining the general reading public in order to shield juvenile innocence "is to burn the house to roast the pig." But how is it possible effectively to control sales to minors?

By the time of the advent of such films as *Deep Throat* and *The Devil in Miss Jones,* efforts at public regulation had gained new impetus. In mid-1973 the Supreme Court, now with several new members, sought once again in a 5 to 4 decision (*Miller* v. *California*) to establish workable guidelines for state action. The threefold standards were whether (1) "the average person, applying contemporary community standards," would find that the work, taken as a whole, appeals to the prurient interest; (2) the work depicts or describes, in a patently offensive way, sexual conduct specifically defined by the applicable state law; and (3) the work, taken as a whole, lacks serious literary, artistic, political, or scientific value. The Court emphasized that local community standards, not national ones, are to prevail, while reliance for the views of the average person is apparently to be on juries. Was the determination of "serious" value an easier standard than "redeeming social importance" or an even more controversial one?

In a related Georgia case (*Paris Adult Theatre I* v. *Slaton*) decided the same day as *Miller*, Justice Brennan, who had written the earlier *Memoirs* decision, suggested in a dissent that the time had come to make a significant departure from past approaches that had not proved workable. His recommendation was that the states might be permitted to regulate distribution (availability to juveniles or obtrusive exposure to unconsenting adults), but that they would have no power to attempt "wholly to suppress sexually oriented materials on the basis of their allegedly 'obscene' contents."

Only a year later the Court further complicated the rule that local community standards are to prevail, when it held in *Jenkins* v. *Georgia* that a jury in Albany, Georgia, was wrong in judging the movie *Carnal Knowledge* obscene. Initial decisions, it appears, may be made by local juries, but the Court will reserve to itself the right to review their reasonableness. In the name of maintaining a degree of national uniformity, the Court placed itself back in the presumably unwanted business of making case-by-case determinations of what is obscene.

Nowhere is the sharp and fundamental difference of opinion over interpretation of this part of the First Amendment clearer than in the majority opinion of Chief Justice Burger and the dissenting opinion of Justice Douglas in the *Miller* and *Paris Adult Theatre* cases. Burger wrote that

> to equate the free and robust exchange of ideas and political debate with commercial exploitation of obscene material demeans the grand conception of the First Amendment and its high purposes in the historic struggle for freedom. It is a "misuse of the great guarantee of free speech and free press." . . . The First Amendment protects works which, taken as a whole, have serious literary, artistic, political, or scientific value, regardless of whether the government, or a majority of the people approve of the ideas these works represent. "The protection given speech and press was fashioned to assure unfettered interchange of *ideas* for the bringing about of political and social changes desired by the people". . . . But the public portrayal of hard core sexual conduct for its own sake, and for the ensuing commercial gain, is a different matter.

For Douglas the efforts of the Court to establish guidelines are well-meaning but go outside its power. The First Amendment makes no exception for obscenity, he said. Moreover, only government action is banned, and no one is compelled to look or listen:

> The idea that the First Amendment permits government to ban publications that are "offensive" to some people puts an ominous gloss on freedom of the press. . . . Its prime function was to keep debate open to "offensive" as well as to "staid" people. The tendency throughout history has been to subdue the individual and to exalt the power of government. The use of the standard "offensive" gives authority to government that cuts the very vitals out of the First Amendment.

"Nine, please"

. . . People are, of course, offended by many offerings made by merchants in this area. They are also offended by political pronouncements, sociological themes, and by stories of official misconduct. The list of activities and publications and pronouncements that offend someone is endless. Some of it goes on in private; some of it is inescapably public, as when a government official generates crime, becomes a blatant offender of the moral sensibilities of the people, engages in burglary, or breaches the privacy of the telephone, the conference room, or the home . . . There is no protection against offensive ideas, only against offensive conduct. Obscenity at most is the expression of offensive ideas. . . .

I am sure I would find offensive most of the books and movies charged with being obscene. But in a life that has not been short, I have yet to be trapped into seeing or reading something that would offend me. I never read or see the materials coming to the Court under charges of "obscenity," because I have thought the First Amendment made it unconstitutional for me to act as censor. . . . As a parent or a priest or as a teacher I would have no compulsion in edging my children or wards away from the books and movies that did no more than excite man's base instincts. But I never supposed that government was permitted to sit in judgment on one's tastes or beliefs—save as they involved action within the reach of the police power of government.

FREEDOM OF RELIGION

The right of free exercise of religion is a cherished tradition in the United States, but this clause and its companion stipulation that there be no governmental establishment of religion have produced a great many intriguing legal controversies. Inevitably there are many situations in which general laws for the health, safety, and welfare of citizens conflict with religious belief and practice, and these conflicts result in headaches for the courts. Significantly, these problems usually involve not a conflict between right and wrong but a conflict between two constitutional rights. For example, the states' power to legislate for the protection of the health of their citizens is unquestionable, just as the right to free exercise of religion is indisputable. When these rights are at odds, the task of the courts is to decide which shall be given effect.

Free exercise Although the free exercise and nonestablishment clauses are intimately related, they pose somewhat different questions and require individual consideration. Most religious belief and practice result in no conflict with the law, so the test cases issue primarily from relatively unorthodox groups and individuals. A well-known case involved the flag salute (*West Virginia State Board of Education* v. *Barnette,* 1943) and was a landmark for many later decisions. At the time all pupils in the West Virginia public schools were required to participate regularly in saluting the flag and reciting the pledge of allegiance. Members of Jehovah's Witnesses refused to permit their children to do so, contending that this constituted bowing down before a graven image, which they felt to be prohibited by literal interpretation of Chapter 20 of the Book of Exodus. When the laws of God and of humanity are in conflict, they said, they are required to grant precedence to the laws of God.

Although the Supreme Court only three years before had upheld a similar requirement in Pennsylvania, it now reversed itself and ruled in favor of the Witnesses. The state, it concluded, had complete right to control the educational program and could require the salute and pledge as a means of inculcating patriotism if it chose to (despite the doubts expressed by many people as to whether this would accomplish the alleged purpose). But such a requirement could not be enforced against those who had religious scruples about it.

After several deaths had resulted from practices of the Tennessee-based Holiness Church of God in Jesus' Name, whose members engage in handling poisonous snakes or drinking poison as a means of demonstrating and spreading their faith, the state legislature acted to ban such practices. Snake handling, said the leaders of the church, was an absolutely central component of their religious belief and exercise; moreover, government had no right to tell competent adults what they might do with their bodies. Ultimately the Tennessee Supreme Court held that the state "has the right to guard against the unnecessary creation of widows and orphans," despite the fact that it would "remove the theological heart" of the church, and the United States Supreme Court in 1976 refused to review the ruling (*Pack* v. *Tennessee*).

The Amish, distinguished in the minds of most people by their mode of dress and the refusal of the orthodox members to use such modern devices as motor vehicles, have always sought to maintain their quiet agricultural life and customs. While desiring to educate their children in basic disciplines and religious precepts, the parents often oppose sending their children to public schools where they will be subject to contamination by the outside world. As a result the Amish have come often into conflict with state compulsory school attendance laws and laws establishing qualification standards for teachers when a sect operates its own schools.

In one Ohio community, where the law requiring attendance beyond the eighth grade had been ignored by the Amish for years, the district attorney decided that his responsibility dictated enforcement, but Amish parents flatly refused in their gentle but firm fashion. The Amish are highly esteemed for personal qualities by their neighbors, and he took the matter to court reluctantly. With equal reluctance the judge imposed minimum thirty-day jail sentences on a group of Amish fathers. They served the sentences but still did not send the children to school. What next? Put the fathers in jail for sixty days? The Amish were obviously prepared to pay the price society exacted for their nonconformity. A handful of people with unshakable religious feeling were involved, and in time Ohio decided to look the other way.

A succession of similar conflicts in several states culminated in a Supreme Court decision in 1972 (*Wisconsin* v. *Yoder*) wherein the right to "free exercise of religion" was given precedence over the interest of a state in universal education. Amish parents of children who were all graduates of eighth grade in public school refused to permit their attendance at high school on grounds of religious belief, and the Court concluded that an exemption for this group did no significant damage to state interests. What might happen if a large group, with a lesser historical record of such belief, were to make such refusal is unclear. It is interesting to notice that Justice Douglas, while agreeing with the decision, dissented in part because of the Court's tacit assumption that the beliefs of the parents represented the beliefs of their high-school-age children.

Some groups have claimed religious belief as license to use dangerous and illegal drugs. Such activities raise some currently unanswerable questions. What is a church? Can any group of people legally constitute themselves a church, formulate sanctioned ritual, and appoint clergy? Are such clergy then entitled to exemption from the draft when it exists? Can a state decide that one group is a legitimate church and another is not? Indeed, how is religious belief to be defined? Such belief is a highly personal matter, and any statement of just how free it is possible for freedom of worship to be is likely to continue indefinitely controversial.

Case Study
RELIGIOUS LIBERTY VERSUS STATE POWER

Karen Johnson, a professional social worker for the county who happened to have been trained also as a nurse, paid a routine call on the morning of September 12 at the tenement apartment of the Richard Roe family. While there she noticed that one of the children, seemingly about three years of age, was obviously seriously ill and was running a high fever. His body was emaciated, and he showed no recognition of what went on around him. "Has a doctor seen the child?" "Oh, no," the mother responded, "our religion teaches that we shouldn't have anything to do with doctors. If the Lord wants Jimmy to live he will live, and if He wants him to die he will die. All we can do is pray, and that we are surely doing." "But God also gave people the ability to learn how to cure sickness." "No, ma'am," came the answer solemnly, "that's not the way I believe."

The social worker left, but, unable to put the picture of the helpless child from her mind, she called the county health officer, who went immediately to examine the child. He told the parents that Jimmy was dying and that he must be gotten to a hospital for medical attention at once. They refused. The doctor asked himself whether parents have a right to decide life or death for their children, but of course the parents would deny that they were making any such decision. As far as they were concerned, it was in the hands of God. Deciding that in good conscience he must act, the health officer went immediately into court, where he secured an order declaring the Roes incompetent to care for the child and establishing a temporary guardianship. Within minutes the guardian authorized medical treatment, and the child was rushed to a hospital where doctors worked to save his life. It was too late. Twenty-six hours later Jimmy Roe died.

Who was to blame? Mr. and Mrs. Roe insisted that the county authorities had killed their son. The county considered prosecuting the Roes on charges of child neglect. What should be done in the event that similar cases arise in the future, as they certainly will? In such a situation, does religious liberty or the power of the state to protect the health of its citizens have priority?

Must an employer grant Saturdays off to an employee for whom that day is the Sabbath, if such an arrangement would violate seniority agreements with a union or force the employer into abnormal expenses for Saturday replacements? Such a question arose in the case of a clerk for Trans World Airlines at a facility that was operated twenty-four hours a day, seven days a week. The case had wide ramifications for employers and workers throughout the country because of the Civil Rights Act requirement that employers make "reasonable accommodations" for employees' religious observances. In this instance the Supreme Court held that TWA was not compelled to take extreme steps nor to discriminate against some employees in order to accommodate others. Protection exists for "majorities as well as minorities," it said (*TWA* v. *Hardison*, 1977).

Increasingly in the focus of public attention are the amazing variety of issues surrounding the "right to die with dignity," the question of whether a medical practitioner should keep alive by artificial means a baby born seriously deformed and lacking minimal mental capacity, the right of parents to refuse medical treatment for a child, and the like. At least one state has now established in law the right of a person to direct in a "living will" that doctors not preserve one's life artificially when there is no further prospect of normal existence. Not long ago much of the nation witnessed the anguish of the parents of Karen Quinlan, who had lain slowly deteriorating in a coma for over a year, as they asked the courts for permission to disconnect her respirator. In an unusual decision the New Jersey Supreme Court authorized such action when no hope exists. The fact that she did not then immediately die re-emphasizes the difficulty of such decisions. Many cases of these types involve matters of deep religious belief.

Separation of church and state   Prohibition of the establishment of religion has produced a great deal of litigation. The constitutional framers were eager to avoid an official tax-supported church with

From *Straight Herblock* (Simon & Schuster, 1964).

"What do they expect us to do—listen to the kids pray at <u>home</u>?"

clergy appointed by government and exercising political power—the situation they were familiar with in most European countries in the seventeenth and eighteenth centuries. What more the framers intended is debatable, but the doctrine of separation of church and state has expanded considerably by interpretation. Probably the most comprehensive judicial statement of the scope of this doctrine appeared in a Supreme Court decision concerning New Jersey's program of aid for transportation of pupils to parochial schools (*Everson* v. *Board of Education,* 1947):

> The "establishment of religion" clause of the First Amendment means at least this: Neither a state nor the Federal Government can set up a church. Neither can pass laws which aid one religion, aid all religions, or prefer

one religion over another. Neither can force nor influence a person to go to or to remain away from church against his will or force him to profess a belief or disbelief in any religion. No person can be punished for entertaining or professing religious beliefs or disbeliefs, for church attendance or nonattendance. No tax in any amount, large or small, can be levied to support any religious activities or institutions, whatever they may be called, or whatever form they may adopt to teach or practice religion. Neither a state nor the Federal Government can, openly or secretly, participate in the affairs of any religious organizations or groups or vice versa. In the words of Jefferson, the clause against establishment of religion by law was intended to erect "a wall of separation between church and state."

Despite this sweeping language and the presence of the wall metaphor, it is not true that no relationships exist. Chaplains are furnished for the armed forces and Congress at public expense. God is invoked in oath taking, and the phrase "In God We Trust" appears on our coins. Church property is commonly exempted from taxation. Low-interest loans are made to church-related colleges. And churches can and do speak to government on a great number of public issues. In the words of Justice Blackmun in the *Hardison* case, "We have acknowledged before, and we do so again here, that the wall of separation that must be maintained between church and state 'is a blurred, indistinct, and variable barrier depending on all the circumstances of a particular relationship.'"

The general rule remains that tax money may not be spent to aid religion, but the boundaries are somewhat hazy. In the *Everson* case, the Court permitted the New Jersey practice because the transportation aid went not to parochial schools, but to the children and their families, and it was said to be basically a matter of protecting the health and safety of the children. The Court soon thereafter invalidated the practice of certain school districts of allocating time each week for local clergy to provide presumably nonsectarian religious instruction in the school buildings. The subsequently developed practice of "released time," whereby pupils could leave school for religious instruction elsewhere, was sustained.

A tempest was unleashed in 1962 when the Court struck down a New York requirement that each public school class recite daily a brief prayer prescribed by the State Board of Regents. (Parents could on request have their children excused from participation.) There was an immediate flood of criticism of the Court in the halls of Congress and from many conservative religious groups, but most of the major church organizations supported the decision as being in accord with the tradition of separation. The Court surely did not "ban God from the public schools," as some people, including certain clergy insisted. Many were intrigued by such a suggestion, for, they asked, if God is God, how is it within the power of the

Supreme Court or any other body to ban Him from anywhere? The Court was quite specific about the limited nature of the decision, saying simply that "it is no part of the business of government to compose official prayers for any group of the American people to recite." The following year the Court also invalidated requirements of Bible reading and recitation of the Lord's Prayer, taking pains to emphasize that government is neither to aid nor to restrict religion but "is firmly committed to a position of neutrality." Such activities do continue in many places where no objection is raised.

Challenges to one sort of government action or another of course continue to arise. In 1970 the Court sustained the practice of property tax exemptions for property owned by religious organizations used solely for religious worship (*Walz* v. *Tax Commission of the City of New York*), remarking that the First Amendment tolerates neither government establishment of nor government interference with religion. "The court has struggled," it said, "to find a neutral course between the two Religion Clauses, both of which are cast in absolute terms, and either of which, if expanded to a logical extreme, would tend to clash with the other."

In a series of cases stretching over several years the Court has sought to draw a line between those expenditures that directly support church-related schools and those that constitute aid to students or have only an incidental and unimportant effect on the religious purposes of the institution. Thus it has struck down grants for instructional equipment or teacher salaries, as well as reimbursements or tax credits for parents who send their children to nonpublic schools. On the other hand, it has sustained public expenditures for secular textbooks, health services, and educational testing in such schools (most notably in *Wolman* v. *Walter*, 1977), construction of buildings for secular purposes at church-related colleges, and even annual grants to such colleges, with a condition that there be no use for sectarian purposes. "Religious institutions need not be quarantined from public benefits that are neutrally available to all," the Court has stated. "Neutrality is what is required. The state must confine itself to secular objectives, and neither advance nor impede religious activity" (*Roemer* v. *Board of Public Works of Maryland*, 1976). Although the Court is rarely unanimous in such cases, there is a basic three-part test that it endeavors to apply: (1) Aid must have a secular purpose, (2) there must be a primary effect other than the advancement of religion, and (3) there must not result any "excessive entanglement" between government and religion.

This discussion merely introduces the welter of issues spawned by these constitutional provisions, but it indicates how lively the protection of religious freedom can be. Perhaps it also helps us understand why generally acceptable settlements of these conflicts are very difficult. Possibly the ultimate problem has surfaced in the recent occurrence of several suits against God. In one instance George Albrecht originally sued the city of Lake Worth, Florida, and a construction firm, alleging that he was injured when a rain-soaked sidewalk collapsed under him. A jury dismissed the claim with the statement that this was an "act of God." Incensed, Albrecht then filed suit against a group of defendants designated as "God and Co.," the codefendants being thirty-two local churches and synagogues. To date copies of the complaint have been delivered to each of the church bodies, but court officials have been unable to serve papers on the principal defendant.

A RIGHT OF PRIVACY

Although the Constitution nowhere speaks of a "right of privacy," it is thought to be implicit in several sections of that document. Over recent years the Supreme Court has gradually constructed such a right from a variety of specific statements in the First, Third, Fourth, Fifth, and Ninth Amendments, and the expression has begun to come into general use. Its full scope, however, is by no means clear and will be determined only through successive judicial interpretations.

Unquestionably the most striking privacy case yet decided took much of the nation by surprise when in 1973 the Supreme Court ruled unconstitutional those laws in Texas and Georgia that prohibited abortion except in situations in which pregnancy caused severe problems of health. Said Justice Blackmun in the pair of 7 to 2 decisions (*Roe* v. *Wade, Doe* v. *Bolton*), the right of privacy "is broad enough to encompass a woman's decision whether or not to terminate a pregnancy." Rejecting contentions of certain religious groups, the Court held that a fetus is not a person and thus is not entitled to protection under the due process clause and that the word *person* applies only postnatally.

Given the deep emotions surrounding this issue and the fact that forty states had basically similar laws on the subject, the impact of this decision was enormous. The Court did not totally prohibit state abortion statutes but rather established a three-stage guideline: (1) during the first three months of pregnancy the decision should be solely that of a woman and her doctor; (2) after that time, state regulations "reasonably related to maternal health" are permissible; (3) a state may prohibit abortion after the stage of viability of the fetus is reached, somewhere between six and seven months, "except where it is necessary in appropriate medical judgment for the preservation of the life or health of the mother." The decision was unusual in that it relies on much clinical detail in order to spell out acceptable state actions. But the most unique feature to any observer other than an American is that so critical a political, social, and religious issue should be resolved judicially. In virtually no other country could this be possible. Efforts to amend the Constitution in order to overrule the Supreme Court have been under way for some time, but Congress has shied away despite strong pressures from the "right to life" forces.

The battles have gone on in both the judicial and the legislative arenas. In 1976 the Supreme Court struck down requirements in Missouri for the consent of a husband to an abortion and for the consent of a parent in the case of an unmarried woman under age eighteen. While Justice White argued that a father's interest "may be unmatched by any other interest in his life," the majority concluded that since only one partner's view can prevail, the balance weighs in the woman's favor. On another aspect White suggested with sarcasm that the Court is becoming "not only the country's continuous constitutional convention but also its *ex officio* medical board" *(Planned Parenthood of Central Missouri* v. *Danforth)*. The following year the Court voided a New York statute prohibiting advertising of contraceptives, giving pharmacists a monopoly on nonmedical sales, and prohibiting all sales or distribution to persons under sixteen. Such a law, it said, is an intrusion on the individual right of privacy, in this case the decision of whether to conceive a child *(Carey* v. *Population Services International)*. In the meantime, in health program appropriations Congress has repeatedly outlawed use of national funds to pay for abortions (although it has sometimes reached a compromise to allow payment when the mother's life was endangered or when the pregnancy resulted from rape or incest), but court challenges delayed effectiveness of the ban for some time. Opponents argued that such action merely discriminates against poor women, many of whom would likely seek unsafe abortions. The right of privacy has only begun to be explored and is likely in the future to give rise to many controversial decisions.

PROBLEMS OF DISCRIMINATION: THE EQUAL PROTECTION CLAUSE

The meaning of the equal protection clause of the Fourteenth Amendment can be stated simply, but its ramifications are almost endless. The intent of the clause was clearly to emphasize that there can be no second-class citizenship in the United States; governments must treat all citizens alike. Although this requirement is applicable to any individual or group and some of its early usage relates to economic matters, the brunt of its effect has been on the problem of racial discrimination. To deal fully with the issues of race relations would require a book, and our discussion must necessarily concentrate on the central constitutional issues.

SUPREME COURT ACTION TO END RACIAL DISCRIMINATION

A great many but not all of the controversies that have shaped present-day interpretations of equal protection have related to racial discrimination in education. A forerunner in a long series of such cases that overturned earlier precedents occurred in 1938 when the University of Missouri law school denied admission to Lloyd Gaines, a black student who was admittedly qualified for admission on every ground except race. Missouri offered to pay tuition for Gaines to attend law school in an adjoining state that made no racial discrimination, but Gaines refused, citing reasons why he wished to study in his home state and insisting that as a citizen who met the academic requirements he was entitled to admission there.

When Gaines's appeal finally reached the Supreme Court (*Missouri ex rel. Gaines* v. *Canada*, 1938), it ruled that although Missouri was not compelled to maintain a law school, if it chose to do so it must maintain it for all citizens equally. Several subsequent cases developed further but different aspects of this theme, some applying to educational institutions, others to public recreational facilities, public transportation, municipally owned cemeteries, and other public services. Facilities supported by the taxes of all citizens must be available to all citizens. At that time, however, the old "separate but equal" doctrine voiced by the court in 1896 (*Plessy* v. *Ferguson*) was still accepted. In substance it held that segregation of the races is permissible provided that equal facilities are made available. Missouri might therefore have solved its problems by creating a separate law school for blacks equal to that provided for whites, but this would have been prohibitively expensive. Texas, in fact, subsequently tried this, but the new law school was patently not equal, and the effort was abandoned under court pressure.

As a steady stream of cases appeared year after year, more and more emphasis was placed on the word *equal* in the traditional phrase, until in 1954 the Court finally discarded the entire doctrine. In the famous case of *Brown* v. *Board of Education of Topeka*, the Court held that "separate educational facilities are inherently unequal" and directed an end to segregated schooling. It subsequently instructed local school authorities to develop plans toward this end, under scrutiny of United States district courts, and to proceed "with all deliberate speed." The reason for this last curious phrase was the Court's recognition that long-established and court-approved customs and physical arrangements could not be totally transformed overnight, but in retrospect progress has been far more deliberate than speedy.

Some states with segregation practices immediately initiated a gradual shift of pattern, but others used every stalling device possible, including a succession of state laws that everyone knew would

be struck down but consumed time in testing before the courts. Late in 1969 the Supreme Court in effect jettisoned the word *deliberate*, unanimously declaring that after fifteen years the time for action was now, but even this did not stop all delaying tactics. The whole process is seriously complicated throughout the country by existing patterns of housing segregation creating de facto school segregation, in contrast to de jure (required by law) segregation, as was the case in southern states.

A different aspect of the complicated equal protection question emerged with a series of cases in which white students claimed to be victims of "reverse discrimination," a series culminating, at least temporarily, in the widely publicized *Bakke* decision in 1978. Allan Bakke, a white pre-medical student denied admission to the medical school of the University of California at Davis, brought suit on the grounds that he had been refused admission on the basis of his race. The university, he said, maintained a separate "minority quota" for admission, and the acceptance of students under that quota system who had lower grades and admission test scores than he did resulted in his exclusion because of a ceiling on the size of the entering class.

The California Supreme Court invalidated considerations of race in admissions, but a sharply divided United States Supreme Court in 1978 struck something of a compromise. The Court ruled (5 to 4, with six separate written opinions and a different group constituting the majority on two different aspects of the question) that Bakke was indeed the victim of discrimination and must be admitted. But this, it said, was because the quota system used race as essentially the sole factor in special considerations and the university dealt with applicants in two separate classes. The Court indicated, however, that race and ethnicity could be *part* of admissions considerations and that efforts to redress the effects of past discrimination were not in themselves unconstitutional. The decision, thus, did not invalidate affirmative action programs in general but left room for a vast amount of future litigation.

Efforts to secure better racial balance, and thus ease possible psychological damage to young victims of discrimination, by busing pupils to schools away from their home neighborhoods have been successful in some communities, but have raised storms of protest in others across the nation. In some northern cities, or more particularly in suburbs, proposals along these lines have been greeted by street demonstrations, boycotts, and even bombings. The opposition has been especially heavy where courts suggested, as in Detroit and Richmond, that entire metropolitan areas should be considered as a whole in establishing nonsegregated public education. Busing of school children for a variety of purposes is of course hardly a new practice. President Nixon made clear his personal opposition to "forced busing" solely for purposes of racial balance, but not long thereafter a unanimous Supreme Court upheld the use of busing, racial balance ratios, and strangely irregular school-district boundaries as possible interim methods of eliminating the vestiges of state-imposed segregation. It gave wide latitude to local authorities but emphasized that United States district court judges were to act in case the local authorities failed to meet their obligations. In June 1974 a sharply divided Court modified the requirements by ruling in the Detroit case (*Milliken* v. *Bradley*) that busing plans could not cut across city and school-district lines to achieve desegregation unless it could be shown that the suburban communities had directly participated in creating the segregation problem.

Three years later the Court further modified the impact of its rulings on this subject by stating that once a school district is in compliance regarding desegregation, it is not required to engage in a continual juggling of numbers to maintain a specific racial balance (*Pasadena Board of Education* v. *Spangler*). An even more delicate problem was that of the segregation practices of private schools.

When two pupils were denied admission to private schools in northern Virginia solely on the grounds that they did not admit nonwhite pupils, the schools claimed that this was a private matter not raising a constitutional issue. The parents sued under the ancient 1866 civil rights law that gave "all persons within the jurisdiction of the United States the same right . . . to make and enforce contracts . . . as is enjoyed by white citizens." The parents claimed that they sought to enter into a contract with the schools, which advertised to the general public, and their position was sustained by the trial, appellate, and Supreme courts (*Runyon* v. *McCrary, 1977*).

Busing became the "sleeper" issue of the 1972 elections and continues to stir heated emotions. Support in Congress has mushroomed for a variety of antibusing amendments to education finance bills, usually barring the Department of Health, Education, and Welfare (HEW) from ordering busing beyond the nearest school (although most such orders were court actions.) Many members who had previously backed all sorts of civil rights legislation sought to rationalize these changed votes by suggesting that busing is not the best way to achieve the desired goal. Knowledge of what the best way is, unfortunately, remains elusive. Some progress was made with special compensatory education programs for pupils from impoverished and ghetto backgrounds. The entire picture was further confused, however, when racial minority groups in some cities began to assert demands for control of "their own" schools and, in a few instances, even for the exclusion of other races. Chinese-Americans in San Francisco staged a protest to claim that their children's cultural heritage would be neglected if they were forced to be educated in schools outside the Chinese neighborhood. Where do fairness and equality lie?

Another sore point in race relations is discriminatory law enforcement and administration of justice. In some sections of the country, the exclusion of blacks from juries, the intimidation of blacks who do serve, and especially the failure of juries to convict whites accused of offenses against blacks even in the face of overwhelming evidence have been chronic problems. Such cases as those in Lowndes County, Alabama, in the middle years of the 1960s, issuing from the murder of a Detroit woman helping the Selma march and the murder of a seminary student working on voter registration, roused the nation's conscience. More recently a number of decisions have indicated a change, and a number of southern juries have convicted whites in racial cases. But the road to equal justice has by no means been fully traversed.

CONGRESSIONAL ACTION TO END RACIAL DISCRIMINATION

Major pieces of national legislation to correct various kinds of inequities have supplemented the court tests of discriminatory practices.

From the Civil War until 1957 very little was accomplished, primarily because the filibuster (prolonged debate or speaking) is permitted in the Senate. In that year the logjam was broken and a bill was passed to aid blacks to secure voting rights where they had been denied. This was thought a logical first step, both because the right to vote seems elementary justice and because increased voting by blacks could be expected to have a fairly immediate impact on the structure of political power in states with large black populations. In recent years solid evidence of this effect has appeared: the black vote has sharply increased, black officeholders have become familiar in the South, and white candidates often actively seek black support.

The Voting Rights Act of 1957 was supplemented by stronger laws on the right to vote in 1960, 1965, and 1968, but the major piece of legislation was the monumental Civil Rights Act of 1964. This was passed after the Senate outlasted three months of filibuster by southern senators and ultimately invoked cloture. Cloture, terminating the debate, was achievable then only by the backing of two thirds of the senators. The 1964 act not only strengthened voting-rights enforcement by the national government, but it also outlawed discrimination based on race, color, religion, and national origin in all manner of public accommodations (including hotels, restaurants, and theaters). It further barred certain discriminatory practices in businesses having effect on interstate commerce (as virtually all do), authorized the withholding of national financial aid to state and local units for programs in which discrimination is practiced, and permitted the national government to intervene on behalf of victims of certain kinds of discrimination.

SEX DISCRIMINATION

Yet another form of discrimination that has come sharply to public attention is social inequity experienced by women. Despite a strong residual sentiment, on the part of large numbers of women as well as men, that the proper role for women lies only in connection with home and family, the justice of the fundamental complaints has been rather rapidly accepted. Innumerable practices involving the legal status of married women, unequal pay scales, and exclusion from certain occupations have stood for centuries largely because they were considered the natural order of things and no one significantly challenged them. But a new awareness and activism have begun to generate a wave of change through both legislative, judicial, and nonofficial processes.

Despite wide acceptance of basic equity changes, provisions in law for more elaborate steps to erase sex discrimination or its effects stirred conflict: Familiar examples are the end of separate physical education classes and most athletic teams in schools and colleges and the affirmative action requirements in employment (that an employer must not only avoid discrimination but actually take positive steps to insure the hiring of more women—and minorities—which some see as reverse discrimination). The conflict tends to arise more from administrative applications of the rules than from the statutes themselves. When HEW sought to prohibit separate sex membership in fraternities and sororities and in service organizations such as Girl Scouts and Boy Scouts, Congress passed amendments stating that this had not been its intent and specifically exempted such organizations. The new standards cut both ways; witness recent decisions holding that widowers must be treated the same as widows in the determination of social security benefits and that men cannot be required to work more years than women in order to be eligible for retirement benefits.

A major feature of public controversy concerns the effort to secure adoption of the Equal Rights Amendment, a proposal that in slightly different forms has been before Congress for decades. This proposed amendment to the Constitution was approved by the House in the fall of 1971 and the Senate in March 1972 by the overwhelming votes of 354 to 23 and 84 to 8. It reads simply: "Equality of rights under the law shall not be denied or abridged by the United States or by any state on account of sex." But despite the congressional vote margins, undoubtedly strengthened to some extent by the desire to pass the buck, securing the approval of thirty-eight states did not prove easy. After thirty, ratification became especially tough. The opposition focused on claims that passage would nullify much protective legislation for women in industry, that it would eliminate existing special advantages such as alimony, that the integrity of the family would be damaged, that privacy between the sexes might be threatened, and that state law-making power would be further interfered with and usurped by the national courts. But whether or not this particular amendment is finally approved, no one can seriously doubt the likelihood of further changes in this very sensitive area of human relations. The equal protection clause has yet to make its full weight felt in this context.

UNFINISHED BUSINESS

Opponents of civil rights legislation protest that such laws are useless on the grounds that "you can't legislate morality," that what is really necessary are "changes in the hearts and minds of people." No one actually suggests that morality can be legislated, but proponents insist that it is possible to control and influence behavior by law and that it is at least desirable to make use of the law and render ethically wrong actions also illegal. Civil rights advocates agree on the desirability of change in hearts and minds, but they do not consider it prerequisite to improvements in the way fellow human beings are treated. During a Senate committee hearing on the 1964 act, a small-city mayor from Maryland remarked in response to a "hearts and minds" comment by Senator Thurmond, "Senator, I too am a Southerner, and I quite agree with your statement. But Senator, something has to happen—it's been a hundred years!"

The battles against segregated lunch counters, separate waiting rooms, and distinct drinking fountains have essentially been won. Now the emphasis in combating segregation and prejudice has naturally shifted. The struggle for the Equal Rights Amendment is in the foreground. Guarantees of special rights for the handicapped are developing rapidly and having considerable impact.

Black people recognize the need to develop their sense of identity and prove their abilities, and are less accepting of too much being done *for* them. The immediate, specific needs are primarily decent jobs, increased educational opportunity, and an end to the ghettos. The situation was etched sharply by President Johnson in a speech at Howard University:

> In far too many ways American Negroes have been another nation, deprived of freedom, crippled by hatred, the doors of opportunity closed to hope. . . . Freedom is the right to share, share fully and equally in American society . . . to be treated in every part of our national life as a person equal in dignity and promise to all others.
>
> But freedom is not enough. You do not wipe away the scars of centuries by saying now you're free to go where you want and do as you desire and choose the leaders you please. You do not take a person who for years has been hobbled by chains and liberate him, bring him up to the starting line of a race and then say, you're free to compete with all the others, and still justly believe that you have been completely fair.

As with most other aspects of civil liberties, equal protection has yet to be fully realized. Significant change in the relationships of federalism has coincided with greater prominence of the rights of national citizenship. What is often not perceived about the national-state conflicts that arise over civil liberties is that they are not cases of constitutional right against constitutional wrong. Each national and state government normally acts with legitimate power, but the grounds of action are quite different. For example, the states commonly insist that control of public education is their prerogative. The national government does not deny this but points out that it has responsibility to its citizens to guarantee that every state treats all citizens equally. When these two rights conflict, which is to have priority? An accurate statement of the resolution is to say that the states have a complete right to run their educational systems as they choose, as long as they treat all citizens of the United States alike. There is only one class of citizenship.

Sign of the times

THE RIGHTS OF PERSONS
ACCUSED OF CRIME

The framers of the Constitution were well acquainted with the many possibilities of arbitrary treatment of individuals accused of crime: forced confessions, secret hearings, imprisonment for long periods without a hearing on the charges, forcible entry into homes to search for evidence, and many others. They sought to protect against such violations in the new nation; yet several of these constitutional protections still raise major controversies. Many people concerned about crime believe that too much protection is provided and that the effectiveness of law enforcement officers is hampered. It is easy to forget the reasons why these protections were introduced and to overlook the fundamental distinction between "criminals" and "persons accused of crime." It is possible for anyone to be accused of a crime at any given moment, perhaps on seemingly convincing evidence, even though the accused may be innocent.

Certain constitutional protections are familiar. An act that was not a crime at the time it was committed cannot be made a crime retroactively (prohibition of ex post facto laws), and no person may be convicted and punished by a legislative act without a judicial trial (prohibition against bills of attainder). Everyone is entitled to an impartial and speedy trial, which in practice means as soon as the court can reasonably get to one's case in a nondiscriminatory order of business. The Speedy Trial Act, intended to become fully effective in 1980, provides for dismissal of criminal charges against anyone who has not been brought to trial within one hundred days of arrest.

Defendants have the rights to know the charges against them, to have legal counsel, and to confront prosecution witnesses. Certain other stipulations—what constitutes "excessive" bail and what are "cruel and unusual punishments"—involve judgment. Such rules have been developed by precedent over many years. Some punishments that were once quite common—boiling in oil, drawing and quartering, cutting off fingers, hands, and ears—are now classed as "cruel and unusual." Yet strangely, throughout most of American history, killing a person by gas or electric shock has not been so classed.

After repeated refusals over the years to rule that capital punishment is "cruel and unusual," the Supreme Court in 1972 on a 5 to 4 vote came finally to that conclusion (*Furman* v. *Georgia, Jackson* v. *Georgia, Branch* v. *Texas*). The majority was not in total agreement about the reasons for holding the death penalty unconstitutional, however. Two judges held it cruel and unusual by its very nature, "a denial of the executed person's humanity," while the three others looked primarily at the fact that its enforcement is arbitrary and discriminatory, affecting largely "the poor and despised": "of all people convicted . . . the petitioners are among a capriciously selected random handful upon whom the sentence of death has been imposed." This view seemed to imply that states might be able constitutionally to enact capital punishment laws, were they to define more specifically the crimes for which it is applicable and to specify standards to be followed by judges and juries. New death penalty laws seeking to follow that approach were enacted in a majority of states; some the Court has sustained, and others it has rejected.

While a majority now says that death penalty laws do not invariably violate the Constitution, it does insist that laws insure that juries be allowed to consider any mitigating circumstances that may exist. A decision that imposition of the death penalty for a rape in which no death occurs constitutes cruel and unusual punishment as a "grossly disproportionate and excessive" penalty casts doubt on whether the Court will sustain capital punishment for any crime other than murder (*Coker* v. *Georgia*, 1977.) The anti-capital-punishment minority of the Court continued a vigorous expression of its belief, in the words of Justice Brennan: "The punishment of death, like punishments on the rack, the screw and the wheel, is no longer morally tolerable in our civilized society."

The protection against double jeopardy means that a person may not be tried twice or punished twice for the same offense. This protection is designed to prevent continuing harassment. It remains true of course that a defendant may appeal a conviction and under certain circumstances seek a retrial. Certain acts (such as robbing a nationally insured bank) may constitute crimes against a state and the national government at the same time and can thus be punished by each government since they are technically separate offenses.

The right to a writ of habeas corpus is a protection against being held without charges or without a prompt hearing to determine the adequacy of the charges, a practice sometimes referred to delicately in totalitarian societies as "protective custody." The writ is actually an order directing law enforcement officials promptly to bring a person in custody before a judge for determination as to whether there appear to be sufficient grounds to hold that person for trial. In cases of major offenses in the national courts the accused is also entitled to have a grand jury determine whether the evidence is sufficient to justify a trial.

Trial by jury in criminal cases in the United States courts is guaranteed. There is much argument over various aspects of the jury system in practice: the fair selection of jurors, the seeming abuse by attorneys of the right to challenge and remove prospective jurors, the possible tendency of juries to reflect prevailing sentiments of dominant groups even when contrary to the evidence, and the desirability of the requirement that decisions be unanimous. Yet the jury tradition is strong, and the system, considered by many to be a protection against possible judicial arbitrariness, will probably continue, although various reforms may be instituted.

UNREASONABLE SEARCH AND SEIZURE

Three other protections and the current interpretations of them have generated more heated controversy. One is the protection against unreasonable search and seizure. The language implies that reasonable search and seizure are possible, and this has meant primarily that an officer must secure an authorization (warrant) for a search in advance from a court. The search warrant must be specific as to time, place, and purpose, the judge presumably having been convinced that there is sufficient likelihood of evidence being found to justify the search. When an offense has just been committed or is being committed, police may search without a warrant under the rule of reasonable cause or suspicion.

The Supreme Court appears to be shifting away from the rigorous insistence, characteristic of the Warren era, on protecting to the maximum possible degree the rights of persons apprehended for suspected offenses. It has permitted greater leeway for police officers relative to "stop-and-frisk" procedures, as the concept of reasonable search undergoes redefinition. The general rule had been that the search of persons who have been arrested should be confined to the removal of such weapons as the frisk has indicated might be in their possession and to securing evidence of the particular offense for which they were arrested. In December 1973 the Court, over the vigorous dissent of the three liberal justices, took a new tack by ruling (*U.S.* v. *Robinson*) that a person in custody as a result of any valid arrest may be fully searched and that evidence of an offense unrelated to the cause of arrest, discovered in the process of search, may be used in prosecution for that separate offense. In this particular case, an officer arrested Robinson for driving while his license was revoked but in the course of search found in an inside pocket a cigarette package containing heroin.

Much of the argument over search and seizure questions has centered on the use of wiretapping and other sophisticated means of eavesdropping to secure evidence. Evidence obtained in this fashion has not been admissible in the United States courts, but not until 1961 was the same rule extended to the state courts. The Supreme Court came to look with approval on an earlier dissenting opinion by Justice Brandeis, in which he said:

> In a government of laws, existence of the government will be imperilled if it fails to observe the law scrupulously. Our Government is the potent, the omnipresent teacher. For good or for ill, it teaches the whole people by its

example. Crime is contagious. If the Government becomes a lawbreaker, it breeds contempt for law; it invites every man to become a law unto himself; it invites anarchy.

Nevertheless the Court has permitted eavesdropping and "bugging" in some situations under strict judicial supervision, and the omnibus crime control act of 1968 authorizes some "emergency" uses by the executive with regard to suspected foreign agents. The Nixon administration claimed a right to wiretap "suspected domestic subversives" without advance court approval, but a unanimous Supreme Court in 1972 rejected the claim. Widespread illegal "bugging" of political opponents, government employees suspected of leaking information, and even "unfriendly" journalists was a central feature of the Watergate affair.

PROTECTION AGAINST SELF-INCRIMINATION

The Fifth Amendment protection against self-incrimination exists to prevent so-called third-degree tactics—namely, securing confessions by coercion. The exercise of this right generated little popular excitement until the protection was extended to persons testifying before televised congressional investigating committees. Many people began to fear, usually incorrectly, that criminals and persons suspected of disloyalty were going free because of this guarantee, and only then did this constitutional right become controversial. The gist of the protection against self-incrimination is simply to require that an individual who has not voluntarily confessed be proved guilty by evidence other than his or her own testimony.

THE RIGHT TO COUNSEL

Most citizens have assumed that every person accused of crime, whether a national or state offense, is entitled to have counsel for defense. Thus it came as a surprise when in 1963 the Supreme Court overruled a Florida conviction in which an indigent defendant had not been provided counsel. Like several states, Florida had assigned counsel for people unable to hire their own attorneys only in cases involving a possible death penalty. This case (*Gideon* v. *Wainwright*), particularly intriguing because the appeal to the Supreme Court had been laboriously printed in pencil by the prisoner from his jail cell, established the right to counsel in all criminal cases, but it did not spell out at what point in the proceedings counsel must be available.

Another case the same year raised precisely that question. Danny Escobedo, arrested by Chicago police on suspicion of murder, was questioned at length by police at the same time that his attorney was seeking permission to advise his client. Escobedo requested counsel, but was ignored. In the course of the interrogation he made some

"Tell him his rights . . . and your city address so he can't claim he was arrested by a nonresident!"

incriminating statements, and the Supreme Court reversed his conviction (*Escobedo* v. *Illinois*, 1963), holding that counsel must be
available through all the critical stages of investigation: "The right to
counsel would indeed be hollow if it began at a period when few
confessions were obtained. . . . Our Constitution, unlike some others, strikes the balance in favor of the accused to be advised by his
lawyer of his privilege against self-incrimination." This doctrine was
elaborated further in the famous *Miranda* case in 1966 (*Miranda* v.
Arizona) when the Court ruled that before any questioning accused
persons must be advised that they have the right to remain silent,
that any statements may be used against them, and that they have
the right to the presence of an attorney. An effort to have the *Miranda*
rule modified failed in a 1977 case (*Brewer* v. *Williams*) in which a
suspect, who had been given a *Miranda* warning but was without
counsel, was led by police officers into a confession even though he
was not directly questioned.

SHOULD THE PROTECTIONS BE PRESERVED?

Recently it has been widely and sometimes bitterly suggested that
such decisions merely "coddle" criminals and that the ability of the
police to protect society is unduly restricted. The evidence does not
support these conclusions, but they are widely believed nonetheless.
Studies indicate that the number of confessions has not decreased as
a result of the decisions and that confessions are a minor aspect of
obtaining a conviction anyway; it is also not true that "vast numbers
of criminals are being released or going unpunished." The rules may
require more careful police work, but that is surely no evil. The

attorneys for Miranda emphasized this point by quoting a 1952 statement by the late J. Edgar Hoover, then director of the FBI: "full use of proper scientific methods should make it unnecessary for officers to use dishonorable methods of detection; this inescapably means increased costs. A laboratory costs more than a strap, and so does the training of those who would use a microscope rather than a whip."

President Nixon pledged during his 1968 campaign to appoint to the Supreme Court justices who would be "tougher" on persons accused of crime, and four Nixon appointees on the bench, joined frequently in votes by Justice White, developed a trend toward the lessening of protection in this area. There was no conservative trend in regard to equal protection or the broad right of privacy, but notable decisions modified the rules on a variety of matters such as the right to face one's accusers, controls on wiretapping, the granting of only limited immunity to a witness compelled to testify, the employment of "stop-and-frisk" procedures by police, allowing states to permit verdicts in noncapital criminal cases by less than unanimous juries, and the like.

A major legislative battle erupted in 1975 with the introduction of a massive bill (750 pages) designed to "reform" and for the first time to codify the entire national criminal law. With that objective of S-1 no one quarreled; the problem was that in the process it also wrote into the code what those concerned with civil liberties termed provisions intended to suppress political dissent, involving weakened entrapment rules, loose interpretations of espionage and sabotage, expanded wiretapping authority, strict rules on release of classified information, and so on. When passage was blocked, the bill returned two years later, minus most of the controversial sections. At nearly the same time (1974, effective in 1975) Congress passed the Privacy Act, designed to protect citizens from invasions of privacy by the national government. For the first time it authorized individuals to inspect information about themselves in the files of government agencies (excluding initially the CIA, law enforcement agencies, and the Secret Service) and to challenge or correct the material. Agencies were directed to disclose the existence of all data banks and files containing information on an individual and were forbidden to make the contents available to any other agency without the individual's consent.

The issue in all the controversies over rights in criminal procedure is fundamentally one of values and priorities. It is possible to have more efficient police forces, in the sense of higher rates of confessions and convictions and more evidence obtained by questionable means, as the secret police in many totalitarian societies have proved. But such efficiency carries a price. In our society the police, whose task is in most respects difficult and often thankless, remain the servants of society. Efficiency is not the only, or necessarily even the highest, social value. The First Amendment freedoms, and the complementary due process and equal protection guarantees under the Fourteenth Amendment, represent the constitutional expression of a higher social value, recognition of the dignity and worth of the individual human being. But while appreciating the existence and importance of these legal protections, one does well to reflect on the words of Judge Learned Hand: "Liberty lies in the hearts of men and women; when it dies there, no constitution, no law, no court can save it."

BASIC CONCEPTS AND TERMS

liberty versus authority
Bill of Rights
Fourteenth Amendment
procedural due process
substantive due process
First Amendment liberties
freedom of speech
doctrine of clear and present
  danger
doctrine of dangerous tendencies
preferred position doctrine
freedom of assembly
freedom of association
loyalty test
freedom of the press
newsmen's privilege
gag order
obscenity control standards
free exercise of religion
separation of church and state

right of privacy
equal protection of the laws
separate but equal doctrine
affirmative action
reverse discrimination
de facto segregation
de jure segregation
Equal Rights Amendment
Civil Rights Act of 1964
ex post facto law
bill of attainder
double jeopardy
protection against cruel and
  unusual punishments
writ of habeas corpus
grand jury
unreasonable search and seizure
protection against self-
  incrimination
right to counsel

POLITICAL BEHAVIOR

4

Who are the people who actually vote in elections? How many people vote? What categories of people produce the best turnouts? What factors most influence their decisions? How well does the political system comprehend and respond to the popular will? The study of such questions is vital to a realistic grasp of politics, and yet, as V. O. Key once remarked, "to speak with precision of public opinion is a task not unlike coming to grips with the Holy Ghost."[*] Launching our investigation of what goes into the political decision-making process in the United States, this chapter attempts to bring into focus the conditioning of patterns of voting behavior, the molding of public opinion in democratic society, and the role playing of interest groups in American politics.

WHY WE VOTE AS WE DO

There are quite interesting patterns of voter turnout among various definable categories of people in our society. Tables 4.1 and 4.2 break

[*]V. O. Key, Jr., *Public Opinion and American Democracy*, Knopf, New York, 1961, p. 8.

TABLE 4.1 Registration as Percentage of Voting-Age Population by Race, Sex, Region, and Age, 1968–1976

Characteristic	Presidential elections			Congressional elections	
	1968	1972	1976	1970	1974
Total	74.3	72.3	66.7	68.1	62.2
White	75.4	73.4	68.3	69.1	63.5
Black	66.2	65.5	58.5	60.8	54.9
Spanish origin[a]	(NA)	44.4	37.8	(NA)	34.9
Male	76.0	73.1	67.1	69.6	62.8
Female	72.8	71.6	66.4	66.8	61.7
North and West	76.5	73.9	67.7	70.0	63.3
South	69.2	68.7	64.6	63.8	59.8
18–20 years	44.2	58.1	47.1	41.3	36.4
21–24 years	56.4	59.5	54.8	40.8	45.3
25–34 years	68.4	68.4	62.3	59.4	54.7
35–44 years	76.5	74.8	69.8	71.2	66.7
45–54 years	80.8	79.3	74.3	76.7	72.5
55–64 years	81.4	80.2	76.8	78.6	75.1
65–74 years	79.5	78.5	74.0	76.4	73.0
75 years and older	69.2	70.7	66.9	69.2	65.2

Source: U.S. Department of Commerce, Bureau of the Census, *Statistical Abstract of the United States, 1977,* Government Printing Office, Washington, D.C., 1978, p. 509.
NA Not available. [a]Persons of Spanish origin may be of any race.

down some of the available registration and voting data by race, sex, region, age, and state. Relatively high average turnout is true of people of middle and high income, of those with higher levels of education, of people in business and the professions, of people in a broadly middle-age bracket, of members of the white race and people removed a generation or more from immigrant status, of adherents of Jewish religious faith, of people living in areas of reasonably strong competition between the major political parties, and of men as compared with women.

Obviously these are not mutually exclusive categories. Nor are they of equal importance as determinants of political behavior. Economic status, education, and occupation are the most significant in this respect and closely related to each other. It is evident, for example, that the relative turnout of different religious groups has little to do with religious belief as such (with the possible exception of a few sects that discourage political participation) and much to do with average education and income of the groups. These differences show up distinctly in a comparison of the various Protestant denominations. Nor does race in itself have any direct bearing, but the close connection has been all too obvious between racial-minority status and low-education and low-economic status.

TO VOTE DEMOCRAT OR REPUBLICAN?

When these patterns of voter turnout are related to patterns of partisan voting, several significant implications can be drawn (see Table 4.3). The clearest lines of classification appear in connection with economic status and occupation. The higher a person's income, the greater is the likelihood that that person will be Republican; the lower the income, the greater is the likelihood that the person will be Democratic. Business and the professions show a strong Republican leaning, whereas labor has traditionally showed Democratic preference. It is evident that a major increase in the number of people voting in a given election will, under normal circumstances (excluding severe economic and military crises or highly unusual personal popularity or unpopularity of one candidate), benefit the Democratic party. Except for young people just attaining voting age, new voters come from the ranks of previous nonvoters, and these are mainly from categories that have ordinarily a Democratic tendency.

Since the 1930s the Democrats have held an advantage in registration and general party identification in the nation as a whole, but this is somewhat offset by their inability to turn out on election day as high a percentage of their registered voters as can the Republicans. Democratic registrants change residence more frequently, and they show party loyalty less consistently in their voting behavior than do Republicans. Thus Republican and Democratic presidential candidates must devise different strategies. The Republican cannot win with Republican votes alone; those voters must be held in line and a significant number of votes must be picked up from both independents and dissident Democrats. Democrats can win if they succeed in keeping their own party substantially behind them and they get even a minority split of the independents, only about half of whom ordinarily vote. There are now more people across the country registered as independent than as Republican, and the number of nonvoters has also been increasing.

After the peak Democratic years of 1964–1965, the Democratic percentage of voters' party identification showed a gradual but fairly steady decrease, until the effect of the Watergate disclosures began to appear in 1973. The parallel Republican gains, however, were smaller as more people in some states classified themselves as independents and others were attracted (often temporarily) to George Wallace's American Independent party. Republican votes for a time increased more rapidly than registrations, and some spokesmen for the party and other observers professed (again at least prior to 1973) to see an "emerging Republican majority" in the nation. Such a majority, they

TABLE 4.2   Voter Registration and Persons Voting, by State, 1976

State	Persons registered		Persons voting		
	Total (thousands)	Percentage of voting-age population	Total (thousands)	Percentage of	
				Persons registered	Voting-age population
United States	105,837	70.5	82,286	77.7	54.8
Alabama	1,865	74.6	1,183[b]	63.4	47.3
Alaska	207	89.7	128	61.8	55.4
Arizona	980	63.0	765	78.1	49.2
Arkansas	1,021	67.9	768[b]	75.2	51.1
California	9,982	65.3	8,137	81.5	53.2
Colorado	1,349	76.1	1,082[b]	80.2	61.0
Connecticut	1,669	75.5	1,408	84.4	63.7
Delaware	301	74.7	236[b]	78.4	58.5
District of Columbia	268	52.1	171	63.8	33.3
Florida	4,094	64.8	3,151[b]	77.0	49.8
Georgia	2,302	68.2	1,467[b]	63.7	43.5
Hawaii	363	60.5	309	85.1	51.5
Idaho	520	91.7	355	68.3	62.6
Illinois	6,252	81.0	4,839	77.4	62.7
Indiana	3,010	82.7	2,279	75.7	62.6
Iowa	1,407	70.0	1,279[b]	90.9	63.6
Kansas	1,113	69.1	958[b]	86.1	59.5
Kentucky	1,713	72.2	1,167[b]	68.1	49.2
Louisiana	1,866	73.7	1,278[b]	68.5	50.5
Maine	696	93.9	486[c]	69.8	65.6
Maryland	1,950	68.1	1,440[b]	73.8	50.3
Massachusetts	2,912	69.8	2,594	89.1	62.2
Michigan	5,202	83.0	3,722	71.5	59.4
Minnesota	2,566	94.3	1,979	77.5	72.7
Mississippi	([a])	(x)	769[b]	(x)	49.8
Missouri	2,553	60.5	1,954[b]	76.5	58.4

Source: U.S. Department of Commerce, Bureau of the Census, *Statistical Abstract of the United States, 1977,* Government Printing Office, Washington, D.C., 1978, p. 512.

X Not applicable. [a]No required statewide registration; excluded from totals for persons registered. [b]Total vote for largest race, president. [c]Total vote for largest race, senator.

argued, would be a coalition based on the "sunbelt states" ranging from Florida to California, the traditional Republicans of the small-town and rural Midwest as well as affluent suburbia, and conservative blue-collar whites in the industrial cities, who have long been Democratic supporters. Such hopes were dashed in 1974, and the road back may be a long one. Some of the most active and vocal elements of conservative ranks today (including a number of the most effective fund raisers) express the feeling that the Republican

| State | Persons registered | | Persons voting | | |
| | Total (thousands) | Percentage of voting-age population | Total (thousands) | Percentage of | |
				Persons registered	Voting-age population
Montana	455	87.8	339	74.5	65.4
Nebraska	841	77.9	624	74.2	57.8
Nevada	251	59.2	206	82.1	48.6
New Hampshire	478	83.3	359	75.1	62.5
New Jersey	3,770	73.1	3,037	80.6	58.9
New Mexico	527	68.4	426	80.8	55.3
New York	8,199	63.5	6,668	81.3	51.6
North Carolina	2,554	66.4	1,679[b]	65.7	43.6
North Dakota	([a])	(x)	309	(x)	71.5
Ohio	4,693	62.9	4,195	89.4	56.2
Oklahoma	1,401	72.3	1,108	79.1	57.2
Oregon	1,420	85.9	1,049	73.9	63.5
Pennsylvania	5,750	68.1	4,621[b]	80.4	54.7
Rhode Island	545	84.1	411[b]	75.4	63.4
South Carolina	1,113	57.6	803[b]	72.1	41.5
South Dakota	426	90.8	301[b]	70.7	64.2
Tennessee	1,912	64.6	1,476[b]	77.2	49.9
Texas	6,319	74.3	4,072[b]	64.4	47.9
Utah	705	89.9	548	77.7	70.0
Vermont	284	86.9	194	68.3	59.3
Virginia	2,124	59.9	1,716	80.8	48.6
Washington	2,065	81.4	1,585	76.8	62.5
West Virginia	1,084	84.6	751[b]	69.3	58.6
Wisconsin	2,566	79.9	2,104[b]	82.0	65.5
Wyoming	195	72.9	160	82.1	60.2

party is a hopeless cause and advocate either a third party or, more realistically, an effort to make their weight felt within both parties. Theirs is, however, hardly a predominant view. Obituaries of one or the other major party have been published fairly frequently in the country's history, always proving premature.

The traditional Democratic sentiment of the South is now quite fragmented, although President Carter, as the first major-party southern candidate in many years, re-solidified the South at least

TABLE 4.3 Percentage Breakdown of Party Vote in Presidential Elections by Population Characteristics, 1960–1976

	1960		1964		1968		
	Dem.	Rep.	Dem.	Rep.	Dem.	Rep.	AIP
National	50.1	49.9	61.3	38.7	43.0	43.4	13.6
Male	52	48	60	40	41	43	16
Female	49	51	62	38	45	43	12
White	49	51	59	41	38	47	15
Nonwhite	68	32	94	6	85	12	3
College	39	61	52	48	37	54	9
High school	52	48	62	38	42	43	15
Grade school	55	45	66	34	52	33	15
Professional and business	42	58	54	46	34	56	10
White collar	48	52	57	43	41	47	12
Members of labor union families	65	35	73	27	56	29	15
Manual	60	40	71	29	50	35	15
Under 30 years	54	46	64	36	47	38	15
30–49 years	54	46	63	37	44	41	15
50 years and older	46	54	59	41	41	47	12
Protestants	38	62	55	45	35	49	16
Catholics	78	22	76	24	59	33	8
Republicans	5	95	20	80	9	86	5
Democrats	84	16	87	13	74	12	14
Independents	43	57	56	44	31	44	25
East	53	47	68	32	50	43	7
Midwest	48	52	61	39	44	47	9
South	51	49	52	48	31	36	33
West	49	51	60	40	44	49	7

Source: The Gallup Poll, Princeton, New Jersey. Used by permission.
Note: The 1968 and 1976 figures show percentages of a three-party vote. For 1968 the third party is the American Independent party of George Wallace. For 1976 the third party is that of Eugene McCarthy; 1976 results do not include the vote for other minor party candidates.
[a]Less than 1 per cent.

temporarily by carrying almost every state in that region in 1976. Some suggested that his election symbolized the return of the South at last to full partnership in the Union. The wooing of the South was of course the goal of President Nixon's "southern strategy": reduced pressure for desegregation, requests for modification of voting-rights laws, and significant political appointments for southerners. While it met with considerable success, it seemed significant primarily in presidential politics, and the early momentum was allowed to slip away when Nixon felt the South to be in the bag in 1972 and as his concerns became principally defensive. President Ford made a heroic effort with a campaign in the South but could not stem the Carter tide, despite the fact that the area remained dominantly

1972		1976		
Dem.	Rep.	Dem.	Rep.	Ind.
38	62	50	48	1
37	63	53	45	1
38	62	48	51	([a])
32	68	46	52	1
87	13	85	15	([a])
37	63	42	55	2
34	66	54	46	([a])
49	51	58	41	1
31	69	42	56	1
36	64	50	48	2
46	54	63	36	1
43	57	58	41	1
48	52	53	45	1
33	67	48	49	2
36	64	52	48	([a])
30	70	46	53	([a])
48	52	57	42	1
5	95	9	91	([a])
67	33	82	18	([a])
31	69	38	57	4
42	58	51	47	1
40	60	48	50	1
29	71	54	45	([a])
41	59	46	51	1

conservative. The South is currently the most rapidly growing section of the country, and a possible power shift is evident from the fact that for the first time in history a majority of the nation's population lives south of the Mason-Dixon line and west of Nebraska.

Many working-class people have been Democrats primarily for economic reasons, since many of them remember the Great Depression and feel that the Democratic party has been more concerned with their economic security; they find less appealing, however, the party's stand on issues like civil liberties and internationalism. Although most of these people remain Democrats for the present at least, the potential for switching has been stimulated by greater

affluence coupled with bitterness over the observation that the affluence of others seems to increase more rapidly and by antagonism to
social welfare programs that have helped the poor but left modest-
income workers as the "forgotten Americans." Lower-income whites
feel threatened by the black push for equality, and "middle America" generally has reacted against what it considers an assault on its
concept of patriotism and its standards of morality and behavior.
Counterdemonstrations by the "hard-hats" early in the 1970s were
clear evidence of this response, if elections, polls, and letters to the
editor were not.

Split-ticket voting, also evidencing the weakening attachment to
parties, continues to increase. Regardless of presidential election
outcomes, the Democrats have retained their overwhelming majorities in Congress. Even while the voters were re-electing Nixon in
1972 by a margin second only to the Johnson landslide over Goldwater in 1964, they returned the Democrats to power in both houses,
increasing their Senate majority. The huge defection of normally
Democratic voters (approximately one-third) from the McGovern
candidacy seemed to reflect for some a vague concern about his
alleged radicalism, while others simply doubted that he had presidential stature. Large numbers of voters found neither candidate
attractive; they opted for the familiar and "safe" incumbent. The
bulk of the Democratic defectors returned to the fold in 1976,
although some Catholics and Jews clearly had concerns relating to
Carter's Southern Baptist positions. On the other hand, an apparent
resurgence of evangelical Protestantism in the nation worked to his
advantage.

The most significant determinant of party preference is family
background. From two-thirds to three-fourths of the voters have the
same party adherence as their parents. Children of Democratic parents are more likely to become Republicans when they move to
higher incomes than children of Republicans are likely to become
Democrats when they move down the income scale. With greater
education, changes in party affiliation become more likely, and shifts
of young people in college are predominantly from Republican to
Democrat or to independent. Besides these considerations the principal influences on partisan affiliation are primary group associations: social circles, companions and colleagues at work, the residential neighborhood and region, and the organizations to which a
person belongs.

DEGREES OF PARTY ADHERENCE

People do not express their party preferences with equal fervor, and
the range of political interest extends from none whatsoever to total
commitment. Party membership in the United States is highly informal and need not consist of anything more than saying that one is a

member, although the voter needs to be registered by party preference in order to participate in the party nominating processes in many states. Viewed from the perspective of party affiliation, the population may be divided into four broad categories. Within each major party is a bloc of solid adherents, those who can be counted on to support the party regularly with little regard to current issues or candidates. Next are the customary adherents, those who support the party most of the time and in most circumstances but who might shift in a crisis or a situation of stress. Third are people who have only a loose party tie and who often do not think of themselves as party members but when pressed indicate a preference. Their allegiance and party dependability are minimal. Finally, there are the people who profess no affiliation or preference.

Most people who have a strong interest in politics are fairly partisan in their political opinions and usually belong to one of the first two groups. Traditionally, most of those who claim no identification and a large percentage of the loosely affiliated have had extremely low interest in and very limited awareness of political events. Although such persons still comprise a major segment of these groups, the percentage has been changing in recent years. As the level of political alienation has increased, the nonvoter category has included a larger number of educated and reasonably informed persons, who because of dissatisfactions with candidates, campaigns, parties, or political performance—and perhaps because of an inadequate understanding of politics and unrealistic or inflexible expectations—have simply stayed home.

AMERICANS ARE MIDDLE-OF-THE-ROADERS

By tradition and habit of mind most American voters tend toward the middle of the road in politics. The preference goes hand in hand with a generally nonideological stance on most issues. The national candidate who can attract support from as broad a range as possible of this middle area usually has the best chance of success, and an opponent who can be forced in the direction of one extreme or the other thereby loses support. This is true of both major parties, but there is considerable distance between the center positions in the two parties. Studies indicate that the leaders of the parties tend to be more sharply differentiated on policy matters than do rank-and-file members.

The political spectrum of how people express their own positions was interestingly portrayed in a Louis Harris poll at about the time of the 1972 elections. Sixty-nine per cent described their political philosophies as either middle-of-the-road or conservative, approximately evenly divided, compared to the 19 per cent who classified themselves as liberal and 3 per cent as radical. Harris pointed out, however, that this indicates a significant change from a comparable study five years earlier. The liberal position had gained 5 per cent and the radical had gained 2 per cent, while the conservative and middle-of-the-road positions each lost 3 per cent (the not-sure category moved slightly, from 10 to 9 percent). The trend toward greater liberalism was most notable among people with college education, among people of incomes over $15,000, among younger age groups, and among people calling themselves political independents. The South moved more toward the middle of the road, while the other regions became more liberal. Party differentiation appeared to be sharper, and Republicans classed themselves as more conservative while both Democrats and independents shifted to a more liberal stance.

In fact, there is apparently a great difference between the average citizen's verbalization of his or her political views (predominantly conservative) and the actual attitude toward what government ought to be doing (predominantly liberal). This often leads conservative spokesmen to believe that they have greater potential support than really exists.

The great majority of the members of both parties have a tacit commitment to the ideal of playing by the rules of the game and abiding by the other criteria of a democratic society that have already been discussed. Not everyone follows this principle, but serious deviations when disclosed result in widespread public and official condemnation. However strong are the feelings over issues and however vigorous is the contest, there remain for most a basic spirit of tolerance for other viewpoints, a belief in the desirability of the free competition of ideas, an acceptance of compromise, and an awareness that the world will not end if the opposition wins. But in every political system, including that of the United States, there are some people whose political attitudes lie distinctly outside the framework of ideas that are common to the majority and that have helped hold the system together.

POLITICAL EXTREMISM

Since we are all exposed, at least indirectly, to the activities and propaganda of people who play outside the rules of the social-political game, some analysis of these extremists, as they are called, and their organizations is important. The wide range of extremist organizations (most quite small), some calling themselves parties, others devoting themselves to political pressure or to propaganda, includes such groups as the Communist party, the Progressive Labor party, the National States Rights party, the American Nazi party, the Christian Nationalist Crusade, and the John Birch Society. Such groups are beyond the range of the usual variations of liberalism and conservatism. Liberals and conservatives in a sense complement one another, the one advocating and introducing change and innovation and the other seeking to preserve the best of what exists. Moderates of the liberal and conservative camps may not be very far apart, and there is a broad spectrum of opinion within each wing. People and groups beyond the fringes of liberalism and conservatism are usually referred to, for want of better terms, as members of the far left and far right.

A remarkable similarity of attitude prevails among most extremist organizations and factions. Their professed goals, like their stands on specific issues of public policy, may be quite different, but their basic attitudes toward politics have much in common. Neither the far left nor the far right has faith in democratic processes, especially when their causes are not supported by these processes, but tolerance of the rejection by the popular will of one's programs and beliefs is, after all, the mainstay of the democratic process. Each extremist faction is convinced that it has all the answers, that it is the repository of ultimate truth in its perception of society. For anyone who believes in the infallibility of personal perceptions, the principle of the free expression of ideas makes no sense: Why, one asks, should error have the same right of expression as truth? If one is certain that one's side is entirely right and the other entirely wrong, why should a victory by the opposition be accepted unless it simply has superior force on its side?

Extremists tend to operate from a conspiracy or devil theory of history. Everything that goes wrong must be the result of an evil conspiracy by the opposition. Problems cannot be the result of social complexities, but somewhere there is a satanic traitor to blame. For the Communist all evil stems from a capitalist conspiracy; for the John Bircher all evil stems from a Communist conspiracy. All issues and events are seen in terms of stark good and evil, with no middle ground; there is a compulsive desire for simple answers and pat solutions to the most complicated problems. The individual extremist tends to be highly doctrinaire and wedded to easy explanations; even to doubt is to be a traitor.

All tactics that seem to accomplish the extremist's purpose are justified: in other words, the end justifies any means, a natural concomitant of the assumption that the extremist has a monopoly on truth. There is no respect for the civil liberties of opponents; indeed, the opposition is seen as an enemy rather than as the "loyal opposition," and a state of war exists until the opposition is liquidated. Extremist organizations of the right are generally ultranationalistic, but all exhibit willingness to use force to solve problems. There seems ordinarily also to be a need to use certain religions or races as scapegoats.

Both the far left and far right evidence a high degree of frustration and a psychology of fear. A perpetual alarmism is reflected in the conviction that the nation is about to be invaded, infiltrated, or subverted; some right-wingers have claimed that the nation's population is being poisoned by fluoridation, and some leftists have asserted that the white majority is planning black genocide. The extremist's inclination is always to believe the worst and to refuse utterly to accept evidence contrary to prejudice or preconception. The extremist heaps hate, venom, and abuse on others who see things differently.

Former Senator Thomas Kuchel of California once cited in a Senate speech a typical example from his daily quota of "fright mail." A constituent wrote in panic, as did many, about "Operation Water Moccasin" then under way in Georgia, claiming that hordes of "barefoot Africans" and Mongolians were being trained under United Nations auspices to take over the United States by guerrilla warfare. He "knew" because he had recently heard a speaker on the subject. The senator, a member of the Armed Services and Foreign Relations committees, patiently wrote back an explanation to the effect that "Operation Water Moccasin" was a United States Army training maneuver and that a few officers from friendly foreign countries were participating as observers. But what was the response?

> Dear Senator Kuchel: . . . I do not accept your statement that I have been the victim of misinformation. It is the other way around. Either you do not know what you have voted for . . . or you are a traitor to the United States.

THE RIGHT TO VOTE

In the American federal system the establishment of qualifications for voting is left to the states. The only stipulation originally in the Constitution concerning participation in national elections was that one had the right to vote if one was qualified to vote for members of the more numerous house of the state legislature. Constitutional amendments later prohibited the states from restricting the right to vote because of race, color, previous condition of servitude, sex, age above eighteen, and the required payment of poll taxes. All states require United States citizenship, although this was not always the case. Most states also require some form of advance registration as a protection against fraud, but some demand this only of people living in urban areas.

Residence requirements for voting eligibility imposed by states and counties, ranging in recent times from three months to a year, in effect have disfranchised millions of citizens in this highly mobile society. While agreeing that states may logically insist that voters be state residents and that election officials need time between the close of registration and the actual election to accomplish administrative tasks, the Supreme Court held in 1972 (*Dunn* v. *Blumstein*) that even three months constitutes an unreasonable exclusion from the right to vote for people exercising their freedom to travel from one jurisdiction to another. The Court suggested that thirty days is probably sufficient, but it later accepted as satisfactory laws in two states setting fifty-day residence requirements.

A concerted effort to further reduce restrictions continues. Since slow or complex registration processes in some states have kept down the number of voters, there was pressure for creation of a nationwide system of registration by mail, a procedure adopted in several states. More recently President Carter recommended that preregistration requirements be abolished and voters with proper identification be permitted to register and vote on election day, subject to severe penalties for fraud. Many Republicans understandably viewed the potential increase in the number of voters as a serious threat to their party, while various other persons feared the possibilities of fraud, even though experience in the few states having such systems seemed satisfactory. That experience also indicated a very high turnout of potential voters. Both to lessen fraud potential and to avoid long delays at polling places, Congress modified the plan to provide that election-day registration be at other locations than the polls themselves. Even so, the proposal was continuously stalled in the face of strong opposition.

Over the years several states in the South devised highly effective ways of preventing blacks from voting, despite the antidiscrimination provisions of the Fourteenth and Fifteenth Amendments. The basic technique was to establish requirements that on their face applied in the same fashion to all citizens but to enforce them in a discriminatory manner. Literacy tests, for example, were not confined to southern states; the question is how they were administered there. Coupled with these were sometimes "understanding tests," allegedly designed to measure the applicant's understanding of the national and state constitutions. The tests usually contained simple questions for people the officials wished to register and other questions like the following from former voter-registration tests in Alabama and Georgia:

If election of the president becomes the duty of the United States House of Representatives and it fails to act, who becomes president and when?

The Constitution limits the size of the District of Columbia to _____.

What is the difference in the Constitution of the United States and Georgia regarding suspension of the privilege of the writ of habeas corpus?

Failure to answer correctly any single question from a sizable list could be grounds for refusing registration.

Other methods included so-called good character tests, supposedly

TABLE 4.4　　Voter Registration in Eleven Southern States, by Race: 1960 and 1976

Registered voters	Total	Ala.	Ark.	Fla.	Ga.	La.	Miss.
1960							
Total white (thousands)	12,276	860	518	1,819	1,020	993	478
Total black (thousands)	1,463	66	73	183	180	159	22
Percentage white	61.1	63.6	60.9	69.3	56.8	76.9	63.9
Percentage black	29.1	13.7	38.0	39.4	29.3	31.1	5.2
1976							
Total white (thousands)	21,690	1,544	817	3,480	1,703	1,445	866[c]
Total black (thousands)	4,149[b]	321[b]	204[b]	410	598[b]	421	286[c]
Percentage white	67.9	79.3	62.6	61.3	65.9	78.4	80.0
Percentage black	63.1	58.4	94.0	61.1	74.8	63.0	60.7

Source: U.S. Department of Commerce, Bureau of the Census, *Statistical Abstract of the United States, 1977*, Government Printing Office, Washington, D.C., 1978, p. 507.
[a]Includes other minority races. [b]Estimated. [c]1975 data.

requiring good moral character of anyone to be registered but with the decision on this in the hands of the local registrar, requirements that new registrants have a previously registered voter "vouch" for them, and various tests of loyalty to party as prerequisite for voting in a primary. For many years certain states restricted participation in the primaries to whites on the theory that the constitutional protections did not apply to primaries, but this practice was invalidated by the Supreme Court in the middle years of the 1940s. Other practices have been invalidated or abandoned in many areas, but all have not yet totally disappeared. Simple economic pressure has been one of the most powerful forces, and such tactics as establishing inconvenient registration locations and hours of operation have been effective.

Growing nationwide recognition of such abuses contributed significantly to the passage by Congress of the series of voting-rights acts mentioned in the previous chapter. These markedly expanded the role of the national government in what had formerly been largely a state preserve, but again the action was in defense of the equal rights of United States citizens. National action would never have been considered had no discrimination been practiced. Both the attorney general and the national courts can now act to guarantee fair registration procedures. Subsequent amendments and extensions of the 1965 act suspended literacy tests generally and authorized appointment of national voting examiners empowered to order registrations in areas previously having literacy tests and in which less than 50 per cent of voting-age residents were registered or had voted in the previous presidential election. While the examiners are rarely used, political participation by minorities has substantially improved. (For recent statistics, see Table 4.4.)

N.C.	S.C.	Tenn.	Tex.	Va.
1,861	481	1,300	2,079	867
210	58	185	227	100
92.1	57.1	73.0	42.5	46.1
39.1	13.7	59.1	35.5	23.1
2,137	828	1,886	5,191	1,794
396	285	271[b]	640[b]	317[b]
69.2	58.4	73.7	69.1	61.6
54.8	56.5	66.4	65.0	54.7

PUBLIC OPINION

In any political system that seeks to express and implement the popular will, there must be constant effort to ascertain and define that will. Elections are of course one device, but a vote in an election may be simply an endorsement of a candidate or party and not a clear expression of opinion on specific issues. Obviously elections do not reflect opinion on issues that arise and must be decided between elections. Newspapers and thousands of organized groups regularly air their opinions, usually in attempts to persuade readers and other people to support their positions. Moreover, samples of the population are frequently polled on public issues. There are in fact many "publics," definable groups having opinions, and vast amounts of money and effort are spent to influence these opinions. Indeed, American citizens are subjected to such a barrage of opinions and queries about their opinions that they may become immunized. They may react with apathy, in order to ignore new arguments, or resort to oversimplification to avoid contradictions, but it is difficult for any American completely to avoid being influenced.

Many determinants help form the opinions of people. First among these is family influence, responsible for most people's political as well as religious ideas. Next are the primary or face-to-face groups to which most people belong in school, in college, at work, in the neighborhood. Third, a person's opinions are broadened and developed by formal education at all stages, from preschool to professional school. Fourth, for some people formal organizations such as labor unions and professional associations cultivate and in some cases virtually require certain opinions as conditions of membership or influence. The entire process is subtle, continuous, and largely unconscious. It enables a society to function. There are, of course, rebels who reject the politics, religion, and standards of their schools and associations; they are free to follow their opinions and to form new parties, religions, unions, clubs, or whatever.

In the last two or three decades the techniques of measurement of public opinion have been developed to a high degree of sophistication and validity by polling organizations, and these polls now exert significant political influence. It appears that polls are capable of reliably measuring opinion on subjects about which opinion has fairly well crystallized or on how people would vote at the moment if a given election were held that day (the major polls were within about 1 per cent of the actual 1972 vote and 3 per cent of the 1976 vote). Pollsters are properly cautious about projecting their findings into the future. The critical element in accurate measurement is obtaining a sample that is an accurate cross section of the population. The number of people polled need not be large (it is rarely over fifteen hundred in a nationwide poll), but they must be typical of the whole. Usually this is accomplished by a system of probability sampling, whereby historically typical and cross-sectional districts are selected and interviewers then call at randomly selected households, gradually correcting for imbalances in income level, education, sex, age, and so on. It is important that questions be framed carefully and pretested, to assure that they are clear and do not suggest particular answers to respondents. Interviewers must be trained not to influence responses, actually to make the interviews where they are supposed to, and so on.

The prediction of election results naturally provokes public interest but is also the most hazardous aspect of polling. Some last-minute event or even the weather on election day can affect turnout and thus a result. There are difficulties in allocating the undecided vote, in predicting the proportion and direction of last-minute changes of mind, of confirming that only potential voters are polled, and of assuring that interviewers achieve real communication with the people of low education and low income who are often inclined to be suspicious and unresponsive. In presidential elections, the electoral college system presents another complication, since in a close election a very small shift of votes in one or two states may shift a big block of electoral votes.

Whatever the problems, polling has become a sophisticated enterprise, as is amply attested by the extensive use of surveys by political and business organizations. No campaign of any size is complete today without at least one or two polls on behalf of each candidate, and in major campaigns there may be many, taken perhaps weekly in the crucial stages. A poll at the beginning can indicate what is the voters' image of the candidate, what they see as strengths and weaknesses, where support and opposition are located, how well the candidate is known, and what issues seem uppermost in the voters' minds. Later readings can shed more light on these matters, showing what progress has been made but also revealing emphases or changes of tactics needed in the campaign.

Pollsters are hired to make confidential reports that serve a purpose different from that of the general public-information releases, although candidates differ in their attachment to them. Many a pollster is no longer merely a recorder of opinions but also a trusted and intimate adviser at the heart of campaign and policy strategy, as Pat Caddell has been to President Carter.

COMMUNICATIONS MEDIA

The press, television, and radio are obviously major instruments in opinion making, but the nature of their roles has changed over the years. In earlier years the press was considered a dominant force in the outcome of elections, but its power nationwide has diminished. Its freedom to play an active political role is protected by the First Amendment, a freedom that is modified slightly in the case of radio and television. Nature imposes a limit on the number of wavelengths available, and in return for the privilege of a license, owners can be required to operate in the public interest.

In assessing the role of the communications media, the extent to which the representatives of the media constitute what is often termed an informal fourth branch of government should not be overlooked. Such persons as James Reston, David Broder, Mary McGrory, Jack Anderson, Marquis Childs, Walter Cronkite, Elizabeth Drew, Harry Reasoner, John Chancellor, and David Brinkley are key figures in Washington. Some correspondents, reporters, and commentators develop intimate relations with exercisers of political power, for they depend on each other. Politicians make news, and publicity is their lifeblood. Reporters of the news, like pollsters, have become much more than mere recorders of the political scene; they are often participants in the actual shaping and achieving of public policy and the making and breaking of public officials.

THE PRESS

Concern has been voiced for a number of years by people within and outside the newspaper profession over the steadily increasing concentration of newspaper control in the United States. This is not primarily a matter of the power of newspaper chains or the dependence of most newspapers (as well as television and radio) on the two wire services (AP and UPI) for national and international news. There is nothing approaching a national newspaper monopoly. But, practically speaking, most people will read for current news a paper published within roughly one hundred miles of where they live, and if they live in a city, it will rarely be a paper from outside that city. What is crucial, therefore, is whether newspaper competition exists within the various cities where the dailies are published.

In 1977 a survey published by *Editor and Publisher* magazine indicated that of 1,511 cities in the United States with daily papers, all but 37 were one-ownership cities. In other words, in 97.5 per cent of the cities there was no newspaper competition. Many cities had two or more papers but all under the same ownership. There are now many states in which there is no city with competing newspapers. This situation is commonly furthered by newspaper ownership of radio and television outlets in home cities. On the whole, greater uniformity is presented to the public, and greater power is increasingly placed in the hands of fewer persons.

Because of the Roosevelt, Truman, and Kennedy victories in the face of majority press opposition, many people jumped to the conclusion that the press no longer carries weight in presidential elections, but it would be a mistake to underestimate its power. Since many factors simultaneously influence election results, it is impossible to isolate any single one and accurately measure its effect, but the news media are at least a major part of the complex of elements determining voter behavior. In presidential campaigns information reaches the voter from a great variety of sources. The further one goes down the list of candidates for other offices, the more potent becomes the influence of the press, for the simple reason that the voter has less information on those races. Press influence is extremely important, for example, in state legislature and local government elections. Although conditions vary around the country, a common politicians' rule of thumb is that a candidate needs approximately a three-to-two registration edge to beat unified newspaper opposition.

Another error would be to assume that the only significant press influence comes from formal editorial endorsements published just before elections, which probably have a very limited effect on changing opinions. Most thoughtful people are aware of the importance of such aspects of influence as the amount and extent of news coverage, the location of stories within a paper and within a page, the use and nonuse of pictures and whether they are flattering or not, and the nature of headlines, cartoons, and captions. Perhaps the most devastating use of this power occurs when a newspaper with no local competition simply gives no coverage whatsoever to a candidate. But what is often forgotten is the long-term effect (also not subject to specific measurement) of conditioning public opinion in the intervals between elections by means of editorials and cartoons and the selective nature of news coverage. This function of the press does not fall under the label "politics," and the reader may be less wary than during a campaign.

Although the nation's daily press is overwhelmingly Republican in orientation (even if ultraconservatives denounce what they see as its liberal bias), this does not impose uniformity on its handling of political matters.* The range extends from papers that confine expressions of opinion to the editorial page and print campaign stories on major candidates in parallel columns to others that frankly write news stories with blatant editorial bias and use the paper as a party tool. It is of course impossible to satisfy everyone, and strong partisans may feel that what an editor considers dispassionate treatment is hostile to them because it does not support their viewpoint. Judgment must also be exercised as to what will be printed, for it is simply impossible to print everything, yet selectivity in what is to be published and when it will be printed allows editors to emphasize their own preferences.

It is disputable whether the biases of the publishers are partly offset by the normally more liberal views of the reporters. Although reporters reflect a variety of opinion, there is a frequent claim that a majority lean toward the liberal and Democratic side. Whether this alleged bias shows up, or is permitted to show up, significantly in published new stories is debatable. After the 1960 election Herb Klein, Nixon's press secretary, remarked sourly in response to a question about newspaper treatment: "Sure we had heavy editorial support, but Kennedy had a band of rooters back in his press bus." Such matters, however, are also influenced strongly by the kind of personal relations each candidate develops with the reporters who travel with him. Nixon's press relations were generally conceded to have been extremely poor in his 1960 and 1962 campaigns, culminating in his famous blast at the press following his defeat for the governorship of California in 1962. In 1968 the candidate and his staff devoted vast attention to the press, with good results, but in 1972 it was deemed unnecessary.

There is a natural and inevitable tension between presidents and the news media, since journalists consider themselves watchdogs on behalf of the public. While relations notably improved under Ford and Carter, the hostility between President Nixon and the media reached a totally unprecedented level. Throughout most of his time in office he held relatively few press conferences. During the 1972 campaign he traveled in virtual isolation from the press. Reporters

---

*In 1976, 62 per cent of the dailies representing 62 per cent of the total circulation editorially supported Ford, while 12 per cent representing 26 per cent of the circulation supported Carter, a slightly more than 5-to-1 margin (*Editor and Publisher,* November 6, 1976, p. 4). The margin in 1972 was a staggering 13.5-to-1 for Nixon over McGovern (71.4 to 5.3), and in 1968 the Nixon margin over Humphrey was 5.5-to-1.

were barred from most of the fund-raising dinners he addressed, and what appeared on television from those addresses was also controlled by the White House. Various administration spokesmen, most notably Vice President Agnew, frequently castigated the news media in public for alleged unfairness and "liberal bias," and many journalists responded with caustic criticism. Administration officials learned quickly that it was not in their long-term career interests to be unduly cooperative with reporters. Especially critical newspapers were cut off from much of their normal access, and exclusive stories were given to their opposition. One of the multitude of interesting documents that surfaced during the hearings of the Senate Watergate investigating committee was a memorandum from Charles Colson detailing a complete campaign against the press, and one of the White House tapes revealed the president's strongly expressed intent to punish the *Washington Post*.

Television and radio, being more vulnerable because they are subject to government licensing, felt pressure most keenly. Although the Nixon administration backed off in the final bill that it proposed for changing licensing procedures, the initial public statements by the director of the Office of Telecommunications Policy carried threats not to renew licenses unless local station managers pursued, in his words, "sense" rather than "sensationalism," avoided "elitist gossip in the guise of news analysis," and counteracted the "ideological plugola" of the networks. Analysts of broadcast journalism concluded that heavy criticism and timidity of advertisers coupled with public indifference resulted in a severe decline in the number of "courageous documentaries dealing with important subjects of controversy." The so-called chilling effect of administration pressure was felt by many to produce a kind of self-censorship that might significantly restrict the flow of news and be seriously damaging to the concept of a free press.

As stories of prolonged secret military operations in Cambodia unfolded in 1973, directly contradicting Pentagon and White House statements, credibility already lessened by the multitudinous facets of the Watergate affair critically decreased. Journalists who believed that they had been consistently lied to and deliberately misled on a scale never before encountered were bitter, although it was hardly a new experience. In June 1973, the board of directors of the National Press Club took the unusual step of asking the president to replace his press secretary, Ron Ziegler, whom it called a "totally programmed spokesman" who had "misled the public and affronted the professional standards of the Washington press corps."

This distrust of presidential attempts at controlling news carried over to make the media more suspicious of Carter than might otherwise have been the case, although Press Secretary Jody Powell succeeded in maintaining generally cordial relationships. Blunders did emerge, nevertheless, and confidence was strained by overzealous efforts to defend Budget Director Bert Lance and top presidential advisor Hamilton Jordan. What information the public is "entitled" to receive, or whether in fact any restriction is justifiable, seems destined to be perennially debated.

RADIO AND TELEVISION

Radio and televison are in a somewhat different situation from the print media, since there could be an unlimited number of newspapers but the number of broadcasting channels is physically limited.. Public controls require broadcasting in the public interest and restrict the number of stations that can operate under a single ownership. Their treatment of news is ordinarily briefer and they have not until recently engaged in editorializing, which tends to be rather limited. However, they are capable of providing immediate, continuous, and comprehensive coverage in an incomparable manner for such affairs as conventions, congressional hearings, and other newsworthy events.

Polls indicate that the public has more confidence in the fairness of television news than in newspapers, principally because people feel they actually see news happen. But there is a growing awareness that what is seen is what the camera crew and editors choose for the viewer. It is in the nature of television to emphasize action and conflict, which generate the most interesting pictures. It is widely thought that public impressions of demonstrations, for example, are seriously distorted. At the time of the 1968 national party conventions, many viewers were disturbed that the television news teams seemed to be advocates as well as reporters, that they provided a nationwide rostrum for anyone with a dissenting view to the virtual exclusion of expressions of majority sentiment, and that they promoted and instigated disputes in order to keep the "show" lively. Another distinguishing characteristic of television news is the temptation on the part of reporters and commentators to "create" news. Thus they may build up a candidate in a few primaries, for example, and then later tear the same candidate down, in the interest of having a continuing dramatic story.

Presidents today make extensive use of television and radio to persuade the public of the rightness of their decisions and actions. Occasionally the opposition secures free time for a rejoinder, but the president has an overwhelming advantage in drawing an audience. Since television lends itself to highly effective dramatic uses and is regarded as having captive audiences for the station-break advertisement, it has long since accounted for the major expense in most

"You've heard both our editorial and a reply to our editorial. Now here is Mr. Ron Emerson, speaking for those who have no opinion either way."

campaigns for major office. Despite the fact that television stations rarely endorse candidates, there is no question that they can if they choose exert influence by the frequency and manner in which they show candidates.

Although it has no power of censorship, the Federal Communications Commission in renewing broadcast licenses is expected to insure that each station or network is operating "in the public interest, convenience, or necessity," in the terms of the law. Broadcasters are also required to make available equal time (in quality as well as amount) to candidates for the same office. A special act of Congress was necessary to authorize the Kennedy-Nixon debates in 1960 without compelling the networks to give equal time to all minor-party candidates, but the 1976 Ford-Carter debates technically were handled as coverage of a news event, an event under the auspices of the League of Women Voters rather than the networks. In addition, the fairness doctrine adhered to by the FCC requires a station that broadcasts a criticism or attack on a person to offer time for rebuttal.

The courts have ruled, however, that the networks are not bound by the fairness doctrine to provide the opposition party time to respond to presidential addresses and interviews so long as they determine that their broadcasting presents a balance of views on the issues discussed by the president. Nor are radio and television compelled to sell time to all groups wishing to air their views; what is required is reasonable coverage and balance. Otherwise, it was said, groups with the most money could dominate the airwaves, and in any case it is manifestly impossible to air every viewpoint.

Opinion: Fred Freed
WHY AREN'T THERE MORE COURAGEOUS TV DOCUMENTARIES?

Problems of a political nature . . . have multiplied rapidly. . . .

To the young and the left we represent the Establishment who keeps their views from being heard and seen. To the blacks we are white racists. To many whites we are apologists for the Black Panthers.

To the South we are anti-Southern. The Midwest thinks we are effete Eastern snobs. The effete Eastern snobs think we are midcult yahoos. The left says we promoted the war in Vietnam. The Pentagon knows we are against them. Cops don't trust us at all.

If you do something controversial, you know you will spend months defending yourself to the government. That's not conducive to doing something controversial.

We are not part of the free press. We are licensed by the government and required always to justify ourselves to a government agency (the Federal Communications Commission). Anyone can complain about us, and a battery of network lawyers will be required just to keep us even.

I work for a commercial network. It is in business to make money. I lose money. I lose money in several ways. First, the programs I do cost between $150,000 and $200,000 to make. That is not because I am extravagant but because the costs of equipment and labor and transportation are very high.

Second, I cost money because the time I take on the network could have been sold to a sponsor for a very considerable sum. My program almost certainly will not be sponsored. Once it might have been. But now people are angry. No one agrees with anyone else. Everything is controversial. Why should a man who is trying to make a good impression on customers sponsor a program he knows will anger many of them? . . .

Third, I cost money because my program will have a low rating. That means it will hurt the programs coming before and after it. Fourth, I cost money because of the controversy that follows my programs.

Reprinted by permission of Fred Freed. The late Mr. Freed, an award-winning producer of documentaries for NBC-TV, spoke these words in an address delivered at Reed College in Portland, Oregon, in May 1972.

Letters will have to be prepared for the FCC, for congressmen, for local officials. Law suits will have to be defended. One year we were sued by various people for $517 million. Finally, I cost money because the programs I do take time to research and pin down. . . .

INTEREST-GROUP POLITICS

One way in which citizens express opinion is through organized groups. Association with like-minded people considerably amplifies the voice of individuals and can make possible the financial resources and publicity required to assure that their voices are heard clearly and frequently whenever and wherever the group wants them heard. Although some groups are organized solely for the purpose of imposing political pressure, most are associations with broader purposes and only a part of their interest lies in politics. Every organized group may have an interest at some time, occasionally or continuously, in what a government does or does not do, and to that extent it may become an interest group, even though its primary function may be as a church, a women's club, or a veterans' organization. Americans have a passion for organizing; a European once remarked, "If three Americans were adrift on a raft, they would elect one president, one vice president, and one secretary-treasurer."

INTEREST GROUPS IN A PLURALISTIC SOCIETY

Some people have the impression that interest groups constitute an evil in politics, but such organizations are a natural and perfectly legitimate and desirable part of the politics of democracy. As long as there is an effort to maintain a government that reflects the popular will, public officials will pay attention to the views of groups, and out of the welter of conflicting views and inharmonious elements they will seek the best approximation of the public interest. It is inevitable that every group will try to identify its own goals, however narrow, with the public interest or the general welfare.

Some writers assert the achievement of the public interest to be a sort of by-product of the competition among the special interest groups representing greatly diverse viewpoints. A countervailing theory of group politics is thus offered to explain and justify American politics. But there is nothing automatic about the process. Certain groups can muster far more power than others; some voices speaking for the general good are very faint, if indeed they exist at all. There is no fully effective consumers' organization to balance manufacturers and retailers (although there have been some notable recent efforts), no American patients' association to match the American Medical Association, no organized opposition whatsoever to the

veterans' groups. It remains the peculiar and vital task of the politician to be the broker among the competing interests—the seeker of that elusive will-o'-the-wisp known as the public interest, or at least the policy that will be broadly tolerable.

A two-party system with a separation of powers is notably hospitable to pressure-group politics. In a multiparty system there may be a party that fairly directly represents the interests of a particular important group; but where each of two parties embraces people of widely varying views, other channels are developed to give effect to more narrow specific interests. Interest groups normally try to bring pressure on both parties, and they commonly insist that they are nonpolitical, by which they really mean nonpartisan. Some groups remain aloof from involvement with either party; most maintain at least a semblance of nonpartisanship, but many of these have close ties with one party, which they look upon as the logical vehicle for exerting their influence.

Interest-group politics reflects the kind of politico-economic system that exists in America—a synthesis of federalism, division of power and responsibility, and mixed economy. Ours is a pluralistic society, one in which many forces and organizations other than government influence and even control our lives. To a great extent public policy decisions are thrashed out by conflict and compromise among competing interests, each seeking achievement of its own goals but recognizing that it cannot have its way entirely at the expense of other interests that also press legitimate claims. In such an environment, voluntary political action through a multitude of groups representing every conceivable interest, with parties playing broker, is perfectly natural and fitting. When polarization within a country becomes so severe that negotiation and compromise as means of resolving public policy disputes are impossible, the very fabric of democracy is threatened.

A party system is vital. Interest-group politics can hamstring the policy process when the spirit of compromise is not present, as Common Cause's John Gardner has cogently pointed out:

> Instead of the United States being run by a well-knit behind-the-scenes power group (as the conspiracy theorists would have it), it is whipsawed by a great multiplicity of special interests. The result is paralysis in national policy-making. All too often each special interest has veto power over one essential piece of a solution, and no one has the power to solve the problem (cf. New York City). No one wants to make the problems unsolvable but collectively they paralyze policy-making. The rule applies to every complex problem we face—inflation, energy, tax reform, transportation: the list is endless.
>
> The special interests are not sinister forces. They are all of us. Yet we are seeing a war of the parts against the whole. Everything is so interrelated today that our capacity to frustrate one another through non-cooperation has increased dramatically.

MINORITY GROUPS

The political role of minority racial, nationality, and religious groups in America is of special interest. It does not fit exclusively within the interest-group pattern, yet it has only occasionally involved separate party activity. As many such groups have begun in recent years to achieve a new sense of pride in group identity and cultural heritage, an associated and long overdue political impact has become steadily more evident. But there are quite varied threads in the history of this development.

In an earlier period certain immigrant groups facing social and economic barriers, perhaps most notably the Irish and the Italians, found that politics allowed upward mobility in society, and rapidly they came to dominate the politics of certain cities. Those whose background made adaptation relatively easy seized their opportunities within the dominant parties of their areas, and in time the effectiveness of a Polish name in candidacy for office in Detroit or Buffalo, a German name in Milwaukee, or a Slovenian name in Cleveland, for example, became potent. Lately this experience is gradually being repeated by Puerto Rican immigrants, particularly in New York City. Likewise, members of the Jewish faith have moved fairly readily and effectively (though certainly not always painlessly) into the established patterns of political activity.

The principal victims of discrimination, the American Indians, the blacks, and the Chicanos or Mexican-Americans, have faced more complex and difficult problems. Afflicted by severe poverty, inadequate education, and poor health, few have possessed until recently any motivation toward political action or any understanding of how to organize and use their potential power. With extremely low voting turnout and little other participation in the political process, these groups have been taken for granted by political parties and other organizations that wield community power. When they did begin to stir, it was hardly surprising that they found it difficult to unite on goals, tactics, or leadership or to build consistent and sustained political effort.

There has developed gradually nevertheless a variety of social movements concerned with the special needs of minority groups, movements that diminish discriminatory practices and benefit from the results, in terms of larger and more highly motivated memberships, better educated and more sophisticated leaders, and the like. Some organizations have focused their efforts on a single problem such as educational opportunity or unemployment; others have functioned as traditional interest groups, with emphasis on lobbying and public relations; still others have moved in increasing numbers to direct support of candidates and parties.

From time to time third-party movements such as the Black Panther party or La Raza Unida have appeared, but candidacies for office are usually only a small part of their activity and are sometimes abandoned in favor of other efforts. Certain groups opt for high militancy, but as violence attracts relatively small numbers of followers and frequently proves counterproductive (although in some instances it unquestionably gets public and official attention), such a stance is often temporary. In general, the largest and most significant organizations have sought to build recognition and support for their causes within the major political parties, in practice principally the Democratic party. They have appealed successfully to conscience but also to solidly practical electoral considerations—if politically active, their numbers can be decisive in an election. It is easy to demonstrate, for example, that black votes provided Jimmy Carter the margin of victory in a number of key states; the problem with such analysis is that in every close election any sizable group can logically claim that the candidate would not have been elected without its support.

Persons from minority groups play a steadily increasing role in serving as party leaders and appointees to high administrative posts, in claiming their share of nominations, and, most significantly, in achieving successful candidacies. The ranks of black and Chicano mayors and councilmen, state legislators, members of Congress, and executive officials are rapidly swelling, and creditable performance in office builds for the future. From 1969 to 1977 there was a 363 per cent increase in the numbers of black political officeholders in the United States—from 1,185 to 4,311. The election of black mayors in Los Angeles, Atlanta, Oakland, and Detroit, adding to earlier successes notably in Gary, Cleveland, and Newark, attracted nationwide attention. Black political activism has progressed furthest (see Table 4.5). That of the Chicano is slowly emerging, and that of the American Indian is embryonic, but increasing momentum is everywhere evident. However painfully slow the accomplishments sometimes seem, the social problems that have been the special plague of these citizens receive attention that was virtually inconceivable as recently as twenty-five years ago. There remains little if any cause for national self-congratulation—we have only begun to traverse the road toward eradication of the inequities that are the heritage of discrimination.

THE MOST POWERFUL INTEREST GROUPS

The most familiar and some of the most powerful interest groups represent major economic interests. The oldest of the agricultural groups is the Grange, but while it is still somewhat a political force in a few states and to a limited extent nationwide, it has now reverted more to its original purpose as a rural social organization. The two most influential are the Farm Bureau and the Farmers Union. The Farm Bureau has nearly nationwide strength and in its policy positions speaks primarily for the large and relatively prosperous farmers. It has recently become less favorable toward the various government programs that guarantee price supports for agricultural commodities, and it has identified itself rather closely, though unofficially, with the Republican party.

The Farmers Union represents to a greater degree the family farm operator and has its greatest membership in the upper Midwest, although it is not confined to that region. It fosters a large number of very successful cooperative marketing and purchasing enterprises and maintains that the health of agricultural economy absolutely depends on sustaining and expanding government services. Though there is no formal alliance, the allegiance of the Farmers Union has been principally to the Democratic party.

Organized business is represented in a multitude of ways; there are trade associations for every kind of industry and aspect of commerce, and many large businesses have their own lobbyists and public relations specialists. Its potency is enhanced by its very considerable ability to raise large sums of money for political purposes. The two principal broad-gauge nationwide groups representing business are the Chamber of Commerce of the United States and the National Association of Manufacturers. While the interests of the two groups may differ on some matters, they naturally seek a favorable business environment and work closely together much of the time. Both not only emphasize lobbying but also engage in huge public relations programs designed to "build a favorable climate of opinion." They produce piles of publications and a number of movies for free distribution to community organizations and to so-called opinion molders, offer speakers free of charge, and promote extensive ideological advertising campaigns. Although the Chamber of Commerce is becoming more moderate, both groups have been generally antagonistic to government social programs. The Business Roundtable, comprised of the top executives of the nation's largest corporations, has been organized to provide maximum lobbying clout.

The AFL-CIO has been the giant among labor interest groups, but several independent unions, like the Railroad Brotherhoods and the Teamsters, wield considerable power too. Some of the larger AFL-CIO unions maintain separate lobby staffs. The merger of the American Federation of Labor and the Congress of Industrial Organizations in 1955 created an organization of vast potential strength, but its political efficacy has been hampered by internal frictions. The withdrawal of the United Auto Workers and its alliance with the Teamsters in the Alliance for Labor Action nearly spelled reversion to the premerger situation. All unions engage in the usual pressure activities, but direct political action of the AFL-CIO groups is channeled largely through the Committee on Political Education (COPE), a semi-autonomous political arm for labor. Labor's strength lies primarily in numbers (although it too can raise sizable campaign funds), but it is rarely able to harness those numbers for a united front. Although its strength is too much concentrated in certain areas to achieve maximum influence in legislative elections (it can help win in a few districts overwhelmingly while being ineffective in most others), the concentration in high-population states with large numbers of electoral votes makes it a force to be reckoned with in presidential elections.

TABLE 4.5   Black Elected Officials, by Office, 1970–1977, and by Region and
            State, 1977

Year, region, and state	Total	U.S. and state legis- latures	City and county offices[a]	Law enforce- ment[b]	Educa- tion[c]
1970 (Feb.)	1,472	182	715	213	362
1971 (Mar.)	1,860	216	905	274	465
1972 (Mar.)	2,264	224	1,108	263	669
1973	2,621	256	1,264	334	767
1974	2,991	256	1,602	340	793
1975	3,503	299	1,878	387	939
1976	3,979	299	2,274	412	994
1977 (July)	4,311	316	2,497	447	1,051
Northeast	541	57	187	77	220
North Central	958	92	536	100	230
South	2,568	138	1,690	215	525
West	244	29	84	55	76
Alabama	201	15	124	38	24
Alaska	2	—	1	—	1
Arizona	14	2	6	2	4
Arkansas	218	4	131	1	82
California	177	13[d]	63	41	60
Colorado	16	4	5	4	3
Connecticut	48	7	26	4	11
Delaware	13	3	8	—	2
District of Columbia	251	1[e]	244	—	6
Florida	91	3	73	6	9
Georgia	225	23	150	9	43
Hawaii	1	1	—	—	—
Idaho	1	—	1	—	—
Illinois	281	22[f]	165	21	73
Indiana	66	6	49	6	5
Iowa	9	2	1	1	5
Kansas	33	6	15	1	11
Kentucky	66	3	43	8	12
Louisiana	276	10	145	40	81
Maine	3	1	2	—	—

Source: U.S. Department of Commerce, Bureau of the Census, *Statistical Abstract of the United States, 1977,* Government Printing Office, Washington, D.C., 1978, p. 507.

Note: As of April, except as indicated.

[a]County commissioners and councilmen, mayors, vice mayors, aldermen, regional officials, and other. [b]Judges, magistrates, constables, marshals, sheriffs, justices of the peace and other. [c]College boards, school boards, and other. [d]Includes three U. S. Representatives. [e]Includes one U. S. Representative. [f]Includes two U. S. Representatives. [g]Includes one U. S. Senator.

Year, region, and state	Total	U.S. and state legislatures	City and county offices[a]	Law enforcement[b]	Education[c]
Maryland	88	20[e]	54	10	4
Massachusetts	24	10[g]	8	—	6
Michigan	251	20[f]	114	30	87
Minnesota	9	2	1	3	3
Mississippi	295	4	175	52	64
Missouri	126	16[e]	79	18	13
Montana	1	1	—	—	—
Nebraska	7	2	1	—	4
Nevada	7	3	—	2	2
New Hampshire	1	1	—	—	—
New Jersey	148	5	71	—	72
New Mexico	4	1	2	—	1
New York	186	16[f]	33	31	106
North Carolina	221	6	157	5	53
North Dakota	1	—	1	—	—
Ohio	159	13[e]	101	19	26
Oklahoma	69	4	46	1	18
Oregon	6	1	1	2	2
Pennsylvania	128	16[e]	45	42	25
Rhode Island	3	1	2	—	—
South Carolina	182	13	99	21	49
South Dakota	—	—	—	—	—
Tennessee	117	12[e]	87	8	10
Texas	158	14[e]	64	12	68
Utah	1	1	—	—	—
Vermont	—	—	—	—	—
Virginia	82	2	77	3	—
Washington	13	2	5	4	2
West Virginia	15	1	13	1	—
Wisconsin	16	3	9	1	3
Wyoming	1	—	—	—	1

Other groups with effective political power include the professional associations representing lawyers, medical doctors, and teachers, religious groups, and the various "good government" or reform groups. The veterans' organizations are very influential, especially on the self-interested matters of veterans' benefits but also on "anti-radical" legislation, law enforcement, patriotic observance, and some foreign policy issues. The most significant politically of these groups are the American Legion, the Veterans of Foreign Wars, and the Disabled American Veterans. A great source of Legion strength lies in its being organized in every community and having within its membership a cross section of the population. Some highly specialized interests have at times shown the capacity for mustering support far transcending their numbers, as in the National Rifle Association's concerted efforts to block extensive gun-control legislation.

WOMEN'S POLITICAL ACTION

For many years before the contemporary women's movement burst upon the scene, a number of national as well as local women's organizations, ranging from highly specialized interests to broadly gauged groups (the American Association of University Women and the League of Women Voters, for example), played significant roles in the political process. Groups such as the League, whose excellent analyses of public policy issues and stimulation of informed popular participation have made a notable contribution to better government across the country, have been interested in general questions of social policy and only rather incidentally in what might be termed distinctively women's issues. Newer women's liberation organizations such as NOW (National Organization for Women) have focused their efforts on problems of sex discrimination and have tended to follow a somewhat more militant line, one result having inevitably been the creation of counterforces like HOW (Happiness of Women). In an effort to bring together as many as possible of the disparate women's groups into a more effectively unified force, the National Women's Political Caucus in 1973 held its first national convention. The variety of goals and approaches represented proved almost too divisive for the organization to be viable, but compromises ultimately produced a constitution and slate of national officers, and the NWPC is now testing its unity and strength as a multipartisan lobbying body and as a fund raiser for campaigns by women candidates. In 1977 the eighteen women members of the House formed a Women's Caucus explicitly to work for women's issues.

The number of women candidates for congressional or statewide offices has mushroomed rapidly in the nation as a whole. There is likewise a considerable increase in female candidacies for city, county, town, and school district offices, where women officeholders

THE BETTER HALF by Barnes, reprinted courtesy the Register & Tribune Syndicate.

"If it makes you any happier, then, yes, I'd vote for a woman for president—but only if she ran as an incumbent!"

were already much more numerous. In part this increase has been stimulated by the women's movement, or at least by the attitudinal environment it has helped to create and the presence of more women in professional and business occupations, although added impetus undeniably has come from the general public desire for new faces in the political arena. Women have long been the mainstay of many party and campaign organizations, but they are now beginning to move strongly toward having a more realistic share of the leadership roles, with every evidence that the opportunities will continue to expand.

HOW INTEREST GROUPS WORK

The principal political tactics of interest groups are essentially of three related kinds: lobbying, public relations, and direct campaign assistance. Establishing personal contact with legislators gets high priority from most interest groups (more detailed discussion of their methods appears in Chapter 9 on Congress), but much time and effort are also spent in lobbying the administrative agencies that enforce the laws with which the interest groups are concerned. Farmer organizations, for instance, want to be sure that the Department of Agriculture is vigorous in maintaining price supports. Occasionally some groups may fight their battles in the courts, as the

National Association for the Advancement of Colored People has effectively done. Most also engage in some kind of public relations campaigning, at least of providing information, designed to create a favorable impression of their objectives and to build public support that will help when policies affecting their interests are under consideration in the legislative and executive branches. Some campaigns are mammoth multimillion-dollar annual programs, such as that conducted by the National Association of Manufacturers, while others are more modest, but the trend is toward continually more extensive public relations efforts.

Since it is always easier to influence legislators who are favorably disposed to begin with, it is not surprising that interest groups are a principal source of campaign funds. Such groups also show strong interest in party platforms. Some endorse candidates, in public or within the group, providing a fair amount of free publicity. They may furnish campaign workers or, depending on the nature of the organization and state laws, may make available free transportation, advertising space, supplies, or headquarters buildings. Certain groups are very influential in some localities in determining who will receive party nominations, and they commonly seek commitments from candidates by raising questions for public response early in the primary campaigns.

It is not true that all interest groups confine themselves exclusively to matters of self-interest. Many support or oppose legislation quite unrelated to their special interests, based usually on broad ideological positions, although such activity may not be their essential purpose. To maximize strength on items thought to be of crucial importance, interest groups often form alliances to support each other's legislation, but such cooperative efforts must be managed with delicacy to avoid negative reactions from legislators and the public.

At least three major groups that have arisen in recent years seek to fill some of the void in representation of broad public interest, Common Cause, Public Citizen, and New Directions. As founder of Public Citizen, Ralph Nader has worked primarily through investigations of both government and private organizations and policies, followed by extensive publicity, using volunteer or minimally paid young people with appropriate training and a commitment to reform. Common Cause, on the other hand, has sought to build a mass-membership "citizens lobby" organization, in which it has achieved unprecedented success. In its first year of existence it gained nearly a quarter of a million members at an annual dues rate of $15, and it has maintained at least that level and more, an incredibly difficult task. Lobbying vigorously and professionally on a variety of issues from peace efforts, environmental improvement, and health care to equal-opportunity measures and overhaul of the criminal justice system, it has come down hardest on reform of campaign practices, financial disclosure, and reform of congressional organization and procedure. It utilizes every legitimate tactic of pressure politics and has proved exceptionally able at mobilizing grassroots influence on the part of individual citizens throughout the country. Now a force to be reckoned with, it has on a number of occasions been publicly credited in Congress with being the decisive element in the winning of crucial battles. The more recently established New Directions, operating in a manner similar to Common Cause, focuses its efforts on promoting a humane and internationalist foreign policy.

Most interest-group tactics are perfectly legitimate, though one may well doubt that there is adequate balance among the groups and their resources. To the extent that questionable tactics or abuses appear, they should be subjected to vigorous criticism, but it is unrealistic to seize on such situations as grounds for condemning all pressure activity. In a system in which parties are coalitions encompassing a wide range of viewpoints, interest groups promoting specific policies are a natural and vital part of the political process. Interest-group politics is, however, highly effective in achieving relatively narrow and specific goals of particular groups or classes of society, but (at least until the advent of the three organizations discussed above) has been lamentably weak in accomplishing goals that reflect the common good, such as preserving cities as habitable and restoring the purity of air and water. For such goals strong political leadership through parties, whose interests are far broader than those of most special groups, is necessary.

BASIC CONCEPTS AND TERMS

voter turnout patterns
partisan voting patterns
southern strategy
middle-of-the-road political
  sentiment
political extremism
literacy and understanding tests
nature of public opinion
political polling
political role of the
  communications media

fourth branch of government
equal-time requirement
fairness doctrine
interest-group politics
countervailing theory of group
  politics
minority-group politics
National Women's Political
  Caucus
Common Cause

PARTY POLITICS

5

"Politicians are the unanointed saints who keep the real saints from cutting each other's throats," an American educator-politician once observed. Not only does democracy depend on politicians, gifted in resolving the conflicts common to any free society, but no democracy of any size has ever functioned without political parties. If a system is to function in such a way that people can influence the actions of government, they will naturally join together to control it. In large-scale societies most complicated tasks and all social programs are accomplished through organizations, and people who share some common political goals recognize this. In a sociopolitical environment individuals become effective in social action involving people other than their friends primarily by achieving influence and leadership in specific organizations.

THE FUNCTION OF POLITICAL PARTIES

Political parties differ from interest groups principally in that interest groups attempt to influence the actions of government whereas parties seek to control and operate the actual machinery of government. The basic purpose of a party is to win and hold public office. Its range of concerns and activities is far greater than that of any interest group, and its emphasis is distinctly different. Major parties, moreover, do not consist of people who are in complete agreement on all goals. They agree on the desirability of gaining and holding power and of exercising it for certain general purposes. The purposes may include achieving certain policies or simply acting in accord with what is conceived to be the proper service or regulatory role of government or perhaps securing jobs and other patronage for the party faithful or a combination of these objectives.

It is largely the political parties that breathe life into the machinery of government institutions. Although far from perfect for the purpose, parties are our principal instrument for determining the popular will and giving it effect. They provide the mechanisms through which the electorate can choose who will hold office and carry the responsibilities of government, including a constant process of recruiting new personnel. They seek to inform the public and stimulate popular interest in political issues and elections. Ideally, they help crystallize from a welter of different issues at any given time broad alternatives that make meaningful voter choice possible. Perhaps most important of all, when a party is elected to power it can give a reasonable degree of cohesion to the different branches of government, which in the nature of the American system are otherwise likely to be uncoordinated. The contribution of the parties to constructive compromise and consensus building is of no small significance.

The major parties in the United States have been not highly ideological but pragmatic and accustomed to pursuing the possible. Each party normally tries to appeal to as wide a spectrum of the population as it can. In general terms, at the national level, the Republican party concentrates on people at the center and of conservative inclination, whereas the Democratic party aims also at people in the center plus those of a liberal bent, although there are conservatives and liberals alike in both parties. The Democratic party in the twentieth century has therefore been much more an agent of change and innovation than has the Republican party. The Democrats also have a much more heterogeneous membership, which is both a strength and a weakness, providing greater numbers but more internal friction.

DEMOCRATS AND REPUBLICANS: SIMILARITIES AND DIFFERENCES

It is instructive to examine the distinction between Democrats and Republicans from several perspectives: orientation toward the desirable role of government in society; attitude on specific public issues and resultant party platform; party votes on a variety of congressional roll calls; and party voters' view of their party and the opposition, to name but a few. A criticism of American parties heard frequently is that there is no fundamental difference between them. If by "fundamental" one intends to suggest that neither party seeks to overturn the existing constitutional system or to alter radically the nature of the economy, the statement is correct. But within the very broad consensus on how to bring about change while preserving what is worthwhile are many and significant differences.

The national Democratic party is much more oriented toward a positive role for government, the active use of government as an instrument for solving social problems, than is the national Republican party, which shows greater distrust of government and urges a larger role for the private sector. These are differences of degree, not absolutes, but differences of degree can be extremely important. Regarding specific policy issues, it is easy in any election year or during any session of Congress to notice fairly clear differences of position on a variety of questions such as taxes, enforcement of civil rights, labor-management relations, and social welfare. There are always some issues at any given moment on which there are no strong partisan differences; there may be general consensus on the issue, or the differences of opinion may run along regional or economic-interest lines. Although it is extremely rare to find all Republicans on one side and all Democrats on the other in any congressional roll call, the roll calls on many major issues show solid majorities of each party in opposition to each other. This is even more apparent if the votes of southern Democrats are tallied separately.

Just as there are clearly wealthy Democrats and poor Republicans, providing exceptions to the generalizations noted earlier about the composition of the parties, other generalizations also must be viewed in the light of majorities rather than totalities. The Democratic party since at least the 1930s has drawn support heavily from people of lower incomes, labor occupations, intellectual pursuits, and racial and religious minority status (blacks and Jews, for example). People in the higher-income brackets lean strongly to the Republican side; and the higher that incomes are, the higher is the Republican percentage of the vote. Similarly disposed toward the Republican party are business and professional people, although occupation and income are of course related.

The popular perceptions of the parties are significant in this respect. It may or may not be completely accurate that the Republican party is the party of business, but there is little doubt that people in business predominantly see the Republican party as their vehicle, just as members of organized labor normally see the Democratic party as identified with the interests of the working class and the

"What we want is a broader base"

economically less fortunate. These relations may not remain fixed for all time and are perhaps already undergoing some alterations, though most people do not change party preference readily. Even when registrations do not change, votes may be switched under the stress of considerations that seem at least temporarily more important than preserving loyalty to one's party, such as war, economic depression, or a crisis over domestic law and order. President Nixon, whose relations with labor were for the most part anything but cordial, successfully wooed significant labor support in the 1972 election by making a number of labor-recommended appointments and agreeing to demands regarding economic controls. Labor backing, or neutrality, resulted in large part, however, from the antagonism of certain labor leaders and a good percentage of the rank and file to some McGovern proposals and to the purely pragmatic conclusion that Nixon was going to win in any case and therefore it was logical to get from him whatever concessions were possible. It was a stormy and short-lived marriage of convenience, ending not long after the election as Watergate disclosures mounted and as labor came to believe that the wage-price freeze was strongly probusiness in its operation. In 1976 Jimmy Carter was generally successful in re-establishing the traditional Democratic coalition. That no category of people can be completely taken for granted by either party is probably an advantage, since both parties seek consensus and compromise in an effort to attract new support. People are not automatons, and the results of elections are certainly not foreordained.

THE MAJOR PARTIES AS CONGLOMERATES

Whatever generalizations are made about the major parties in the United States, one must view them as essentially conglomerate bodies accommodating considerable internal variation in structure, policy, and attitude, Moreover, the parties are based strongly on the states. Some states like Illinois and Pennsylvania have sharp and fairly continuous party competition, while others like Louisiana and Nebraska are traditionally one-party domains. The parties in some states are tightly organized; in others they are quite fragmented; in still others they are essentially the personal instruments of strong individual political leaders, such as a governor or United States senator.

Political scientist James MacGregor Burns asserts the existence of a four-party system at the national level, since there are presidential and congressional wings with divergent interests within each party. The presidential wing centers its attention on the election of a president and on congressional races in the close districts that often swing with the presidency. It focuses on national and international policy and generally has a moderate-to-liberal stance by the standards of that party. The congressional wing in each party is concerned not only with the numerical control of Congress but also with the exercise of power within that body. It is dominated by the committee chairmen and elected leaders of each house. Seniority thus plays a major role in the distribution of power, which lies principally with members from safe districts and states. The congressional wing is basically conservative, and its heartland is the rural and small-town areas, in contrast to the dominantly urban orientation of the presidential wing.

THE INDEPENDENT VOTER

We have noticed previously that most people who are actively interested in political matters are likely to be partisans and that many of those professing no affiliation are likely to be relatively uninformed. But much depends on what one means by the term *independent voter*. The polls indicate that about one-third of the voters classify themselves thus, but many independents have fairly definite party preferences even when they have no active party affiliation. They frequently mean by adopting this label merely that they do not consider themselves bound to one party or set of candidates and that they do not vote a straight ticket. Yet in our voting system no one is in fact bound, so this is not a very meaningful distinction. Preferential leanings are more important. Sometimes the term *independent* is applied to those who are simply undecided in a given election. A significant percentage of the independents never vote; they merely describe themselves as independent when the less honorific *indifferent* would be more accurate.

Persons who want to exercise power or influence within a party must be "regular" enough for others to feel that their influence is warranted, but the system is far from rigid. Party membership is not at all well defined. In general, if people say they are Republican, then they are, and if they say they are Democrats, they are. There is little, if any, party discipline, and only a small percentage of members contribute even modest financial support to their parties.

Although the percentage of unaffiliated voters is increasing, as noted earlier, the claim that the independent is the deciding force in politics remains highly dubious. Both parties do indeed devote considerable effort to wooing the independent vote, but they do so more through persuasion than concession, particularly since independents have no unified viewpoint or set of goals. The independent must choose among candidates offered by the parties and is removed from the nominating process by not indicating a party preference in registration. The independent recognizes belatedly, if at all, that many important decisions are in fact made within the parties. It can reasonably be argued that the most truly nonpartisan discussion of issues occurs within the parties and not in debate or contest between them. Within a party there is more likelihood of an issue's being debated on its merits, but once party positions have been established and the issue is thrust into the midst of a campaign, the independent voter is hardly likely to hear a dispassionate presentation.

The common stress on independence, however unrealistic, has doubtless contributed to the antipolitical and antipartisan attitudes so prevalent in the United States. These attitudes reflect a kind of nonpolitical view of politics, perhaps an unconscious attachment to the belief that the "bad guys" will always be headed off at the pass by the cavalry. How often do we hear people claim piously that they vote not for a party but always "for the best candidate"? And how is the "best" candidate determined? If the voter means selection of the candidate whose political views seem most nearly in accord with one's own, there is no ground for argument. But such language almost invariably implies a quite different standard. We rightly view with mixed amusement and annoyance someone who votes for or against a candidate because of a mustache or a haircut. Should we not feel the same about votes based on other irrelevant factors?

The "good candidate" approach to politics is exhibited by the voter who ignores the political stand of a candidate and bases choice on certain allegedly good characteristics of a candidate, perhaps one who does not smoke or drink. We may be happy that a candidate is kind to mothers and does not kick dogs, but we do not ordinarily elect people to represent our views on dog treatment. Public figures must deal with crucial issues of domestic and foreign policy.

Equally simplistic is the assumption that a good candidate elected to office will always "do what is right." And what is right? In a world where all decisions were either right or wrong, human judgment would scarcely be needed, but whoever has held public responsibility knows well the incredible mixture of right and wrong, good and bad, advantages for some and disadvantages for others, that almost every significant issue presents. Yet in each case a decision must be made.

A strong case could be made for voting as a rule for the candidates of the party best representing one's viewpoint, at least if one sees merit in achieving a greater degree of party responsibility. (One would, of course, always reserve the option to vote for a candidate of another party in the few instances in which one feels the party nominee to be completely unacceptable and the position of the opposing party candidate reasonably satisfactory.) The notion of maintaining party responsibility refers to the situation in which the voters can elect a party to office and expect it to carry out its program as set forth in its platform and in the statements of its leaders. Voting for the candidate rather than the party clearly makes such party responsibility unlikely, especially since the government system in the United States also militates against party responsibility. Yet we often hear a party condemned when it fails fully to accomplish its announced program. Many other considerations, such as regional differences in social and political attitudes and the conglomerate nature of our parties, further complicate the problem of responsibility. Then, too, party faithfulness works both ways. A party that expects dependable support from voters must consistently offer programs and candidates that are generally acceptable to a broad cross section of the population rather than cater to an ideological minority.

THE TWO-PARTY SYSTEM AND THIRD PARTIES

Political parties perform several functions in a democratic society: they help crystallize public opinion and define the decisions to be made; they inform and educate the public politically; they bear responsibility for operating the government and providing leaders for the nation or alternatively serve as the responsible opposition in providing criticism; they seek out and develop the personnel who will assume the leadership of government; they contribute a degree of unity to a system of government created with more emphasis on separateness of its branches than on unified operation; and they perform (much less than in the past) social services in such ways as aiding the poor and assimilating newcomers from foreign lands.

The two-party system has remained strongly entrenched in the United States as a result both of traditional factors, like voter expectation that one of the major parties will always win, and of certain institutional features, like the electoral college and the single-member legislative district. Although a two-party system may be somewhat less representative and less responsive than a multiparty system, thus offering less clear-cut choices to the voters, it does have certain advantages. Its greatest claim is that it normally affords a high degree of stability. Political activity is less fragmented, and everyone can expect that one party or the other will normally hold majority control after each election. This eliminates any need for constructing coalitions of parties to constitute a legislative majority, and coalitions often prove to be shaky. Furthermore, since a two-party system frames many political questions in terms of either-or, choices for the voter are made less complex.

Another feature of a two-party system is that both parties tend to be moderate, rejecting attitudes of extremism. Not only do the parties in such a system sufficiently define issues for voters, but when necessary they can temporarily blur certain issues that are too sharply divisive for the society to bear. Such issues cannot safely be ignored or neglected, but given time they can usually be worked out, whereas an immediate confrontation might be totally destructive. The parties then serve as brokers for the compromise necessary for a solution. The most notable instance in which the parties were unable to perform this function adequately was the period preceding the Civil War.

Nothing illustrates better the solidity of the American two-party system than the common practice of referring to every minor party, however many there may be at any given moment, as a third party. It is sometimes suggested that a distinction should be made between a third party, referring to that which poses a serious threat to the major parties, and a minor party, referring to any small movement (like the Prohibition and Socialist Labor parties) that has no real chance in elections, but customary speech blurs such a distinction. All but the major parties are somehow assumed by the public to be just a bit outside the norms of political behavior, despite a recognition that third parties appear regularly on the scene and are wholly legitimate. There have been many third parties throughout history, but most have lasted for only an election or two. A few have had great durability, but they achieved no substantial public support.

The cards are largely stacked against the successful rise of a third party to major-party status. Gaining nationwide attention and support requires considerable organization and vast amounts of money, neither of which is easily and quickly attainable by most third parties. To be effective, they must organize comprehensively at all levels with slates of candidates for all offices, not just nationally or regionally. Attaining these objectives is both difficult and time consuming. Of central importance, of course, are traditional popular attachments to the major parties.*

The winner-take-all aspect of the electoral college in presidential elections makes it necessary to win states to secure electoral votes. A third party may win respectable percentages of the popular vote in many states without getting a single electoral vote, a result that is most discouraging to its followers. Congressional structure and electoral processes also sustain the two-party system; indeed, several practices of Congress, such as the committee system, could have developed only in a context of two strong parties. Even the typical voter who favors a third party is always confident that one of the major parties will win and is likely to vote for the major party considered to be the lesser of two evils rather than waste a vote. Despite the enthusiasm generated in some quarters for the candidacy of George Wallace in 1968, for example, what appeared in September to be a strong vote dropped by election day to a level disappointing to his supporters. Moreover, experience has suggested that an issue promoted by a third party that gains sufficient popularity may be embraced by one or both of the major parties, thus taking the wind out of the third party's sails. With little if any chance of ever achiev-

---

*It is sometimes suggested that the coming to prominence of the Republican party in the middle of the 1850s is an example of the rise of a third party to major-party status, but this party was actually the natural heir of the Whig party (and its predecessor the National Republican party), which quietly folded as the Republican party took its place.

ing power, the third party must find satisfaction in seeing some of its goals attained by others.

Some third parties have generated nationwide interest; others have had a regional base and concentrated on state and local issues and elections. Most of these parties have had an effect on the political system, and a few have played significant roles in American history. Certain of them have succeeded in electing some of their candidates in a number of state and local governments. They have also served usefully in times of stress as a vehicle for the expression of protest—a safety valve of sorts.

Third parties have occasionally been a weight in balance of power, in effect determining which major party achieves victory even when unable to win itself. Because third parties ordinarily pull away votes principally from the party to which they are closest, the usual and ironic result is that the election is handed to the party they most strongly oppose. One of the best-known illustrations of this is the 1912 Bull Moose Progressive party's defection from the Republican party, which clearly resulted in the election of Woodrow Wilson, the Democratic candidate. Although he received less than 1 per cent of the nationwide vote in 1976, Eugene McCarthy drew more votes in Iowa, Maine, Oklahoma, and Oregon than the narrow margins by which Ford carried those states, which in slightly different circumstances might easily have altered the outcome. Attention has centered recently on the possibility that a third party capable of acquiring some electoral votes could, in the event of a close race between the major-party candidates, succeed in throwing the election into the House of Representatives. The third-party candidate could thus have significant bargaining power, and it was this openly avowed prospect that helped fuel the 1968 Wallace campaign.

ORGANIZATION OF THE
TWO MAJOR PARTIES

In looking at an organization chart it is natural to assume that power increases as one goes up the hierarchy. In political party organization this is not completely true, at least in the sense of the ability of each party level to exercise control over the units below it. Within the major parties, power decreases the higher one moves up the structure; in other words, county organizations have more control over the wards and precincts than the state organizations have over the counties, and the states have more control over the counties than the national committee has over the various state parties. The scope of activity is of course much greater at the top, but, despite some trends toward national consolidation, American parties are remarkably decentralized (see Figure 5.1). In the American federal system, state

FIGURE 5.1   Organization of a Major Party

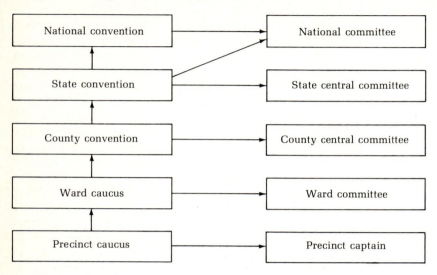

election laws determine the party structures or allow the parties to do so. The Republican party in Nebraska may be quite different from the Republican party in Maine.

Since the fundamental purpose of parties is to win elections, it is natural that their organization should reflect that of the districts administering elections. On paper the pattern is essentially the same throughout the country, but in practice there is considerable variety of operation among states and regions. The normal organization can be described, but the broad regional variations should also be indicated.

PRECINCT, WARD, AND COUNTY

The basic unit of major-party organization is ordinarily the precinct caucus (or convention), which is simply a meeting of all the voters of that particular party living in the precinct who care to attend. Precincts are administrative subdivisions of cities or counties set up for the conduct of elections, and each precinct contains approximately the number of voters who can reasonably vote in one polling place in one day (usually two hundred to six hundred people but occasionally many more, especially where voting machines are used). Except during a struggle for control of the party, attendance at the caucuses is normally light, partly because the public lacks interest and fails to understand their importance and sometimes because the group in power keeps its meetings as quiet as possible. At any rate, every resident member of the party is entitled to participate in this biennial grassroots meeting of the party.

The central function of the precinct caucus is twofold and is usually accomplished quickly. It must elect a precinct executive, usually called a precinct captain or chairman, who is primarily responsible for carrying on the work of the party in that precinct for the next two years. Then it must select delegates who will represent the precinct at the ward caucuses, the next higher level. At times there may be vigorous discussion of issues or proposed resolutions. Since all the higher caucuses and conventions are meetings composed of delegates, the precinct caucuses are the foundation, and control at the grassroots is necessary to control the higher levels. In some areas precinct captains are appointed by city or county organizations, in which case delegate selection is the only formal responsibility of the precinct caucus.

In well-organized areas the precinct captain and assistants, if there are any, are probably the most important single element in the electoral success of a party. This is the point where the individual voter can be reached personally. A good precinct captain seeks to develop a friendly acquaintance with every member of the party in the precinct and with as many other people as possible. If help can be secured, the captain can extend the limits of effectiveness through the use of block workers, individuals responsible for the voters living in a single block of the precinct. The precinct captain directs local fund raising, distributing of literature, and getting out the vote on election day. Although electronic media have changed the nature of campaigning in many respects, a good precinct worker is still invaluable.

But the most useful tool is acquaintance and friendship, aided by the average citizen's recognition of the precinct captain as an activist who is well informed about politics. The average citizen is not well informed and turns naturally to someone in whom he or she has confidence for advice and counsel when an election is imminent. Everyone who has done any kind of party work, even on a small scale, has had the experience of people telephoning in the days just before an election to ask whom they should vote for (or of people remarking, "Say, why don't you just mark this sample ballot for me?"), especially in the case of the lesser-known offices. Not every precinct captain, however, is active and efficient; some precincts may be completely leaderless or undertake active work only in a pre-election period, whereas others are too divided factionally. Then the voter depends more on the news media.

The wards (which may not exist as party structures in every area) are larger subdivisions incorporating a number of precincts, anywhere from half a dozen to thirty or more, depending on the size of the city and its governmental form. In cities having a district system for council elections, the wards are the districts from which council members are elected. The ward caucuses, held in in many places the same night as the precinct caucuses, perform the same two functions.

They elect delegates to the county conventions, and they choose the ward chairman and a few other officers to serve as the ward committee for the next two years. Such caucuses may also address themselves to issues of city politics and at times pass resolutions or provide instructions for delegates to be conveyed to higher caucuses. Ward officers are expected to deal with all such matters and to furnish aid and direction to the precinct officers.

The county convention normally lasts all day, rather than the evening meeting typical of precinct and ward caucuses, and its range of activity is broader, although some of its responsibilities are similar. It may discuss, formulate, and adopt a set of resolutions on government policies, and it usually endorses candidates (or actually nominates if there is no primary) for local government offices, such as that of sheriff, and often for state legislators. It elects delegates to the state convention and members of the county central committee. While the county convention is in session, it has extensive power over party affairs in the county, but in the intervening two-year periods the central committee is the party's governing body. The county chairman, ordinarily elected by the central committee, is a key figure in county politics and often is influential in state politics as well.

STATE

The state convention, usually scheduled to occupy a two- or three-day weekend, adopts a state platform, endorses or nominates candidates for statewide office, and in similar fashion to the counties elects the state central committee. Every four years it selects the state's delegation to the national convention, except in states in which the delegation is chosen in a presidential preference primary (see Chapter 6). State central committees tend to be rather large, of up to several hundred members in some states, although that size is rare. This committee is responsible for all statewide campaigns, fund raising, and party programs, but because of its unwieldy size the normal practice is to choose a state chairman, the top figure in the formal state organization, and an executive committee to carry on the regular day-to-day activities.

NATIONAL

National conventions are familiar to all as the mechanism for nominating presidential and vice-presidential candidates. Their internal operations will be discussed in the following chapter; here it will suffice to notice that in addition to their nominating and platform-writing functions, provision is made for continuing activity during the subsequent four-year period. In this case, however, the national committee is only nominally elected by the national convention. The

convention simply ratifies the persons selected in each of the states
for committee membership. Traditionally the national committees
consisted of one man and one woman from each state, but the
Republican party early in the 1960s decided more accurately to represent party strength in the states by providing that the state chairman
should also serve on the national committee if the chairman's state
voted Republican in the preceding election. More recently the Democratic party shifted to allocating seats on the committee on the basis
of state population and the percentage of the state vote that went to
the Democratic candidate in the preceding election.

Although the national committee in theory has broad responsibilities, its activities tend to be quite limited. It has officially overall
responsibility for running the presidential campaign (though candidates tend to set up their own organizations), authorizes national
fund raising by a finance chairman, and generally supports the full-
time professional staff of the national headquarters in Washington. It
initiates the arrangements and organizes the machinery for the next
national convention. Although the committee technically elects the
national chairman, this person is in fact designated by the party's
presidential nominee and usually serves as the nominee's campaign
chairman. The national committee has been known after a defeat to
replace a chairman with someone of its own choosing, as happened
in the Republican party after the 1964 election and in the Democratic
party after 1972. An incumbent president can determine just about
how active the party's national committee will be.

Recently a trend toward larger professional staffs for the national
party organizations—public relations experts, fund raisers, researchers, and pollsters—has developed, and the Republican party is distinctly in the lead with this effort. Both parties have on public policy
questions experimented with prestigious "advisory boards" composed of officials and prominent private citizens, but they have not
had notable success. Neither presidents nor congressional leaders
have been enthusiastic about permitting others to tamper with their
prerogative of speaking for the party on policy matters.

PERSONALITY IN THE PARTY ORGANIZATION

At the conclusion of a discussion of party politics, one sometimes
hears the question, "But where do bosses and machines fit into the
picture?" Our language in response must be imprecise. To some
extent these terms are merely derogatory labels for the opposition:
"My party has an organization; the other side has a machine. They
have a boss; we have a leader." Aside from such rhetoric, it is usually
assumed that a machine is a tight organization controlled from the
top down by a boss. In turn, a boss is considered to be a person
who exercises nearly complete political power, presumably largely

through undesirable tactics such as coercion and questionable use of money, and who often seeks personal or group goals rather than the public interest. The line between a strong leader and a boss is clearly not easy to draw in real life. Bosses, much less common today than in the past, have cropped up most frequently in local politics. There have been fewer state bosses, but some, like Huey Long, have been politically very powerful.

REGIONAL VARIATIONS

The party structure described here is the normal form, but it does not appear uniformly across the nation. The more one learns about the politics of any state, the more one perceives its distinctiveness. But certain broadly regional characteristics may be noted. The normal pattern prevails generally throughout the East and Midwest, but often in the trans-Mississippi Midwest and the West the precinct level is not fully staffed or really operative except during campaign periods, if at all. In the South there has often been only limited formal organization except on paper; the system there has traditionally depended on personal politics, but this may be changing. The parties in some New England states also evidence personalized politics. California, the state with the largest population, has had for many years no official precinct or ward organizations at all, and county central committees are elected in the primaries.

In a number of states, unofficial political bodies bearing in some fashion the major party names, such as a Democratic Council or a Republican League, have sprung up, particularly since World War II. These generally have been groups of activists banded together to control more effectively the official machinery or to act in matters neglected by the official machinery. When state laws do not provide for local organizations, for example, such bodies can create their own, or when state laws prohibit the official organizations from endorsing candidates before a primary, the extralegal organizations can endorse and put the weight of their money and effort behind the candidates they wish to see their parties nominate. In a few states, as in California a few years ago, groups of this kind have at times come to be, at least temporarily, a sort of tail that wags the dog.

THE FUTURE OF THE PARTIES

From time to time proposals are made for the reform or restructuring of party organization, the thrust of most suggestions directed toward achieving a higher degree of party responsibility. In the 1950s a committee of the American Political Science Association offered specific recommendations that have generated continuing controversy. The committee members believed that the parties were too weak and irresponsible for meeting the demands of the last half of the twentieth century. It recommended that greater unity and responsiveness could be achieved by holding national conventions every two years and constituting a fifty-member party council to control party affairs in the interim, interpret party policy, and propose advance platform drafts. National committees would be made representative of population and party strength instead of treating each state equally, and in several ways the national party organizations would be made more powerful. Party leadership and the committee system in Congress would be reorganized to reflect more accurately and effectively the popular will.

Although many people hailed these proposals as constructive, some observers have insisted that a decentralized system fits the peculiar needs of the United States and that it is unwise to sharpen divisive issues and require greater conformity of representatives through more rigid party discipline. The broadly inclusive nature of American parties, they suggest, and the interest-group character of our politics are simply not conducive to high party discipline, and the price of change would be a less free and less open political system. Just how directly responsive the system ought to be remains in dispute.

A version of some of these proposals surfaced in the recommendations of the Democratic party reform commission that functioned in the aftermath of the turbulent 1968 national convention. In addition to changes in the selection of convention delegates, to be discussed in the following chapter, these included the establishment of a national policy conference to meet in the even-numbered years when there is no presidential election, the creation of a national executive committee to include congressional and party leaders, the establishment of a national membership and finance council, and an increase in the size of the national committee, whose members would be selected according to state populations and previous Democratic vote. These suggestions predictably did not meet with universal enthusiasm, but the 1974 conference drafted a charter or constitution for the party and incorporated most of these features.

What will be the future of these conglomerate American parties? One needs no crystal ball to anticipate some trends that are already evident, but many uncertainties remain. Among the serious problems they must face is the apparent steady decline in party loyalty and perhaps even party interest from the general public. There is perhaps some increase in single-issue voting unrelated to party, as on environment questions, for example, but more important has been the widespread disaffection from politics to which we alluded earlier. If the parties continue to be weakened, there are potential dangers to the entire political system. Without effective parties to provide linkage, will we not have even poorer coherence among the components of government than in the considerably less-than-perfect situation that now prevails? Lacking the guidelines afforded by party positions, will not the rationality of voter choice be seriously reduced? There is evidence that in nonpartisan elections, decisions are more likely to be made on the basis of personality and other essentially nonpolitical factors. Nonpolitical decision making will likely mean continued one-party dominance of Congress, as incumbents find re-election relatively easier. If parties do not adequately perform as brokers among interest groups, are we not likely to be even more dominated by special-interest politics? Are there conceivable realistic alternatives to parties for the essential task of building the coalitions of popular support needed to accomplish social goals?

For a few years much was heard of the "new politics," although the term remained ambiguous and ill defined. In essence it seemed to imply a departure from the old and presumably tarnished organizations, leaders, and campaign practices in favor of a greater concentration on issues and principles, leaders and workers oriented more toward social goals than personal power, and emphasis on participatory democracy. Whether in fact those who claimed to be practitioners of the new politics were possessed of purer motives than others is debatable, but the movement introduced some new blood and helped instigate a variety of reform efforts.

There is likewise no clear agreement as to the meaning of participatory democracy. Most people agree on the desirability of widespread active participation in the democratic process, but in practice advocates of a politics with this label have often been marked by a refusal to work through parties and other such institutions, instead emphasizing political decision and action by individuals, ad hoc groups, and mass meetings.

The upshot is often confusion and chaos: uncoordinated groups seeking the same goals as well as many groups in conflict; demonstrations answered by counterdemonstrations; a demand for action as opposed to discussion and negotiation; the appearance of talented demagogues adept at mob psychology. The experience of other nations during the twentieth century demonstrates all too clearly how such an approach easily degenerates into political decision making based on whichever faction can turn the largest mass of followers into the streets at any given moment. Force rather than reason can readily dominate. But if the political parties are to remain attractive and workable, they must prove their continued ability not only to adapt to change but also to lead the way in effecting the kinds of constructive change that a modern society needs and demands.

That the parties have been highly adaptable in the past should occasion some optimism for the future.

Many writers are fond of referring to the contemporary era as that of the postindustrial society, and one may thus likewise speak of postindustrial politics. The term refers to the fact that we are at a point in economic history where manufacturing is less important than services and the marketing of knowledge. Over one-third of our gross national product is now accounted for by the production, distribution, and consumption of knowledge, and a large segment of our population is involved in the process: educators, communications specialists, government employees, foundation personnel, consultants, researchers, data processors, and the like. Some observers suggest that the creation of a new class identified with knowledge may lead to greater polarization in politics, since its relative social liberalism will conflict with a conservative-populist coalition struggling to maintain its status and to reaffirm the old patriotic and religious virtues.

The end result might be groups, cutting across party lines, that are dominated by activist ideologues and attracted to relatively extreme programs. Their fervent style may be effective in winning primaries but does not produce candidates or issues attractive to a broad spectrum of the public in general elections and may contribute to further weakening of the parties. Despite some evident trends in these directions, Jimmy Carter as a centrist managed, at least in the short run, to succeed in the traditional fashion of making himself acceptable to the widest possible range of the populace. The mix combined emotional issues like amnesty for Vietnam objectors and tighter controls on nuclear weaponry with effective emphasis on populist themes (jobs, control of big business and bureaucracy) and the solid virtues of honesty and attachment to church and family.

Talk of a possible realignment of the two parties along more clearly defined liberal-versus-conservative lines has been perennial in American politics, but throughout the historical shifts in group support and changing regional patterns of that support the parties have remained heterogeneous. The potential realignments of the foreseeable future pose several interesting questions. The remarkable and somewhat unlikely coalition that for more than four decades has made up the Democratic party and rendered it the national majority—labor, the traditional South, civil libertarians, low-income groups, intellectuals, minorities (racial, ethnic, and religious), and internationalists—appeared to be breaking up until revivified by Carter, and it may yet do so. Can the Republicans, aided by reaction against racial integration, high cost of government, social welfare programs, and changing standards of acceptable social behavior, forge a successful conservative coalition—sometimes termed a status

"And so I say ask not for whom the bells tolls. It tolls for moderate Republicanism."

quo or "no change" coalition? If so, for how long could this kind of essentially static party retain support? Can the party find a moderately activist role acceptable to its clientele?

The issue of the party's collective sense of direction is most crucial for the Republicans, who are out of power both in Washington and in the great majority of the state capitals but, even worse, are faced with a situation in which only about 20 per cent of the population is willing to identify with the party. By contrast 44 per cent identify themselves as Democrats, and approximately 35 per cent take the label independent. Both parties are accustomed to internal divisions, but the Republican party now finds itself bitterly torn between opposing viewpoints as to its fundamental role. Effective control of the party machinery lies with its very conservative wing, the result of years of hard and unremitting effort on its part, and that wing is utterly convinced, in the face of considerable evidence to the contrary, that its path of ideological "purity" (primarily a stance of opposition) leads in the direction the country is hungering for.

The party's moderate-to-liberal faction argues that if the party is to have a future, it must erase its negative image. offer affirmative progressive programs, and open its doors to a much wider variety of people, whose ideas will likewise be varied. Without a broader base, they say, the GOP elephant is an endangered species. Some pragmatists who are hardly liberals agree. No less a lifelong conservative than Gerald Ford frankly identified the problem in an address several months after his election defeat:

> Too many people see our party as old, tired, wedded to the past . . . a tool of big business, indifferent to the needs of minorities, unfeeling toward the poor and the unemployed, an enemy of progress and a staunch defender of the status quo. The longer this false impression persists, the weaker our party will grow. . . . A contest within our ranks to prove who is the purer of ideology will not attract the American people. This is a moderate nation of moderate people to whom ideology is far less important than practicality.

But neither is the course of the future clear-cut for the Democrats, who always face factional strife. Can the party successfully maintain the old coalition, or can it forge a new coalition based primarily on the minorities, youth, intellectuals, the poor, and people dedicated to international approaches to world peace? If such a coalition were created, could it become a viable political party, given the low levels of voting and civic participation of some of these categories of people? Could enough people deeply concerned about environment issues be added to the number of people committed to peace and social justice to form a majority? Or are these likely to be essentially the same people? What will be the effect of continual expansion in the number of college-educated people? What, indeed, is the effect of extensive political alienation? What other kinds of party alignment or coalition are conceivable and, more importantly, feasible? Or are somewhat reorganized and reconstituted conglomerate parties, devoted to peaceful problem solving and avoidance of polarization, still the most likely outcome?

BASIC CONCEPTS AND TERMS

political party
functions of political parties

distinctions between
Republicans and Democrats

NOMINATIONS,
CAMPAIGNS,
AND
ELECTIONS

6

Genuine popular excitement over elections in American politics is not continuous but periodic, occurring in most states in even-numbered years and reaching a climax every four years in presidential campaigns. American elections are both a participant and a spectator sport of heroic proportions but with most serious objectives. The full range of human feelings is expressed in the campaigns, and the atmosphere for people close to the battle is frequently charged with the deepest emotions. In a national election campaign, tons of newsprint, scores of polls, and countless hours of television and radio time are committed to informing and persuading citizens. The dramatic moments of the contest are watched by a nationwide audience of a size rarely matched by any other attraction.

THE DIRECT PRIMARY

The political parties nominate their candidates for public office either through conventions of delegates elected by party voters to represent them for this purpose or through the direct primary.* The latter device has been commonly adopted throughout the United States for most offices other than those of president and vice president. In most states it is also possible to nominate a candidate by petition, a practice used by new and minor parties or by so-called independent candidates. Many people are confused by primaries, largely because they fail to appreciate the fact that primaries are simply one means by which party members can choose their candidates to run against the nominees of the opposition party. Primaries are not intended to be elections to office. They are, in other words, an alternative to nominating conventions, and evaluation of the various kinds of primary is much more realistic if this distinction between primaries and general elections is kept clearly in mind. One must remember, however, that in form and structure a primary is run as an election.

KINDS OF DIRECT PRIMARIES

The most common form of primary is the closed primary, so labeled because only party members are allowed to participate. No one would reasonably argue that a Democratic convention should permit Republicans to help choose the party's nominees, or vice versa, and for the same reason closed primaries are restricted to people who can show evidence of party affiliation. The usual evidence is advance registration in the party, but in some instances the filing of a formal statement is acceptable. Thus a Republican voter, say, has a ballot listing all people seeking the Republican nomination for each office and chooses among those aspirants. Ordinarily the high person in each case becomes the party's nominee, but a few states, all in the South, stipulate that if no one has a clear majority a run-off primary must be held between the two highest vote getters for each office. A party member may become a candidate for nomination on the primary ballot by the fairly simple procedure of paying the required fee (designed to protect against frivolous candidacies, although courts in a few states have recently declared such fees unconstitutional) and submitting a petition signed by a specified number of registered voters of his party, usually not a large number.

In the open primary, used in seven states, the voter must choose among the possible nominees of one party but is not required to indicate party affiliation publicly in advance. The voter registers merely as eligible, without declaring a party, and at the polls on primary day the most common procedure is to give the voter the ballots of both parties. In the privacy of the polling booth the vote is

---

*The word *direct* is used to distinguish primaries in which candidates are actually nominated (as a result of balloting) from primaries which are merely advisory or in which convention delegates are selected (as in the presidential preference primaries).

cast in the primary of one party or the other, and no one else has any way of knowing which one it is. In this situation independents, or even opponents, have the same weight as active party members in selecting party candidates.

Such a system obviously makes it possible for people to become "one-day Democrats" or "one-day Republicans," voting in the primary of the opposition party presumably in hopes of helping to nominate the weakest possible candidates. To be really effective, however, such "raiding," as it is called, would ordinarily have to be a well-organized effort on the part of a large group of people, and this rarely occurs. A major restraint on raiding rests in the fact that in order to do so one denies onself the opportunity of choosing among candidates for *all* the offices in one's own party, and this is usually unattractive. Experience indicates that in practice a voter who does raid the other side most often does so to "buy political insurance"— that is, to help choose someone reasonably acceptable should the voter's preferred party's candidate lose in the general election.

The blanket primary, which exists only in Washington and Alaska, goes one step further than the open primary by making it possible for the voter to shift between parties for different offices. One might thus choose among the candidates for the Republican nomination for governor, among the Democratic candidates for the senatorial nomination, among the Republican candidates for the nomination for members of Congress, and so on. This is virtually an invitation to raid, and it is common but not on the scale that would be expected. The blanket primary is defended as giving the voter a freer choice, but it clearly confuses the purpose of a primary with that of a general election, and it makes it impossible to hold a party organization responsible for the quality of its nominees.

Another system that also confuses the two chaotically is cross-filing. Now almost extinct but still finding advocates, this system operated in California for nearly fifty years until it was abolished in 1959 and has been in limited use in a few other states. This was a closed primary as far as the voter was concerned, but it permitted candidates to seek not only the nomination of their own party but that of the opposition party at the same time. It gave a huge advantage to incumbents and to candidates with the fattest campaign funds and resulted in serious weakening of the parties.

People who favor party responsibility understandably tend to favor the closed primary, in which no one but a party's voters is involved in choosing candidates, although with a few exceptions the open primary also works fairly satisfactorily. Closed primaries appear to have the best rate of voter participation. Primaries provide a good test of candidate attractiveness, and they give the average voter a feeling of playing a larger role in the nominating process than if there were no direct primaries.

CONVENTIONS VERSUS PRIMARIES

Interest has increased recently in the use of conventions for nominations. The gist of argument is that conventions more closely and clearly reflect the choices of the people who maintain active interest in politics and do the work in campaigns, that they are far less expensive and minimize the pressure on candidates, and that they are not as destructive of party unity as primaries. The normal motivation of a convention is to seek ultimately to heal breaches and effect party unity, even though this cannot always be successfully accomplished. In contrast, a primary by its very nature provokes battles within a party and fosters publicity for such conflicts; thus a primary will often split a party, creating wounds that are sometimes long in healing. Furthermore, a convention provides a representative base for the important task of platform making.

It is also becoming more and more evident that those who vote in primaries are generally not representative of the total electorate and thus may distort the selection system. The turnout in a primary is ordinarily much lower than in a general election, and those who do vote are more likely to be of higher socioeconomic status, more strongly issue oriented, and perhaps more "extreme" in their views. Thus the qualities or tactics needed to win primaries may be quite different from those needed to win elections. Many voters also behave differently in a primary, for example, casting a protest vote for a candidate they would never actually support for office "because, after all, the primary doesn't elect anybody."

Combinations of primaries and conventions exist in some states and are significant as possible compromises. One system is that of the preprimary convention, in which party activists can endorse the candidates they favor in a convention before the primaries. Endorsed candidates receive considerable boost toward success in the primary, but they are certainly not guaranteed victory. Furthermore, these conventions enable representative delegates to draw up a platform, something that is seriously lacking in ordinary primary systems. The challenge primary presents another compromise method. In essence it involves nominations by convention, which may in most cases be final, but provision is made for any losing candidate who polls at least a certain sizable percentage of the convention vote to demand a primary. In effect, the primary becomes a sort of popular referendum on the actions of the convention.

PRESIDENTIAL PREFERENCE PRIMARIES

When one moves from consideration of the direct primary to the presidential preference primary, it is necessary to shift mental gears. Although they may look much the same on the surface, they are essentially different breeds. The most notable distinction is that the presidential preference primaries do not nominate anyone; it is of course the national conventions that nominate presidential and vice-presidential candidates. The basic functions of the presidential preference primary are (1) to express preferences of the party voters in a state as to whom they want the convention to nominate and (2) to permit those voters to select the state's delegation to the national convention, in most cases pledging them in some degree to a particular candidate. Twenty-six states and the District of Columbia hold some form of presidential preference primary, and in three other states delegates are chosen in a primary but without opportunity for voters to express a candidate preference.

The delegates are elected in some states on a statewide winner-take-all basis and in others by congressional districts or some system of proportioning, now required by the Democratic party, in which cases the state delegation may be divided between two or more candidates. Slates of proposed delegates are formed by each candidate or campaign manager; and although voters are often under the illusion that they are voting for a particular candidate, they actually vote for a slate of delegates pledged to support that candidate at the convention. In one or two states the election of delegates and the expression of preference are separated on the ballot, and the preference vote merely informs the delegates rather than pledges them.

The national importance of these preference primaries varies greatly from state to state and sometimes shifts from one election to the next. Lively contests often develop in only about half of the primary states in a given presidential election year. The significance of some primaries is likely to be exaggerated, simply because public attention is focused on the contest even though the state may be in no sense typical of the country as a whole. New Hampshire, for example, is not a politically powerful state, and its convention delegations are small, but its primary invariably achieves national importance because it comes first. It is bathed in a glare of publicity and besieged by poll takers, commentators, and television crews. Whether or not the results prove anything about party opinion in other states, the news media catapult a winner, even with a minority of the vote, into tremendous national prominence. In 1976 a relatively little known ex-governor of Georgia drew 23,396 votes (hardly the vote of one moderate-size city) in the New Hampshire Democratic primary, 28.4 per cent of the total and only six percentage points above his nearest rival, and was instantly transformed by the media into the "front runner," a position he never really relinquished. One study indicated that the New Hampshire primary received 170 times as much network news time on television per Democratic vote as did the New York primary.

Certain primaries may assume special importance in a given year because of unique circumstances at that time, as was the case in 1976 in Florida, where Carter needed to prove that he could defeat George Wallace in a head-to-head contest in a southern state. Winning in several states with early primaries creates vital momentum for the later state campaigns, tends to obscure a few later losses, and has an effect on convention psychology. Nor is the margin of victory the most important aspect. Carter edged Udall, for example, in Wisconsin by 1 per cent and in Michigan by 0.3 per cent. What counts is having more votes than anyone else. It is also true that Carter was greatly aided by the fact that the liberal wing of the party was dividing its votes among four or five candidates.

THE SHORTCOMINGS OF PREFERENCE PRIMARIES

The number of states holding preference primaries has sharply increased in recent years, so that many more national convention delegates are now chosen in primaries than by state conventions (about 75 per cent to 25 per cent). No longer can a candidate have hope of nomination without a number of primary victories, but whether the primaries will determine the convention nomination depends on whether or not several candidates secure significant numbers of delegates. The widespread expectation in early 1976 was that the Democratic convention would be fragmented, resulting in a heated contest on the floor, but Jimmy Carter succeeded in winning enough delegates from both convention and primary states to have the nomination sewed up before the convention began. Despite their importance, the political effect of the preference primaries as now operated remains subject to certain limitations.

First, the primaries are held at different times in different states, and the results in the early states have an effect on the later states. This snowball effect may be somewhat unpredictive, depending on the states involved. A candidate may have great popular support in the nation as a whole but be little known in two or three states that happen to have early primaries. Or the reverse can be true. We have already noted the potency of New Hampshire despite its low population. It has been said that this primary can be won with a minority of the vote in a minority party in a state with one-third of 1 per cent of the population of the United States.

Second, mechanisms for insuring that delegates selected in primaries vote in accord with the will of the party voters who elected them are highly variable and sometimes unsatisfactory. The convention does not attempt to enforce these instructions to delegates, since this matter is the state's business; even the delegate who is technically bound can therefore change a vote if willing to risk punishment by the party on the return home.

Third, and perhaps most important, is that in most preference primaries all the candidates do not appear on the ballot, and thus the decision of the voters is rendered much less meaningful. Although some primaries are hotly contested by two or more candidates, others are entered by only one major contender, and still others are the sole domain of a "favorite son." Since anyone can win against no opposition, primaries in this situation prove nothing. Also subject to misinterpretation are situations in which a heated campaign between two candidates does not include a third whom many people would have preferred.

There are several possible reasons why candidates may not enter certain primaries. An incumbent president seeking re-election normally can effectively eliminate most opposition and needs to enter only a limited number of selected primaries. Ronald Reagan's challenge to President Ford, which came within a mere 117 convention votes of success, was therefore a highly unusual situation, but Ford was not an elected president. Occasionally a candidate has impressive strength built up throughout much of the country and feels no need of contesting all of the primaries. As a rule candidates understandably want to enter only primaries in which they feel they have a respectable chance. There is little point in going into a state where an opponent is known to have solid support, only to invite a shellacking that will inevitably have bad psychological effect. An unwritten rule is that one does not "invade" the home state of another candidate (though it has happened on rare occasions); a candidate gets a free ride in his or her own state even though the voters may desire to vote for someone else. This rule fosters the use of favorite-son candidacies, usually on the part of the state's governor or senator, as a device for staving off a first-ballot victory by some leading candidate or to prevent a primary battle that might split a state party. Favorite-son candidates may of course also come from states where delegates are chosen by conventions. At times a favorite son may harbor hopes that a divided or deadlocked convention will nominate him or her, but more often the motive behind such a candidacy is to keep the state delegation uncommitted as to the major candidates and thus preserve that delegation's favorable bargaining position.

In an attempt to guarantee the voters a meaningful choice, several states now operate free-for-all primaries, in slightly differing versions. Instead of the candidates' having to file in the primary, as is the case elsewhere, state officials automatically place on each party's ballot the names of all persons mentioned seriously as possible party candidates. One can usually have one's name removed only by a formal request stating that one is not and does not intend to be a candidate. Such a system can be rough on the candidate who has not had time to build a following in that particular state, but it is highly attractive to the voters and renders that state's primary more significant nationwide.

PROPOSALS FOR CHANGING PRESIDENTIAL PRIMARIES

"The [presidential primary] system has gotten to the point where it is insanity compounded—demeaning to the participants and exhausting to candidates as well as resources . . . counterproductive, inconclusive, wasteful and confusing," or so Robert Finch (Republican former secretary of Health, Education and Welfare and adviser to President Nixon) maintained. Senator Daniel Patrick Moynihan, a former White House adviser and a Democrat, added that "the present system is half crap-shooting and half trial by ordeal. It rewards the possessed. . . . We are getting an atomized electorate, which is by definition an unstable one." Such criticisms are louder and more frequent as awareness of the shortcomings of present arrangements increases.

In addition to the problems of unrepresentativeness and lack of realistic choice, as already discussed, there is no question that candidates are worn to a frazzle by the series of primaries spread over three and a half months. Voters too become exhausted. Expenditures are staggering. Voting turnout in primaries tends to be low, and voters may behave in a manner different from what they would in a general election. When successive battles must be fought, a front-runner candidate may be destroyed by "gang-up" tactics of competitors in one or two contests (and even the secret intervention of the opposition party) despite the fact that the candidate remains perhaps the nationwide favorite of party voters and the most electable candidate. This situation is exacerbated by the arbitrary assumption of the press that a front runner who slips in virtually any primary is finished. To prevent opposition invasions the national Democratic party has sought to outlaw open primaries.

As has been said, primaries commonly create serious splits within a party. If both parties are split, the effects may cancel each other out, but such balance is rare. The situation is most serious when one party has a bitter primary contest and the other has no contest at all, perhaps when it is renominating an incumbent. The result is highly advantageous to the incumbent, in addition to advantage already possessed by virtue of being in office.

In the light of these criticisms suggestions for change are hardly surprising. Perhaps most common has been creation of a single nationwide direct primary held on a single day. In the version advanced by former Senate majority leader Mike Mansfield, there would be a run-off between the top two contenders if no candidate received 40 per cent of the vote in the initial primary. Such a system, it is argued, would make it possible for all voters in the country to participate and choose from among all the serious contenders in their party, would do away with snowball effects, and would notably shorten the primary campaign. Opponents claim that two nationwide nomination campaigns would be even more expensive and probably as exhausting as the present series of contests, that well-known and publicized candidates would have vast advantages since a new candidate would have no chance to build recognition gradually in individual states, that wealthy candidates or those with established financial backing would have even greater advantage than at present, that a nationwide primary would be ultradivisive, that the two in a run-off might often be representative of party extremes, thus almost guaranteeing ultimate defeat, and that it would never be possible to draft a candidate who was reluctant to run.

A regional primary system as proposed by Senator Robert Packwood would provide for one primary a month from March to July in each of five regions of the country. The order would be determined by lot, and which primary was to be next would be made public only seventy days before the date. After each primary, each candidate would appoint delegates to a national convention from each state in proportion to the vote received, and the convention would make the nomination. A limited experiment occurred in 1976 when three neighboring states in two different areas set their primaries on the same date—Oregon, Idaho, and Nevada on one date, and Kentucky, Tennessee, and Arkansas on another. An effort to establish a New England primary foundered on New Hampshire's desire to remain first and Maine's subsequent unwillingness to move to an earlier date, although Connecticut, Massachusetts, and Vermont arranged a common time.

Yet another possibility is to continue to leave to the states the decision as to whether they will use a primary but to require those that do to hold them either on the same day or on one of three specified dates. Each proposal has its merits and shortcomings, and none satisfies all the criticisms of primaries. Stronger voices have lately been heard advocating return to a system in which all delegates to national conventions would be chosen by representative state conventions.

THE NATIONAL CONVENTION IN ACTION

When the delegates, currently almost twenty-three hundred at the Republican convention and about three thousand at the Democratic convention, swelled by at least an equal number of alternates, arrive at the convention city, they become participants in a uniquely American drama. Once dubbed "the American substitute for the Roman circuses," the national convention is a curious mixture of carnival and deadly serious decision making in which the stakes are very high indeed. The two conventions attract a national audience of tens of millions of people, and with the advent of satellite relays they are now followed with intense interest in other countries throughout the world.

The delegates are watched by several thousand reporters and employees of the three major television networks alone, which in one year may spend more than $25 million on the two conventions. What were once activities taking place largely "within the party

GRIN AND BEAR IT by George Lichty. © Field Enterprises, Inc., 1978. Courtesy of Field Newspaper Syndicate.

*"Testing . . . I am not a candidate . . . testing . . . after reassessing
my position, I AM a candidate . . . testing . . ."*

family" have become pageants choreographed for television, complete with program directors, special lighting arrangements, and professional advisers on how to speak most effectively, what to wear, how to act at the podium, how best to be made up, and how to read a teleprompter without seeming to do so. The most private caucus is spotlighted by bird-dogging reporters and television floor crews.

Except for conventions that renominate an incumbent president or ones where for other reasons the nominee is a foregone conclusion, a

national convention is likely to operate in a white heat of emotional-
ism and under conditions that test the stamina of the hardiest. There
are long hours of pressure and suspense, ceaseless caucusing, and
continual revamping of strategy to meet unforeseen developments—
all amid a hubbub of noise and confusion and a constant flood of
rumor. Even the individual delegate is caught up in this, and for the
leaders the tension can be overwhelming. To the uninitiated
observer the scene at times appears to be utter chaos, but although
conventions seem often about to founder on the shoals of anarchy,
there are an underlying order and direction and experienced hands
at the helm.

Candidates and their managers work for months to control the
course of events. When a candidate has been successful in this, the
progress of the convention seemingly follows a script, but the best-
laid plans can go awry and there can be no relaxation. If it is an open
convention, with two or more major contenders dividing initial
support, a scattering of favorite sons and potential dark-horse minor
candidates, and uninstructed delegations, all keeping the situation
fluid, the struggle for delegate votes can be a totally fascinating
drama. It has been some time, however, since a convention has gone
to more than one ballot. The last Republican convention to do so was
in 1948, and only one Democratic convention (1952) has done so
since 1936.

PRELIMINARY WORK

Convention committees perform much of the preliminary work of
the convention. The platform committee meets and begins to hold
hearings at least a week (and often several weeks) before the opening
of the convention, preparing the draft platform to be presented on
the floor. The rules committee recommends the procedure for the
convention, ordinarily suggesting acceptance of past rules but occasionally proposing a change that touches off a major controversy, as
have some attempts to require pledges of loyalty to the nominee of
the convention. A rule proposed by the Reagan forces at the 1976
Republican national convention to require each candidate to
announce his choice of a vice-presidential running mate in advance
of the presidential nomination balloting (jocularly termed "the misery loves company rule" because Reagan had already named his
choice) brought a vote that clearly forecast the relative strength of
Ford and Reagan. The function of the committee on permanent
organization is to recommend a slate of permanent officers for the
convention, also usually accepted in routine fashion. Sometimes,
however, a battle over the powerful permanent chairmanship also
serves as a tip to the outcome of a contested nomination.

More excitement usually surrounds the work of the credentials committee. At almost every convention disputes erupt over the seating of one or more state delegations, a situation that arises when there is a split in a state party and two delegations arrive at the national convention, each claiming to be the official representative of that state. The credentials committee certifies the legitimacy of all delegations, but its primary responsibility is to investigate all contests and to recommend to the convention which delegation should be seated. Sometimes the decision is clear, but there are cases when neither side has a better claim than the other and the decision is made, practically speaking, on the basis of which candidate each delegation supports. Recommendations must be approved by the full convention once the uncontested delegates have been seated. Floor battles may ensue from some of these contests, and the outcome may indicate the ultimate nomination, as when the Eisenhower rather than the Taft delegations from Texas and Georgia were seated in the 1952 Republican convention.

The convention opens with a keynote address, designed to whip up enthusiasm among the delegates and to instill them with optimism and crusading zeal. Following this, the convention considers the reports and recommendations of the committees, and usually the most heated debate is provoked by the presentation of the platform. Only rarely, however, are amendments to the platform successfully added from the floor.

THE CONVENTION NOMINATES

With such matters out of the way, the convention is ready to move to the nominating and seconding speeches. Each state (in alphabetical order in the Republican convention and in an order drawn by lot in the Democratic convention) has the opportunity to place names in nomination; but there is considerable jockeying for position, since states at the head of the list not desiring to make a nomination may yield to another state for that purpose. The demonstrations that have traditionally followed the placing of each name in nomination are part of the pageantry and perhaps a means of reducing tension, though they are unlikely to change votes. The supporters of each major candidate want to insure that the demonstration for their candidate runs at least as long as that for any other, so the presiding officer must try to enforce a uniform time limit. Both conventions now seek to bar nondelegates from the floor, since demonstrations had come to be staged in part by "professionals" who entered on signal to whoop it up for a candidate, sometimes regrouping to come back later in support of another.

The great reduction in the number and length of convention speeches has been one of the healthy consequences of television coverage. The indulging of everyone in the act has at times reached ludicrous proportions, as in 1936 when the nomination of Franklin Roosevelt was seconded with no fewer than fifty-six speeches. In the days before television, the long intervals of waiting for committees to complete their work were filled with redundant oratory, but sessions are generally now held only when business is at hand and are in fact carefully scheduled for prime television viewing hours.

BALLOTING

The dramatic high point of any open convention is reached when all the nominating speeches and demonstrations have run their course and the chairman bangs down the gavel to announce in resonant tones: "The clerk will call the roll of the states." The balloting proceeds in alphabetical order, but a state may pass when its name is called, to be called again at the end of the list. The chairman of each state delegation announces the total vote for that state, the delegations usually caucusing between ballots. As everyone keeps a tally, tension builds, then crackles when a significant shift is noted. Convention psychology reflects the powerful influence of steady growth, and an unwritten rule that it is fatal for a candidate in the lead to slip back on any ballot seems to operate. A clear majority is required for nomination.

Occasionally, an individual delegate, claiming that the chairman

President and Mrs. Ford acknowledge cheers after winning the nomination of the 1976 Republican national convention.

Wide World Photos

for a state did not report the vote correctly, will demand that the delegation be polled, necessitating a roll call of the entire delegation. A perceptive observer will notice that the result of the individual tally rarely differs from what the chairman reported, and one can conclude that typically the real motive behind the demand is to delay, perhaps to buy time for representatives of some candidate to work on a wavering delegation further down the list.

The permanent chairman of a convention exercises considerable influence, and people chosen to be chairmen are normally of great prestige and long experience in high office and have the confidence of most delegates. Presiding over a convention is no task for an amateur. The stress is intense and constant, and it is important that the convention operate under strict rules of parliamentary procedure. The chairman decides on the outcome of voice votes, when the galleries often shout along with the delegates, and must rule on many questions of parliamentary order. The chairman determines who will speak in a situation in which hundreds want to do so. Ordinarily recognition must be arranged with the chairman in advance, and a delegate who simply seeks recognition from the floor is asked a traditional question: "For what purpose does the gentleman (lady) rise?" If the purpose is, say, to make a parliamentary inquiry, it may be stated; if the purpose is to make a speech, recognition will be refused. Should the person try to continue anyway, the microphone will be cut off—there are certain advantages to modern technology. The chairman must also decide which motions are in order, a matter of no small import, and by a variety of actions can either drag down or speed up the proceedings of the convention.

Vice-presidential nominations are likely to be anticlimactic, particularly since the convention accepts the choice of the presidential nominee if one is made, and usually one is. Many who were contenders for the presidential nomination will have been virtually forced out of this competition by the incessant questions of reporters during the preliminary campaigning as to whether they would consider the vice presidency. Candidates who admit that they might do so are written off by the news media as serious presidential aspirants, so the candidate must either refuse flatly to accept the second spot or follow a difficult course of evasion. The interest in offering a well-balanced ticket further restricts vice-presidential possibilities. A well-balanced ticket can mean one that achieves geographical balance. Other considerations may include differences in ideological wings of the party (provided the differences are not too sharp), age, political experience, religion, and attractiveness to certain large interest groups.

Jimmy Carter's choice of Walter Mondale was a highly successful example: Mondale was from a northern state, possessed the Washington experience and contacts that Carter lacked, and as a senator was very highly regarded by colleagues on the hill. Although he and Carter were very compatible, his strong liberal credentials were such as to reassure and bring into the fold many Democratic liberals who had been a trifle uneasy about Carter's seemingly ambiguous ideological stance. Most important, he was recognized as a well-qualified successor, should that need arise.

In his final drive to wrest the Republican nomination from President Ford, Ronald Reagan took the virtually unprecedented step of announcing his choice of a running mate a few weeks before the convention. That in itself was something of a surprise, but the selection of Senator Richard Schweiker of Pennsylvania startled friend and foe alike: the conservatives in particular complained that this was carrying ticket balancing too far, even if done by their champion. Schweiker was considered at the time perhaps the most liberal Republican in the Senate, his voting record the preceding year having been given a remarkable 89 per cent favorable rating by the liberal Americans for Democratic Action and 100 percent by the AFL-CIO. He had voted opposite to the positions of the majority of his party in the Senate 81 per cent of the time in that year. The decision by both men was especially striking in the light of Schweiker's previous statement that a Reagan nomination would be a disaster for the party leading to a defeat of the same magnitude as 1964, and Reagan's comment only two months earlier: "I do not believe you choose someone of an opposite philosophy in hopes he'll get you some votes you can't get yourself, because I think that's being false with the people who voted for you and your philosophy." Schweiker apparently brought no additional convention votes to Reagan, and both lost credibility; the plan clearly backfired. Ford, on the other hand, forced by conservative pressure to drop Vice President Rockefeller early in the game, bided his time, ultimately choosing Senator Robert Dole, a vigorous campaigner but a fellow midwesterner with a similar congressional background who brought to the ticket no noticeable new sources of strength.

CONSTRUCTIVE COMPROMISE

Clearly an essential ingredient of the convention process, as it is of all democratic politics, is constructive compromise. Not everyone can win the presidential nomination; the convention must agree on one candidate, and thus some aspirants must lose. Axiomatic as this is, many citizens seem to overlook such evident facts and are highly critical of the conventions because of their compromising nature. But what alternative do such critics propose? A convention seeks all the common ground it can find within a conglomerate party and serves as an arena in which conflicts within a party can be resolved. These are created not by the convention but by the nature of a free society and open political process. The convention tries to find the basis on which rather disparate groups, which nevertheless have much more in common than they do with the opposition, can work together toward electoral victory.

It may be useful to follow the logic of this reasoning one step further. Let us suppose that after a couple of ballots in a convention candidate C concludes there is no chance of being nominated, despite control of a fairly sizable block of delegates. Of the other candidates, candidate C feels that candidate D is far superior to either A or B, in terms of electability and as a potential president. The decision therefore is to swing support to D, and as a result D is nominated. Let us further assume that D is elected and subsequently appoints C as secretary of commerce. Is there something corrupt or reprehensible about this? Such implication is cast on the situation by many critics. But if C was in fact sufficiently well qualified to be seriously considered as a presidential nominee, does it not make sense for the president to use that person in a position of responsibility? Why should unsuccessful candidates be cast on a figurative ash heap? Is it reasonable that aid to the president in being nominated and elected should be grounds for disqualification for appointment?

CONVENTION REFORMS

In the wake of widespread criticisms, particularly of the 1968 national conventions, both parties have devoted considerable effort to reforming the conventions, with most attention focused on improving the quality of representativeness. The greatest change occurred in the Democratic party as the result of studies and recommendations of two special commissions. Guidelines for the states specified approximate percentages of minority groups, youth, and women that should be included in each delegation, and these tended to be interpreted as rigid quotas. As a result the percentage of women delegates, for example, jumped from a 1968 figure of 13 per cent to 40 per cent in 1972. Control of the party shifted dramatically, as over 80 per cent of the delegates to the 1972 convention had never attended a convention before.

Convention committee structure was altered to give more representation to the larger states; all delegates were required to be elected through conventions or primaries (in a few states they had been appointed by party leaders such as a governor); delegates were required to be elected within a few months of the convention rather than a year or two earlier, as had sometimes been the case; free participation of all party voters in each state was to be guaranteed; all meetings of committees were to be open to the public and the press; and a considerable variety of procedural changes was made. Rules effective in 1980 required the states to give candidates the proportion of delegates reflecting their percentage of the primary or state convention vote, provided they achieved a "threshold" level (ranging from 15 to 20 per cent), thus eliminating winner-take-all arrangements. It was also specified that only Democrats might be permitted to vote in Democratic primaries, thus in effect banning the use of open or blanket primaries for this purpose. The Republican convention of 1972 established a new representation formula effective in 1976, generally favorable to the smaller western and southern states and increasing the total size of the convention. Specific guidelines for minority representation were debated but rejected in favor of general recommendations to the states. In 1974 the Democratic party modified the representation rules to insure that the special group guidelines not be interpreted to exclude large numbers of the party's most faithful leaders and workers, as they had two years before. The subsequent 1976 convention seemingly evidenced a good mix.

Efforts to democratize can be worthwhile, but the parties find it also necessary to insure continuity and reasonable responsibility to the interests of each national party as a whole. The conventions have probably been better political instruments than they have been portrayed to be. Studies indicate that delegates constitute a fairly good cross section of their parties (although they tend predominantly to be in the higher socioeconomic groups), that they are above average in intelligence and education, and that they are far better informed than party voters generally. The division on issues between delegates to Republican conventions and delegates to Democratic conventions is much sharper than such divisions between the ordinary voters who support the Republican party and those who support the Democratic party. Conventions have generally nominated people of ability who have been quite acceptable to the great majority of party voters.

THE CAMPAIGN IN CONTEMPORARY AMERICA

All who have become accustomed to presidential candidates' behaving, as an acute observer once put it, "like a couple of hyperthyroid squirrels on a treadmill," would find almost inconceivable the picture of William Henry Harrison defeating Martin Van Buren in 1840 without making a single public speech and without leaving his home state of Ohio. As late as 1904 Judge Alton Parker announced, "I shall do nothing and say nothing to advance my candidacy," and true enough his candidacy against Theodore Roosevelt did not advance. (Parker and his eighty-year-old running mate, Henry G. Davis, were described as "an enigma from New York and a reminscence from West Virginia.")

THE INFLUENCE OF MODERN TECHNIQUES

Today every technique of modern merchandising is used to build a favorable image of a candidate while the candidate keeps up a pace that is more than a test of stamina for the job. A candidate is accustomed to making from six to twelve appearances a day and is whisked back and forth across the country by jet aircraft in a state of seeming perpetual motion. Every waking moment is scheduled by campaign managers, and at every appearance he or she must somehow appear bright and amiable, brimming with vitality, alert, and fully informed on all conceivable topics. The candidate's hand is crushed a thousand times, and diet becomes subject to all manner of indignities. The same basic speeches will inevitably be used, but something new must be provided every day or two for the benefit of the headline writers and to insure variety for each major television appearance. An incumbent with a good likelihood of re-election can of course take things easier, and there are endless ways in which an office can be used to advantage.

Television has become the most important tool of campaigning and accounts for the greatest single item in the campaign budget; over $15 million was spent in 1976 by the presidential contenders alone. If production and promotion costs are added to station and network charges, the total amount allocated for television in campaigns at all levels reaches around $100 million. The range of television exposure for candidates includes formal addresses, appearances on panel shows, spots on comedy and talk programs, and brief station breaks. The short plugs are probably the most effective, since they catch viewers between their favorite programs. Television also allows dramatic presentations and documentaries portraying the candidate as involved in widely different activities. Debates between major candidates, initiated by the Kennedy-Nixon series in 1960 and carried on by Carter and Ford in 1976, are always a possibility, but the better-known candidates are not eager to help an opponent secure a wide audience. An incumbent president ordinarily will be especially reluctant to engage in debate and may anyway be under certain restraints as president concerning matters that can be freely discussed. President Ford was an exception, since he had not been popularly elected and was the underdog according to the polls.

Despite the fact that television can introduce the candidate indirectly into millions of living rooms, it has by no means replaced personal contact. Voters still like to see their candidates in person, and most candidates thrive on the stimulation of crowd response. Political rallies probably sway few votes, but they are quite effective in collecting together the faithful to be inspired and motivated to work for the candidate. The 1960s made the American people altogether too conscious of the possibilities and likelihood of political assassination in this country. Yet neither candidates nor presidents want to or can be kept in bullet-proof cages. Great efforts are now being made to minimize risk, but such risk cannot be eliminated completely.

ROLE OF PERSONAL CONTACT

Even in the electronic age the importance of the individual campaign volunteer should not be underestimated. Much recent evidence argues that the personal contacts of a precinct worker still pay great political dividends, and "new politics" campaigns perhaps even more than others have relied heavily on the time-tested process of person-to-person contact. Many traditional campaign devices have merely been supplemented rather than replaced by new techniques, although 1976 saw a sharp reduction in the use of such items as buttons and bumper stickers, at least for presidential campaigns, largely because of limitations on campaign contributions and spending.

Campaigns for Congress and other offices differ from the campaign for the presidency mainly in scope. Some tactics from presidential campaigns may be less feasible for aspirants to lesser offices, as, for example, would be the use of television in a district that is only part of a large metropolitan area. In congressional and lesser campaigns, there is also more emphasis on the politics of personal acquaintance and on the candidate's being a member of numerous and varied organizations. Candidates at all levels are often frustrated by the limited opportunity for discussion of issues in depth; the billboard and the station break can accommodate little more than a picture and one or two words such as "honesty" and "integrity."

ADVANTAGES OF INCUMBENTS

Although there are periods, usually in the aftermath of some scandal, when the public is inclined to turn against incumbent officeholders generally, incumbents in almost any office under normal conditions have impressive advantages making them favorites for re-election. While it is true that an incumbent has a public record to defend and is thus potentially more vulnerable than a challenger who can devote more time to attack, an incumbent possesses the great benefit of name recognition in the mind of the citizen and identification of the name with the office. Moreover, there is a continuous flow of publicity attached to the office; at least in the case of major offices, the actions and statements of the official are almost automatically deemed newsworthy. A competent public relations person on the staff can additionally find ways to achieve maximum mileage from every event and announcement. In the case of a president, the news may to at least some degree be "managed," timing release for the most favorable effect, spreading items over time, restricting certain information, staging events in a manner most likely to catch attention.

Case Study
A PRESIDENT'S USE OF THE POWER OF INCUMBENCY

President Gerald Ford's uses of incumbency in 1976 were not unusual, merely the most recent examples. They included:

1 An administration announcement shortly before a presidential trip to the Midwest of sharp increases in grain price supports, despite the fact that the Department of Agriculture had stated only the day before that there was "no economic justification" for an increase.

2 Numerous speaking engagements throughout the country on the part of Cabinet members and other high officials, at little or no cost to the campaign treasury on the grounds that these were official statements rather than campaign speeches.

3 A presidential speech on nuclear policy, in Cincinnati late in the campaign, wherein it was disclosed that a new uranium enrichment plant would mean "6,000 new jobs for southern Ohio."

4 A well-timed trip to the Middle East that automatically received massive media coverage, symbolically stressing the role of the president as a world leader.

5 An announcement in the final days of the campaign by United States mass transit officials, who went to New York City for that purpose, that New York would receive almost $90 million for subways and other commuter travel systems.

6 A series of messages to Congress lecturing it on the need for budgetary restraint, each of which, as a presidential statement, made headlines.

7 A White House announcement, one day before the president was to meet with Jewish leaders in Brooklyn, of intent to provide Israel with new, highly sophisticated weaponry that had been previously denied.

8 An offer to a group of local television newscasters in Illinois, during a campaign swing just prior to that state's primary, of an opportunity they would ordinarily never have—an exclusive interview with the president of the United States.

If such time and exposure had had to be purchased, the dent in campaign funds would have been considerable.

Every member of Congress is provided with a professional staff, paid from the public treasury, as an aid in carrying out the responsibilities of office. No one challenges the necessity for such assistance, but the research, the writing, the daily responsiveness by mail and by telephone to constituents, and the like have a vast impact upon re-election prospects, and this is never out of mind. In addition to a Washington office, the member may also maintain and staff at public expense one or two offices in the district of representation. While this is justified in the name of improved service to constituents, through ease of accessibility, it is also true that field staff can serve as invaluable eyes and ears in the district and help in a multitude of ways to keep local fences mended and the legislator's actions before the voters. There is no way to draw a clear line between service to the public and the process of continuous re-election campaigning. Even a staff member who temporarily goes off the public payroll to work in a campaign during the official period has already been trained, is in tune with the candidate and organization, and is knowledgeable about issues and people in the district.

Subject to some limitations that are not too serious, a member of Congress may travel, send mail, and telephone extensively at public expense, although there are practical restraints during the official campaign period. Available are the research services of the Legislative Reference Service and legal counsel, in addition to personal staff, capable of providing information on virtually every subject. Moreover, requests for information from any agency of the executive branch are ordinarily given preferred treatment. It is no wonder that a member is likely to want to talk about specific legislative issues in a campaign, for to a considerable extent issues can be chosen, perhaps from personal involvement with some of them, reams of information can be secured, and on certain topics an opponent can be made to look a bit foolish, since the challenger does not have public resources at command.

The legislator is, of course, also in a position to do a variety of minor favors for the voters of a district, from answering requests for information to smoothing the way for citizen contact with administrative agencies. Most people remember such things even if they have no knowledge of how their representative voted on important issues. If the representative is also successful in getting military installations or other public facilities located in a district or helping to bring in other large employers, those who secure the jobs are not likely to forget who was responsible (and in any case will hardly be allowed to forget).

Since it is certainly legitimate for a respresentative to seek to keep constituents informed and, for that matter, to endeavor to learn their opinions on various public issues, widely distributed newsletters and questionnaires emanating from legislative offices are standard fare. At a minimum these greatly enhance name recognition, but recipients who read them may be impressed with the concerns, accomplishments, and diligence of their representative; many voters, moreover, are flattered to have their opinions asked. At rather nominal cost facilities are provided in the congressional offices that enable members to tape television and radio programs that can be made available to broadcasting stations at home. The value of these perquisites of congressional office to a re-election campaign is variously estimated at from $200,000 to $750,000 each term, a truly formidable advantage. Ninety-three per cent of House incumbents were re-elected in 1976, although for a complex of reasons the percentage was not quite as high in the Senate.

Prestige, established contacts, demonstrated attitudes, the power attaching to seniority, and the favorable odds on re-election all combine to make campaign fund raising notably easier for incumbents than for the average challenger. An especially important aspect is the fact that incumbents usually also find it easier to raise funds when they count the most—early in the campaign. Finally, there appears to be a factor in popular psychology that is advantageous to incumbents. Barring occasional times of economic crisis or scandal that produce a "throw the rascals out" fervor, there is an evident, though perhaps not overwhelming, inclination to stick with a known quantity rather than to chance an unknown.

IMAGE MAKING

One of the most significant developments in campaigning in the last few decades has been the rapid growth in the use of professional campaign-management firms. A few firms deal almost exclusively with campaigns, although most combine campaign management with general public relations and advertising activities. They may be hired by a candidate or party to run a campaign in a given region, using expertise gained from involvement in many more campaigns than the average political worker will ever see together with intimate familiarity with the practices and personnel of the news media. Such management firms generally wish to plan and direct all advertising, schedule events, determine the issues to be emphasized, organize and train volunteers, and as much as possible control the behavior and utterances of the candidate. They concentrate on the mass media, especially television, and emphasize image building for the aspirant.

The transformation of certain candidates accomplished by some public relations firms has been striking, although this hardly instills confidence in the integrity of the system. The same firm that first labeled Ronald Reagan a "right-winger" while working on behalf of another candidate of the same party managed his campaign for governor of California only four years later and successfully sold him

"With a good public-relations team on the job, Senator, you'll come through as a smart guy who happens to be inarticulate, instead of a guy who doesn't know what the hell he's talking about."

to the voters as a "moderate." Many political observers have serious qualms about the tendency of such firms to try to merchandise candidates as if they were toothpaste or cigarettes, to be interested in issues only as tools for the manipulation of public opinion, and occasionally to engage in highly dubious tactics in order to keep their win-loss average marketable for the future. The firms are not identical in their procedures, and such strictures do not apply equally to all. A number are very responsible management organizations well worth their fees, and in this age of specialization they are likely to continue to be with us.

THE LESSONS OF WATERGATE

When at 2:30 A.M. on June 17, 1972, a somewhat inept group of political spies in the employ of the Republican Committee to Reelect the President was arrested while seeking to improve their wiretaps inside the offices of the Democratic National Committee in the Watergate buildings in Washington, D.C., the door was opened on the biggest political scandal of the nation in generations, perhaps in its history. Centered in matters of campaign tactics and finance, the scandal was gradually discovered touching in an almost unbelievable number of directions countless facets of the national administration. President Nixon succeeded until after the election in dismissing the initial disclosures as merely a "deplorable incident" which was perpetrated by a few misguided people and in which no one on the White House staff had been involved.

Persistent investigative reporting, however, especially by the *Washington Post,* aided in time by the testimony of implicated individuals who found themselves threatened with prosecution, brought to light a web of intrigue that staggered imagination. The details were filled in by hearings before several congressional committees, plus the work of special prosecutors and grand juries.

As the complex story unraveled there was exposed to public view, in addition to the break-in at the Watergate, activities such as the following: an elaborate program of spying on opposition candidates, including the planting of employees and volunteers in the staffs of Democratic candidates to copy mail, steal campaign plans, and the like; widespread wiretapping and other types of illegal and legal surveillance of government employees, private citizens, and journalists critical of the administration; an extensive effort to hide White House and campaign committee connections to the Watergate burglars and people involved in other illicit activities, which included repeated lies to press and public, withholding of evidence from Congress and law enforcement officers, destruction of records and other information relevant to criminal charges, obstruction of an FBI investigation, attempts to get the CIA to take responsibility by claiming that its efforts to counter foreign espionage were involved, burning of possible evidence by the acting director of the FBI, and payment of cash (ostensibly for expenses and legal fees) in hundreds of thousands of dollars to those undergoing trial (or convicted) apparently in order to buy their silence—all acts that are criminal as a deliberate obstruction of justice. Other activities included improper handling of campaign funds, with tactics such as "laundering" money in and out of a bank account in Mexico in order to make it difficult to trace; the promise of ambassadorships in return for campaign contributions; the establishment of lists of "political enemies" who might be harassed by government agencies such as the Internal Revenue Service; political use of legally confidential government records on private citizens, such as income tax returns; the burglary of a psychiatrist's office in an effort to steal the doctor's confidential records on Daniel Ellsberg, who had given the Pentagon Papers to the press; efforts to damage economically newspapers and broadcasters that were critical of the administration or exposed Watergate-related matters; and acceptance of large campaign contributions from individuals and corporations under circumstances raising suspicions that favorable government actions were being purchased.

A special group operated, during the primaries and the general election, what came to be known as the "department of dirty tricks," its principal emphasis having been efforts to destroy leading Democratic contenders in various presidential primaries. Some of its more infamous efforts included a leaflet, printed on what appeared to be Senator Muskie's campaign stationery and distributed during the Florida primary, that accused Senators Henry Jackson and Hubert Humphrey of sexual misconduct; a multitude of telephone calls made in the middle of the night to New Hampshire residents from people identifying themselves as representatives of the Harlem for Muskie Committee and urging support for Muskie because he was for blacks; bogus orders for entertainers and expensive quantities of food, liquor, and flowers at a candidate's campaign dinner; a letter published in a New Hampshire newspaper fraudulently alleging derogatory comments by Muskie concerning persons of French-Canadian origin in New England; and a pamphlet falsely claiming to have been published by a labor organization and titled "Why Labor Can't Support George McGovern." Campaign aides also rigged the results of a Washington television poll by stacking the responses and spent tens of thousands of dollars sending to the White House telegrams and letters that were then cited to show public support for the mining of Haiphong Harbor.

The president, determined in the words of one aide to "tough it out," injured his public credibility by seeming to drag his feet in cooperating with investigations and by making successive admissions only when forced by events to do so. He stated that he had been misled by some of his staff and insisted that he had not known until the spring of 1973 of any wrongdoing on the part of White House staff members, a statement he later admitted was false. In an address to the nation in which he took technical responsibility as chief executive, he indicated that many of the criticized activities had actually been undertaken as matters of "national security," a claim that columnist Mike Royko promptly labeled as the president's "bold new effort to achieve burglary with honor." Just as everyone felt that all disclosures had surely been made, it was revealed that the Nixon White House was equipped with automatic devices in every room in which the president met visitors, that recorded all conversations without a visitor's knowledge, whether staff aide, member of Congress, or head of a foreign state. (For the confrontation between the president and both Congress and the courts over access to these tapes, see Chapter 7.)

From *Herblock Special Report* (W. W. Norton & Company, Inc., 1974).

"I'll approve whatever will work and am concerned with results, not methods," wrote the president's former chief of staff H. R. Haldeman across one report, a statement that seemed remarkably symbolic of the attitude that produced the Watergate affair. A permeating psychology of fear and suspicion led easily to acceptance of the idea that the end justifies any means. Personal loyalty to the president and his organization became more important than loyalty to the nation (though the two were commonly equated) or to ethical standards. Political opponents were frequently viewed as enemies rather than as persons with different opinions on what constitutes desirable social policy. Since the public was not to be trusted either, the logical procedure was to manipulate its opinion by providing false and misleading information or by withholding information, as the circumstances surrounding United States military operations in Cambodia from 1969 on so cruelly illustrated.

Some of the problems arose precisely because this was so much a closed administration supremely confident of its own rightness. Governing power was increasingly pulled away from the operating agencies and concentrated in the White House staff. It had campaigned on a theme of law and order but seemed to assume that it was above the law. The picture of the former attorney general of the United States, the nation's chief law enforcement officer, was hardly edifying as he defended his failure to act upon or even report what he knew to be criminal actions, on the grounds that he felt it was more important at the time to get the president re-elected. There was a chilling effect in John Ehrlichman's stout insistence that the president is not subject to the usual constitutional and legal restraints if he deems an action to be concerned with "national security," a theme reiterated by Nixon in his 1977 television conversations with David Frost. And one could feel the anguish of L. Patrick Gray, former acting director of the FBI, as he admitted to the Senate investigating committee that he had at the request of a White House staff member burned papers relevant to the Watergate case and subsequently lied about having done so. "I permitted myself to be used to perform a mere political chore," he said softly; "I shall carry the burden of that act with me always."

The Watergate scandal was strikingly different from most of the other famous political scandals of American history, such as the Teapot Dome episode during the Harding administration. Those were largely matters of personal greed and financial corruption. Watergate involved not primarily motives of personal gain—"I stole no money," said John Mitchell rather plaintively, and President Nixon himself returned to this theme in his farewell to the White House staff, in an attempt to claim that no serious wrongdoing had occurred. It involved instead a fundamental corruption of the political process on which democracy depends. These men, said columnist Joseph Kraft, "are loyal, hard-working, disciplined, patriotic family men cut in the spitting image of the strong-jawed, steely-eyed executive. Watergate, in other words, expresses the shame of the managerial class. It presents the spectacle of what happens when a president gives great power to administrators uninformed by any larger purpose than winning big." It recalls the prophetic words of Justice Brandeis in 1928: "The greatest dangers to liberty lurk in insidious encroachment by men of zeal, well-meaning but without understanding." The Watergate affair damaged the president and the presidency and complicated a host of domestic and international problems but most serious of all was the inevitably severe damage to the credibility of government and the citizen's faith in the democratic process.

Yet is it already evident that in the longer run some good may be found among the debris. Certain tactics condoned too long in American politics will not soon be practiced again. People in public service have had a sharp reminder that their highest loyalties lie properly to the public they serve and the ideals that have been the true strength of the country. The public may be more alert to threats to liberty and to the fundamental need for greater, not less, attention to politics— that process by which democracy can be wrecked or made a vital and living force for humanity. The danger is that people become rapidly immunized, tiring even of scandal, in this case confused by sheer magnitude, and lose sight of the real issues and lessons to be learned from them. The political system, of course, did not fail; human beings can make mistakes or become corrupt in any system. The system, in fact, provided its own correctives, and as these ground inexorably along, many a critic, both at home and abroad, conceded, even if reluctantly, that there remained far more to praise than to condemn. The thoughtful comment of a British scholar is apropos: "To shocked Europeans who say 'where else but America could one have . . . a Watergate affair?' the true answer is, 'Anywhere—but where else would it have been publicly exposed?'"

MONEY AND ELECTIONS

Any discussion of modern campaigning makes amply evident that this aspect of politics has become an extremely expensive enterprise, but few people have much awareness of just how expensive it is. The best information comes from educated guesses, for it is impossible to develop accurate figures on what is spent by others in behalf of a candidate in addition to what is spent by the candidate's personal organization. Finally, there has been established no requirement that all these expenditures be reported to a central body. And how does one fix an accurate price for the services of corporate or other organization executives lent to a campaign while remaining on the company payroll, even if the information were readily available?

The total cost for a presidential campaign, both primaries and general election, now runs to about $120 million. The estimated cost for races at all levels throughout the country is well over $400 million. In a highly populated state, a contested race for a Senate seat or a governorship will easily run over $1 million (the high in 1976 was $3 million), and one gubernatorial candidate in a major state was reported recently to have spent $7.7 million on his successful effort.

The expense is, of course, appreciably less in a small state. A respectable contested race in a congressional district can hardly be run for less than $30,000 and may go much higher.

Why are these huge expenditures made? We tend to forget the magnitude of the populations with which candidates deal in almost every case. Even the costs of a presidential race amount to less than fifty cents per person in the country. The expense of postage stamps alone (not including paper, envelopes, and printing) to send a single letter to every registered voter in the average congressional district is about $15,000. A half-hour of prime time on a single nationwide television network costs between $100,000 and $150,000 for air time alone, to which must be added very sizable production costs. A twenty-second station-break advertisement on one major metropolitan television station can cost $3,500, and spot commercials are often repeated several times a day for at least a few weeks. One page in the *New York Times* can cost up to $12,000. Travel expenses, staff salaries, and the cost of publishing literature rapidly increase the totals. Even so, it is well to remember that the costs of a presidential campaign are dwarfed by the combined advertising budgets of four or five major corporations in a single year.

The money for political campaigns other than presidential general elections must be raised by contributions from individuals and organizations, and interest groups are the prime contributors. Ideally, every candidate would like to get financing in small contributions from great numbers of people in order not to feel heavily obligated to any single person or group; but while large sums can sometimes be raised in this way, the amount is rarely adequate, and collection is slow and difficult. Despite partially successful efforts to broaden their base of support, both parties still depend heavily on the big contributors. While corporations and labor unions are forbidden by law to contribute directly to political campaigns, there are indirect ways for both to do so. They operate primarily through separate political organizations called political action committees, supported largely by voluntary (but solicited) contributions. Corporation executives are often given bonuses to compensate for personal contributions.

Nationwide, the Republicans have generally been much more successful than the Democrats in fund raising, and their expenditures have therefore been correspondingly higher. In the 1968 campaign the Republicans spent three times as much as the Democrats did; moreover, the national Republican party remained solvent, while the national Democratic party ended the campaign $8 million in debt. In 1972 McGovern raised $22.8 million and Nixon raised approximately $60 million, not all of which he found necessary to spend. As Watergate illustrated, the availability of too much money may constitute a dangerous temptation. In the words of one Washington attorney, "It's the kind of money that tempts you to do things you wouldn't think of otherwise." The onset of public financing and stringent contribution limits in 1976 means that figures for that year are not comparable to those for previous years, but expenditures by the two major parties were roughly equalized.

After years of inconclusive haggling over a possible new law to regulate campaign contributions and expenditures, replacing the outdated and generally ineffective Corrupt Practices Act of 1925, Congress finally passed such an act in 1971. But with the example of Watergate-era financial transactions fueling public indignation, it was rather quickly superseded in late 1974 by a major reform law that has significantly altered the whole picture of campaign financing in the United States. As further amended in 1976, this law restricts contributions to $1,000 from any individual ($5,000 from an organization) for a candidate for national office for each primary, run-off, and general election, with a $25,000 aggregate maximum to all such candidates.* Extensive records and reporting by candidates are required. Provisions in the original act for expenditure ceilings and for limits on the amount that candidates and their immediate families might put into the campaign from personal funds were declared unconstitutional (as a restriction of free expression) by the Supreme Court. Enforcement of all regulations is made the responsibility of an independent Federal Elections Commission.

The truly revolutionary change, however, lay in the establishment of public financing of presidential campaigns, utilized for the first time in 1976. A candidate may choose whether to accept public financing for the general election campaign, and if that option is chosen, no private contributions may be accepted. Ford and Carter each received $21.8 million in public funds in 1976. Matching funds up to a maximum of $4.5 million each are also available for candidates in presidential primaries who prove themselves serious contenders by raising $100,000 in private contributions, including at least $5,000 from each of twenty or more states. Only the first $250 of each contribution may count for matching purposes. General election financing for major-party candidates is guaranteed; third-party candidates may claim public finance reimbursement if they succeed in polling a certain percentage of the vote. The latter provision is presumably to discourage frivolous candidacies, but it also means a very considerable handicap since one must gamble expenditures with an uncertain prospect of recovery. Sizable allocations for the

---

*The largest contribution from one individual to a single campaign (Nixon's) in 1972 was $2,056,145, coming from Chicago insurance executive W. Clement Stone. Richard Mellon Scaife, heir to the Mellon banking fortune, gave approximately $1 million to the Nixon campaign and additional funds to various House and Senate races.

financing of the two major-party conventions ($1.8 million each in 1976) are also available. All money for these purposes comes from the special fund created through the voluntary opportunity for taxpayers to indicate on their income tax returns each year that one dollar from their taxes should go toward campaign finance.

The basic argument for public financing is that candidates should be freed from dependency upon special interests to pay for their campaigns, interests that ordinarily want something in return, whether specific benefits or simply ease of access to the seats of power. Cleaner politics, it is contended, is well worth the price. Moreover, in a system of free elections the public should have adequate information and reasonably equal access to different points of view, so the financing is properly a public responsibility.

Nevertheless, the 1974 act has hardly met with universal approbation. Some criticisms relate to specific problems in its administration: what some people feel are overly burdensome reporting and bookkeeping requirements demanding a vast amount of staff time, the need to hire accountants for even a modest campaign in order to be protected against some technical violation of the law, the inequities resulting from the existence of limits on contributions of money but not of time or from the fact that indirect donations are not covered. A case in point was a fund-raiser concert given by a rock group for candidate Carter that netted his campaign $60,000, although a direct contribution of that amount would have resulted in prosecution. There are endless comparable illustrations. Some also contend that fund-raising pressures are even greater than before because contributors have been frightened off and one now spends as much time wheedling a $250 contribution as was formerly spent getting one of $50,000. Both individual candidates and groups have turned to massive direct mail solicitation, which is extremely expensive and may soon reach a point of saturation. Removal of the ceiling on contributions to one's own campaign has placed a premium on wealthy candidates: the successful Senate campaign of H. John Heinz in Pennsylvania in 1976 saw an infusion of $2.5 million of his own money as the major portion of a $3 million campaign.

Other criticisms are of a broader policy nature, the central line of argument (in addition to complaints of third-party exclusion) being that the present limitation on contributions makes the law an "incumbents' guaranteed re-election act" because of the vast advantages already possessed by them. It remains true, however, that incumbents can raise large sums more easily than challengers if the limits are removed. One persuasive suggestion is that the ceilings should be higher for challengers than incumbents in order to provide at least a modicum of equalization. This problem of imbalance would be even more significant if the proposals to extend public financing to congressional campaigns are adopted. Despite the assumption that incumbents would be advantaged by public financing in the sense that they would simply have that much more added to already disproportionate resources, some members of Congress take an opposite view. To them it looks like nothing more than making their future opponents more effective. Beyond a certain point added resources do not necessarily mean a great increase in votes, and the fact is that at present a great many challengers are unable to raise anywhere near enough money to mount a realistic campaign. It appears, therefore, that whatever the shortcomings, public financing would at least mean that with attractive candidates meaningful contests could be waged in each district. There is little doubt of the omnipresence of special-interest influence under current circumstances: With the beginning of public financing of presidential campaigns, interest-group contributions to congressional races (predominantly for incumbents) doubled.

THE ELECTORAL COLLEGE

Although it has been the target of much criticism over the years, the electoral college system of electing the president, with the now customary practice of winner-take-all elections by states, has so far withstood all proposals for change. In part this is because of the complexity of constitutional amendment and general reluctance to change institutions, and also it is simply that most people do not get excited about the matter unless the system actually distorts the results of an election enough to produce a minority winner or comes close to doing so. Presidents who have had fewer popular votes than an opponent have been elected, though not in this century. Yet a minority president remains always a distinct possibility. It is interesting to speculate that a rather miniscule shift of only 5,558 votes in Ohio and 3,687 votes in Hawaii would have resulted in the election of Ford over Carter, despite the fact that Carter's total popular vote was 1.7 million greater. Figures 6.1–6.4 show the distribution of states' electoral votes in the 1964, 1968, 1972, and 1976 presidential elections.

Each state is entitled to the number of electoral votes equal to the total number of senators and representatives that it has in Congress. Under present practice a candidate receives all of a state's electoral votes if he or she wins a plurality of the popular vote in the state. An absolute majority of the total electoral vote is required to elect a president. The intent of the framers was that a group of distinguished citizens be elected in each state and meet after the passions of a congressional campaign had died down to select someone they believed would make a good chief executive. But the electoral college system rapidly adapted to the realities of a party system, especially after the passage of the Twelfth Amendment.

Many citizens assume that they are voting for a president; they are actually voting for a slate of electors who, it is presumed, will support their party's nominee. There is nothing to compel them to do so, however. Once elected, each one is a presidential elector and legally free to vote for anyone. Elector candidates are selected by each of the state party organizations, and the posts are generally considered honorary, a reward for outstanding service or for large contributions to the party. Their function is expected to be routine, and it almost invariably is. Yet four times since World War II electors have voted for someone other than the candidate on whose slate they were elected, and a few states now endeavor to bind electors by law.

The Constitution provides that in the event no candidate receives a clear majority in the electoral college, the House of Representatives will elect a president from among the three highest contenders. The hitch here is that each state has one vote, and thus twenty-six votes are required to elect. Hence we are faced with the seemingly irrational situation in which California's forty-three representatives caucus to decide by majority vote how California's one vote will be cast, while Delaware's member of the House caucuses alone to determine that state's vote. The potentialities hardly need elaboration. In these circumstances a vice president would be elected by the Senate. Each senator has one vote, but the states are equally represented. Only twice have presidents been elected by the House—Jefferson in 1800 and John Quincy Adams in 1824, but the House election in 1800 resulted from an unforeseen complication in electoral college voting procedure rather than from any question that Jefferson was the intended choice.

Third-party candidates have from time to time entertained hopes of securing enough electoral votes to throw an election into the House, which is always a possibility if the race between the major-party candidates is close. They do not ordinarily expect to be elected but anticipate being in a position to bargain for concessions from one of the major candidates.

The electoral college system has had other effects (see Figure 6.5). Presidential campaigns have concentrated heavily on populous states with big blocs of electoral votes. (The geography of President Carter's victory was substantially the same as those of Franklin Roosevelt and John F. Kennedy: The South plus most of the big industrial states of the East, with enough of the Midwest to push the electoral vote over the top. He carried only four states in the Midwest, but a shift of only 18,000 votes would have given him three others constituting a large electoral vote block.) Presidential candidates have come most often, though not entirely, from a few large states, and vice-presidential candidates have come most often from a

FIGURE 6.1   State Electoral Vote in the 1964 Presidential Election

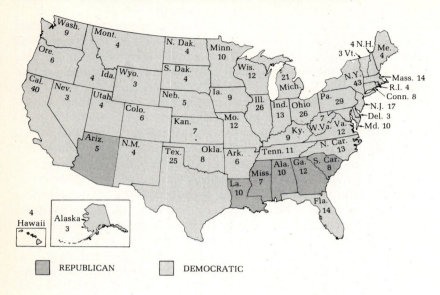

FIGURE 6.2   State Electoral Vote in the 1968 Presidential Election

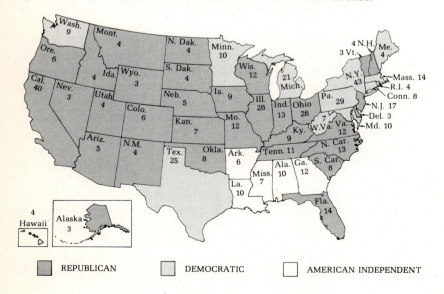

FIGURE 6.3   State Electoral Vote in the 1972 Presidential Election

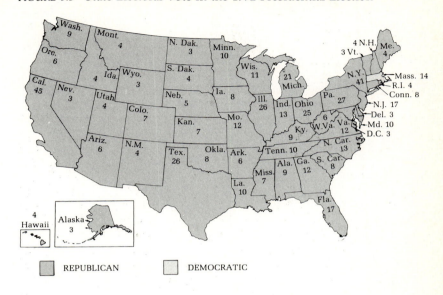

FIGURE 6.4   State Electoral Vote in the 1976 Presidential Election

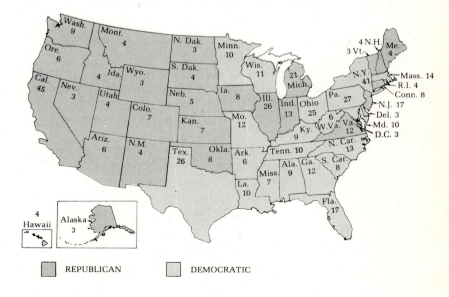

FIGURE 6.5   States' Sizes in Proportion to Their Electoral Votes

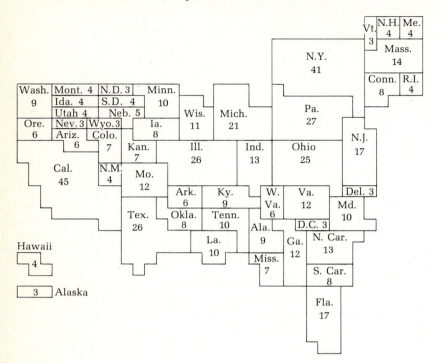

different state and region. The opportunity for any third party to gain nationwide strength has been severely limited. Election to the presidency depends heavily today on winning large pluralities in the major metropolitan areas of the nation, which can swing big states. The location of certain minority groups in big, closely contested states has given those minorities a political influence out of proportion to their numbers.

The seeming inappropriateness of the electoral college system to modern presidential elections and the dangers of seriously distorting the democratic will that it entails have led to a fairly steady stream of proposals for reform. The most obvious possibility would be simply to abolish the electoral college and choose presidents by popular vote, as is done for other offices. This would of course diminish the importance of the states as such in the election process. Moreover, some people argue that as long as Congress is "stacked for the conservatives" by the district election system, it is appropriate that the electoral college system give an advantage to a liberal presidential candidate (because of the importance the system gives to the big cities, which normally have a preponderantly liberal vote).

A modest proposal for change is that the discretionary freedom of the electors, or even the electors themselves, be abolished, leaving the rest of the system intact. The electoral vote of each state would be cast automatically for the candidate winning the state's popular vote. This would correct no other deficiencies but would at least eliminate the prospect of individual electors violating the expressed will of the voters in their states, and it would prevent the recent tactic in a few states of choosing unpledged slates of electors who might try to bargain in a close election. Part of this proposal is the frequently made suggestion that 40 per cent of the electoral vote be sufficient to elect when there are more than two candidates and that, if no candidate has 40 per cent, there be a run-off between the top two. There would then be no possibility of an election being decided by the House.

Still another recurrent proposal involves the choice of one elector from each congressional district in the state and two electors at large from each state. Each voter would vote for two statewide candidates for elector and one in the congressional district. The division of popular sentiment would be somewhat more accurately reflected, because one party might win certain districts while the opposite party won others. It would still be a distorted reflection, however, owing to the arbitrary division of voters into district groupings. The most serious objection to this proposal is that it would notably increase the motivation, even more than currently, to draw congressional district boundaries in a way that favors the party in power.

The proposal that until a few years ago had seemed to garner the most support, and in fact once passed the Senate as a proposed constitutional amendment, was that for proportioning the electoral vote of each state on the same basis as the split of the popular vote. In other words, if the popular vote in the state divided 52 per cent for A, 45 per cent for B, and 3 per cent for C, those would be the percentages of the state's electoral vote automatically assigned to each rather than the 100 per cent that A now receives. This would eliminate most of the shortcomings of the electoral college arrangement, although it would still slightly overrepresent the states with the smallest populations, since each state has a minimum of three electoral votes (two senators and one representative). It is interesting that, had this system been in effect, five presidents would have been different: Tilden rather than Hayes in 1876, Hancock rather than Garfield in 1880, Cleveland rather than Harrison in 1888, Bryan rather than McKinley in 1896, and Nixon rather than Kennedy in 1960 (despite the fact that Kennedy had the larger popular vote).

Since this system still permits distortion of the popular will, the greatest support for change today is for a shift to straight popular election, most proposals incorporating the principle of a run-off if no candidate has 40 per cent of the vote. Such a proposed constitutional

ANTI-DIRECT ELECTION

POPULAR VOTE

ELECTORAL COLLEGE ROULETTE

From *Herblock's State of the Union* (Simon & Schuster, 1972).

"Don't be chicken—try it just once more"

amendment, authored by Senator Birch Bayh, is under active consideration, but the roadblocks to constitutional change both in Congress and in the states make the task of securing approval awesome.

BASIC CONCEPTS AND TERMS

direct primary
closed primary
open primary
raiding
blanket primary

cross-filing
nominating convention
pre-primary (endorsing)
  convention
challenge primary

presidential preference primary
weaknesses of preference
  primaries
favorite-son candidate
free-for-all primary
platform committee
rules committee
credentials committee
selection of vice-presidential
  candidates
convention reform
incumbent advantages
image making
professional campaign
  management
lessons of Watergate
campaign finance control
public financing of campaigns
electoral college system
electoral college reform

THE
MODERN
PRESIDENCY

7

"No nation has ever been so ready to seize the burden and the glory of freedom," said President John F. Kennedy in 1962. No phrase more aptly characterizes the nature of the American presidency than "the burden and the glory." The person who holds this office bears a burden of responsibility that mere words cannot convey yet has also in hand the potentiality for service to humanity on a scale unequaled in any other position in the world. The prestige attached to the office makes it, at its best, a tremendous force for moral influence, though as in all human situations abuse is also possible. The great presidents have been able to embody the needs, hopes, and dreams of the people and to inspire them more nearly to live up to the finest qualities that lay within each of them. The office of president, an equal and coordinate branch of the government, was conceived for strong people capable of difficult decisions and endowed with a vision of the future. It was never intended as a job for amateurs; it is a position to be filled by the ablest politicians the nation can produce.

THE NATURE OF THE PRESIDENCY

The president and vice president are the only elected officials who have the entire country as a constituency, and the second office is always in the shadow of the first. The American system expects the president to be many people at once, a sort of monarch and prime minister combined, both head of state and head of government. The president is the natural focal point of public attention regarding issues of public policy, heads what is probably the largest administrative organization in the world, must perform a multitude of necessary ceremonial functions, such as the receiving of foreign dignitaries, and should be an effective leader of a political party. At times the person who is president seems to be wearing several hats at once but at any rate must constantly be taking off one and putting on another.

The burden of the presidency is not exclusively or even primarily a matter of volume of work, though that should not be underestimated. Some details can be shifted to subordinates. The real burden lies in the responsibility for making decisions about matters on which ride the fate of more than 200 million fellow citizens and, indeed, of the entire world. No one is more conscious of the fallibility of human judgment, no one more aware of the limitations of available information, despite the tremendous resources at his command. Often there surely must be the desire to postpone action until results can be more accurately forecast, yet decisions must be made. Always there is the knowledge that failure to act is also a policy decision that has its own consequences. The consciousness of how much depends on personal judgment can never be escaped, day or night, as long as the president is in office.

President Truman kept on his desk a sign that read "The buck stops here." It is a paradox that, in this office where a person is constantly surrounded and besieged by people, every president in modern history has spoken feelingly of the loneliness of the position. It is the loneliness of power that cannot really be shared, no matter how many advisers may be consulted. The president lives with the constant knowledge that the slightest offhand remark may be a headline within minutes, that there are few persons who can be spoken to freely and in utter confidence. Woodrow Wilson, speaking of Lincoln, remarked on the "very holy and terrible isolation for the conscience" of the person who must preside over the destiny of a nation. "That privacy," he added, "no man can intrude upon. That lonely search of the spirit for the right perhaps no man can assist."

Yet the power of the president is by no means absolute, and it is incredibly difficult to manage. It is less a power to command than a power to influence and persuade. It must operate within the constitutional framework and the limitations imposed by the other branches. Some responsibilities are the president's alone; others are shared with Congress. But the fundamental responsibility for giving leadership to the nation arises more out of the inherent needs of a political community than out of constitutional obligation. From time to time suggestions have been made for reducing the burdens of the office, but the conclusion invariably reached is that, although administrative details can be delegated to others, the essential responsibilities must inescapably lie upon a single individual. The very nature of the office insures that it will tax the resources of the most energetic and competent person.

This being the case, people have commonly asked, "Why would anyone want to be president?" Many would not; the office requires a very special sort of person, possessed of great ambition, tremendous self-confidence, and love for the exercise of power. No other position presents a challenge of such scope and magnitude. The president paints on a broader canvas than other human beings, and success in guiding the nation to new and significant levels of accomplishment assures that person a place in history. It is an office that some individuals will always seek.

CONSTITUTIONAL STIPULATIONS

The Constitution is specific in its stipulation that a person must be thirty-five years of age to be eligible for the presidency. It is less clear when it requires that he or she be a "natural born citizen" and originally unclear whether the vice president was intended to become president in the event of the death or disability of the president. Whether or not a person born to American parents outside the United States is to be deemed a natural-born citizen has not yet had to be officially interpreted, though the possibility has occasionally arisen. It is generally assumed that the courts would probably rule that such a person is eligible for the presidency.

SUCCESSION AND DISABILITY

It is possible to read the original succession statement in two ways: in the event of presidential death or disability, the vice president should become either president or acting president. The language used is that "the powers and duties" of the office devolve upon the vice president. Some interpreters of the Constitution have contended that had the framers intended that the vice president be sworn in as president, they would have said so. In any case the argument is an academic one by now, for the precedent, established by Vice President John Tyler in 1841 in taking the oath as president, and formalized in the Twenty-fifth Amendment, has been followed ever since. Uninterrupted continuity of government responsibility is vital, especially in times of crisis. National law provides that the next in line of succession after the vice president will be the speaker of the House, followed by the president pro tempore of the Senate and then by the Cabinet officers. Except in the event of multiple catastrophe, the Twenty-fifth Amendment has made such succession inoperative by providing a mechanism whereby the office of vice president can promptly be filled.

President Eisenhower's first heart attack in 1955 focused public attention on the uncertainty over presidential disability that had prevailed since the beginning of the republic. At what point should a vice president take over the reins and at what point relinquish them? What if a president were incapable of performing the duties of the office but refused to concede that this was so? After prolonged discussion of various alternative approaches, Congress finally proposed an amendment sponsored by Senator Birch Bayh that was ratified as the Twenty-fifth Amendment in 1967. Its provisions sought to resolve most problems in this area as completely as could be done by law:

1 Whenever there is a vacancy in the office of vice president, because of succession or other reasons, the president will nominate a vice president, subject to confirmation by majority vote of the Senate and the House. (We have previously noted that presidential nominees are ordinarily able to pick their vice-presidential running mates, so this is hardly a revolutionary idea.)

2 When a president in writing declares inability to discharge the powers and duties of the office, the vice president becomes acting

The inauguration of President Carter in 1977. Chief Justice Burger congratulates the new president after administering the oath of office.

United Press International

president until the president in writing indicates ability to reassume the office.

3 If it is concluded at any time by the vice president and a majority of the Cabinet (appointees of the president, it should be remembered), and so stated in writing, that the president is unable to carry out the duties of office, the vice president at once becomes acting president.

4 The president can subsequently resume office by a written declaration that no inability exists, unless the vice president and the Cabinet majority reassert their belief in incapacity, whereupon Congress must decide the issue, needing a two-thirds vote of both houses to determine that the vice president will continue as acting president.

The first application of the new provisions for filling vacancies in the vice presidency was made in an unexpected fashion in the fall of 1973. To an administration already beleaguered as a result of the Watergate disclosures, there could not have been news much worse than the word that the U.S. attorney in Maryland was prepared to secure indictments against Vice President Spiro Agnew for tax evasion and other charges in connection with alleged payments to him when he was governor of Maryland (and earlier, while he was a county executive) in return for lucrative government contracts. Agnew vehemently denounced the prosecutors and branded the accusations as lies, insisting in public speeches that he would clear his name and would never consider resigning. Technical uncertainties existed as to whether he could be brought to trial while still holding office or whether he would first have to be convicted and removed from office through impeachment proceedings. But speculation ceased abruptly with a dramatic series of steps one October morning when Agnew, his letter of resignation as vice president delivered to the secretary of state only moments before, strode into the courthouse in Baltimore to plead "no contest" to the charges of income tax evasion. By pre-arrangement, other charges were dropped and he was sentenced on this count, leaving his office as a humiliated and discredited man.

President Nixon, who had of course originally picked Agnew in 1968 and who was obviously anxious to avoid a battle with Congress over the new nomination, which might well arise if he chose a person with a strong national following, nominated Representative Gerald Ford of Michigan, the House Republican floor leader and a safe team player, to fill the vacancy. As if nothing untoward had happened to make this nomination necessary, the president's choice was made public in a kind of White House television spectacular before a sizable gathering of members of Congress, the foreign diplomatic corps, and the press, a process admirably designed to place possible critics at a severe disadvantage (and jocularly referred to in Washington as "the coronation of Jerry Ford"). Although normally favorably disposed toward one of its own, Congress conducted fairly extensive investigations and hearings, to establish a precedent as much as anything, and then approved Ford with only minimal dissent. Although in light of the Watergate investigations the possibility of succession was very real, the chances seemed remote to most people, and few anticipated that within eight months Gerald R. Ford would be president of the United States. After congressional approval of President Ford's choice of Nelson Rockefeller for vice president, the nation was in the unprecedented situation of having both a president and a vice president who had not been elected to those offices.

The Agnew case caused some second thoughts about the way vice presidents are chosen, and a variety of changes have been suggested. Among them are: (1) at least forty-eight hours should elapse at a convention between the nomination of a presidential candidate and announcement of his choice for vice president, allowing time for more careful investigation; (2) the runner-up for the presidential nomination automatically should be the vice-presidential nominee; (3) candidates for a presidential nomination should be required to state their vice-presidential choices in advance, making widespread scrutiny possible; (4) persons seeking a vice-presidential nomination should be required to run in the preference primaries: (5) the presidential nominee should choose from a list selected by a panel of party leaders; and (6) instead of vice presidents being elected, they should be nominated by presidents after their own election, subject to confirmation by Congress. Others have advocated elimination of the office, with arrangements to be made for a caretaker government in the event of loss of a president, until a special election can be held to fill the vacancy. Each proposal has its problems, and further change would no doubt be very difficult to bring about, but the present system is not necessarily permanent. Understandably, the Twenty-fifth Amendment also underwent renewed scrutiny. Proposals for change included returning to the old system of succession, using a special election, holding of a popular referendum on the president's choice, or reconvening of the electoral college to make the choice. After an initial flurry there seemed a general consensus that despite the fact that these had been highly abnormal circumstances, the system had worked reasonably well, and that no alternative seemed clearly superior.

It is interesting that the office of vice president, once ridiculed and considered a political dead end,* has in recent years acquired much

---

*Thomas Marshall, Wilson's vice president, compared the position to that of a cataleptic: "He cannot speak; he cannot move; he suffers no pain; yet he is perfectly conscious of everything that is going on about him." And John N. Garner, Franklin D. Roosevelt's first vice president, warned Lyndon Johnson in 1960: "The vice presidency isn't worth a pitcher of warm spit."

greater political significance. Nine vice presidents have succeeded to the office of president, and events of the last few years have brought greater public awareness of the person who stands "just a heartbeat from the presidency." Presidents from Harry Truman on have given attention, commonly lacking in the past, to insuring that the vice president is fully informed and prepared to take over the reins, should the occasion demand. They have also assigned to the office administrative and political responsibilities and have frequently used the vice president as a temporary roving ambassador. Some vice presidents, like Agnew, have served as effective political "hatchet men," carrying the attack for the administration and thus allowing the president to avoid what some might consider unseemly, vehement attacks upon the opposition, while others, like Ford, facing different circumstances, have played the role of conciliator and party strengthener. It is not purely by chance that modern vice presidents or former vice presidents are presidential aspirants more frequently than in the past, even though their role while holding office is no more independent now than in former times. President Carter went considerably further than any of his predecessors, making Vice President Mondale to a far greater degree than other vice presidents a real partner in the executive office. Mondale was a major element in planning the transition to the Carter presidency, in the selection of top-level appointees such as the Cabinet members, and in day-to-day liaison with Congress. He rapidly became a highly valued adviser to the president on the whole range of the chief executive's responsibilities.

THE TWO-TERM LIMIT

Still another amendment, ratified in 1951 (the Twenty-second), established a two-term limit on the presidency, a requirement that is still often debated. Many argue that the political limitations on a president's holding office are quite sufficient and that the people should not be restricted in their choice. It is likewise a common feeling that a president's influence is severely limited in the last year or two of office when it is known that he cannot run again; on the other hand, it can be argued that during that period the president acts with a great deal more freedom than previously.

IMPEACHMENT

One other aspect affecting tenure and succession is the possibility of removing a president from office, an action that has never occurred, although Nixon's resignation in 1974 occurred because impeachment and conviction were essentially certain. A president, like other civil officers of the United States, may be impeached (formally charged) by vote of a majority of the House of Representatives for "treason,

" . . . But is it a high crime or misdemeanor?"

bribery, or other high crimes and misdemeanors." A trial is conducted before the Senate, with a two-thirds vote being required to convict and thus remove the president from office. Impeachment was clearly intended as a highly extraordinary procedure; only Andrew Johnson, of all the presidents, has been impeached (in the heat of post–Civil War passions), and he was not convicted. Although one occasionally hears political threats of impeachment, most are never acted on seriously; thus the extended controversy over impeachment of President Nixon was virtually unique. The impeachment process, it may be noted, applies in practice only to officials of the executive and judicial branches, since simpler proceedings are available for removal of a member of Congress. Military officers are excluded, and minor administrative officers would as a rule never be involved because they can be removed by their superior officers. Impeachment is a political action (which does not necessarily mean partisan), and the only penalty on conviction is removal from office. Should the officeholder also be alleged to have committed a crime, charges and trial could follow after return to private citizen status.

Since the Constitution is not explicit and precedents are extremely limited, a number of uncertainties surround the impeachment process, most notably the question of precisely what constitutes an impeachable offense. The Nixon case naturally brought these uncertainties to the fore. What did the framers mean by the phrase "high crimes and misdemeanors"? Some years earlier, when he was unsuccessfully seeking the impeachment of Supreme Court Justice William O. Douglas, then Representative Gerald Ford asserted that this meant whatever a majority of the House said it meant. The opposite view was expressed vehemently during the Nixon investigation by a number of House members who believed that they could not vote for impeachment unless it was conclusively proved that the president had committed a crime or, as one dramatically phrased it, "unless we have found the president with a smoking gun in his hand."

The weight of expert opinion is that the framers used the term "*high* crimes and misdemeanors" to distinguish impeachable offenses from mere maladministration. The concern was to be with major political offenses such as abuse of the powers of office or failure to carry out responsibilities under the oath of office. Imagine, as columnist William Buckley has suggested, the totally improbable situation of a newly elected president who secludes himself at Camp David to live a life of luxury and refuses to go to Washington to carry on the work of the office. Would anyone seriously claim that he ought not to be impeached and removed, even though he has violated no criminal statute?

Prior to the culmination of the Nixon case, there was widespread public misunderstanding of the meaning of the term *impeachment*. It apparently sounded to most people like some terribly drastic action. Even when the polls showed heavy majorities believing that the president was personally implicated in the scandals, many of the same people hesitated to advocate impeachment. To some extent this merely reflected popular respect for the office, but the results of one poll, long before all the evidence had come out, pointed up sharply the extent of misunderstanding: When asked whether the president should be impeached, only 41 per cent of those polled said yes; but when asked whether the House should bring formal charges against the president, to be followed by a trial in the Senate to determine guilt or innocence, 73 per cent replied affirmatively.

The events leading to the resignation of President Nixon provide the only example in modern history of the presidential impeachment process. As the full scope of the Watergate affair was gradually untangled during 1973, the probability of direct presidential involvement steadily appeared greater. Despite initial promises to cooperate fully with any legitimate congressional inquiry and with the special prosecutor's office, the president throughout the entire period of investigation released almost no information voluntarily and delayed as much as possible in acceding to every court order. He was forced into progressively tighter defense perimeters: first claiming that no one in either the White House staff or the Committee to Reelect the President had been involved, then drawing the line around the White House, then requesting the resignations of his closest and highest-level staff assistants H. R. Haldeman and John Ehrlichman, as well as that of White House counsel John Dean, then conceding staff involvement but maintaining his own innocence.

In April 1974 the president, facing demands for tapes and other records from both the House Judiciary Committee and the special prosecutor, sought to stem the tide by releasing edited transcripts rather than the tapes themselves. Many of the transcripts of conversations nevertheless proved severely damaging, and the effect was compounded when the committee later received the tapes from the courts and released its own transcripts showing that incriminating material had been excluded from the president's version. For example, the president, who had from the beginning insisted that whatever the actions of his subordinates he himself had not participated in the cover-up (withholding of evidence, perjury, and various diversionary tactics), could be heard on tape directing his aides in these words: "I want you all to stonewall it, let them plead the Fifth Amendment, cover up or anything else, if it'll save it—save the plan." The conflict with his frequent assurances to the public that he was doing his utmost to bring all the facts to light hardly needed elaboration.

With more prosecutor's subpoenas for specific tapes in hand, the president took his claim of refusal based on executive privilege to the Supreme Court, which deferred its normal summer recess to hear arguments on the appeal in an unusual July session. Its subsequent, unanimous (8 to 0) decision (*U.S.* v. *Nixon*) written by Chief Justice Burger, a Nixon appointee, held that the president could not use this claim to withhold evidence in a criminal trial and that the tapes must be surrendered at once.

When the House authorized its Judiciary Committee to study the situation and bring recommendations as to whether or not the president should be impeached, it set in motion a lengthy, thorough, and detailed investigation, involving not only the 38-member committee (all lawyers) but a professional staff of 104. Although at times criticized for slowness, the committee under the astute chairmanship of Representative Peter Rodino was well aware of the essentiality of leaving no stone unturned. It needed to be scrupulously fair, to steer clear of even an appearance of a "rush to judgment," and to avoid strictly partisan votes. Because of a Democratic majority in the House, the commiteee was composed of twenty-one Democrats and seventeen Republicans.

In the judgment of most observers the committee and its staff performed very responsibly. The comprehensive evidence presented lacked only that which the president had refused to yield. On an impeachment issue there were inevitably strong differences of opinion, and for every member of the committee the investigation and decision-making process was an exhausting and emotionally draining experience. The seriousness of the issue produced a deep seriousness of behavior. Though initial hearings and discussions were closed, the final debate and votes of the committee, which followed the release of no less than thirty-eight volumes of evidence and information amassed by the staff, took place before television cameras. The fears of many persons that this might encourage grandstanding proved unfounded; polls showed in fact that the popular impression of Congress was materially improved as a result.

The House Judiciary Committee, its study of the mountains of evidence and its debate concluded, voted to recommend to the House articles of impeachment on three counts: obstruction of justice, abuse of the powers of the presidency, and violation of the oath of office by refusing to respond to subpoenas from a committee of Congress carrying out constitutional responsibilities. The long effort of the White House to force a party split on the committee and thus make the action appear to be merely a partisan attack was to no avail. Six Republicans joined twenty-one Democrats on the first article and seven on the second, although on the third only two Republicans voted yes while two Democrats joined the no's. The president's defenders on the committee did not in general dispute the fact that a multitude of improper and illegal actions had taken place; instead, they contended that the evidence was not conclusive that the president was personally involved. But by then a heavy vote in the House for impeachment was considered a certainty.

As the president's supporters planned strategy for the floor debate and the Senate moved toward completing arrangements for the trial, the final bombshell exploded. Faced after the Supreme Court decisions of July with the need to turn over sixty-four tapes to the district court, President Nixon tried to take some of the sting from one crucial conversation by public release of a transcript accompanied by his own explanatory statement. This tape of conversations with Haldeman on June 23, 1972, showed that, contrary to the president's oft repeated claim that he had known nothing of White House staff involvement in the cover-up before John Dean's report to him on March 21, 1973, he had in fact been deeply involved only six days after the Watergate break-in. He admitted to having lied about this and to having withheld vital information not only from Congress and the prosecutor but also from his staff and his personal attorney. Conceding that he had shown bad judgment and that he undoubtedly would be impeached, he appealed to the Senate, contending that he had committed no offense serious enough to warrant removal from office.

The last line of defense was shattered. "I guess we have found the smoking gun, haven't we?" Representative Barber Conable, Jr., until then a Nixon supporter, asked wryly. The president's support almost instantly eroded to the point at which there was talk of a near unanimous impeachment vote and general agreement to reduce sharply the time allocated for debate. Every previous supporter of the president on the Judiciary Committee announced a switch in favor of impeachment, as did the Republican floor leader and a host of other former defenders. Most spoke sadly or bitterly of feeling betrayed. Nor was the situation in the Senate, where the president had been counting on at least the thirty-four votes needed to stave off conviction, appreciably better. No more than ten to fifteen votes were believed to remain at best. Demands for resignation flooded in from Republican leaders and candidates throughout the country as well as from the Republican members of Congress; everyone seemed certain that the Republican party faced disaster at the polls if the president stayed in office even a few more weeks, but he continued to insist that he would not resign. Finally a solemn delegation, consisting of the Senate and House Republican leaders and party elder statesman Senator Barry Goldwater, visited tbe president's office to tell him his chances of survival were gone. The congressional ultimatum was clear: resign or be impeached and convicted. On the evening of August 8, 1974, Richard Nixon, only a year and a half into his second term following a landslide re-election victory, now disgraced but conceding nothing but a "few mistakes," went before the American people in a somber television address to become the first president in history to resign from the office.

Although it did not run its full course because of the resignation, the impeachment process had clearly worked as the framers had intended, serving as a final protection against misuse of power. As

President's Nixon's emotional farewell speech to White House staff at the time of his resignation.

United Press International

millions of citizens the following day watched the swearing in of a new president in a brief and simple ceremony, they could remark on this peaceful transfer of power, without armies or mobs in the streets. And despite the attempt of the former president for many months to identify his personal positions and interests with the institution of the presidency and thus instill fear that impeachment would result in disaster for the future of the office, it was evident to all that, however sadly, only a man had fallen—the presidency still stood.

SOME PERQUISITES OF THE OFFICE

Presidents from the beginning of the nation's history have been well provided for in a material sense. Today, in addition to a $200,000 salary, the president is supplied with the executive mansion and its upkeep, a personal Air Force jet airplane (and additional planes as desired), a yacht if desired, a fleet of automobiles, several helicopters, a comfortably appointed mountain retreat in Maryland, extensive entertainment and expense funds, a very large personal staff in addition to the personnel who operate the above-mentioned facilities and provide medical care and security protection, and a host of other relatively minor benefits. The White House professional staff (excluding personnel such as security forces, gardeners, military chauffeurs, and cooks) totals over five hundred, in addition to numerous people detailed to the White House from the payrolls of other government departments.

Congress has been generally disinclined to raise questions about the expenses of running the White House establishment, just as the president ordinarily does not question budgets for operation of the legislature. In 1973, however, there arose a major public controversy concerning the nature and magnitude of public expenditures for the improvement of private property owned by President Nixon at Key Biscayne, Florida, and San Clemente, California. When questions were first raised by a Santa Ana, California, newspaper, the president's press secretary stated that the government had spent $39,525 for security at San Clemente, but within a few weeks that figure was revised to $703,367, and ultimately the General Services Administration reported that the total expenditure for protection, improvement, and operation, mainly at the two homes but including other occasional vacation spots, was a staggering $10 million, more than five times what the president paid for the properties. Approximately $6 million of this amount was for military facilities, mainly communications.

No one is likely to question expenditures for protection of the president and family wherever they may be. The controversy arose, rather, over the legitimacy of spending tax funds for improvements having only a remote, if discernible, relation to protection, cases in point being such listed expenditures as $76,000 for septic tank repairs at San Clemente (relatively few citizens own homes where house, land, and facilities together are valued at that amount), $13,-500 for a new heating system, and lesser but sizable amounts for a swimming-pool heater, a beach cabana, and the like. A home belonging to Vice President Agnew also received an air-conditioning system and full carpeting under the heading of security. Even the property of a multimillionaire friend of the president in the Bahamas, where the president liked to visit, benefited from additions (for the use of accompanying personnel) as well as security devices. None of these was government property, and all expenditures for actual improvement (as distinct from military communications and the like) obviously enhance the market values for the private owners by approximately the amount of such expenditure.

Even if all such expenditures could be justified in the name of security, however, a still more basic question has to do with how real the need is that taxpayers support extra vacation retreats, given the accommodations already provided for the president. Obviously no expenditures of this type would be needed if a president did not insist on frequent visits to personal homes, which then must be made into virtual White Houses away from Washington. It is estimated that each time a president makes a trip across the country for a few days, the cost to the public (for planes, crews, communications, up to two hundred accompanying personnel, and so on) is somewhere in the neighborhood of a quarter of a million dollars, and this does not include any portion of the huge costs of acquiring and maintaining the jet and helicopter fleets.

When President Nixon resigned, he was provided $200,000 in transition expenses. In addition, as do all ex-presidents, he continued to receive a considerable range of benefits (all of which would have been lost had he been impeached and removed): a $60,000-a-year lifetime pension, a $96,000-a-year allowance for staff assistance, free office space, the franking privilege for mail related to official business, and the right of his wife to a widow's pension.

PRESIDENT OR MONARCH

It is evident that in modern times the presidency had become surrounded with a vast panoply of ceremonials and rituals, typified by the omnipresent Marine Corps band playing "Hail to the Chief" to herald virtually every formal appearance, as well as the perquisites just discussed. Coupled with the vast powers attaching to the office and the natural tendency of the public to look on the president as almost a potentate, it is hardly surprising that attitudes arose justifying the label placed on the office by Arthur Schlesinger, Jr., that it was an "imperial presidency." If it were true, as many believed, that Richard Nixon and some of his top associates came to view the position in essentially monarchial terms—justifying the propriety of acting above or outside the law on their personal concepts of what the public really needed, for example—this was but the culmination of a long-growing idea that an election gives the president a mandate to rule and that his only responsibility is to the electorate at the next election rather than to constitutional restraints, Congress, party, or interim public opinion. Yet it is important, without approving of excesses, to recognize a dilemma inherent in the role of the president. If he is to be an effective leader, some of the symbolism of power may be necessary to the achievement of goals.

For years there had been many academicians and journalists as well as political figures who stressed the theme that only the chief executive could provide significant forward-looking leadership. Congress was presumably stagnant and hidebound, incapable of initiative and perhaps even of action: the times demanded presidents who could dominate the policy-making process. Interestingly, it was primarily the liberals, desiring an activist government eager to deal with social problems, who promoted this viewpoint. Only belatedly did they come to realize that perhaps they had been identifying with the personalities and goals of certain individual presidents rather than with an institution; the powers of a strong presidency could be used to prevent action and change as easily as to foster it. With the tragedy of Watergate, liberal disillusionment touched bottom, and the shift of liberal and conservative alike was sharply toward a reform and rehabilitation of Congress, seeking to make it once again an effective counterbalance to presidential power and a promoter and protector of public interest.

President Ford was widely praised when he entered office with an implied pledge to reduce the aura of "Caesarism" that had come to surround the presidency, and he indeed made notable strides in that direction. Jimmy Carter set out to do even more to "restore the presidency to the people" and wipe out any vestiges of monarchy. Here too was symbolism, however sincere, skillfully employed as a means of building support for exercise of the governing power, but it was a self-consciously opposite style, labeled by one critic "conspicuous humility." Even if the label were accurate, the efforts met with a generally favorable public response. The folksy gestures fit easily the president's background and seemed to most people a welcome change from the pomp and isolation prevalent in the past: walking hand in hand with his family down Pennsylvania Avenue rather than riding in a limousine for the inaugural procession, enrolling daughter Amy in a District of Columbia public school, participating

"Here's the latest, Mr. President. The people like you better this afternoon than they did this morning but not as well as yesterday."

in town meetings around the country (and staying overnight in private homes), delivering an energy policy television address to the nation while sitting before a fireplace and wearing a casual sweater, ending the practice of playing "Hail to the Chief" except for rare formal occasions, ordering an end to the availability of personal limousines and various other perquisites for most top government executives, conducting a radio call-in show for questions to the president, practicing drop-ins to executive departments for informal talks to employees, urging citizens to write the president their concerns and suggestions (which brought a deluge of mail, necessitating additional office employees and thus, to some consternation, at least temporarily wrecking his pledge to reduce White House staff).

In reality, the need for effective executive leadership is as vital as ever and a weakening of the presidency would probably be unwise. The goal is properly a restoration of balance, and a leadership thus more closely responsive to public control.

Every president invests the office with something of his own personality and style, leaving it in certain ways a bit different than he found it. Are there definable types of presidents and, if so, is it possible that we might be able to predict general patterns of probable behavior before electing a person to the office? Political scientist James David Barber, in a fascinating analysis based on the lives of thirteen twentieth-century presidents, contends that prediction of the nature of presidential performance is indeed feasible.* What is necessary is to understand the personal style, character, and world view of the individual, all of which can be ascertained from a study of his early and formative years as well as his previous political behavior. Once well established, those behavioral patterns are unlikely to change.

Barber describes four basic types of presidential character: (1) the active-positives, who are oriented to achieving goals, are self-confident and flexible in adapting to changing circumstances, and who genuinely enjoy the exercise of power (typified by Franklin Roosevelt and John Kennedy); (2) the active-negatives, compulsive hard workers driven by a sense of obligation but getting no real satisfaction from accomplishments, whose tendency toward self-righteousness, distrust of others, and inflexibility can easily lead to disaster (typified by Wilson, Johnson, and Nixon); (3) the passive-positives, who lack self-confidence, devote their efforts largely to seeking reassurance and affection, and are genial and cooperative but unlikely to produce notable accomplishments (typified by Taft and Harding); and (4) the passive-negatives, individuals who serve from a sense of duty but resent the time and effort, caretakers who withdraw from leadership and offer instead a rhetoric of vague principles (typified by Coolidge and Eisenhower).

THE PRESIDENT AS CHIEF EXECUTIVE

The breadth of the president's responsibility as chief executive is enormous, embracing as it does general direction of and control over the vast administrative machinery and the many services of the entire national government. In the tremendous scope of these activities, the president's direct personal involvement must be minimal despite great influence on administrative policy and, at times, on a surprising amount of detail. In practice, Congress may to some degree limit presidential administrative discretion by attaching

---

*James David Barber. *The Presidential Character*, 2d ed., Prentice-Hall, Englewood Cliffs, N.J., 1977. Few books are more rewarding for an understanding of politics and the presidency than this very readable and provocative study.

restrictions to appropriations and specific programs. In other words, Congress does control the purse strings.

PRESIDENTIAL ADVISERS

Every president struggles to find more effective ways to sharpen policy leadership and to manage a giant bureaucracy, the style of each one differing a bit from that of the others. Although pre–Civil War presidents sometimes wrote out their own letters, modern presidents have been provided a very sizable personal staff. The press secretary and the chief of staff are frequently in the public eye, but few if any of the dozens of other high-ranking special assistants and presidential aides are known at all to the average citizen. To those inside government, however, they are well known as the keys to the center of power. They are arms, legs, ears, and sometimes voice for the president, acting on behalf of that office on many matters.

Some observers close to the White House in recent administrations are deeply concerned that staffs may become too eager to protect and please the president, thus encouraging dangerous isolation from the realities of public opinion or from differing viewpoints within the administration. The risks are obvious if virtually all information is filtered through one or two aides, especially if they seek to tell the president primarily what they think is wanted. In addition, actions of top-level staff taken in the president's name may also entail considerable risk. President Carter avoided designating a chief of staff in order to minimize the filtration process, but his principal political adviser, Hamilton Jordan, soon came to perform many of the functions of that office. Some concentrated staff control is probably essential.

The Cabinet has rarely played the major role that many people assume it has. The extent to which it is used, and in fact whether it is used at all, is entirely at the discretion of the president; each president has ideas of how much and in what way the Cabinet will be used. The Cabinet has no clear-cut constitutional status, and it takes no official actions as a body. It has traditionally consisted of the heads of the principal administrative departments, twelve currently,* but a president may add others, such as the vice president and the ambassador to the United Nations. It meets when the president summons it and considers what he wishes to have brought before it. It can be a useful forum for the exchange of information and ideas and for coordinating administrative policy, but a president who may seek the opinion of the Cabinet is in no sense bound by it.

---

*Until the post office was changed from a department to a government corporation, the postmaster general was a Cabinet member.

Almost at the beginning of the republic, John Adams shrewdly observed that a president may often be obliged to act on "his own mature and unbiased judgment, though, unfortunately, it may be in direct contradiction to the advice of all his ministers." As individuals, the members of the Cabinet have their own important departmental responsibilities; as a group, they remain purely an advisory body to the president to be used at will. They are his appointees and hold office only so long as he thinks them satisfactory.

Probably there has been no president who has not found it desirable to have close at hand a few trusted personal friends, frequently holding no official position, who can provide informal confidential advice and information and serve as sounding boards for ideas. They certainly do not replace Cabinet officers and other officials, but as independent persons having an easy relation with the president and sharing confidences, they can play a different and uniquely valuable role. At the same time, when such a person holds high office, as did Bert Lance as President Carter's budget director, any actions involving questionable ethics reflect immediately upon the president.

An additional part of the formal mechanism for executive management is the body of specialized agencies and advisory bodies grouped together as a part of what is termed the Executive Office of the President. The one with the broadest responsibility is the Office of Management and Budget. It not only acts as the president's arm in the huge task of developing a national budget each year but is supposed to provide continuous suggestions on executive reorganization and management improvement. Further, OMB acts as a clearing-house and coordinator for all departmental advice regarding legislation and recommends action that it believes the president should take relative to these proposals. The National Security Council is expected to advise on all policies, foreign and domestic, that have a bearing on national security, but its emphasis has been almost entirely on foreign relations and military affairs. The staff researches and recommends policy, the high-level council itself seeking to clarify alternatives through discussion before final decisions are made. The Council of Economic Advisers analyzes, interprets, and projects domestic and international economic trends, recommending policies designed to maintain as nearly as possible a healthy economy and full employment. Among other things, it develops the president's annual economic report to Congress. The functions of the advisory councils and committees on science policy and on the environment are self-evident in their titles.

President Nixon sought a major restructuring of the administration in order to achieve tighter control in the White House. Five presidential assistants (promptly labeled a "super-cabinet"), for domestic affairs, foreign affairs, economic affairs, executive management, and White House administration, were to report directly to the president. The old departments were demoted to second-class status. This arrangement had barely been created when the Watergate affair shattered the existing White House staff and made the idea of more concentration of power in the White House considerably less attractive, however logical it might appear managerially. The plan was informally demolished. President Carter, perhaps reflecting his engineering training, also placed great emphasis on administrative reorganization, though not in the same patterns, to achieve greater efficiency and economy. These are always popular themes. Some observers, in fact, were disturbed that he at times seemed more concerned with the procedures for making and implementing policy than with what the policy ought to be.

THE POWER TO APPOINT

The presidential appointing power is broad and constitutes one of the most significant instruments of control. Appointments to major offices, such as heads of departments, justices of the Supreme Court, and ambassadors to foreign nations, require by constitutional directive the advice and consent of the Senate. Other officers of the government are not subject to Senate confirmation, except when this is stipulated by law for specific offices. Congress has tended, understandably, to seek to expand the number of appointments requiring confirmation, and presidents have usually strongly resisted. The power to select people who hold the principal positions of responsibility is a major force in the influencing of policy, and it may be helpful indirectly in building congressional support. Although most national government personnel are appointed within the agencies under merit systems, several thousand positions are filled by presidential appointment.

No one who cannot appoint and control principal subordinates can reasonably be held responsible for an administration. In recognition of this, the Senate has rarely refused to confirm appointees to Cabinet and other major administrative posts, and the same has generally been true of Supreme Court nominations, the Haynsworth and Carswell rejections during the first Nixon administration being notable exceptions. There may be verbal fireworks, but approval is usually forthcoming. In instances in which a rejection occurs or there is at least a significant battle, the reason is most often some sort of ideological opposition to the nominee rather than doubt regarding technical qualifications. Appointments to various commissions have been more vulnerable, as Presidents Nixon and Ford discovered when the Senate began to balk at their practice of appointing to regulatory commissions individuals who were officials of the kind of business that were supposed to be regulated. Strong pressures to appoint persons representing various groups (handicapped, blacks, women, Hispanics, Polish-Americans, and so on) have of late raised further complications.

SENATORIAL COURTESY

Presidential appointments to national government posts located in the states, as distinct from positions located in Washington or abroad, are invariably governed by senatorial courtesy. This is commonly misunderstood as presidential courtesy toward senators. It is instead reciprocal courtesy among senators; under their threat of refusal to confirm appointments, the president is forced to appoint persons chosen by senators. The effect of threat is to transfer the power of appointment from the president to senators of the president's party in the states concerned. Presidents, therefore, usually follow a standard procedure.

If, for example, a Democratic president has a district judgeship to fill in Idaho, and there is at least one Democratic senator from that state, the president will notify the senator of the vacancy and invite recommendations. The senator may offer a few names or submit only one. As long as one of these persons is nominated, confirmation is ordinarily routine. But should the president be brash enough to nominate someone else, the senator need only state in the Senate that the nominee is "personally obnoxious" (the formal way of informing the Senate that the nominee is not the senator's choice), and confirmation will be refused. Every senator expects similar treatment when the need appears. No president is required to consult opposition-party senators, though they sometimes do. If both senators are of the president's party, he will usually notify both and let them work out who will make the recommendation, a privilege that is customarily rotated.

Senatorial courtesy can at times place presidents in extremely uncomfortable positions not of their own making. If an appointment proves to be bad, the president is likely to be blamed even though he was unable to exercise real choice in the appointment. Sometimes the president is faced with a virtually impossible dilemma and will be condemned for any action at all.

Case Study
PRESIDENTIAL APPOINTMENT AND SENATORIAL COURTESY

In 1965 a vacancy occurred on the Fifth Circuit United States Court of Appeals, which serves states of the deep South and is therefore continually involved in the crucial civil rights controversies. President Johnson wanted to appoint a judge who would accept the position of the

Supreme Court on civil rights, but by tradition the vacancy had to be filled by a person from a specific state. The next in line was Mississippi, where racial moderates with good legal qualifications and, especially, good political credentials were almost as scarce as snowflakes in August. Not only was it necessary, according to tradition, to consult the senators from Mississippi, but the initial stage of confirmation, and thus absolute power over it, lay with the Senate Judiciary Committee. Its chairman was conservative Senator James O. Eastland of Mississippi. The court needed its full quota of judges, but the president spent a year seeking a person who would meet his own qualifications and would be acceptable also to the two senators. James P. Coleman was an able former district attorney and a former governor; to reach the governorship he had campaigned the way campaigning was done in Mississippi. Yet as governor, despite signing certain segregationist bills, his had been the record of a man who would be fair and moderate. He had, in fact, lost his second try for the statehouse because he looked too liberal to the segregationists. The attorney general talked with him at length and was convinced of his reasonableness.

Persuaded that this was the best appointment available under the circumstances, and having gotten the agreement of the Mississippi senators, the president submitted Coleman's name, only to unleash a torrent of protest. An overflow crowd of militant civil rights supporters packed the confirmation hearing before the Senate committee while others picketed the White House. Oblivious to the restraints upon the president's power of appointment, they demanded a liberal integrationist on the court. The president was forced to decide whether to stay with his choice, practicing "the art of the possible," or withdraw the nomination and seek another solution. In the end he rode out the storm and most senators agreed with his view of the practical realities; Coleman was confirmed by a vote of seventy-six to eight.

THE POWER TO REMOVE

The president's extensive power of removal is limited in certain ways. Judges are not affected by it, since they receive life appointments during good behavior and thus may be removed only through impeachment proceedings. In general, the president may remove from office most officials of the executive branch, but Congress may create specialized agencies (notably the regulatory commissions) whose heads perform functions that are not only administrative but also partly legislative and judicial. The courts have held that heads of these agencies may be removed only on grounds specified by Congress. Occasionally Congress has tried to pressure the president into removing a particular officer and has even sought to prevent the payment of his salary, but such efforts are strongly resisted. The most effective approach, though one not always feasible politically, is to abolish the position or the agency. The broadest limitation on removal power, applying to people below top-level administrative positions, is found in the tenure provisions of the civil service statutes, but these are by no means absolute protections.

OTHER EXECUTIVE POWERS

Much discretionary authority is conferred on the president by the broad constitutional directive that he shall see "that the laws be faithfully executed." The president is thus the chief law enforcement officer of the nation, and it is obvious that the legislature neither can nor should try to spell out all the details of enforcement of the laws it enacts. The president interprets the meaning of a law and decides the level and nature of enforcement within the general boundaries fixed by Congress. There remains a broad grant of power, as presidents have often demonstrated. In recent years, for example, some presidents have vigorously enforced the antisegregation decisions of the Supreme Court while others have been more passive in that area.

Still another major tool of administrative authority is the president's power to prepare the budget. Although appropriations must be made by Congress, it works from a set of proposals developed by

President Carter at work in the Oval Office in the West Wing of the White House.

Official White House Photograph

a staff under the direction of the president. Internal financial control is vital to management of the panorama of administrative agencies. The ability to do a particular job and the level at which it will be accomplished always depend on financing.

Other important presidential powers arise from the position of the president as commander in chief of the nation's armed forces and from his prerogative to conduct relations with other countries. It is, in fact, in these two areas that the president possesses the widest freedom of action, despite a recent limitation on war powers. His relative independence in these realms is a striking contrast to the varied legal and political restrictions evident in connection with many other responsibilities. In much of modern history, international affairs have dominated the political scene, and it is thus on that stage that presidents have been able to make some of their most dramatic actions.*

The president also has the power to grant pardons, amnesties, commutations, and reprieves. This clemency power is a carry-over from the past, when monarchs could mitigate what seemed to be undue harshness of law or miscarriage of justice, and has generally been transferred to elected chief executives. The president's power extends to all offenses against the United States. Most governors have this power with regard to offenses against individual states. Conviction in an impeachment proceeding is not covered by the clemency power, because the only penalty in that situation is removal from office.

A pardon is a complete forgiveness and theoretically restores an individual to the status held before the offense was allegedly committed. An amnesty is a pardon granted to a group or class of alleged offenders. A commutation of sentence simply terminates a sentence before its completion, without a pardon. A reprieve is a delay in the execution of a sentence. A president cannot of course, personally review the many hundreds of applications for clemency but must be guided primarily by the reviews and recommendations of officers charged with this responsibility in the Department of Justice.

On the Sunday morning of September 8, 1974, President Ford took even his own staff by surprise with the announcement of a pardon for former President Nixon "for all offenses against the United States . . . which he has committed or may have committed or taken part in during his years as President." He acted, he said, because it was time to put the whole Watergate affair behind us and because his predecessor had already suffered enough. (Ford had indicated at an earlier date that a pardon would be inappropriate.) Instead of closing the door on the episode, this action unleashed a torrent of protest throughout the country. Many who would not have objected to a

*See Chapter 12 for more detailed discussion of these powers.

pardon if the former president had been tried and convicted on criminal charges considered a pardon at this time a frustration of normal processes and a further whitewash. Most significant, the public's sense of justice was offended by a situation in which underlings were being sent to prison while the man at the top went free. Nor were most sympathetic to the argument of Nixon's having already paid a great price: the price was principally removal from office, which was not a possession or right but a public trust (and one that had been violated). Should it be accepted, for example, that if a bank president and a junior clerk in the bank are both found guilty of embezzlement, the bank president should receive the lesser penalty or none at all because his public disgrace is greater and he has more to lose? Acceptance of the pardon, President Ford indicated, was obviously tantamount to an admission of guilt, but despite its acceptance Nixon continued to insist that he had committed no crime.

At a later date President Ford entered another highly emotional field by offering a very limited amnesty for Vietnam draft evaders and deserters. The record might be cleared by swearing allegiance and performing up to twenty-four months' alternative service if required. Since most considered theirs to have been an act of conscience that, they contended, had subsequently been proved justified, the number accepting on those terms was relatively small. President Carter, who promised during his campaign a general amnesty for draft evaders of the 1964–1973 period as a means of helping to heal the nation's wounds, brooked severe criticism and made that his first official act following his inauguration. A few months later Congress prohibited the use of Justice Department funds to implement the program, but this action was largely symbolic.

THE PRESIDENT AS CHIEF LEGISLATOR

Although our most common designation for the president is that of "chief executive," we do not evaluate presidential performance primarily on administrative ability. Distinctions between greatness and mediocrity rest largely on presidential success as policy leader of the nation, ability to sense and give direction to the goals of the people. The president is not a member of the legislature, as are chief executives in parliamentary systems, but his legislative influence, both formal and informal (that is, both legal and political), is great.

THE PRESIDENT'S PROGRAM IN CONGRESS

A principal means by which the president may influence legislation is the power to recommend policy to Congress, exercised not only in the constitutionally established state of the Union message but in any number of communications throughout the year. It is expected that the president will submit at the opening of each session of Congress a series of recommendations representing his and his party's program of action for the nation. The state of the Union message has become much more a policy statement than a review of the past; it is delivered to Congress but is at the same time a powerful appeal for popular support.

This series of proposals, supplemented from time to time throughout the session by special messages, is a major part of the agenda of Congress. Congress ordinarily does not accept the entire package, but all the president's proposals are given serious consideration. Administration measures, as such proposals are termed, are often given favored treatment, which varies, of course, according to the party composition of Congress, the effectiveness of its leadership, the popularity of the president and his program with the public, and the length of time the president has been in office. Traditionally a president has the best chance of getting a program enacted during the honeymoon period, the congressional session immediately following his election.

Although the bulk of specific individual communications to Congress are in writing, modern-day presidents ordinarily deliver the

President Carter addressing a joint session of Congress.

Official White House Photograph

state of the Union message orally before a joint session of the two houses (a tradition since Wilson, broken only at the beginning of Nixon's second term). This practice places great emphasis on the recommendations and creates a dramatic event attracting public attention and providing the president with an opportunity to build popular backing. Other personal appearances before Congress are usually limited to national emergencies. In times of crisis or when announcements of major importance are to be made, a president may also make a televised report to the nation. Prime time is made available by the networks whenever the president requests it. The importance automatically attached to a presidential statement guarantees a vast audience and represents a significant if indirect method by which the president may bring pressure to bear on Congress.

The Constitution authorizes the president to call Congress into special session, a power of less consequence now that Congress ordinarily stays in session most of each year. The president, however, has no power to control the agenda of a special session, as a number of governors do, though recommendations can be made. A call is usually for one or more fairly specific purposes, but Congress may or may not do anything about them. The feasibility of such a move depends entirely on the circumstances of the times. President Truman used a call to special session in 1948 after the party nominating conventions to dramatize what he termed the "do-nothing" character of the Eightieth Congress, and he successfully made the "do-nothing Congress" into a major issue of the subsequent campaign.

VETO POWER

One of the most familiar presidential prerogatives is the veto power, which in effect gives the president a potential voting power equal to the votes of one less than two-thirds of the members of each house. It may be rather rarely exercised, but the possibility is always present. In order to become law, all legislation (with rare exceptions) must be signed by the president after passing both houses of Congress; the president approves most legislation. A veto is a formal refusal to approve, a statement of the president's objections being returned with the bill to Congress. If both houses, despite his objections, then repass the bill by a two-thirds vote, it becomes law, but that two-thirds vote under the circumstances of presidential opposition is usually difficult to achieve. Few vetoes are overridden. Because overriding is unusual and newsworthy, we hear much more about it and thus may be disproportionately impressed. Of course a president cannot personally study all legislation but receives analyses and recommendations continually from all executive departments and agencies as well as from the White House staff.

There are rare occasions when a president, being unhappy with a particular bill but finding it better than nothing, may express mild disapproval by allowing it to become law without his signature. This requires only that the ten days (excluding Sundays) allotted for consideration of a bill expire without his taking any action. But should this occur near the end of a legislative session, and should Congress adjourn during the ten days, a bill is killed absolutely by the president's refusal to sign. This so-called pocket veto (the president seemingly having pocketed the bill) is much more significant than many people assume, because a large volume of important legislation that has required extensive study and discussion or that has been long held up in committee is often passed in the closing days of a session. Vehement argument arose when President Nixon announced late in 1971 the pocket veto of a bill, passed by both houses almost unanimously, for grants to medical schools and hospitals to train more general practitioners. Congress was on a five-day Christmas recess when the ten days expired. Was this an "adjournment" that prevented return of the bill to Congress, in the meaning of the Constitution? President Ford sought to utilize the same tactic, but after losing court tests of the matter, initiated by Senator Edward Kennedy, he announced abandonment of pocket vetoes except at the ends of sessions.

In terms of total impact on the course of legislation, the threat of veto may be of greater consequence than an actual veto, which is a last resort. The veto threat can be most influential early in the legislative process. Put yourself for a moment in the position of a president. When you saw introduced legislation that you believed to be undesirable, would you wait for it to pass and then veto it? Or would you exert every effort to block or modify the bill before it came to that sort of showdown? In such circumstances a president's normal reaction is first to let the author of the bill and the chairman of the committee to which it has been referred know the nature of objections. They may at that point find it possible to make changes resolving the most serious differences. If not, the president may subsequently let it be known to the committee, probably through a member who is a close friend, that passage of the bill in its present form would, "to his deep regret," compel veto. Proponents of the bill then have a clear choice: they can continue trying to push the bill through, which will now be more difficult, and ultimately face the need for a two-thirds vote to override a veto, or they can amend the bill to meet some of or all the president's objections and thus at least neutralize opposition. Most of the time the president does not need formally to put Congress on notice, for the mere statement of his concern or opposition makes his position clear.

The president's veto power is an all-or-nothing matter, since bills must be accepted or rejected in their entirety. This means that the president may be forced to swallow disliked features in otherwise desirable bills. This is particularly true of appropriation bills, which are usually passed in the last stages of a session or near the end of a fiscal year. The president must have the funds to operate government services, and Congress has at times added riders (unrelated legislation that it is suspected the president would not approve separately), hopeful that the president cannot afford to veto the appropriation bill. But presidents are quite aware that Congress cannot, any more than they, simply permit a necessary program to die. Presidents have on a few occasions accepted a bill but announced that there were certain features they did not intend to enforce or money appropriated that they did not intend to spend.

To deal with such problems, the governors of forty-one of the states are authorized to exercise an item veto in regard to appropriation bills, "blue penciling" and sending back to the legislature sections of a bill while approving the rest. This represents a considerable increase in executive power and responsibility, justified largely in the name of economy. The item veto may also result in some buck-passing, when a legislature approves items to please interest groups, confident that these particular items will be vetoed by the executive. There have been frequent recommendations to grant the president an item-veto power, but Congress so far has not been inclined to view with enthusiasm proposals to strengthen the presidency in its relations with the legislature.

THE POWER TO PERSUADE

The many informal means of influencing legislation (exercising the power to persuade) available to the chief executive are often more significant than some of the formal ones. The ability to command a national audience and thus appeal "over the heads" of Congress to the public has already been mentioned. This power was made most effective by the advent of television, although the device was perfected by Franklin D. Roosevelt with his famous "fireside chats" over radio. His mastery of this approach was such that some opponents flatly refused to listen to the chats, admitting that they soon found themselves agreeing with him.

A related device also developed in its modern form by Roosevelt is the presidential press conference, now considered virtually integral in governing the United States. It places the president in a highly exposed position, subject to persistent and sharp questioning on every conceivable topic; even a response of "no comment" to a question becomes grounds for speculation. But it is also another means of reaching the public, of pushing Congress, and of stimulating administrative agencies or pressure groups. President Eisenhower permitted the taping of press conferences for later broadcast after editing. President Kennedy moved a step further by permitting live telecasting. President Johnson preferred brief conferences, called on the spur of the moment, and President Nixon used both of the latter approaches, though he cut down sharply the number of press conferences. Greater frequency and ease of communication were restored by President Ford and were continued and expanded by President Carter.

Still other techniques for focusing public attention on a particular problem, for building popular support for a policy, and thus indirectly for bringing pressure on Congress are the appointment of a presidential task force or commission and the calling of a White House conference of specialized persons from across the country. These can be useful, but they are also inherently risky. The widely publicized report of the commission or conference may make recommendations of a nature contrary to the president's policy or at least of an insupportable kind or magnitude.

Effective influence on members of Congress, however, is far less likely to be exerted in mass efforts than in person-to-person contacts. The prestige of the presidency and the attendant publicity of an invitation to the White House and a presidential request for assistance can be seductive. It is not solely because presidents are normally gregarious people that they entertain so often. Members of Congress may be present at breakfast, lunch, or dinner for exchanges of views and the subtle reciprocal influence that takes place under

President Carter fields questions at a press conference.

Official White House Photograph

such circumstances. (Most people seem more amenable to reason when they are being fed.) In any walk of life it is well recognized that far more can be accomplished by spending a few minutes of conversation over a cup of coffee than by writing interoffice memoranda for weeks. In addition to the merits of the case at hand, long-time personal friendships may be called upon, the needs of the party emphasized, the possible advantages to a legislator's district noted.

The role of the president as head of his party normally has some effect on his fellow partisans in Congress. Most members of Congress, though not all, feel some degree of commitment to the well-being of the party. Further, the visible support of the president may be extremely helpful to their own re-election. Patronage is not the weapon it once was, but the president's appointing power may still be important to many members. Moreover, there are a number of other ways in which a president can be helpful to cooperative legislators, not least in budgetary allocations favorable to a district. They know full well the dangers of incurring the displeasure of a president. The member who has been a consistent problem to the president and seeks an irrigation project, a new post office facility, or expanded defense contracts may discover that funds for these purposes are strangely lacking.

It would be naive to overlook the fact that the various administrative agencies under the president's control also wield influence. Their actions and services have an impact on the legislators at home, and many of the agencies have their own constituencies—sizable and important interest groups—that may help put pressure on the legislature. Any agency of size has its own lobbyists on Capitol Hill, although they are not so labeled, and staff members who devote much attention to acting on the requests and otherwise serving the needs of members of Congress. Legislators and administrative agencies can be and are of considerable help to one another. The presidential power to persuade, then, extends itself in many directions.

Finally, it should be recognized that a sort of quasi-legislative function is continually performed by agencies of the executive branch in the exercise of their rule-making power. As noted earlier, Congress must legislate in fairly broad terms, establishing policy and setting the boundaries within which the administration can act in carrying out that policy. The detailed rules and regulations for day-to-day operation are written by the administrative agency concerned with the particular program. These range from purely procedural matters, such as prescribing the form on which one applies for a social security number, to major regulatory controls, such as fixing rates and specifying standards of service on railroads and airlines or stipulating health standards and quality grades for the inspection of meat. Administrative rules and regulations are published in the *Federal Register* and have the force of law. Contrary to what some people assume, the development of important rules is by no means an arbitrary matter; it is normally a thorough process involving extensive preliminary consultation with people who will be affected as well as a careful determination of the public interest.

RELATIONS BETWEEN THE PRESIDENT AND CONGRESS

In a system of separation of powers in which the executive is independently elected, some degree of friction or conflict among the branches of government is inevitable. The president and members of Congress are elected on quite different bases, and different alignments of voters are necessary for success. The president has a national constituency and usually a predominantly national view; senators and representatives have a state or (even smaller) district constituency and thus have on some issues a more parochial view. The position of chief executive is by its nature one of an activist: the president recommends ideas, initiates policy, leads a political party, enlists support for programs, and takes responsibility for accomplishment. The natural motivation of a large collegial body like a legislature is to keep what exists unless and until there is compelling reason and pressure to change. The complex machinery of the legislative process does not move easily, and once a settled question is reopened there may be all manner of unforeseen results. Where there is a party or ideological difference between the two branches, the frictions are likely to increase.

These differences and the resulting conflicts are not necessarily all bad. It is possible to argue that they may produce wise decision making. Certainly they are part of the cherished American tradition of balance, though they can also produce frustration. The preservation of this delicate balance results in continual pulling and hauling between the president and Congress, insofar as each tends to believe that its prerogatives are threatened by an expansion of power in the other branch. Especially in times of crisis, whether military or economic, there is a natural expansion of executive power because executive action is the central need. In fact, in a crisis Congress ordinarily delegates additional powers to the president. After the crisis, the pendulum swings back, and Congress reasserts its independence of action.

CONFLICT OVER WAR POWERS

From 1970 onward the Senate devoted frequent and lengthy attention to a struggle with the president over presidential freedom of military action in Vietnam and Cambodia and its own right to be consulted.

Opponents of the war contended that executive action such as Nixon had taken was illegal without specific authorization by Congress, while the president relied for justification on his constitutional prerogative as commander in chief and his inherent obligation to protect the nation and American personnel abroad. The Senate sought repeatedly to use the congressional power of the purse to restrict the president's actions, even setting dates beyond which no further war expenditures could be made, but it could not gain majority support in the House.

Following the accomplishment of a presumed peace in Vietnam and the return of American troops and prisoners, the sentiment of both the public and Congress was overwhelmingly against further military involvement in Southeast Asia. Continuation of massive bombing in Cambodia and funding of Thai mercenaries in Laos, despite a specific prohibition in a defense appropriation act, therefore precipitated a kind of ultimate confrontation between the two branches. This time the House agreed to an outright ban on further money for the Cambodian bombing, whereupon the Defense Department indicated that it would simply transfer funds from other accounts for this purpose. When that too was banned, the president announced that he would veto the congressional actions on Cambodia, arguing that he would be deprived of all effective bargaining power for achieving a peace settlement in that country. In a test of will over where the superior power lay, the president finally gave ground, and a face-saving compromise was agreed upon, whereby the final bombing date was fixed and the president was required to secure congressional approval for extension. Although this obviously also eliminated any bargaining power based on force, he made no request for extension. The principle established was of no small significance, but the episode surely did not mark the end of executive-legislative tensions over this question. A few months later, Congress, overriding a presidential veto, imposed a sixty-day limit on the president's power to commit troops abroad without congressional approval. (This will be discussed at greater length in Chapter 12.)

IMPOUNDMENT

Another area of perennial executive-legislative conflict has also to do with the power of the purse. While it is true that only Congress can appropriate money and can thus limit the president, it has been questionable whether the president can also limit Congress by refusing to spend money it has appropriated. The issue is hardly new. Jefferson was the first to balk, refusing to pay certain officials. In more modern times, Truman refused to increase the Air Force from forty-eight to fifty-eight groups. Kennedy did not spend certain funds on weapons development, and Johnson did not allow the

Pentagon to build a new type of plane that it desired, although in all cases Congress had appropriated funds specifically for those purposes.

Each such case was, however, a rather isolated instance, so that prolonged battles did not develop. The matter came to a head during the second Nixon administration, when the president announced that he would veto any appropriations exceeding his budget proposals if he considered them seriously inflationary and that, if they were passed over his veto, he would simply impound (set aside and refuse to spend) the funds. The congressional majority reacted with indignation, pointing out the president's constitutional obligation to "take care that the laws be faithfully executed." It was particularly incensed because it felt that the president considered relatively modest amounts for environmental protection or meeting domestic social needs to be dangerously inflationary, while multibillion-dollar military appropriations were not. His contention in return was that military expenditures were vital and unavoidable, that reasonably adequate and increasing amounts were being spent on social programs, and that somebody had to hold the line on government spending to prevent runaway inflation.

The issue reached a climax early in 1973 when the president vetoed a series of appropriations bills and announced the impounding of a variety of funds for housing, pollution control, agriculture, highways, and social welfare. He withheld, for example, $6 billion of an $11-billion two-year appropriation for improved sewage treatment to correct water pollution, although his veto of this bill had been massively overridden, with a great many of his party deserting him on the vote. Congress sought to insert in subsequent legislation language specifically directing that all money appropriated by the bill be spent, but this had no apparent new effect. Various groups thereupon began to bring the third branch of government into the fray. The state of Missouri, for instance, sued for the release of money allocated to it from the Highway Trust Fund, and the Eighth Circuit Court of Appeals ultimately ruled the withholding illegal. In rapid succession other courts ruled on comparable matters. Finally in 1975 a unanimous Supreme Court held that President Nixon had exceeded his authority when he refused three years earlier to allocate to the states $9 billion in water pollution funds (*Train* v. *City of New York*). The Congressional Budget and Impoundment Control Act of 1974 presumably virtually eliminates any unilateral impoundment.

EXECUTIVE PRIVILEGE

In a system of separation of powers, it is natural for each branch of the government jealously to guard its prerogatives and independence. As a part of that protective reaction, presidents have from time to time refused Congress access to certain documents or other information on the grounds that internal decision making of the executive branch was involved and that if Congress could pry into such matters at will, it would clearly destroy the equality of the branches. For the most part, it has been assumed, the branches would cooperate fully in the exchange of information, but presidents retain the right to decide when some item—details of the current negotiations on a treaty with another nation, for example—must remain confidential. Likewise, it has been contended, if the president is to be truly independent in making necessary decisions, advice from personal staff must not be subject to disclosure. Any such refusals of information to the other branches are termed a claim of executive privilege.

The legitimacy of such privilege under certain circumstances has been widely accepted, and Congress has not seriously contested most claims, even though disagreements over the justification in individual situations are understandably common. The doctrine was intended never as an extension to the presidency of an unlimited and undefined royal prerogative but simply as a practical matter of independence relative to the president's specific constitutional responsibilities. As has been noted previously, the Constitution's framers obviously did not intend to create branches of government isolated from each other or totally independent, for they also established the elaborate system of checks and balances.

As it did in so many ways, the Watergate affair sharpened executive-legislative conflict over the doctrine of executive privilege, ultimately resulting in a confrontation of historical proportions. While asserting that executive privilege might apply to some matters involved in the investigations, President Nixon stated at the outset that the claim would certainly not be used in connection with any criminal actions. Moreover, he said, "executive privilege will not be used as a shield to prevent embarrassing information from being made available, but will be used only in those particular instances in which disclosure would harm the public interest." Nevertheless, although it appeared that White House aides might be implicated, it was announced that they would not be permitted to testify before the Senate investigating committee, a position from which the president subsequently backed away.

Other controversies arose over specific memoranda and the like, but the real crisis emerged when the story surfaced that the White House possessed tapes of all conversations in the executive offices in which the president had been involved. Presumably these would show the accuracy, perhaps truth or falsity, of much crucial and conflicting testimony based on recollection. In particular they would sustain or disprove President Nixon's statement that he had known nothing about the cover-up and the involvement of White House staff until the middle of the spring of 1973. Both the Senate investigating committee and the government's special prosecutor sought access to a few tapes covering specific conversations about which there had been significant testimony. The president, however, despite the risk of public reaction that he had something to hide, refused to make them available to either, indicating that the tapes did not in fact resolve the central issues and that relevant material was inevitably intertwined with a great deal of necessarily confidential conversation. He likewise refused to permit the committee to listen to the tapes in a session closed to press and public or to permit the chairman and vice chairman to hear selected portions. He did state that he had listened to some of the tapes in question and that they substantiated his own public statements on the matter but that others might place different interpretations on words spoken in a general discussion.

With the breakdown of negotiations to secure the tapes, both the committee and the prosecutor served subpoenas upon the president of the United States, only the second time in history that such a step had been taken. Since he continued to refuse, there occurred the unique circumstance of one branch filing a lawsuit against another. There were those who wondered whether Congress was wise to accept the premise that the judicial branch was entitled to arbitrate a conflict between the two other branches or whether it should not have relied exclusively on its own powers. In any case the die was cast, and the president responded through his attorneys to the trial judge that he was "answerable to the nation but not to the courts": "The courts, a coequal but not a superior branch of government, are not free to probe the mental processes and the private confidences of the president and his advisers." The same principle, of course, applied to Congress. Moreover, he said, even if it meant that some guilty persons went free, "the public interest in a conviction, important as it is, must yield to the public interest in preserving the confidentiality of the president's office."

The special prosecutor, who at the time of his appointment had been promised complete independence and full cooperation, insisted that access to the tapes was vital to the accomplishment of the responsibility vested in him and the grand jury, and a court ordered the president to comply. President Nixon directed Attorney General Elliot Richardson to order Special Prosecutor Cox to make no further attempt to secure by judicial processes any tapes, notes, or memoranda of presidential conversations. Richardson responded that at the time of his confirmation as attorney general he had given solemn assurances to the Senate that he would allow the special prosecutor full independence and that he could not in conscience act in a contrary fashion.

The sensational events that followed on the fateful weekend of October 20, commonly referred to as "the Saturday Night Massacre," took Washington and the nation by surprise. The president called in the attorney general and ordered him to fire Cox, whereupon

Richardson, unable to comply, resigned. When the order was next transmitted to Deputy Attorney General William Ruckelshaus, he likewise resigned, and the directive was finally carried out by Solicitor General Bork. The nation reacted with an almost unprecedented outburst of indignation. As Alexander Haig, the president's chief of staff, conceded, the White House had misjudged the public temper; and as what he termed the "firestorm" mounted, the president was forced to retreat. Three days later Nixon's attorney appeared in Judge Sirica's court, where he was expected to argue reasons for refusal to accept the court order, but he stunned the hushed courtroom by announcing quietly that the president would surrender the nine tapes in question, which he had previously sworn never to do. Shortly thereafter it was further announced that a new special prosecutor, Leon Jaworski, had been appointed and that, moreover, he had been promised the very independence of which Cox had just been deprived.

But the end was not yet. A week after agreeing to surrender of the tapes, the White House announced that two of them "did not exist" (although it had been known for months which ones were wanted), and the two missing tapes covered periods of crucial conversations. Again a public furor was fanned. The president had hardly finished telling a governors' conference that there would be "no more bombshells" when it was disclosed that in the middle of one vital tape there was an eighteen-and-a-half-minute gap in the conversation, resulting from what two panels of experts concluded was a manual erasure. With this the credibility of the president plummeted, and his approval rating in the polls reached a level lower than that of any president in history, since polling began.

There were subsequent further confrontations with the new special prosecutor over refusals of requested materials. But taking over the center of the stage were the investigations by the House Judiciary Committee on the question of whether President Nixon should be impeached. Repeated subpoenas from the committee were defied, and this refusal of cooperation became one of the grounds on which impeachment was ultimately recommended. This particular question of legislative-executive conflict thus never was resolved by the courts, Congress relying instead on its own processes. The ability of a president to withhold, solely on grounds of executive privilege, properly subpoenaed materials from prosecutors and grand juries in a criminal proceeding was, however, unanimously denied by the Supreme Court.

IMPROVING EXECUTIVE-LEGISLATIVE COOPERATION

Despite these situations, everyone concedes that the two branches ought not primarily to be competitors but that they are charged with a common responsibility, which necessitates a reasonably high degree of cooperation. A number of suggestions have been made as to how this executive-legislative harmony might be increased, but most have not met with wide support. In fact some steps appear to work in the opposite direction, such as the more and more frequent practice of Congress's writing into legislation provisions giving itself (usually either house) power to invalidate by a resolution, which is not subject to veto, any administrative regulation issued under that particular law. Presidents have strongly resisted the development of this "congressional veto," which they see as an invasion of their authority to execute the laws, and the constitutionality is being challenged in the courts.

The most extreme proposal for improving cooperation is that for changing to a parliamentary system comparable to the British pattern, but acceptance of so complete an alteration either by government officials or by the public is remote. Some have suggested modified versions, such as selecting all or part of the Cabinet from among members of Congress or giving to the president power to dissolve Congress and call new elections when Congress rejects much of the president's program. The former proposal would certainly create much greater unity in some senses but probably a new complexity of relationships as well. The dissolution power is a means of going back to the voters for a mandate when the government is stalemated, and the implication is presumably that if the voters sustain the position of Congress, the president should resign. At this point the vice president would hardly seem a logical successor, and the speaker of the House may or may not be. An interim presidential election would be no small undertaking. To be meaningful a dissolution would have to include all members of both houses, which is complicated by the overlapping terms of senators. Perhaps much of the goal of this suggestion could be accomplished by electing all members of Congress for the same term and at the same time as the president, it thus being somewhat more likely to have the same party holding responsibility in both branches. A four-year term for House members, the elections to be held in presidential election years, was proposed unsuccessfully by President Johnson, and the principle was supported also by President Nixon.

A more modest proposal offered rather frequently would grant to Cabinet members the privilege of the floor in both houses of Congress, where they could participate in debate and be subject to interrogation. This would make the relations more direct and open, but Cabinet members, as we have seen, are not free agents but agents of the president; they would need to clear statements with him or at least be confident that their views were in accord with his. In practice, Cabinet members now appear regularly before committees of Congress, which is where much of the work is done.

The proposal with the greatest likelihood of acceptance is one to establish a joint executive-legislative council, meeting on a regular basis to screen proposed legislation, set priorities, coordinate efforts, and plan strategy for accomplishing a program. Several versions have been suggested, some consisting of the president and a few top advisers joined by the party leaders and key committee chairmen in each house, others consisting of a specially selected group of senior legislators, but in each the general pattern is the same. Most modern-day presidents have met fairly regularly with the legislative leadership, but these proposals would formalize the relation, which now depends entirely on the initiative and will of the president, and foster somewhat broader activities than is customary at present. An executive-legislative council would require no structural changes but could possibly have some impact on current congressional leadership practices.

Whatever the ultimate success of any such proposals, it can be assumed that some stresses between the two branches will continue, for the reasons previously advanced. There will be times when cooperation is not seen to be a primary objective, and one branch will conclude that its most vital role for a period is that of protecting the nation against the wrong-headedness of the other. Nevertheless, improved cooperation and more effective party responsibility are worthy goals. No doubt there will continue to be gradual increase in the powers of the presidency as conditions of the modern world create a great demand for effective executive leadership, but this does not in any sense mean that the legislative branch will wither on the vine. Tinkering with the machinery may now and then be useful, but each new president and Congress must gradually work out their own ways of getting along together, achieving constructive results, and easing the frictions that inevitably arise. Neither likes to be taken for granted, be surprised, or be abused in an effort to curry public favor; each is defensive of its prerogatives. Same-party control of the two branches is normally helpful but certainly provides no guarantee of automatic cooperation. As with most aspects of human relations, satisfactory harmony between the executive and legislative sides requires continuous careful cultivation by people who are both realistic and reasonable. The presidency and Congress have both proved to be institutions of tremendous adaptability in a country that has undergone almost incredibly rapid change.

A president is, in the nature of the position, supremely political. The point was effectively made by George Reedy, press secretary to President Johnson, in recent testimony against a proposal to establish a single six-year term for the president:

> Are presidents really more effective when they are separated from the political process? I doubt it. I think there is strong reason to believe that modern presidents can be effective only when they understand the political process thoroughly and engage in it enthusiastically. Presidents politic

all the time, not just to be re-elected but because there is no other way they can gain support for their programs. Effectiveness and political support are tied together and any effort to separate them will work against the interests of our nation.

The presidency is indeed the focal point of power in the American system, but it is also inevitably in the center of the storm. The potential for tremendous achievements of leadership lie ready to the president's hand, but if he should prove too small for the job, the nation and perhaps the world may be the worse. It remains also true that events over which he has little or no control may suddenly make of him either a hero or a bum. One may in fact be seen as both, all within an amazingly short period of time, and may be deeply loved and savagely attacked simultaneously. No one has caught better than John Steinbeck (writing primarily with President Johnson in mind at the time) this peculiar and unique relation between Americans and their president:

Not all our Presidents have been great, but when the need has been great we have found men of greatness. We have not always appreciated them; usually we have denounced and belabored them living, and only honored them dead. Strangely, it is our mediocre Presidents we honor during their lives.

The relationship of Americans to their President is a matter of amazement to foreigners. Of course we respect the office and admire the man who can fill it, but at the same time we inherently fear and suspect power. We are proud of the President, and we blame him for things he did not do. We are related to the President in a close and almost family sense; we inspect his every move and mood with suspicion. We insist that the President be cautious in speech, guarded in action, immaculate in his public and private life; and in spite of these imposed pressures we are avidly curious about the man hidden behind the formal public image we have created. We have made a tough, but unwritten code of conduct for him, and the slightest deviation brings forth a torrent of accusation and abuse.

The President must be greater than anyone else, but not better than anyone else. We subject him and his family to close and constant scrutiny and denounce them for things that we ourselves do every day. A Presidential slip of the tongue, a slight error in judgment—social, political, or ethical—can raise a storm of protest. We give the President more work than a man can do, more responsibility than a man should take, more pressure than a man can bear. We abuse him often and rarely praise him. We wear him out, use him up, eat him up. And with all this, Americans have a love for the President that goes beyond loyalty or party nationality; he is ours, and we exercise the right to destroy him.*

*From *America and Americans* by John Steinbeck. Copyright © 1966 by John Steinbeck. All rights reserved. Reprinted by permission of The Viking Press, Inc.

BASIC CONCEPTS AND TERMS

the burden and challenge of the
  presidency
rules of presidential succession
impeachment process and
  grounds
the imperial presidency
presidential symbolism
types of presidential character
executive powers of president
role of the Cabinet
presidential appointing power
advice and consent of the Senate
senatorial courtesy
presidential removal power
budget proposal power
pardon

amnesty
commutation
reprieve
state of the Union message
veto power
pocket veto
rider
item veto
power to persuade
rule-making power
war powers of president
impoundment
executive privilege
congressional veto
executive-legislative council

ADMINISTRATIVE POLITICS: THE MANAGEMENT OF MONEY AND PEOPLE

8

Under the broad executive authority of the president lies a vast administrative organization with the task of providing the multitude of day-to-day services of the central government. With approximately 2.8 million civilian employees and an annual budget of more than $500 billion, our national government qualifies as probably the largest administrative organization in the world (see Figure 8.1). In size, variety, and complexity it staggers the imagination. Yet to look at it as a single huge organization is in a sense highly misleading. We speak often of what "the government" is doing or might do, but in fact it never acts as a whole and no one ever has dealings with "the government" as a single entity. It functions through the actions of frequently small agencies or sections of agencies; the citizen actually and realistically sees government as the soil conservationist (in a farming area), the Old Age Insurance counselor, the Park Service ranger, the postal carrier, the Action volunteer, or, inevitably, the Internal Revenue Service.

Hence our discussion of administrative organization is primarily not about machinery but about people. People use administrative

FIGURE 8.1   Distribution of National Government Civilian Employment
(Estimate for Fiscal Year 1979)

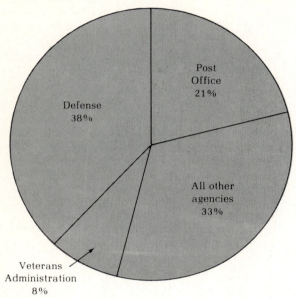

Source: Office of Management and Budget, *Special Analyses: Budget of the United States Government, Fiscal Year 1979,* Government Printing Office, Washington, D.C., 1978, p. 202.

structures, money, and communications systems as tools, to be sure, but the fundamental questions are always about values and social priorities: What *should* government be doing? Among the nation's many needs, which should come first? How can a job be accomplished most effectively? In what ways can we get the best return for the taxpayer's dollar? These questions involve matters of judgment on the part of the public, members of Congress, presidents, and judges, but also especially everyday decisions by the multitude of administrative officials.

THE POLITICAL ROLE OF ADMINISTRATIVE ORGANIZATIONS

Tradition has it that administrators are concerned exclusively with carrying out policy that is made by legislators, but such a view is a gross oversimplification. Administration does indeed have as its central responsibility the translation of legislative intent into practical services to citizens, but it also in reality has much to do with making and developing that policy.

Although final determinations rest with the legislature, much legislation is initiated by administrative agencies, and the necessary and ongoing process of revising and updating statutes depends considerably on the experience of people who have worked with these statutes over a period of time. Recommendations from the appropriate administrator are likely to make up much of the material with which the legislator must work, and the administrator is normally consulted at almost every stage of the process of formulating policy. Furthermore, every sizable agency has on its staff specialists in legislative relations, some of whom are in effect lobbyists for the agency and others who keep track of and analyze every bill that might have some effect on the agency.

It is true not only that administrative agencies exert vast influence on legislative policy making but also that they make a great deal of policy themselves. For example, it is obviously necessary that Congress legislate for the most part in fairly broad terms, setting forth objectives and general procedures. Within this framework much specific policy for day-to-day public services must be made. Moreover, a large amount of rule-making authority is commonly delegated to certain agencies, most notably the regulatory commissions.

Most administrative organizations have special constituencies, such as business associations for the Department of Commerce or Legionnaires for the Veterans' Administration, which can be counted on to mobilize pressure on Congress and the president when needed. In fact, the mere existence of such organized interest groups, representing sizable blocs of votes and capable of providing potent favorable or adverse publicity on elected officeholders and campaign funds, is influential even without overt action. Agencies that lack a strong domestic constituency, notably the State Department, are at a serious disadvantage. Competitive mobilization of support, from outside and inside the government, is a necessarily constant feature of administrative life, as each agency struggles to protect its sphere of responsibility and make its voice heard above others as new priorities are being established during each season of budget preparation. Most also devote attention to the related effort to build a favorable image of their activities in the public mind, none more than the Department of Defense, which annually spends some $30 million on public relations campaigns.

Although they are under the direction of the president, administrative agencies commonly have extremely cozy relations with certain powerful congressional leaders and with the committees with which they must regularly deal, especially the subcommittees of the two appropriations committees, which handle their budget requests. This is a matter of mutual political advantage for they can be useful to each other. While there may or may not be a direct quid pro quo, agencies hope for favorable treatment from friendly legislators both on desired program bills and on budget. Their friendship may be nurtured by locating government facilities or maintaining a particularly high standard of service in the right congressional districts, expeditiously handling congressional requests for information on behalf of constituents, and so forth. Thanks to a former senator of great seniority who held the right chairmanships, the state of Georgia has so many military and naval installations as to be wryly referred to in some circles as "the U.S.S. Georgia." Close personal relations are built over the years; presidents and Cabinet officers come and go, but senior committee members and civil servants may work closely together for decades. In fact, one of the most familiar patterns is that of the "triangular alliance": an intimate cooperative relationship among an administrative agency, a congressional committee majority, and an interest group, for each of which primary concern focuses in the same problem area.

Of particular irritation to presidents and others charged with general administrative responsibility is the practice of many committees in insisting that administrative agencies within their sphere of policy or financial authority secure advance "clearance" of all important administrative decisions from the committee chairman. Thus Representative Jamie Whitten of Mississippi, long-time chairman of the subcommittee on agricultural appropriations, has sometimes been jestingly referred to as the "permanent secretary of agriculture." Congress, to be sure, has a responsibility to oversee the quality of administration and to insure conformity to the purposes of the legislation that established the program (a responsibility that is rather spottily performed). In addition to the possibility of appropriation cuts, a committee has other tools to force administrative agencies to comply with its wishes. Basic is the prospect of altering the law under which the agency operates. More immediate is the threat of a congressional hearing on a specific issue that will be time-consuming, perhaps agonizing, and will draw extensive publicity. In extreme cases there may be a request for authority to conduct a full-scale legislative investigation. Yet syrup may still be more effective: an administrator is no less susceptible than other humans are to praise by committee members in the presence of the press.

Nevertheless, large administrative organizations have their own momentum and, in practice, often a high degree of independence of action. They make long-term commitments. Their established modes of thinking and behavior are extremely difficult to change, even by a president possessed of considerable zeal for that change. Given their size and complexity, the procedure of decision making within the organizations is an elaborate political process not too unlike that which occurs within Congress.

ADMINISTRATIVE ORGANIZATION

KINDS OF ADMINISTRATIVE BODIES

There is no single structural pattern of administration in the national government, but the various forms fall generally into three or four categories. Most familiar are the great departments, like Commerce, Treasury, Justice, and Health, Education, and Welfare, whose secretaries are members of the president's Cabinet. Some of these, such as Justice, are engaged in a single function, but many are in effect giant "holding companies" giving central direction to a number of large semi-autonomous agencies whose functions are in some way related to each other. The Department of Agriculture, for example, embraces such subunits as the Consumer and Marketing Service, whose activities range from meat inspection to school lunch programs; the Rural Electrification Administration; the Soil Conservation Service; the Agricultural Stabilization and Conservation Service, concerned principally with price support; and no fewer than fifteen other agencies.

There are also several other administrative units, such as the General Services Administration and the Veterans' Administration, organized like the departments but lacking Cabinet status, thus often termed quasi-departments. Where the task to be performed is an activity very much like a business, such as a transportation system or the development and sale of electric power, the structure used has sometimes been the government corporation, of which the best known examples are the U.S. Postal Service and the Tennessee Valley Authority. A government corporation is controlled by a board of directors appointed by the president, which customarily hires a professional general manager to supervise day-to-day operations. Finally, there are the various independent boards and commissions, many of which are primarily regulatory agencies, such as the Federal Communications Commission and the Interstate Commerce Commission. Bodies of this kind, with several members, are considered especially appropriate for jobs that are quasi-legislative and quasi-judicial in nature—that is, they make rules and settle disputes in the particular area being regulated.* The commission bears the responsibility for actions under its jurisdiction, but it is of course aided by professional staff.

Different kinds of organization have naturally been evolved to meet varying kinds of needs, and one kind is not necessarily better than another except in terms of a particular purpose. Nor is it ordained that every agency preserve forever its original form; the

---

*Other administrative organizations also have rule-making authority, within broad guidelines set by Congress. The range of rules that can be made is large, and criminal penalties may be attached to violations.

Post Office was only rather recently transformed from a department into a semi-independent corporation. Every president leaves a mark on administrative structure, and in recent years none did more so than President Nixon. His most notable (and controversial) moves were in the direction of downgrading the Cabinet departments and concentrating decision making on the most critical and important areas of policy in a greatly expanded White House staff. Much of the real power over foreign policy, for example, moved from the State Department to the president's adviser on national security matters; planning for environmental improvement shifted from the Department of the Interior to the White House Domestic Council; a good deal of the policy development in response to urban crisis was concentrated in the hands of the president's urban affairs counselor rather than in the departments of Housing and Urban Development and of Health, Education, and Welfare. Most of those shifts have since been reversed, and President Carter gave more independence to Cabinet officers than any president in years. Under Nixon there was also created a super-Cabinet-level agency known as the Office of Management and Budget, which supersedes (and in practice is perhaps not too different from) the former Bureau of the Budget and whose head is intended to be a general manager with responsibility not only for overseeing budget development and control but also for seeing that presidential directives are carried out and for propelling newly authorized programs into action.

FORMAL AND INFORMAL ORGANIZATION

In any organization there is likely to be some difference between the formal pattern of hierarchy, which presumably delineates the internal power structure, and the way things actually are done. There are individuals who do not necessarily hold the formal leadership positions but who by reason of their personal attractiveness, ability to articulate forcefully, and role in nonofficial organizations may exercise great influence on their fellow workers and determine the group's understanding of what constitutes "a good day's work." This informal organization, which denotes the structure of influence and leadership apart from the official structure, is of considerable importance. Awareness of its nature and potential is often as vital to successful administration as any other aspect of the job, and such awareness is likewise necessary for an accurate understanding of how policy is actually made.

But the workability of formal organization is also a matter of interest, especially the way in which different elements of an entire government relate and divide responsibility. The natural tendency has been to create new organizations as new government functions have been undertaken, while at the same time there has been a gradual expansion of the activities of existing units. Over the years, in an organization the size of the United States government, a certain amount of duplication and conflict result. Some corrections can be accomplished by executive order; others require congressional action. For a number of years presidents have been authorized to submit reorganization plans that go into effect in sixty days unless vetoed by either house of Congress. That authority must be renewed from time to time, and Congress is rarely enthusiastic about granting so much freedom of action to the executive. President Carter at the beginning of his administration faced something of a struggle before persuading Congress to grant an extension.

GOVERNMENT REORGANIZATION

As noted previously, most presidents undertake efforts at streamlining what always appears to them to be a rather unwieldy bureaucracy. Probably the most significant of the broad-gauge reorganization efforts was the work of the first Hoover Commission, created by President Truman and headed by former President Herbert Hoover. Its task forces probed into all aspects of national government and developed extensive recommendations toward more efficient organization. What proved notable in this case was that ultimately about three-fourths of the recommendations were put into effect, although some of the most important ones were neglected. Agencies opposed to change and having strong interest-group support, such as the Veterans' Administration, are able to muster congressional allies and stave off restructuring that might affect their independence of action or alter their jurisdiction.

Attempts at reorganization have often been useful, but of course study groups are as fallible as any other group and no magic or validity automatically attaches to their proposals. Often the press acts as if the recommendations had been pronounced from heaven and frequently attacks public officials having the temerity to question any specific recommendation. Moreover, administrative reform does not fan a wild light of excitement in the eye of the average citizen; the only way to get the public interested is to press upon the pocketbook nerve, which is often the most exposed. Recommendations are normally touted as great money savers, and considerable public misunderstanding often results because of such promises. First, the savings are likely to be in securing more and better service for the same amount of money, and although this is clearly a saving in business terms, the average taxpayer is merely frustrated when the tax bill is not reduced.

More important, many people are unconsciously misled because they assume when they hear that seemingly vast savings could be achieved, say, in the operation of the Fish and Wildlife Service of the

"—uh—Don't expect the walls to come tumbling down right away"

Department of the Interior, that these savings will result in distinct reductions in the national budget. Although such economy might be worthwhile if it could be achieved without injury to a valuable public service, it would be naive to view such a step as having any visible impact on the total budget. The Fish and Wildlife Service could be completely eliminated without perceptible effect on government spending totals; indeed, elimination of the entire Department of the Interior would result in only a very minor budgetary change.

So-called sunset laws as an idea for controlling bureaucracy have attracted widespread popular, interest-group, and legislative support in recent years, becoming in fact something of a fad. In essence, such laws simply provide that all executive branch agencies, their programs, and their appropriations automatically expire at the end of rather brief, fixed time periods (six years in new national legislation) unless Congress takes affirmative action to re-establish them. Thus periodic regular legislative scrutiny and budget review is presumably forced.

Such a system has yet to prove its workability. Detailed study of every program and "zero-base budgeting" (compelling a justification of every item of each budget request, starting from scratch), which was strongly advocated by President Carter, involves a staggering workload for already busy congressional committees. Is the process really necessary for every agency? No one, for example, really thinks that air traffic control is going to be allowed to expire. But if some are not to be included, how is this determination to be made? Of something over 1,000 current budget accounts, 14 of them represent 50 per cent of the expenditures, and 998 of them are responsible for only 10 per cent. Furthermore, if every program must be periodically re-established, the blocking potential and bargaining power of determined minorities in Congress will be magnified immensely— the use of delaying procedural technicalities, the power of committee and subcommittee chairmen, the filibuster in the Senate, and the impact of presidential vetoes only begin the list. If all appropriations are to be regularly reconsidered, should that not be true also of so-called tax expenditures, the extensive array of deductions, credits, exclusions, and exemptions that constitute a loss to the treasury just as much as direct payments? Proposals to include these seem notably less attractive to many affluent and powerful individuals and groups.

THE CRUCIAL ROLE OF FINANCE

It is hardly news that in every aspect of life financial considerations often dominate or at least significantly modify our decisions as to what we would like to do, and government is no exception. Rarely can a new public policy be implemented simply because it is desirable. Unless it can be financed, a new program will not materialize. Where does a proposed policy fit into the scheme of relative priorities? Does the program have political support? Can it compete successfully for funds with long-established programs that have their own powerful constituencies? Can the additional money required be raised without serious political repercussions?

TAXING AND SPENDING POWERS

The taxing and spending powers of the national government are very broad. The tax restraints imposed by the Constitution are minimal and are mostly concerned with insuring that there will be no discrimination against any particular area of the country. In general, it is technically possible for Congress to tax almost any object at any

FIGURE 8.2   The Budget Dollar: Sources of United States Government
Revenue (Estimate for Fiscal Year 1979)

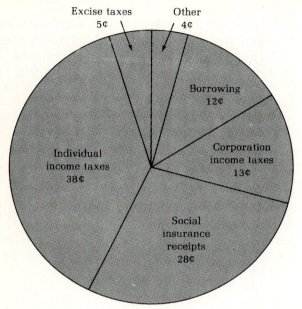

Source: Office of Management and Budget, *The Budget in Brief, Fiscal Year 1979*, Government
Printing Office, Washington, D.C., 1978, inside front cover.

rate, and for that matter both the nation and the states may tax the
same object at the same time, as is the case with gasoline. The
meaningful restraints are political and economic, and both are sufficient limitations. The spending power is in a sense even more
extensive, since Congress can spend funds in support of functions on
which it probably could not legislate directly. If we assume, for
instance, that the national government could not create and operate a
system of public education, that being a matter under state and local
jurisdiction, still the national government can and does allocate
money for the support of public education.

By far the greatest revenue producer for the national government is
the individual and corporate income tax (see Figure 8.2). Substantial
revenue also comes from inheritance taxes, customs duties, and
various excise taxes, which are taxes on the sale or use of a particular
item, be it cigarettes, air tickets, or telephone calls. The bulk of the
income of the national government is from taxes, although a fair
amount is derived from service charges, such as those for postal
service. Taxes are presumed always to exist for the purpose of
securing revenue, but some taxes are used also as a means of regulation, as is the case, for example, with the control of legal as compared

"Book me for 8 weeks in Paris and hang the expense"

with illegal sales of drugs. Although in the past the courts did strike down tax laws if it seemed that the actual purpose of a law was regulation rather than revenue, the modern practice is to accept a law that produces any revenue whatsoever, regardless of any regulatory effects. At one time the Supreme Court invalidated use of the taxing power to control child labor, on the grounds that the raising of revenue was not the true purpose of the law, but such an interpretation would almost certainly not prevail today.

Grumbling about taxes is at least as old as recorded history, but most reasonable people recognize that they are necessary. The significant questions deal with the kinds of taxes to be used, their fair distribution over the population, and the harmonizing of different kinds of taxes with each other. In the abstract, tax reform is always a popular theme, but trouble arises as soon as it is discovered that a reduction of the tax burden on certain people means that others will have to pay more. The most serious criticisms are directed at the exemptions, write-offs, and allowances that have made it possible for many wealthy individuals actually to pay little or no income taxes. In each of several recent years nearly three hundred individuals with incomes in excess of $100,000 paid no tax at all, and thousands more paid only a relative pittance. In the major tax revision act of 1976 Congress did succeed in placing some new restrictions on tax shelters and increasing the minimum tax now established to prevent wealthy persons from avoiding taxes altogether through extensive deductions. The system is still geared to the advantage of the business executive.

Popular criticism of loopholes and write-off techniques jumped sharply when it was disclosed that President Nixon had paid total national income taxes of only $5,969 for the three years 1970 through 1972. The payments in 1970 and 1971 were equivalent to those of a family of four with an income of $8,000. The Internal Revenue Service and congressional investigators concluded that some income, such as certain capital gains from sales of property, had not been reported, but the major action was disallowance of a claimed deduction of $482,018 for donation of his vice-presidential papers to the national archives. Whether or not done with the president's knowledge, the gift had been made after a change in the law that allowed such deductions (for items that obviously were public property), and the donation papers had been back-dated to make it appear legal. There were a variety of other disputed situations as well, but the upshot of the total investigation was an agreement by President Nixon to pay a total of more than $467,000 in back taxes and interest for the years 1969 through 1972. Because of large business equipment purchases in the year before he became president, Jimmy Carter owed no taxes for that year, but in the interest of public relations he submitted a voluntary payment of $6,000.

Tax policy is a continuous battleground on which powerful economic interests engage, and legislation in this area is so incredibly complex that Congress has often hesitated to embark on revisions. Recently it has been somewhat more willing to deal with the problem, in the face of widespread public protest bordering on a taxpayers' revolt.

The widely heralded "tax revolt" that spread across the nation in the wake of a successful 1978 tax limitation initiative measure in California began as an attack on local property tax rates but had far broader implications. Despite some of the accompanying rhetoric, it was basically a simple protest against high taxes rather than a move to cut governmental services or to remove inequities. Polls consistently showed that most persons voting for such measures also wanted a high level of public services continued and clung to a vague belief that the money would be found somewhere, especially if "waste" (usually undefined) were eliminated. The popular antitax sentiment was promptly seized upon by some politicians and party organizations as the key to election success, and the conservative push for less government and greater emphasis on regressive taxes received at least a temporary boost. Perhaps more than anything else the revolt demonstrated the need for what is known as the *indexing of tax rates*: automatic sliding adjustment of tax rates to stay in balance with changes in average income levels or property valuations, rather than allowing the rates to remain fixed while incomes and property values inflate. In a fixed rate situation a person's taxes may increase substantially with inflation, even though the individual's purchasing power remains static or actually declines.

Case Study
WELFARE PAYMENTS FOR THE RICH

I think most Americans would probably be intensely surprised to find in their morning's newspaper an account such as the following:

Washington, D.C.—Congress today completed action on the final part of a revolutionary welfare program that reverses the usual pattern and gives huge welfare payments to the super-rich but only pennies per week to the very poor.

Under the program, welfare payments averaging some $720,000 a year will go to the nation's wealthiest families—those with annual incomes of more than $1 million.

For the poorest families—those earning $3,000 a year or less—the welfare allowance will average $16 a year, or roughly 30 cents a week.

The program, enacted by Congress in a series of laws over a period of years, has come to be called the rich welfare program after its principal sponsor, Senator Homer A. Rich, who, in a triumphant news conference told newsmen that the $720,000 annual welfare allowance would give America's most affluent families "added weekly take-home pay of about $14,000. Or, to put it another way," the Senator added, "it will provide these families about $2,000 more spending money every day."

Total cost of the program—the most expensive welfare program ever voted—comes to $77.3 billion a year.

Political observers have been surprised by the manner in which this huge sum has been allocated. Experts have calculated that only about $92 million—about one-tenth of 1 percent of the total—will go to the 6 million poorest families in the country—the under $3,000 income group.

By contrast, experts said, Congress has voted about 24 times that

From testimony by Philip M. Stern, former legislative assistant to Henry M. Jackson and Paul H. Douglas, in *Hearings before the Subcommittee on Priorities and Economy in Government of the Joint Economic Committee*, 92d Cong., 1st sess., January 13, 14, and 17, 1972, pp. 74–77, 82–83.

amount, more than $2.2 billion, for families with incomes greater than $1 million a year. Informed government sources said there are roughly 3,000 such families in the United States.

Moreover, Congress has allocated nearly 15 percent of the total, more than $11 billion annually, in welfare payments to families with annual incomes of $100,000 or more. Revelation of this fact brought angry protests from consumer groups here in Washington who pointed out that this $11 billion outlay for the rich is five times the expenditures to provide food stamps for hungry poor families and 1,000 times the federal outlay for health programs for migrant farm workers.

Of greater consequence, political analysts here believe, is the potential discontent among the middle-classes, those in the $10,000 to $15,000 income group, for whom welfare payments under the Rich scheme will amount to $650 a year, or about $12.50 a week. While this is considerably more than the 30 cents a week allocated to the very poor, political pundits here feel that Congressmen who supported the Rich Plan might have trouble explaining to middle-class constituents why the very rich should receive welfare payments of $60,000 per month, in contrast to the $55 per month allocated to middle-income families.

Reporters asked Senator Rich whether the new plan would require wealthy families to work in order to receive their welfare payments, a usual requirement with most welfare programs. Senator Rich seemed puzzled by the question. "The rich? Work?" he said; "why, it hadn't occurred to me." Congressonal experts advised newsmen that the program contains no work requirement.

The new program promises to be one of the most controversial acts ever passed by Congress. Countering the protests from the poor, glittering names from among the superrich have showered Congress with praise. "These generous welfare payments will at long last give the wealthy families of this country the incentives they need to invest in American enterprise," said one Pittsburgh heir to a large fortune, who declined to be identified by name. "The public will soon realize," he added, "that this is just what America has needed to bring jobs and prosperity for all."

This view was reinforced by a spokesman for the Yacht Builders Association of America, who predicted a great resurgence in the yacht industry. Christopher P. Wainwright III, President of Luxurama, builder of luxury resort homes in the Bahamas, was similarly ebullient about the future of his company.

Admittedly, the above news story sounds implausible, if not unbelievable. Yet that news story is essentially true. The facts and figures in it are real. Such a system is, in fact, part of the law of the land.

Only the law isn't called a welfare law. . . .

It is the basic income tax law of the United States.

Now, since a tax law takes money from people rather than gives it to them, what connection does the tax law have with the topsy-turvy welfare system in the news story?

The connection lies in the way Congress has played fast and loose with the 16th amendment to the Constitution, the one that authorized the original income tax. It empowered Congress to levy taxes on "incomes, from whatever source derived." But, over the years, as you

CHART 1   1972 Tax "Welfare" Program

If you make	Your *yearly* tax "welfare" will be	You'll get added *weekly* "take-home" of
Over $1 million	$720,000	$14,000
$500,000 to $1 million	$202,000	$3,900
$25–50,000	$4,000	$75
$15–20,000	$1,200	$21
$5–10,000	$340	$7
Under $3,000	$16	$0.30

know, Congress has put in this deduction or that exemption or exclusion or waiver or special rate. And every time it did that it excluded someone from paying what could and would have been collected if Congress had adhered to the 16th amendment.

To give a concrete example, Jean Paul Getty is one of the richest men in the world; he is said to be worth between $1 billion and $1.5 billion, and to have a daily income of $300,000.

If Congress were to apply to Mr. Jean Paul Getty the standard of the 16th amendment, and were to tax his entire income, "from whatever source derived" at the current rates, Mr. Getty would, each April 15, write a check to the Internal Revenue Service for roughly $70 million. But Jean Paul Getty is an oilman and, as is well known, oilmen enjoy a variety of special tax-escape routes. As a result, according to what President Kennedy told two U.S. Senators, Mr. Jean Paul Getty's tax, at least in the early 1960s, amounted to no more than a few thousand dollars. Annual tax saving to Mr. Getty—at current rates—$70 million.

Compare the consequence of that $70 million tax forgiveness that Congress bestowed on Mr. Getty with the effect if Congress had, instead, voted him a $70 million welfare payment directly from the U.S. Treasury.

What is the difference between a tax forgiveness of $70 million and a direct welfare payment out of the Treasury to Mr. Getty of $70 million? I suggest there is no difference. In both cases Mr. Getty ends up $70 million richer. In both cases the U.S. Treasury is $70 million poorer. And in both cases the rest of the U.S. taxpayers have to pay $70 million more to make up the difference.

The fact is, there really isn't any difference between a tax forgiveness and a welfare payment, so all those special exemptions and exclusions—for the lowly as well as for the mighty—amount to welfare payments.

Who are the fortunate citizens who get those welfare payments, and how much do they get in tax welfare payments each year?

. . . If you are one of those lucky 3,000 families that makes over $1 million a year, your annual welfare will be $720,000 or, to put it in more conventional terms, your added weekly take-home comes to $14,000 a week.

In the $500,000 to $1 million class, the yearly welfare payment is $202,000.

Getting down into more normal ranges, at the $25,000 to $50,000 income level, the annual welfare is $4,000; and the $15,000 to $20,000 range, it is $1,200 or $21 a week.

Now we come to where most of the taxpayers are, in the $5,000 to $10,000 range, where the need is greater. There, the welfare payment is $340 a year, or $7 a week.

And in the poorest range, for families with incomes under $3,000, the annual welfare is $16 or 30 cents per week.

Now, how is the $77 billion of tax welfare distributed among various income groups? Is it distributed fairly? I think chart 2 of my prepared statement presents the matter graphically. In the under $3,000 income category, there are 6 million families and, of the total $77 billion, they get $92 million or one-tenth of 1 percent of the total.

By contrast, in the over $1 million income category, there are only 3,000 families; yet they get 24 times as much as these 6 million families in the under $3,000 groups. In all, those 3,000 super-rich families receive tax "welfare" of over $2.2 billion, the same amount that Congress has voted in total for payments for food stamps for hungry poor families in America.

Now, there are two particular tax preferences . . . that I would like to mention.

The first is income from tax-free bonds, bonds that are sold by states and municipalities. . . .

Those clearly are owned only by financial institutions and by the very wealthy. . . .

Bear in mind that the income from these not only is tax-free; it doesn't even have to be reported on income returns. The chart shows that the tax "welfare" from tax-free bonds that goes to the over $1 million group is $36,000 a year. For the $500,000 to $1 million group, the annual tax "welfare" comes to $19,000 a year. Even in the $25,000 to $50,000 group, not a bad income, annual "tax welfare" from this tax preference is only $24; and in the $10,000 to $15,000 and the $5,000 to $10,000 you can see the annual "welfare" comes to just 80 cents per year, 10 cents per year, respectively.

I come, finally, to what I think is recognized at least by many as the tax preference that most flagrantly discriminates against the poor and in favor of the rich. I refer to the favored taxing of capital gains—the profits that are made from the sale of property, stocks and bonds, buildings, lands, real estate and the like.

The first point to be made about this is that only one taxpayer in twelve reports any capital gains. Eleven taxpayers out of twelve report

CHART 2   Who Gets Tax "Welfare"?

Income group	Number of families	Total yearly tax "welfare"
Under $3,000	6,000,000	$92 million
Over $1 million	3,000	$2.2 billion

none at all. This is a phenomenon of the rich and only of the rich. As you know, capital gains realized during lifetime are taxed at just one-half of the rate of earned income, and capital gains held until death are taxed at a zero rate. . . .

In the over $1 million group, $641,000 a year counting both capital gains during lifetime and at death. In the $500,000 to $1 million group, annual "welfare" is $165,000 a year, more than $3,000 a week.

Now, let's get down to where most people are, in the $20,000 to $25,000 range, where the tax "welfare" comes to just $120 a year. In the $5,000 to $10,000 range, it amounts to $9 a year; and in the $3,000 to $5,000 income range, the yearly "welfare" from capital gains is only $1.

. . . If we went back to the 16th amendment to the Constitution of the United States, which is a fairly revered document, and taxed income "from whatever source derived," it would be possible to reduce all tax rates by 43 percent and to have a tax rate schedule running from 8 to 40 percent rather than the present tax rate schedule of 14 to 70 percent. I am not necessarily advocating exactly that kind of schedule but I should think that a lowering of tax rates of that sort would be of immense interest to those who now bewail the high marginal rates that supposedly inhibit incentive, individual initiative, and the like.

The main point of my testimony is that it would be unthinkable for Congress to vote a welfare program of the sort that has been described in those charts, that would give welfare grants of $14,000 a week to the nation's wealthiest families versus 30 cents a week to the poorest. Yet Congress has done indirectly in the tax law what it would never dream of doing directly.

PROGRESSIVE VERSUS REGRESSIVE TAXES

The principal taxes levied by the national government are progressive, to the extent that this quality has not been undermined by the system of exemptions mentioned above. Moreover, national taxes are considerably more progressive than are state and local taxes. Reform battles often center around the question of the progressive versus the regressive nature of certain taxes, and the distinction is important. A progressive tax is one in which the rate of the tax increases in direct relation to increased ability to pay. A regressive tax is one with greater impact on the person who is less able to pay.

It is important to understand that the impact on the taxpayer is of greater consequence than the amount of the tax alone. That is, the effect on the taxpayer is more important than the dollar amount actually paid. To illustrate, let us examine the comparative effect of a general sales tax on two hypothetical heads of families, each with four children. Family A has an annual income of $50,000 and family B an income of $5,000. It is obvious that A will pay larger sales taxes than B, though by no means ten times as much, simply because A has more money to spend. But though undoubtedly a minor irritation, the effect of a 3 or 4 per cent sales tax on A's standard of living is inconsequential. In contrast, for the $5,000 a year family, *any* amount that must be paid in taxes is literally food out of the children's mouths and clothes off their backs. So the impact in B's case is tremendous. A sales tax is thus considered to be regressive, because it hits hardest those with the least ability to pay, although its negative impact can be modified somewhat by exempting certain necessities like food and medicine. Graduated income taxes with higher rates for the higher-income groups come closer to equalizing the impact on all taxpayers and are thus termed progressive.

The nature of the taxes on which a government relies reflects almost as much about its social attitudes and goals as does the pattern of its spending policy. It must be remembered, however, that local governments are usually subject to severe state limitations on the type and level of taxation. Very legitimate bases for evaluating governments are the scope, nature, and quality of public services; others are the fairness and equity with which the cost of government is shared. To insure fair and equitable treatment of all citizens, a good tax system should be based fundamentally on the principle of progression: rates scaled according to ability to pay.

It is important also to realize that the tax and spending powers are more and more consciously used as a mechanism to help stabilize the economy of the nation. Government fiscal policy is a huge factor in the contemporary economy, and its intelligent use can aid greatly in providing a stimulant or a restraint when necessary, thus helping to level out the cycle of prosperity and depression, of "boom and bust." Such use of government powers was anathema to much of the business and financial community only a few years ago but is now widely accepted as public policy. The role of the Federal Reserve System in influencing the expansion and contraction of commercial credit is another major government device toward the same objective, a healthy rate of economic growth without severe fluctuations that may be disastrous. To this end the Federal Reserve Board stipulates the percentage of assets that member banks must hold in reserve, raises or lowers rediscount rates, buys and sells government bonds, and provides advice to banks on economic trends.

PREPARING THE BUDGET

Preparation of the annual national budget is also a huge task vital to effective executive management. The budget is a most important tool for control of the whole administrative structure. It is also the point at which the best overview of the entire scope of government operations is possible and where basic questions of priorities must be resolved administratively and politically. Even though a heavy percentage of the expenditures is fixed cost, there are large areas where choices must be made and emphases determined. Resources are always limited, and every agency is in a constant struggle to secure its share.

Budget planning is the point at which policy goals and choices confront the hard realities of financial feasibility. What programs should be undertaken? At what level must they be supported to be effective? Will it be necessary to sacrifice one service to expand another? Allocation of available resources through a budget expresses to a considerable degree the order of values and the social viewpoint of the government at the moment. One president may want most of all to keep expenditures down and the budget balanced, with almost no regard to social effects. Another may stress improvement of conditions for the disadvantaged. Yet another may see himself as forced to sacrifice desirable domestic programs in order to meet defense responsibilities abroad.

Often there is a tug-of-war between the president who prepares the budget and the Congress that must approve it. Congress may add to a budget as well as subtract from it, though a president may sometimes, as we have noted, attempt to refuse to spend money that has been added. Much-publicized cuts may be restored later by deficiency appropriations. Repeated vetoes by Presidents Nixon and Ford of increased funds for such programs as housing, medical training, education, or environmental improvement were most often successful, yet they suffered more overrides than any other presidents in modern times. The politics of the budget is always at the heart of the political drama.

Preparing the budget involves a complex planning program that begins well over a year before the start of the fiscal year in which the money will be spent. It is in fact a continuous process for the budget staffs of every department and agency and of the Office of Management and Budget, which is the president's arm for this purpose. The agencies prepare their plans and requests each spring, and by midsummer the OMB reviews these and makes preliminary estimates

ARMS PROGRAMS

©1974 HERBLOCK

Hunger

available for the president. At the same time the president receives projected estimates of revenue and general economic outlook and on the basis of all this information must establish guidelines for the budget and general financial policy, indicating especially the aspects to be emphasized or de-emphasized.

The OMB then returns to the agencies for further discussions, and gradually the specific final requests are hammered into shape and adjusted to each other. The end result, the president's budget, is submitted to Congress in January, whereupon traditionally the appropriations committees began detailed examinations and hearings on every request. The final budget bill passed by Congress appropriates funds for the fiscal year beginning October 1. It is common practice for a Congress passing any policy legislation to authorize in the same act the appropriation of funds up to a certain amount but actually to appropriate the money in a separate act at another time. Thus the legislative policy in effect runs two gauntlets, and the appropriations committees have almost life-and-death power over any policy set by Congress. Once the funds are appropriated, the Office of Management and Budget is also responsible for general supervision of expenditures by the various agencies to insure their orderly and economical use.

A central problem has been that Congress has had no adequate mechanism for looking at a budget as a whole and thus making meaningful judgments about the nation's priorities. Instead, chunks of it have been handled by a dozen subcommittees, each of which viewed only part of the picture and whose decisions were rarely changed. After two years of study and discussion, Congress in the summer of 1974 passed the Congressional Budget and Impoundment Control Act, designed to restore an effective congressional role. It created a professionally staffed Congressional Budget Office, to provide research and to reduce dependence on the executive's OMB, and established radically altered procedures for budget enactment.

Congress is now required to establish overall spending totals and tax targets each May, on the basis of the recommendations of newly created powerful budget committees in each house, which have the authority to deal with the entire budget picture rather than merely with fragments. The breakdowns by function are then parceled out to the appropriations subcommittees. After the various separate appropriation bills have been passed, Congress in September votes on the budget as a whole. At that time it is required to reconcile actual appropriations with the ceilings and estimated tax revenues, making spending cuts, raising taxes, or authorizing borrowing as necessary. The act also limits severely the president's power to impound appropriated funds, a power already restricted by the courts.

WHERE DOES THE MONEY GO?

In trying to describe and explain national expenditures it is easy to get lost in a mass of figures. Some figures are necessary, but they are not important in themselves, for they change from year to year. They are important because they give some idea of the pattern of national spending and a sound basis for making value judgments. There is much public discussion of government spending, but a great deal of it is hopelessly out of touch with the facts. Few people know, for example, that since World War II state and local expenditure and debt have increased more rapidly than national expenditure and debt.

CURRENT BUDGET PATTERNS

The grand total of the president's proposed budget for 1979 was $500.2 billion, a figure of astronomical proportions difficult to grasp. But this includes payments out of a number of revolving trust funds administered by the government—such as veterans' life insurance, social security, and the railroad retirement program—that are not a charge against general tax revenues. These are insurance trust funds into which participants pay premiums and from which benefits are paid. If these are subtracted, there remains an administrative budget of approximately $338.6 billion, of which about $85 billion goes to state and local governments as grants-in-aid and revenue sharing.

It is informative to examine this budget by sampling a few major categories of expenditure, looking at percentages of the administrative budget rather than dollar amounts (see Figure 8.3). By far the largest single item is defense, which alone accounts for 34.8 per cent of the budget. Veterans' benefits and services amount to 5.7 per cent; space research and technology, 1.1 per cent; international affairs and aid, 2.3 per cent; and interest payments on the national debt, another 14.5 per cent. In effect, most of this 58.4 per cent of the administrative budget is devoted to past, present, or future wars, and only 41.6 per cent remains to finance all the nation's other activities—agricultural programs, highway construction, domestic and foreign commerce, social welfare, the courts, and environmental protection, to name but a few.

The relationship of the defense and veterans' budgets to war conditions is amply clear. Space technology has been predominantly, though not entirely, related to defense. International assistance often reflects, quite legitimately, a mixture of humanitarian and national interests, and in any case it is not a large part of the total. The national debt has accumulated mainly in times of war or cold war. Only a small part of it is attributable to deficit financing in times of economic depression. Thus portions of the latter three amounts may be discounted slightly, but we are still left with almost three-fifths of the budget in war-related categories. As an indication of changing times, the $3.8 billion designated for space research and technology in 1979 is more than the total national budget for all purposes in 1931, in the depths of the Great Depression, when there were extensive demands on government. While the purchasing power of the dollar today is much less than it was then, the comparison is still interesting. Even more striking is the fact that interest payments on the

FIGURE 8.3   The Budget Dollar: United States Government Expenditures
(Estimate for Fiscal Year 1979)

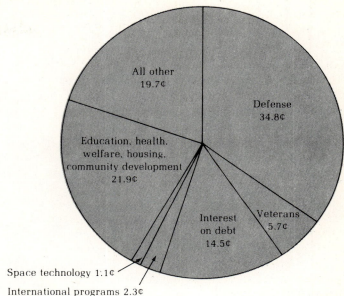

All other
19.7¢

Defense
34.8¢

Education, health,
welfare, housing,
community development
21.9¢

Interest
on debt
14.5¢

Veterans
5.7¢

Space technology 1.1¢

International programs 2.3¢

Source: **Office of Management and Budget,** *The Budget in Brief, Fiscal Year 1979,* Government Printing Office, Washington, D.C., 1978, pp. 76–82. (Adapted to show percentages of the administrative budget.)

national debt are now double the amount of the total national budget just before World War II.

It should be pointed out that much expenditure for defense and space as well as for other purposes is not purely "outgo" in the sense of its simply disappearing. There is some circular effect, as military and space procurement constitute a major demand on industry, resulting in a large volume of employment and high purchasing power—income incidentally, on which taxes are paid. From research and experiment in these fields have also come many by-products of value to the society in other ways.

DEFENSE VERSUS WELFARE-STATE SPENDING

In view of the often heated arguments over whether we live in a welfare state, a look at the welfare portion of the budget is also in order. The merits of each specific program are always subject to debate, but seen from a financial standpoint all social welfare programs account for only about 22 per cent of the administrative budget. This is based on an extremely broad definition that includes

"Now let's be absolutely certain I have this all straight. Your taxes, regardless of circumstances, are not—I repeat <u>not</u>—to be used for waging war, manufacturing munitions, financing espionage, or for any other activity designed to subvert the legitimate democratic aspirations of peoples at home or abroad. Rather, these moneys will be spent to reduce poverty, advance education, fight pollution, and, in short, to do whatever is necessary to improve the human lot and make this planet a viable habitat for mankind once again."

aid to the poor, the blind, dependent children, and other groups in need, health services, education, and housing and community development. In addition, as noted earlier, there are large social insurance programs in health and welfare whose annual payments approximately equal these amounts.

To see why budgets reach the heights indicated by our totals, it is helpful to look at a few examples of current costs, especially where the heaviest expenditures are made. An Air Force F-15 fighter plane costs $15 million; each MX missile, $100 million; a Trident submarine, $1 billion; and a nuclear-powered aircraft carrier, $2.4 billion (plus $3 billion for the ninety combat planes that it carries.) The estimated total cost of the original moon landing was $24 billion. Such items add up.

Yet the average person confronted with such figures becomes quickly immunized. Their magnitude is such that they cease to be meaningful, nor are pictograms of stacks of ten dollar bills the height of the Empire State Building of much help. It may be more helpful to think what else these sums could buy. One's imagination may be stirred, for example, by the realization that for the cost of one nuclear-powered submarine a basic dietary supplement could be provided daily to sustain the lives and health of *1 million* of the world's hungry children for nineteen years and eight months. One nuclear-powered aircraft carrier costs a little more than thirty colleges, each with a hundred-acre campus complete with buildings and equipment to serve fifteen hundred students! Decisions on defense expenditures do not of course depend on the United States alone, and many people would argue that if the United States seriously weakened its defenses, all its other services might become inconsequential. Nevertheless there is a crying need for clearer understanding of what carriers and submarines cost in comparison with other social goals.

SOCIAL PRIORITIES

Clearly, the question of social priorities is eternally fascinating. What things will the public think so important that there will be no question of paying, whatever the cost? If choices must be made, what will come first? How do we relate social needs to national ability to pay? Do we apply the same standards of judgment to private expenditures as to public? One interesting aspect of priorities is the percentage of presidential budget requests actually approved by Congress. In one recent year Congress granted 98 per cent of the president's request for the National Aeronautics and Space Administration and 99 per cent of his requests for military construction. By contrast, it granted 88 per cent of the request for the food stamp program, 53 per cent for elementary education, and 20 per cent for rent supplements.

Vice President Walter Mondale, when a senator, pointed out accurately in a newsletter to constituents that we seem to apply a different yardstick to our military-space programs than to programs to aid human beings:

A good illustration is the manned moon shot. When in the early sixties we determined to go to the moon, we didn't ask ourselves, "how near the moon can we get for 5 billion dollars," but rather, "how many dollars will it take us to get to the moon?" We then appropriated $24 billion over the years to do it.

But when it comes to education, or food stamps, or low-cost housing, we never seem to ask ourselves "how much will it take to meet the problem?" Rather we appropriate a set amount of dollars that will meet only a portion of the problem. If this amount feeds only some of the hungry, or educates only some of the children, or houses decently only some of the poor, so be it.

I believe it is time that we began thinking in terms of the final product in our social programs, just as we do in our defense-space programs.

The reason most often advanced for inadequate funding of certain programs is that the nation is already taxed to the limit and cannot afford more. If we leave aside the question why one activity can be financed while another cannot, it is important to take a closer look at the trends in public expenditures from another perspective. Most discussions deal only in dollar amounts and stress the steadily

From *The Herblock Gallery* (Simon & Schuster 1968).

"We've got to get the fat off of you"

FIGURE 8.4   Budget Outlays and Receipts as a Percentage of GNP for Fiscal
Years 1969–1983

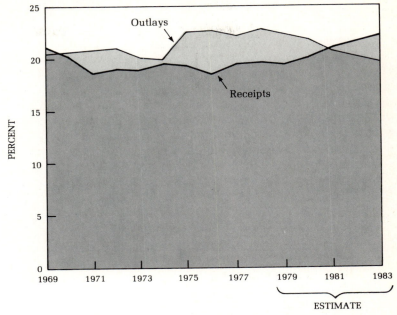

Source: Office of Management and Budget, *The Budget in Brief, Fiscal Year 1979,* Government
Printing Office, Washington, D.C., 1978, p. 18.

increasing level of spending, but it is vital to relate expenditure totals
to the national ability to pay. Put another way, we may ask whether
national government spending has grown more rapidly than the
gross national product (the total value of all goods and services
produced in the nation during a given year). The answer is clearly
that it has not. During the peak cost year of World War II, administrative budget expenditures amounted to 47 per cent of the GNP, but
in subsequent years, as national productivity boomed, this figure
dropped sharply. For the past fifteen years, despite a continual
increase, public spending has constituted a fairly steady 15 to 16 per
cent of the GNP. Even if total budget rather than administrative
budget figures are used, the percentage is currently only about 22
percent (see Figure 8.4). Taxes are never popular, but the nation
evidently has the capacity to finance whatever programs, within
reason, it really wants to support.*

---

*Although more dollars are now being spent than formerly on the alleviation of
poverty, on education, and on pollution control, the *percentage* of national income
devoted to such matters has increased only a small degree. Government has still not
plunged into a really major reallocation of resources.

FIGURE 8.5   Publicly Held National Debt as a Percentage of GNP for Fiscal
Years 1955–1979

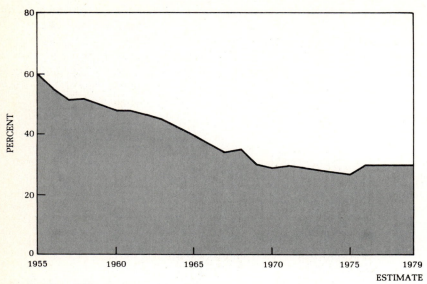

Source: Office of Management and Budget, *The Budget in Brief, Fiscal Year 1979,* Government
Printing Office, Washington, D.C., 1978, p. 87.

Likewise it is common to bemoan the size of the national debt, and
it may be reasonably argued that there should be serious effort
toward gradually reducing it. But however much one condemns the
size of the debt, the average citizen, faced with a choice between
helping reduce it and being able to buy a new television set, finds
the choice easy. When a budgetary surplus looms, the cry is for tax
reduction, not debt reduction, although the only way to reduce the
debt is for revenue to exceed expenditure. Again, the significance of
the debt can be most readily seen by relating it to the gross national
product. In most years since the Great Depression of the 1930s there
has been some dollar increase in the debt, but since World War II it
has steadily and markedly declined as a percentage of the GNP. Thus
in 1959 the publicly held national debt equaled about 50 per cent of
the GNP, but twenty years later, in 1979, it equaled only 30 per cent
of the GNP (see Figure 8.5).

It is natural and proper that there be differences of opinion on
specific programs for public action. But criticism couched in such
generalities as "let's get rid of waste" accomplish little. Quite often
one individual's waste is another's treasured public service. And
everyone wants to economize—in someone else's congressional district. Many a local business organization sees no inconsistency in

passing, even in the same evening, resolutions demanding government economy and urging construction in the city of new national facilities, such as post offices or veterans' hospitals.

As long as public spending is not far out of balance with national productivity, and taxes are not an undesirable drag on the economy, one can persuasively argue, as many have done, that Americans spend a disproportionate amount on personal gratification to the neglect of such vital public needs as eliminating poverty, cleaning up polluted air and water, and remedying inadequate transportation. Military costs aside, it should be obvious that as population increases and society becomes more complex, social expenditures will continue to rise. The need is to outgrow vague complaints and focus on the real issues: determining policy priorities, getting the best dollar's worth for each dollar spent, using the financial powers of government to control fluctuations in the economy, and developing the fairest and most equitable systems of securing public revenue.

THE CIVIL SERVICE

The average person often thinks of public employees as administrators or clerks, but in fact government employs persons with virtually every known skill—specialists in linguistics, medical doctors, poultry experts, research physicists, aircraft engine mechanics. Only about 17 per cent of the nation's civilian public employees work for the national government (only about 10 per cent of those work in Washington), and the other 83 per cent work for state and local governments (see Figure 8.6). Understandably, a larger percentage of college-trained persons than of the general populace works for government. Almost any type of professional preparation may lead to government employment, but in the last three or four decades special college training for career public administration has become widely available. Public service offers some of today's most interesting and challenging opportunities offering the satisfactions of service to others, whether one deals with domestic problems or international affairs.

THE BUREAUCRACY

Social objectives sought by policy makers are achieved mainly by those who bear the day-to-day administrative responsibility, known collectively as the civil service and often called the bureaucracy. To many people bureaucracy is a dirty word, though basically it means simply an organization with some system of hierarchical internal

FIGURE 8.6   Federal, State, and Local Government Civilian Employment at End of Fiscal Years 1949–1979

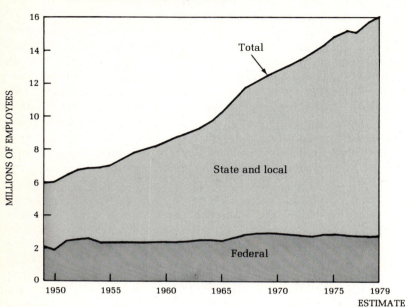

Source: Office of Management and Budget, *Special Analyses: Budget of the United States Government, Fiscal Year 1979*, Government Printing Office, Washington, D.C., 1978, p. 208.

control, job specialization, and a formal pattern of entry and promotion. Virtually any large organization, public or private, is thus a bureaucracy.

Employment in the administration of the national government is in two broad categories. One of these consists of political appointees chosen by the president or his assistants, most in top-level policy-making positions but a few in policy or confidential jobs in the various agencies as well as on the presidential staff. The other category comprises the merit-system appointees, about 90 per cent of the total. Because of traditional emphasis on a merit system as a means of eliminating spoils politics, there is a common but curious attitude that political appointees are somehow of a lower moral order. Yet the fact is that those selected through the political route are usually at least as highly qualified as the others and have certain orientations and skills that may be uniquely valuable.

No one seriously suggests that a president should be unable freely to choose as department heads persons who generally share his viewpoint, can be counted on for policy direction in accord with his goals, and will maintain personal loyalty. The chief assistants to department heads are usually in a similar category. Their roles are simply somewhat different from those of the permanent civil servants, though the differences are mainly of degree.

Excepting policy and confidential positions, the original reasons for establishing a merit system of employment are still valid, especially in dealing with so large a number of employees. To have all appointments on a patronage basis would be chaotic and disruptive of coherent service, and the pressures on the president and other top executives would be unbearable. Recruitment and retention of employees by merit makes a professional and specialized public service easier, places a premium on first loyalty to the government rather than to partisan affiliations, and relieves public employees of being campaigners and campaign contributors except by choice.

VETERANS' PREFERENCE

Detailed discussion of personnel administration practices is unnecessary here, but some attention should be given to aspects of it that are particularly controversial. Veterans' preference in the civil service, for instance, has long been a bone of contention. On the theory that the national government owes a debt to veterans, and under pressure from veterans' organizations, Congress has provided that all veterans may have five points added to their examination scores if a basic eligible score is achieved. Beyond this, disabled veterans, spouses of disabled veterans who are unable to work, and unmarried widows or widowers of veterans receive a ten-point bonus. Under the doctrine of "absolute preference" disabled veterans with eligible scores must be certified for job vacancies before all other eligibles. Further, veterans receive special privileges for seniority and job tenure.

Unbiased studies have concluded that veterans' preference is detrimental to the public service, but veterans' benefits understandably tend to be emotional matters and change is difficult. All the veterans' organizations but one, the relatively small American Veterans Committee, have vigorously supported civil service preference. Opponents agree that government has an obligation to veterans, especially the disabled but would meet it in ways other than public jobs. They argue that special preference, whether to veterans, Democrats, Masons, or Elks, is plainly contrary to the purpose of a merit system. And they suggest that it results not only in hiring less than the best but also in a morale problem, an occasional attitude that "you can't fire me no matter what I do," a motivation to get around the rules, and the discouragement of many qualified nonveterans even from applying. These problems are greater in some jobs than others and are relatively minor at the professional level.

RESTRICTIONS ON GOVERNMENT EMPLOYEES

Another controversy centers on restrictions of political campaigning imposed on civil service employees. The Hatch Act of 1939 prohibits merit-system employees of the national government from active participation in campaigns for partisan offices. They may belong to political organizations and express their political ideas "privately"; they may not serve as an officer of a political club or engage in public campaigning. The number of persons affected by this law was later expanded to cover state and local employees who receive part of their salaries from national grants, and a total of some 5 million persons is now under the law.

The purpose of such regulations is obviously to prevent the building of partisan machines composed of public employees and to encourage performance of duties in a nonpartisan way. Critics insist that such dangers are remote today and point out that public employees show about the same split in party preferences as the general public. They also argue that the system denies many of our best-informed and most interested citizens a significant part in the political process and unfairly restricts their rights of citizenship. The courts, however, have consistently held that the controls are reasonable, most recently in 1973 (*U.S. Civil Service Commission* v. *National Association of Letter Carriers*). Legislation has been introduced to remove most restrictions other than those on candidacy for partisan office and solicitation for political contributions, but support for change has so far not been heavy.

BASIC CONCEPTS AND TERMS

political role of administrators
department
quasi-department
government corporation
independent board or
  commission
Office of Management and
  Budget
informal organization
Hoover Commission
sunset laws
zero-base budgeting
the taxing power
indexing of tax rates

progressive tax
regressive tax
Federal Reserve system
fiscal policy and social priorities
budget-planning process
current budget patterns
national debt policy
civil service
bureaucracy
merit-system appointees
political appointees
veterans' preference
public employees and political
  action

CONGRESS
AND THE
LEGISLATIVE
PROCESS

9

Congress, as well as the president, has frequently been "the nation's whipping boy," and indeed it has its faults, in terms both of the institution and of the individuals who are its members. Yet it stands at the heart of our representative form of government, and its history of accomplishment is great. It has its men and women of singularly outstanding ability and its hacks; though an above-average sample, it reflects with surprising accuracy rather typical behavior patterns of the American populace, with all the characteristic virtues and vices of that populace—humanitarianism and selfishness, idealism and materialism, magnanimity and pettiness, tolerance and intolerance, innovation and fear of change. In broad perspective it is now, as it has been in the past, one of the democratic world's most notable representative deliberative bodies.

THE POLITICS OF REPRESENTATIVENESS

The political character of a given Congress is determined in the elections in the fifty states and 435 congressional districts. Campaigns turn in part on national issues and often to a greater extent on local issues; no member can long disregard the special interests of the district or state. The old dilemma of whether a member of Congress is properly to be primarily a national legislator or an agent reflecting district or state attitudes cannot be resolved one way or the other. In practice, this dilemma is likely to be resolved by representation of special interests of constituents when those interests are clear and compelling and by reflection of the broader interest when it is felt to be of overriding importance or when constituency opinion is divided, weak, or nonexistent. There is likely to be no clearly delineated district opinion on most issues before Congress, but the tough problems arise when the national interest and the local interest appear to conflict. Is a member of Congress elected to mirror constituents' views or to exercise his or her best judgment? If the former, how is he or she to determine realistically the "view" of a constituency now averaging approximately 500,000 people per House member?

Winston Churchill once remarked that the first duty of a representative is to get elected (or, as is often said, "You can't be a good congressman unless you're a congressman"). A representative under a district system of election inevitably devotes a good deal of time to taking care of the district. There is nothing necessarily wrong with this attitude, provided that the national interest is well served and provided that a representative does not serve simply the selfish interests of a highly vocal minority or of those who pay the campaign bills. The outstanding members of Congress are usually those who arrange a reasonable harmony between national and local considerations. At times it must give a thoughtful person pause to remember that the continuing presence of a leading national figure in a position of public responsibility depends wholly on the will of a plurality of the voters in single districts in states as diverse as Oklahoma and Vermont.

But the results of elections to the House may also turn in part on things other than issues, personalities, and meticulous attention to such items as defense contracts for local industries—most significantly, the party composition of the district and the way in which the boundaries have been drawn. Although districts of reasonably equal size are now required by the courts, it is really less consequential how many voters are included than which voters. One section of a community normally will show a Republican preponderance; another, a Democratic preponderance. Where the line is drawn makes a difference. Since the establishing of congressional districts and state legislative districts after each census (conducted every ten years) is ordinarily a function of the state legislatures, whose members have a considerable personal stake in the outcome, it is hardly

FIGURE 9.1   Five Gerrymandered Congressional Districts

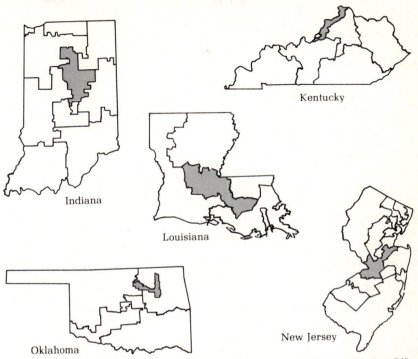

Kentucky

Indiana

Louisiana

New Jersey

Oklahoma

Source: 1977 Congressional Directory, 95th Congress, 1st Session, Government Printing Office, Washington, D.C., 1977, pp. 955, 958, 959, 971, 977.

surprising that the majority party seeks to protect its own future by judicious map drawing.

FAIR REPRESENTATION VERSUS GERRYMANDERING

The time-honored tactic of the gerrymander is the process by which the party in control of the state legislature draws the district boundaries in such a way as to favor its own candidates in subsequent elections (see Figure 9.1). There are, of course, no guarantees that voters will always behave in the expected manner, but a careful study of registration figures and the records of votes in past elections gives a fairly reliable guide to the future. The exact same region commonly may be made to produce either a solid Republican majority or a solid Democratic majority depending on which side carves it up. One familiar device is the use of the "loaded district," one that includes all the opposition party voters possible. The opposition may win this district by a four-to-one margin, the bulk of their votes thus being wasted, while the party in power wins four or five surrounding districts by very small margins.

Inequities of representation are most serious when there are also extreme differences in population among the districts, but this situation has been changed in recent years principally as a result of court decisions. Through a series of reapportionment cases beginning in 1962, the United States Supreme Court developed its emphatic one man–one vote doctrine,* applied originally to state legislatures but with the principle logically extended subsequently to both congressional districts and districts for electing local governing bodies.† The Court has held that population inequality—which means that a vote in a small population district is worth much more than one cast in a large population district—denies equal protection of the laws. Although it ruled in 1969 that electoral districts must be exactly equal in population, four years later it relaxed this a bit to permit a modest degree of arithmetical discrepancy among districts if they are drawn to conform to boundaries of local governments (*Mahon* v. *Howell, City of Virginia Beach* v. *Howell, Weinberg* v. *Pritchard,* 1973). As a consequence of the Court decisions, redistricting has increased representation for urban and, especially, suburban areas in which the bulk of the nation's population is located. It should be remembered, however, that even with reasonably equal population districts, gerrymandering is still possible.

When has a state been gerrymandered? The answer may seem obvious, but indeed it is not. Since populations are constantly shifting, absolute equity is not possible for long. Lines must be drawn somewhere, and wherever they are drawn someone will scream "foul." The minority party in the state legislature almost invariably makes all the political capital possible by claiming it has been the victim of a gross and callous gerrymander; court suits, which rarely occur, are threatened. Judgment concerning any redistricting must be on the degree of fairness or unfairness. A district system of elections insures various kinds of inequities, not the least of which is that in every district some majority is getting 100 per cent of the representation while some minority or minorities are getting no representation at all. Unless there is a willingness to move to a system of proportional representation, these inequities will persist. Not to be overlooked is the fact that a party can often injure itself in the long run by creating a large number of safe districts. They are

---

*Most notably *Reynolds* v. *Sims* (1964) and *Wesberry* v. *Sanders* (1964).

†The broadest statement, applying this principle to every type of elective governing body, appeared in *Hadley* v. *Junior College District of Metropolitan Kansas City, Missouri* (1970). It was modified in 1973 by making an exception of a water district where all expenses were paid by landowners and they alone possessed votes, weighted according to acreage owned—despite the fact that one corporate farm had had enough votes to control the district for twenty-five years (*Salyer Land Co.* v. *Tulare Water District*).

safe not just for the party but for the incumbents, and incumbents who no longer need the party's help may cease to show responsibility to the party.

MAINTAINING EQUAL REPRESENTATION

In 1929 Congress fixed the number of seats in the House "permanently" at 435 (although there was a temporary two-seat increase at the time of admission of Alaska and Hawaii) to prevent its size from becoming unmanageable. This means that since population shifts and grows unevenly, there will be a certain amount of reshuffling of seats after each census. An increase in representation can be accepted enthusiastically, but losses are likely to be a rather traumatic experience, and for every gain in one state some other must lose. It is especially difficult when a state discovers that with the same or even slightly larger population it can lose representation, simply because it did not grow as rapidly as some other states. Following the 1970 census California gained five seats; Florida, three; and Arizona, Colorado, and Texas, one each. New York, although it gained 8 per cent in population, lost two seats, as did Pennsylvania. Alabama, Iowa, North Dakota, Ohio, Tennessee, West Virginia, and Wisconsin lost one each. Each state, regardless of population, is entitled to at least one representative in the House.

Each state is entitled to two senators, and this creates inherent inequality of representation. This unequal representation is in no danger of being declared unconstitutional, however, for it is a part of the Constitution, one of the original conditions of union. It is interesting, however, to notice the change that has occurred in the nature of the Senate. Originally intended as the representative of the states, while the House was to be the representative of the people, the Senate has in modern times come to have a more national outlook and generally a somewhat more liberal perspective than the House. In part this may result from the special role of the Senate in foreign affairs, but it results also from the longer term and greater independence of senators. Perhaps even more important is the fact that the shift of population to the cities has meant that in most states election to the Senate now requires strong support in urban areas, which are ordinarily more liberal than rural areas and small towns.

One of the most difficult districting problems of recent years involves the question of whether it is desirable and legitimate to draw boundaries in such a way as to insure (as nearly as possible) the election of minority-group persons to legislative bodies. The argument for doing so is, of course, that minorities traditionally have been underrepresented, often because concentrations of minority population have been divided among two or more districts or submerged in multimember districts. It is impossible to resolve to everyone's satisfaction the perennial argument over whether blacks can be represented effectively only by a black, Italian-Americans by an Italian-American, and so on, or whether ability and attitude are more important than racial or national background. A case can certainly be made concerning the necessity for role models and for concrete evidence that the achievement of leadership positions is possible.

If drawing boundaries deliberately to exclude minority representation is unconstitutional (a denial of equal protection), as the Supreme Court held in 1960 (*Gomillion* v. *Lightfoot*), then is the deliberate effort to guarantee election of a minority person by drawing boundaries to exclude others equally unconstitutional? The Court decided in 1976 that there is no constitutional requirement that districts be drawn to insure representation of minorities proportional to their percentage of the population (*Beer* v. *U.S.*), but the following year it concluded that the use of racial quotas and criteria in legislative districting is not unconstitutional (*United Jewish Organizations of Williamsburgh* v. *Carey*). It is obvious that the *Williamsburgh* case and *Gomillion* v. *Lightfoot* fit uncomfortably together, even if distinctions can be rationalized. Intriguingly, the *Williamsburgh* case pitted the interests of two minorities against each other, for the challenge was brought by a closely knit community of Hasidic Jews, which argued that its being split between two districts in order to reduce the white populations of each diluted its votes and deprived it of its rights under the Fourteenth Amendment. It is probably true that wherever boundaries are drawn, some group is disadvantaged.

THE JOB OF A MEMBER OF CONGRESS

The newly elected member of Congress encounters a job larger than one person can handle if everything that is presumably expected is to be done carefully and personally. The new member must quickly learn to handle a variety of activities and to depend a great deal on staff and colleagues. The sheer volume of proposed legislation is staggering: In one recent session 20,805 bills were introduced. Much of a session could be occupied with merely reading all the bills, let alone seeking information necessary to understand their implications. The member must concentrate on bills that she or he believes most important, are the responsibility of committees on which she or he serves, and will in fact come to a vote (many bills are winnowed out in committees). Even so, one cannot be an expert on all enacted bills or on the incredible variety of topics covered.

The natural consequence is specialization. Each member of Congress tends to specialize in the areas of his or her committee membership, and in time friendships are developed with members of

DUNAGIN'S PEOPLE

"Funny how much more tolerant you become of inflation, unemployment and taxes after you're elected . . ."

other committees who can be counted on for information and advice regarding bills within their special competence. Lobbyists and constituents provide volumes of additional information that consume a considerable amount of time. Though the public tends to view the member of Congress as a general legislator, to a considerable extent the task is that of committee member. This is where much of the work is done, where personal power is built, and where reputations are established.

THE MEMBER AND CONSTITUENTS

The senator and the representative have other responsibilities. Many constituents seem to look upon them as errand-runners in Washington, and they are deluged with requests for help on everything from obtaining government publications on the treatment of whooping cough to securing hotel reservations to getting someone's relative out of the army. Some things can be done and some cannot, but the members try, for voters are much more likely to forget issues than they are to forget personal favors. Some members of Congress estimate that over half their own and their staffs' time is spent in this kind of activity, much of it contacting administrative agencies on behalf of constituents.

Whether successful in providing assistance or not, the member must respond to constituents to indicate the efforts that have been made. In addition to specific requests for help, mail dealing with issues before Congress arrives daily by the sackful. The average representative receives several hundred letters and telegrams and a good number of phone calls each day, and a senator from a large state may receive from fifteen hundred to three thousand pieces of mail or even more when a highly controversial issue is in the news. Each person who has taken time to share wisdom with a member of Congress feels entitled to a personal reply and is offended at the receipt of a form letter in response, even though a few standard replies would adequately cover much ground.

Technology comes fortunately to the rescue. There are machines capable of turning out thousands of letters identical except for name and address, each individually typed and "personally signed" by the member. Many organizations stimulate mass "write your member of Congress" campaigns, sometimes having great numbers of letters typed by machine and sent out for individuals to sign and mail. In imagination one may envision the intriguing picture of batteries of machines in different parts of the country tirelessly corresponding with each other. But beyond this sort of mass enterprise, there is much correspondence that demands individual attention and response.*

Most members of Congress believe that it is a useful public service and an aid to re-election to render fairly regular reports to their total constituencies. As noted earlier, newsletters and columns prepared for local newspapers are common. Radio and television broadcasts may be taped, if the district is one in which their use is feasible and stations are willing to contribute public service time. In addition, most members feel an obligation to aid their party in various ways as the need arises. With all these demands on time, further complicated for the House member by the shortness of a two-year term that

---

*Even though a few letters they receive are vicious, most members provide serious response rather than risk stimulating further bitterness. Occasionally the provocation is too great. Former Senator Stephen Young of Ohio achieved some fame for his "let the chips fall where they may" rejoinders; one of the classic correspondence-stoppers he sent to writers of what he deemed "nut letters" read as follows: "I thought you would want to know that someone has been writing me crackpot letters and signing your name to them."

demands that the next campaign begin as soon as an election is over, a conscientious member of Congress leads a highly pressured and hectic existence. Yet it is a fascinating existence that few voluntarily leave.

THE MEMBER'S STAFF

There is probably no key more significant to success in the job of a legislator than a first-rate personal staff. The staff can make or break a member of Congress. There is financial allocation for hiring staff— equal for all members of the House except its leaders, and for senators related to the size of the state they serve. Committee and subcommittee chairmen also have committee staff at their disposal. The top person on any member's staff is the administrative assistant, commonly known on Capitol Hill simply as the AA. The AA is responsible for office operations generally and ideally serves as a sort of alter ego for the senator or representative, acting in legislative matters, constituent relations, and campaign leadership. Other staff members may specialize in legislative research or public relations, for example, but all must be flexible to cope with constantly shifting pressures. The attitude and competence of secretaries and reception-ists are vital, too, for most citizens gain an impression of the member of Congress from the way in which they are treated by the staff members with whom they first come in contact.

Some people assume that a member can be evaluated by how hard she or he is working, and many members emphasize this diligence in their campaigns. To evaluate them on this basis alone is unrealis-tic, however. Hard work is one criterion for judgment, as is ethical stance, but a member's stands on public policy ought to be the voters' central consideration. In other words, a member may be working a killing schedule but, from the voters' perspective, for the wrong things.

CONGRESSIONAL PRIVILEGES AND RESTRAINTS

Members of both houses are currently compensated by a salary of $57,500 per year, with additional allocations for staff, travel, and office supplies. It is certainly not unreasonably high pay for the level of responsibility and the many legitimate expenses incurred, includ-ing for most the need to maintain a home in the district they represent as well as in Washington. A postal-franking privilege enables members to send mail free on official business, though the line is not always easily drawn between what is official and what is personal.

To prevent harassment, senators and representatives are immune to arrest for minor offenses. Such incidents are rare, and most are caused by traffic violations; thus the privilege of immunity is infrequently claimed, probably because it is felt that such claim will result in undesirable publicity.

The term *congressional immunity* customarily refers not to these privileges but to one much more likely to arouse controversy: the privilege of absolute freedom of speech on the floor of Congress. In order to protect members of Congress against intimidation by slander suits, which might restrain them from saying some things they cannot clearly prove but believe ought to be said, the Constitution provides that no member will be subject to legal action for statements made in Congress. In practice the protection applies to statements in committees as well as in sessions of either of the houses and to news media reporting of what is said. Any special privilege carries with it, of course, the possibility of abuse, and the question is always whether need outweighs danger. In this case the public depends on the exercise of common sense and discretion by the people it elects to Congress, and most members have proved worthy of trust. A few, notably in recent history Senator Joseph McCarthy of Wisconsin, have acquired vast publicity by irresponsible use of the privilege. Such techniques as his practice of making a steady succession of sensational charges and personal attacks, in succession rapid enough that each seized the headlines away from one immediately preceding, making questions and counterproofs extremely difficult, have subjected congressional immunity to serious criticism.

Each house, acting independently of the other, has complete power to control the behavior of its members, but in such bodies there is a natural reluctance to discipline colleagues unless the circumstances are highly provocative. The "club spirit" is strong. Various kinds of informal pressure can be used. Beyond this are three levels of formal punishment that can be imposed. The simplest is a reprimand from the chair, which may seem inconsequential but carries with it bad publicity, always of vital concern to a person in public office. More serious is a resolution of censure, following full-dress charges and debate in the house of which the individual is a member; in this case the publicity is likely to be damaging to the member's political future. The only recent cases other than McCarthy are the censure of Senator Thomas Dodd in 1967, for personal use of funds contributed for campaign purposes and for improper relations with private-interest groups, and of Representative Robert L. F. Sikes in 1976, for failing to disclose certain financial holdings and for sponsoring legislation that would benefit his personal real estate interests.

The most serious penalty is expulsion, which requires a two-thirds vote of the house concerned, but until 1969 the same result could sometimes be accomplished by refusing to seat a newly elected or re-elected member, and this required only a majority vote. In 1967 the House of Representatives denied a seat (for one term) to veteran Representative Adam Clayton Powell of New York after the Democratic caucus had earlier stripped him of his committee chairmanship. The charges were misuse of public funds, refusal to honor a court judgment for damages against him, and noncooperation with House committees investigating his case. Powell challenged the authority of the House to deny him his seat and ultimately won a Supreme Court judgment. The Court ruled that while either house may expel a member for any reason, neither can refuse to seat a duly elected member except for failure to meet requirements specified in the Constitution: age, citizenship, and residence in the state (*Powell v. McCormack,* 1969). It had been assumed in the past that each house was free to determine what would constitute grounds for punishment. During World War I, the House of Representatives refused a seat to a Socialist who had been duly elected, presumably because of his opposition to the war. In the early days of Utah's statehood the House balked at seating Mormons who were polygamists, although there is no formal stipulation that monogamy is a qualification for membership.

There is little question that Congress has been extremely tolerant of much questionable conduct on the part of its members. When disciplinary action has been taken, it has usually been only after prolonged abuse has occurred and after public sentiment has been aroused. This behavior is the more striking because members of Congress have been very quick to criticize alleged ethical deviation by officials and employees of executive agencies and of the courts. It is also true that the media tend to create distortions, giving massive publicity to a "sex scandal," such as the Wayne Hays affair, but focusing only minimal attention on such matters as illegal oil company campaign contributions or numerous congressional trips to Taiwan paid for by a front organization financed by the Taiwan government, itself long subsidized by the United States.

In order to establish more definite standards and "avoid even the appearance of impropriety," both the House and the Senate in 1977 adopted fairly detailed codes of ethics and created ethics committees to investigate complaints and recommend penalties, if needed. The codes require full disclosure of personal finances, limit the amount of income (15 per cent of salary) that can be earned at outside jobs (predominantly lecturing and writing), prohibit affiliation with professional firms or partnerships while serving in Congress, place restrictions on mass mailings under the franking privilege during periods prior to primaries and elections, prohibit acceptance of gifts aggregating more than $100 in any year from a lobbyist or lobbying organization, prohibit working as a lobbyist for one year after leaving Congress, and establish a variety of lesser stipulations. A number of members contended in vain that restrictions on outside job earnings discriminate in favor of those who are personally wealthy and have large incomes from investments. Although they insisted that full disclosure is an adequate control, heavy pressure for passage of the bills without major amendment prevailed.

Case Study
A LEGISLATOR'S RESPONSIBILITY: CONFLICT OF LOYALTIES

In 1973 the self-styled Marxist government of President Salvador Allende in Chile was overthrown by a coup and was superseded by a repressive military junta. In the course of this takeover Allende lost his life. Because the Central Intelligence Agency of the United States was known to have been active in that country and to have opposed the Allende regime, questions were raised as to whether it had played a role in the coup. Several administration spokesmen provided public assurances, including testimony before a congressional committee, that it had not been involved.

Several months later Representative Michael J. Harrington received information causing him to doubt those assurances, and he asked for the opportunity to examine secret testimony that had been given to the House Armed Services Committee by a high official of the CIA. The committee granted him access to the material, stamped "Top Secret," but in accord with its rules required that he sign a pledge not to reveal its contents to any unauthorized persons. He signed, and on two occasions he studied the information in some detail. Harrington was shaken. In his opinion the secret testimony completely contradicted the public statements, showing that in a nine-year period the CIA had spent $11 million first to try to prevent the election of Allende and later, in the words of the agency official, to "destabilize" his government in order to help bring about its downfall. Whether or not it had directly participated in the coup, it seemed evident to the representative that the CIA had contributed heavily to making it possible.

Harrington faced a serious dilemma. As he saw it, these were immoral actions. Moreover, efforts at destabilization violated the non-interference clauses of two treaties to which the United States is a party, and the cover-up involved perjury before a committee of Congress. He was being asked, he felt, to be guilty of an offense himself—failure to report illegal actions of which he had knowledge. Yet he had made a pledge of secrecy. The more he thought about the situation, the more he was convinced that the public had to be made aware of these acts done in its name—nor were they apparently isolated acts or ones of a type that might not occur elsewhere if they remained secret. He had signed a pledge of secrecy pursuant to the rules of a committee; that pledge now seemed to him to conflict with the oath of office that he had taken and his fundamental responsibility to his constituents. He broke his pledge and brought the CIA Chilean operations to congressional, press, and public attention. Was his action right or wrong?

Months later, in a closely divided vote, the Armed Services Committee in effect rebuked Harrington by denying him further access to committee files and referring his case to the House Ethics Committee for investigation. No censure or other formal punishment occurred.

CONGRESSIONAL ORGANIZATION AND POWER STRUCTURE

There is in Congress a kind of dual organizational structure, based on formal congressional hierarchy on the one hand and on the hierarchy of the political parties on the other. In many ways, however, the two structures are closely interrelated. The basic units of party structure are the Democratic and Republican caucuses in each house, to which every member automatically belongs. The most important function of the caucus occurs at the opening of a new Congress every two years, when each caucus selects its officers and its nominees for leaders of its house and its committees. During the course of a session the caucuses meet from time to time as a forum to hammer out party policy and to promote maximum cooperation

The first official portrait ever made of the House of Representatives in session, February 25, 1964.

National Geographic Photographer George F. Mobley, courtesy U.S. Capital Historical Society

among members, but there is no significant effort to make the decisions of the caucus binding on party members in their votes on the floor.

FLOOR LEADERS

Since there is normally a straight party vote on organization, it is a foregone conclusion that the majority party will elect its nominees for speaker of the House and president pro tempore of the Senate. The minority goes through the motions but does not name floor leaders, because its nominees for top offices in fact take those posts after they are defeated in this ritualistic election. The floor leaders serve as field generals and chief spokesmen for their parties in the day-to-day work of Congress, and the floor leader of the party that controls the White House is expected to be something of an administration spokesman as well. The House speaker is ordinarily re-elected as long as his party holds power; and if it loses its majority, he reverts to being House minority (floor) leader. The position of House floor leader has come to be considered a steppingstone to the speakership, although such a promotion is not automatic. The president pro tempore of the Senate holds a more honorary position; the most powerful figure is actually the majority floor leader.

The party officers ranking next in each house are the whips, often aided by assistant whips, whose main function is to serve as a two-way channel of communication between the leadership and the members, to keep track of the location of members at all times, and to be able to round them up when needed for a vote. A good whip should know where each party member stands on every key issue and how each can most effectively be persuaded if necessary.

THE HOUSE SPEAKER

The speaker is at the same time the head of his party in the House and the chief officer of that body as an institution. He both presides over the House and gives direction to its activities; his support or opposition may be vital to the passage or defeat of legislation. The speaker has often been called the second most powerful person in Washington, second only to the president of the United States, although the actual amount of influence he wields varies depending on who holds the office, how long he has held it, and the respect (or fear) he inspires in the membership of the House. His power is a mixture of the formal prerogatives of the office and the influence stemming from personal relationships built up over many years. This is not a position to which a member comes automatically on the basis of seniority, but neither is it one to be held by a novice.

The formal powers of the speaker include the power to determine whom to recognize on the floor and whether that which a member wishes to say is in order, to rule on all points of parliamentary order, to decide the outcome of voice votes (though a record vote may be demanded), and to refuse to entertain motions that he deems dilatory (designed merely to delay action by the House). The speaker also has power over the assignment of bills to committees, and the fate of a bill is not uncommonly sealed by that assignment. One of the most famous illustrations of the significance of the power of referral occurred in the Senate when the Civil Rights Bill of 1964 was sent to the Commerce Committee, which was certain to recommend it, rather than to the Judiciary Committee, where its death would have been equally certain. It is the speaker's privilege to appoint the members of conference committees and various select or special committees created from time to time. Very little of importance takes place in the House without the speaker's having been consulted in advance, and he is quite capable of expediting or delaying matters. There are many favors he can grant or withhold, as every member well knows, and his relations with the other principal power brokers, the floor leaders and committee chairmen, are in most cases intimate. Speakers rarely enter debate, but when they do step down from the chair for this purpose, the chamber gives them marked attention.

The speaker runs the House in close cooperation with the majority floor leader and is in constant contact with the minority leader as well. These people fight their party battles on the floor and before the news media, but they are usually personal friends who have worked together for many years and feel a common responsibility for the institution of Congress. In the Senate the floor leaders function in a similar spirit of cooperation, however vigorous the policy battles may be. The vice president, who votes only in case of a tie, acts generally as an impartial presiding officer, but if highly regarded is in a position to exert considerable personal influence.

COMMITTEES AND THE SENIORITY SYSTEM

In American legislative practice a large percentage of the work is accomplished in the standing committees, one of which in each house covers each major area of congressional responsibility (agriculture, foreign affairs, and so on), where it is determined whether and in what condition a bill is to be considered by the full house. Congress, it is often remarked, is a collection of "little legislatures." The power structure within the committees, then, is of overwhelming importance. The seniority system remains the heart of the committee power structure, although there have been significant recent modifications. A committee chairman, who has great political power, normally reaches that position by continuing to be re-elected and by remaining on the same committee. By long-established tradition the chairmanship of each committee has gone to the member of the majority party with the greatest seniority on that particular committee (not necessarily the greatest seniority in the house as a whole), although in both houses there is now a vote on each chairman and ranking minority member in the party caucuses.

The majority party in each house holds a majority on all committees, the proportions on each committee ordinarily being approximately the same as that in the house. Thus the majority party holds all chairmanships, which is logical if party responsibility is to have meaning. New members are given committee assignments by the party caucuses acting on the recommendations of committees that strongly represent the leadership. Each member can indicate preferences, which are usually honored as far as possible, but certain committees are much more powerful than others and thus much more widely desired. A member may have a special interest or background that makes a particular assignment logical, but the choice often is determined by what is thought most significant for the district and thus improves chances for re-election. A legislator from a rural district, for example, may seek to serve on the Agriculture Committee. A member who does not get an assignment of first choice (whether one does or not depends largely on the number of seats available to the party on that committee) may switch to the preferred assignment in the next Congress if re-elected and if a committee vacancy exists, but in this case the member will relinquish the committee seniority already established. A member who

The Senate Judiciary Committee, after completing hearings, votes on a presidential nominee for a Cabinet position.

Wide World Photos

switches committees begins on the bottom rung of the new committee, and a person defeated and then restored to office again at a
subsequent election likewise starts at the bottom.

A representative who manages to stay in office moves up the
seniority ladder only as those ahead retire, die, or are defeated for re-
election; the speed with which this occurs is thus extremely variable.
Several of the senior majority members of each committee are able to
hold subcommittee chairmanships, which are in themselves positions of considerable power. The operation of the seniority system
has been until lately extremely rigid, because everyone already
within the system has had a personal stake in its continuance. It is a
common saying on Capitol Hill that the seniority system seems very
bad when a member first comes to Congress but looks better the
longer one remains. One of the best examples of the system's inflexibility is the case of Hubert H. Humphrey. Senator Humphrey served
as a senator from Minnesota for sixteen years and had reached the
post of majority whip. He was then elected vice president and
presided over the Senate for the next four years, after which he was
his party's candidate for president. In two years he again successfully
ran for the Senate. But now he was a freshman member and at the
bottom of the seniority ladder! The only bits of deference paid to his
past service were that he was given seniority over other new members of the committees to which he was assigned and, in time, a
largely honorary post as deputy president pro tempore.

A member's seniority status is almost never tampered with, but
the party caucus controls seniority and there have been a very few
cases of disciplinary reduction of seniority. At the opening of the
1965 session, the Democratic caucus in the House stripped seniority
from Representatives Albert Watson of South Carolina and John Bell
Williams of Mississippi because of their active campaigning for
Barry Goldwater, the Republican candidate for president. It was
recognized that as individuals they were perfectly free to support
whomever they wished, but the real question was whether under
these circumstances they were entitled to hold positions of power in
Congress granted by the Democratic party. Watson soon switched
his registration to Republican, and Williams became a successful
candidate for governor of Mississippi. American parties are generally remarkably tolerant of deviations from party regularity. Even an
officeholder can often sit out a party campaign with impunity; Watson and Williams, however, stepped beyond the line of tolerance.

Strictly speaking, each member has at least two seniority rankings,
one in the house and the other on a committee or committees. A new
member's rank among other new members on a committee is determined by seniority in the house. Since the system permits no equality, elaborate devices are used to establish rankings of all new
members at the beginning of each Congress. Former Senator Gale

McGee liked to tell of his·experience coming to the Senate as one of
fifteen new members in 1958. Precedence was given to former members of the House, according to their previous relative seniority, and
eight new members benefited from this. Next were former governors
and a former lieutenant governor, accounting for three more. The
leadership then went back to the Buchanan administration for a
precedent and assigned others on the basis of the date of admission
of their states to the union. Oddly, this did not fully solve the
problem since two came from states admitted in the same admission
act, so final resort was to alphabetical order of the state names. In this
fashion Senator McGee, of Wyoming, became ninety-eighth in
seniority out of the then ninety-eight senators!

COMMITTEE CHAIRMEN

The seniority system has guaranteed experienced people in the
chairmanships, but it also has tended to throw power to safe districts
and one-party areas, where individuals, once elected, are virtually
irremovable. These districts are the most politically static areas of the
country and their representatives are least likely to be amenable to
change and innovation. Local and regional politics are the bases on
which legislators most often achieve seniority, yet this power is
translated into the power to decide national policy. Some districts are
so solid that their representatives could vote to make Fidel Castro an
honorary citizen of the United States without their tenure being
threatened in the slightest. Such representatives are not in any
significant fashion held accountable by the voters, nor do they feel
any sense of responsibility to the national party with which they are
identified. Some have been known to work against an administration of their own party, and powerful committee chairmen can strip
party responsibility of meaning. Others have held on to the reins of
power far beyond the age at which they were completely competent.

Yet despite the constant criticisms of the seniority rule, it has been
difficult to reach agreement on an alternative. Many are dubious of
the bargaining for position that would occur if each committee freely
elected its chairman, and many fear the power of the speaker if there
were a return to the old system under which he appointed chairmen.
A strong case can be made for either approach or for a mandatory
retirement age for chairmen. But more than the lack of an acceptable
alternative, a basic reason for resistance to change is the stake each
member has in the status quo.

Given this fact, the changes made in the House by the Republican
caucus in 1971 and the Democratic caucus in 1973 are truly remarkable. The Senate in 1975 followed suit with essentially comparable
provisions. The rapid influx of new and often younger members,
predominantly of liberal persuasion, in both houses in recent years
has brought much greater motivation for change.

" . . . And while I may be ignorant about the subject, Gentlemen, don't forget that my seniority on this committee makes me an authority!"

Rather than a free-contest election of chairmen or ranking minority members by the caucus, there is a yes or no vote on the member on each committee whose seniority makes that member eligible for the position, even if he or she currently holds it. In the event of defeat the caucus elects a new chairman, usually but not always the next-ranking member in seniority. Under these circumstances chairmen become considerably more responsive to the wishes of their party colleagues. Even if not rejected, no one is interested in having a large negative vote reported, and the size of such votes does vary. What is significant is the establishment of the principle that chairmen are responsible to their caucuses and that the caucuses are responsible for the persons they put in those positions. Initial use of the system produced no defeats of sitting chairmen, but in 1975 the House Democratic caucus deposed the long-time chairmen of the Agriculture, Armed Services, and Banking and Currency committees. In the latter case the fourth-ranking member, a highly regarded expert in the field, was named to head the committee.

The power wielded by committee chairmen in both houses in the past was multifaceted. They were generally able to determine which bills would be brought up for consideration before their committees and when, thus commonly having power to block by inaction those they opposed. In addition, they possessed a great deal of control over the time and frequency of committee meetings, again a potential force for either speeding or stalling action. The new reforms require that bills assigned to a committee be referred to subcommittees within two weeks and stipulate written rules for each committee that specify regular meetings and further limit the powers of the chairmen. Nevertheless, they retain significant power and influence; the changes have served largely to restrain arbitrariness.

A major element of the reform movement was not only to restrict the powers of chairmen with formal rules, but also to strengthen the role of the subcommittees, thus giving greater importance to middle-level members of the majority party. Subcommittees have been authorized to draft legislation independently of the full committee and manage bills on the floor, to have their own professional staffs (both majority and minority), and to have fixed jurisdiction so that the committee chairman cannot, for example, refer a bill to what he or she deems to be a subcommittee antagonistic to the bill. Every committee in the House is compelled to have at least four subcommittees, and the majority caucus can designate the chairmen. Sharp restrictions have been imposed on the number of committees and subcommittees that one member may chair, and both houses have lately seen the unprecedented situation of senior members turning down committee chairmanships in order to retain a key subcommittee chairmanship on a much more powerful committee. All these developments diffuse power, giving more members greater responsibility and making the houses more freewheeling, open, and unpredictable. By the same token they make overall leadership and the achievement of a coherent legislative program far more difficult.

THE MOVE TO CENTRALIZE RESPONSIBILITY

At the same time that these trends toward decentralization (and perhaps even fragmentation) have been occurring, there has been a countertrend, particularly in the House, toward strengthening the central leadership, with a view toward significantly increasing party responsibility. Again, younger members have been instrumental in this movement. Party Steering and Policy committees, which operate as a sort of executive committee for the caucuses to plan and push policy programs and to move the often cumbersome machinery of a legislative house, have been given renewed life and added authority, notably to suggest assignment of members to committees and to recommend nominees for the committee and subcommittee chairmanships.

But it is the position of speaker that has benefited most. In addition to the general powers previously discussed, the speaker has been given, as part of the reform movement, the power to appoint all the members of the extremely important Rules Committee and to name eight of the twenty-four members of the majority Steering and Policy Committee. He is himself automatically a member of this latter committee, as are the whip (whom he appoints), the majority leader, and the caucus chairman; thus the formal leadership accounts for half of the committee. (The other twelve are elected by six regional caucuses.) With the decline of the Rules Committee and the Ways and Means Committee as independent czardoms, the speaker today has greater power to lead the House than has been true for many decades. Yet it is a more difficult House to lead, as we have noted. Former speakers needed only to deal primarily with the so-called barons, the once virtually all-powerful committee chairmen, but a modern speaker must involve himself in the total legislative process, dealing with the multitude of more decentralized power centers.

UNOFFICIAL ORGANIZATION

In addition to the formal structures, there exists within each house a variety of rather specialized ad hoc groups organized to promote particular interests or concerns. Their collective weight is more potent than the sum of individual voices. The result is what some have termed "the Balkanization of Congress." Many groups have existed in one form or another throughout most of the history of the nation, such as those designed to promote the economic interests of a region, like cotton production or a particular manufacturing industry. More recently created have been the Black Caucus, Women's Caucus, Hispanic Caucus, Rural Caucus, the "frost belt" and "sun belt" groups, and broader-gauged associations devoted to particular causes, such as Members of Congress for Peace Through Law, which is concerned with constructive internationalist foreign policy. Organizations like these cut across party lines. Within each party there are also ideological factions, typified by the Democratic Study Group as a voice of liberal Democrats or by the Wednesday Club and the Republican Study Group, respectively seeking to speak for moderate Republicans and conservative Republicans.

HOW A BILL BECOMES A LAW

Bills may be introduced in any quantity by members of each house, and the volume each session is massive. The most prolific sources of

FIGURE 9.2   How a Bill Becomes a Law

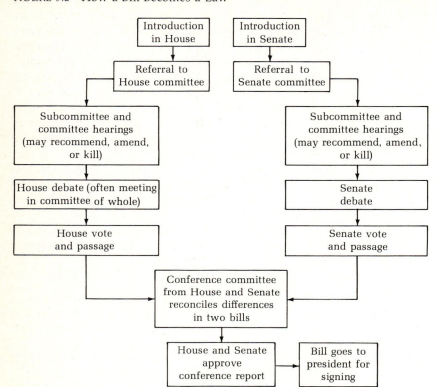

legislation are the multitude of interest groups and the administrative agencies, but they must find legislators willing to act as sponsors, and for this purpose the most powerful members are much sought after. Members ordinarily choose bills that fit their personal philosophies and, where possible, those likely to be popular enough to add to their political capital. Certain bills may be introduced merely as a favor to some group, without a commitment for active support. In addition, most members of Congress have their own favorite projects, as well as a host of actions of concern to their home districts. It is quite common for bills, particularly major ones, to be introduced in both chambers at approximately the same time so that the legislative process may proceed without the delay arising from one house's having to wait for the other. Figure 9.2 indicates the typical route by which proposed legislation is enacted into law.

REFERRAL TO COMMITTEE

Except in rare emergency situations when Congress has acted on certain bills almost immediately, all bills are referred to committees.

Most do not get beyond this stage. Those deemed important are considered in detail, the controversial ones ordinarily being given public hearings before a subcommittee or, occasionally, a full committee. Proponents and opponents are marshaled to make presentations; often a verbatim record is kept and subsequently published. Various amendments may be adopted in the process of working out agreement, and ultimately the committee votes on whether to recommend the bill. If it does so, the bill is placed on one of the calendars of the house, which list the bills in the order that they are reported out. Since much time is required for work on major legislation, such bills are likely to be reported out late in a session.

However valuable it may be to have specialized groups consider potential legislation, the committee system militates against a coherent legislative program, as James Reston has observed:

> The President will go to the Hill and define the State of the Union in iambic pentameter. He will speak in continents and epochs and define the challenge of change.
>
> Then after partisan applause . . . the vast panorama of the nation in the world will be cut up into little pieces, each committee chairman will vanish into his privileged sanctuary with his special part of the picture and the vast decentralized Congressional machine will begin to grind. . . .
>
> They are not looking at the same picture. They are talking across each other. . . .
>
> Congress operates not as a unified institution but as a loose federation of virtually autonomous committees. . . . Thus the function of Congressional leadership is scattered among the chairmen of almost two hundred committees and subcommittees whose activities are seldom coordinated. . . . *

Still another criticism of some committees concerns the tendency to compose them primarily if not exclusively of members who in effect represent the special interest with which they deal. It seems at first glance eminently logical, for instance, that members with a professional background in banking should be assigned to the House or Senate Committee on Banking and Currency, but it is not necessarily true that the public interest will be served best by a committee made up of former bankers. Agricultural policy is a concern of city dwellers as well as of farmers, but the committees with life-or-death power over it are likely to be composed almost entirely of representatives from rural districts.

THE POWER OF THE HOUSE RULES COMMITTEE

In the House, once a bill is on a calendar, its fate lies to a great extent in the hands of the Rules Committee. This has traditionally been

New York Times, January 7, 1963.

"There are days, Hank, when I don't know who's President, what state I'm from, or even if I'm a Democrat or a Republican, but, by God, I still know how to bottle up a piece of legislation in committee."

considered to be one of the two or three most powerful committees in the House because it determines, subject to ordinarily routine House approval, which bills (other than those on revenues and appropriations) the House will take up and in what order. It also determines generally the time limits for debate on each bill and the extent to which, if at all, amendments may be offered on the floor. Since some bills are obviously much more important than others and since bills do not go on the calendars in order of importance, few will dispute the proposition that there must be some mechanism for establishing priorities for House action. Yet there has been constant argument about whether the Rules Committee is the appropriate mechanism as well as about the way the committee has functioned.

The power to decide which bills will be considered implies the power to decide which will not be considered. The Rules Committee has thus been the burial ground of much proposed legislation already recommended by the subject-matter committees. In killing legislation, it has often in the past acted without much regard for the wishes of the majority of the House or of the majority party that is trying to carry out a program. This committee was customarily loaded with senior members of both parties from safe districts who felt relatively little sense of party responsibility. Several of its chairmen were famous for exercise of immense, almost unrestrained power. In all fairness, however, it should be pointed out that the Rules Committee is also often used by members of the House as a means of avoiding blame for killing a bill. There are times when many do not want to vote against a bill for personal political reasons, but they expect the Rules Committee to sit on it so they will not be forced to vote at all.

The frequently arbitrary actions of the Rules Committee in the past in its control of the agenda of the House have led to a variety of attempts to curb its power. Two or three times the power of the Rules Committee was reduced for one session by a special rule that permitted the speaker to bring up a bill that the committee had held for twenty-one days or more, but the conservative coalition (an informal Republican–Southern Democrat alliance) each time succeeded in restoring the committee's absolute power. In the wake of the reform movement the committee, still functioning as the traffic cop of legislation, has become an instrument of the majority leadership rather than an independent empire. Responsibility is thus placed where it properly belongs: much more squarely on the majority party.

THE HOUSE APPROPRIATIONS, BUDGET, AND WAYS AND MEANS COMMITTEES

The other committees wielding the greatest power are the Budget Committee, the Ways and Means Committee, and the Appropriations Committee. Virtually every policy proposal of consequence, and even most amendments to existing law, involve expenditure of public funds. Whenever this is the case and whatever the amount, a specific amount of money must be approved by the Appropriations Committee, after approval of the bill by the subject-matter committee to which it was originally referred. Without money a program is effectively dead, even if it was previously authorized in principle. Fundamental responsibilities of the Appropriations Committee include studying the president's proposed budget each year, forcing the various administrative agencies to justify their requests in hearings, and ultimately recommending the detailed appropriations legislation to the House. In practice this large committee works primarily through subcommittees specialized in the areas of responsibility of the major executive departments and agencies, and its subcommittee chairmen commonly hold tremendous power (so much so that they are now subject to caucus vote, the same as committee chairmen). With the recent advent of a more formalized congressional budget procedure, Budget committees in each house develop overall budget targets each spring and recommend final ceilings in early fall. These committees and the professional staff that they employ are intended to make the Congress much more effective in the vital process of determining national priorities and to end its previous, nearly total reliance on the executive branch in that area. It is the budget that really determines the nature and course of action of the entire government.

Since in one way or another money must be raised to pay for most legislation that has been approved, action by the Ways and Means Committee is also required. This body has responsibility for all taxing and borrowing legislation and has come to have a central influence on the entire spectrum of national economic policy. Its chairman is always a key House figure whose support must be cultivated by every president. It is evident that the gauntlet that almost every major bill must run before being voted on by the houses themselves is a grueling one, and its life may be snuffed out at any stage: approval by the basic subject-matter committee, by Appropriations, by Ways and Means, and by Rules, preceded commonly by the judgment of a number of subcommittees; and most of the same hurdles must also be surmounted in the Senate.

THE HOUSE COMMITTEE OF THE WHOLE

Once a major bill is up for action the House usually considers it in what is known as a Committee of the Whole, which is simply the House of Representatives acting as a committee to expedite business. The procedural rules are simpler in committee, and only one hundred members are required for a quorum. Proponents and opponents are given equal time, and ranking majority and minority members of the committee that originally handled the bill usually allocate that time among various speakers. Time limits are ordinarily set in advance, but debate may also be cut off by the familiar process of adopting a motion "calling for the previous question." After debate and amendments, the vote of the Committee of the Whole is on whether to recommend the bill to the House, since a committee cannot pass legislation. The committee is then dissolved, the members reconstituting themselves as the House for brief floor debate and a final vote.

SENATE PROCEDURE

Senate procedure is basically similar to House procedure, but there are several significant distinctions. We have already noted that there is no officer in the Senate comparable to the speaker of the House; the floor leaders and policy committees are more powerful in the Senate. Bills are for the most part referred automatically to the committee requested by the authors, except where there are formal requirements. The Rules Committee of the Senate is primarily a housekeeping committee and has no power over the calendars, unlike its counterpart in the House. Instead, the establishment of priorities for bills is largely the responsibility of the majority leader, working in consultation with the party's Steering and Policy Committee and with the minority leader. A strong case can be made for this arrangement, since it places responsibility on the majority party even more clearly than is true under the new rules in the House.

The best-known difference between the procedures of the two

Respite from a filibuster. Senator Henry Jackson catches some sleep on an anteroom couch during an all-night session of the Senate, September 28, 1977, while a filibuster against deregulation of natural gas was in progress.

houses is the possibility of unlimited debate in the Senate, praised by some members as making the Senate the last bastion of completely free debate in the world. Privileges are subject to abuse, however, and in the name of free debate it is possible to deny others meaningful freedom of debate and to frustrate the process of democratic decision making by thwarting the majority will. The filibuster, the practice of talking indefinitely in order to prevent action on a bill or to force concessions, is not a frequent occurrence, but it can be devastatingly effective. In fact, the mere threat of a filibuster may sometimes exert the same pressures as an actual filibuster.

The Senate does not have the familiar mechanism for closing debate by a majority vote on a motion to take up the "previous question." Since senators may speak as long as they wish and may yield the floor to each other, it is possible for a group to monopolize the floor interminably. A one-person filibuster can be broken simply by outwaiting the limits of physical endurance, although some senators have demonstrated truly remarkable stamina. The current record for the longest filibustering speech is held by Senator Strom Thurmond of South Carolina, who spoke for twenty-four hours and eighteen minutes in opposition to a civil rights bill in 1957. Debate in the Senate is supposed to be germane to the subject at hand, but each senator is judge of what is germane. Members have been treated to the delights of a Louisiana senator's recipe for "pot likker," have had *Pilgrim's Progress* read to them, and have even been subjected to random selections from an unabridged dictionary. To be sure, during the course of a filibuster no one but the person speaking is likely to be on the floor except the unfortunate presiding officer (that duty can be rotated), the clerks, and one member from the proponents' side who is there "to keep the speaker honest."

In an effort to break a filibuster the leadership can keep the Senate in session continuously twenty-four hours a day. Cots are moved into the cloakrooms, for the proponents cannot allow themselves to be caught without a quorum available. That would automatically adjourn the Senate until the next day, providing respite for the filibusterers. An associate of someone speaking at three o'clock in the morning, for example, can give the speaker a brief period of relief by entering the chamber to suggest the absence of a quorum. This cannot be done repeatedly, but the quorum check necessitates a roll call, which occupies perhaps twenty or thirty minutes. Members are forced out of bed to answer the roll, after which they can return to sleep.

The Senate has been notoriously reluctant to cut off debate, although a method is available. It is likely only if something of a state of exhaustion has set in, if the public or group pressure for the legislation is great enough, and if a sufficient number of members are strongly determined. The cloture (or closure) rule permits sixteen senators to file a motion for closing debate; after two days the question is put to a vote. A three-fifths majority of the entire Senate (sixty if there are no vacancies) is then required to terminate debate (reduced in 1975 from a requirement of two-thirds of those present and voting), although each senator is entitled to speak for one hour after such a vote has occurred. Cloture has been successfully invoked less than twenty times. Probably the most famous instance was in connection with the Civil Rights Act of 1964, when cloture was finally achieved only after the Senate had been tied up for three full months, the longest filibuster in history. More than half the successful cloture votes have occurred since that time. Under ordinary circumstances the time limits for debate in the Senate are set when a bill is taken up, on recommendation of the leadership and by unanimous consent of the Senate. In recent years a supplemental tactic of delay has been perfected, sometimes termed *filibuster by amendment.* A filibustering group, facing the probability of cloture, may introduce scores (sometimes even hundreds) of amendments to the basic bill, which it can then call up for vote one by one after cloture has been invoked.

Further efforts emerged during the 1977 session to restrict some of the technical ways in which a minority can delay proceedings even after cloture has been voted (such as demands for verbatim reading of the journal or conference committee reports and the like), and a few modifications were achieved. One can make a strong argument that in a bicameral legislature one house should have freer rules of debate than the other, but it is certainly hard to square with democratic theory that a small minority should be able to block the will of the majority indefinitely. One might argue for longer time limits and greater flexibility to guarantee full expression for the minority, but should not a legislative body ultimately be able to come to a vote?

THE BILL GOES TO CONFERENCE

Once a bill has been passed by both houses in identical form, it goes to the president for signing. But after each house has worked over an important or complex bill through this elaborate process, the two versions are unlikely to be identical. The method of resolving the differences is through the use of conference committees. A separate conference committee is appointed to deal with each bill in dispute, the members being designated by the presiding officers of each house. From three to nine members are appointed by each house, and the chairman and ranking minority member of the committee that originally handled the bill are included in each case. Their function is to seek the compromises necessary to iron out the differences between the two versions.

When a majority of House conferees reaches agreement with a

majority of the Senate conferees, their recommendation goes back to both houses, where it has priority for action and must be accepted or rejected on an all-or-nothing basis. If one house rejects, the conferees try again, but ultimately agreement must be reached or there is no act. There has been much criticism of this system because of the tendency to shove conference committee reports through the houses with little consideration, the ability of the committees to change the bills drastically, the possibility that majority wishes may not be vigorously represented, and the secrecy of the committees' proceedings. Recent changes limit the ability to make major substantive alterations and have opened most conference committee meetings.

HOW LOBBYISTS WORK

It would be unrealistic to discuss the legislative process without taking more fully into account the part played by lobbying. The lobbyists (or in more genteel language "legislative advocates") are often referred to somewhat sarcastically as the "third house," and theirs is in truth a vital role. In a democracy every group must be free to express its views to legislators, and lobbyists can frequently be most helpful. As specialists in particular areas they can provide a great deal of expert technical information to the legislator who must deal with a fantastic variety of subjects and who lacks the research resources available to the executive branch. The viewpoints they represent need to be considered in the legislative process, although the legislator is certainly under no compulsion to accept them. The biased perspective of the lobbyists' views can be recognized, and they can be balanced against the views of other groups.

Lobbyists are a source of a large share of all proposed legislation, and to a surprising degree they function much like members of Congress without a vote. After getting someone to introduce a bill, the lobbyist must urge its consideration by a committee and appear at hearings to speak in its behalf and answer questions. The lobbyist seeks to build support among other legislators and often develops alliances with other pressure groups. If successful in committee, the next step is to try to get a green light from the Rules Committee or the majority leadership, and so on through the entire process. This is essentially what a legislator does in attempting to get bills passed. There may be considerable logrolling with other legislators, which is a kind of reciprocal back scratching: "You help me with my bill, and I'll help you with yours." While most people assume that all the pressure is from lobbyists on legislators, there is pressure in the other direction too. Legislators often seek the aid of lobbyists and their organizations in getting legislation passed.

The popular image of the lobbyist is a sort of cartoon version of a fat man carrying a cigar and tossing hundred-dollar bills about. But most lobbyists are solid citizens representing perfectly legitimate interests in a responsible fashion. One may surely agree or disagree with the goals of any particular group, and criticism of questionable tactics is certainly proper, but neither of these attitudes is an objection to the institution of lobbying. While "wine, women, and song" lobbying has not disappeared, its influence is minor. Entertainment of legislators is rarely if ever a matter of buying votes but is rather a method of acquiring access. Time is at a premium, and easy access to a legislator through personal friendship is extremely important. Campaign contributions are another channel of access, and it is in connection with these that most dubious practices are likely to arise.

The effective lobbyist is one who develops acquaintance with as many legislators as possible, knows a vast amount about each of them and their attitudes, understands the legislative process, and above all builds a reputation for honesty and for knowing what he or she is talking about. The lobbyists' most priceless asset is the confidence that legislators have in their reliability. Members of Congress know that a lobbyist is paid to represent only one side of a question; but if they are ever victimized by dishonest information, the lobbyist's usefulness in dealing with them is ended.

Lobbyists registered with the clerk of the House or the secretary of the Senate outnumber members of Congress by more than two to one, and there are many occasional lobbyists not included in such tabulations. Expenditures of interest groups to promote or oppose legislation in the halls of Congress alone run to many millions of dollars a year. Many have had notable and continuing success even in the face of strongly contrary public opinion, as has been evidenced by the ability of the National Rifle Association to prevent effective gun-control legislation and the American Medical Association's success in staving off a general program of public health insurance.

Efforts to regulate undesirable practices in lobbying concentrate primarily on publicity. Full-time lobbyists are required to register with the clerk of the House and the secretary of the Senate, indicating by whom they are employed and what amount they are paid. They must then file quarterly reports itemizing receipts and expenditures and indicating what legislation they seek to influence. All such information is published in the *Congressional Record*. Despite the fact that there are numerous loopholes, it appears that the regulatory requirements have been somewhat useful. It is probable, however, that more significant than the formal requirements is the floodlight of publicity focused on public officials, and to some extent lobbyists as well, by the news media. Such publicity is somewhat erratic and often incomplete, yet it can be devastatingly effective.

Because of the many loopholes, a major attempt at legislation for more effective regulation of lobbying has been under way for a number of years, actively pushed by Common Cause. The most important features are provisions to require registration and reporting from the multitude of lobbyists who engage in that activity only as a part of their responsibilities as officers or employees of organizations and to require reports by paid "grassroots lobbyists" who work to persuade other persons to communicate with members of Congress. Determining who should be covered, and the extent to which contributors should be disclosed, generates vehement controversy.

CONGRESSIONAL INVESTIGATION

At the height of a flurry of legislative investigations several years ago, cartoonist Herblock began referring to the three branches of the government as the executive, judicial, and investigative. Because they may often be relatively sensational, investigative activities by congressional committees are likely to steal the headlines, and television coverage has magnified their public impact. Nevertheless, they are supplementary and supporting activities to the main responsibilities of Congress. Investigations are authorized for one of two basic purposes: developing information as a foundation for possible legislation or helping to hold the administration or individual administrative agencies accountable by checking on the way their duties are being handled. They are also frequently used as a means of bringing pressure on an administration to adopt a policy favored by the investigators, as was done in hearings on United States policy in Southeast Asia by Senator William Fulbright and the Senate Foreign Relations Committee late in the 1960s and early in the 1970s.

Throughout the history of the country, investigations have frequently made notable contributions in both categories. Excellent studies have formed the basis for legislation in such areas as regulation of the stock exchanges, immigration control, and business monopolies. The story of falsified bombing reports from Southeast Asia was uncovered in this way after the formal end of the Vietnam War. The notorious Teapot Dome oil scandal during the Harding administration was exposed in the same fashion, the Watergate investigation is widely familiar, and there have been others of a less sensational nature. This potential for significant accomplishment should not be lost sight of as one examines the criticisms of congressional investigations, which have been numerous and vehement. The investigative power is second only to legislative and budget direction as the most important tool of Congress in dealing with the executive.

Many investigations have been careful and thorough; others have not. Some have been used for mere publicity, for the personal aggrandizement of a chairman, or for inflicting personal or partisan damage. Certain committees have devoted their attention to the political opinions and alleged disloyalty of individual citizens and organizations, with little apparent concern for either the overseeing of administration or the studying of potential legislation. The courts, though under great pressure to impose further limitations, have generally interpreted the scope of the investigative power broadly, suggesting that it can extend to any subject on which Congress *might* legislate. The Supreme Court has indicated, however, that the scope is not unlimited, even though it is still reluctant to impose restraints in practice, except in guaranteeing freedom from self-incrimination under the Fifth Amendment. In *Watkins* v. *United States* (1957) the Court said:

> The power of Congress to conduct investigations is inherent in the legislative process. That power is broad . . . but it is not unlimited. There is no general authority to expose the private affairs of individuals without justification in terms of the functions of Congress. . . . Abuse of the investigative process may imperceptibly lead to abridgment of protected freedoms.

A few committees have given legislative investigations a bad name, and there are a number of justifiable recurrent criticisms of practices such as (1) hearing only one side of a case and then recessing indefinitely; (2) failing to establish the reliability of witnesses and even using paid informers; (3) granting to "friendly witnesses" (who can be counted on to say what the committee wants to hear) free rein to say whatever they wish while restricting "unfriendly witnesses" to answering questions; (4) bullying witnesses and using the related tactic of reacting to the answers to loaded questions with an air of disbelief; (5) refusing an individual who has been subjected to attack before the committee the right to confront and question accusers; (6) giving to the news media unverified and unevaluated materials about individuals as if they represented committee findings; (7) refusing to accept responsibility for the accuracy of materials that damage a person's reputation; (8) including in committee files only derogatory information and excluding anything that might convey a favorable impression; (9) making sweeping allegations against entire groups on the basis of "guilt by association"; and (10) conducting "road shows," a series of hearings in different cities across the country in which the same witnesses are heard and the same documents produced, obviously developing no additional data.

The logical road to improvement is to correct abuses rather than to seek to destroy the investigative power; the ways to correct the specific abuses listed above are implicit in their statement. Each house is perfectly able to control its committees more adequately if it chooses to do so, but there has been a reluctance to interfere with personal prerogatives. Codes of ethical procedure have been proposed from time to time; although most have not been formally adopted, there have been some limited improvements. Much depends on the personal qualities of the chairman of an investigative committee as well as on the temper of the country at the time of the investigation.

THE "REFORM" OF CONGRESS

It is always easier to point out shortcomings than to offer constructive and acceptable solutions. Over the years Congress from within and without has been the subject of numerous studies proposing reforms. The Legislative Reorganization Act of 1970, like its predecessor in 1946, took steps to improve research and information services, but it went further in guaranteeing greater fairness of operation. It provided, for example, that in both houses a majority of any committee could call a meeting if the chairman refused a request, and it restricted the freedom of conference committees to change a bill significantly beyond the scope of the versions sent to it by the two houses. Committee staffs were increased, with one-third of the staff (and one-third of the funds available for staff) guaranteed to the minority. Its greatest achievement, however, was to end the practice of secret unrecorded votes in committees, a device by which members were often able to escape responsibility for their actions.

This act seemed to push the door ajar, and there followed during the next few years a whole series of reforms that will have a lasting impact on the openness and effectiveness of the legislative process. Congress had become weary of being characterized as the weakest of the branches and the least rapidly adaptable to changing times, and there was within it increasing recognition that its own house must be put in order if it were effectively to reassert itself vis-à-vis the presidency. Powerful external force was applied, principally by Common Cause, which for some time focused its lobbying and publicity on congressional reform and has been given much credit by leaders of the movement within both chambers. But the most significant factor for change has been the changing composition of Congress itself and the resultant shift of attitudes.

A new generation had come to political power, and many able and articulate newcomers impatient with the old ways were eager for a piece of action. Agitation for reform that had been urged for the preceding five or six years by young liberals in both parties, notably the Democratic Study Group and the Republican Wednesday Club, suddenly began to bear fruit. The automatic caucus votes on chairmanships have already been mentioned, but there have been a number of other actions of equal importance. Both houses, after considerable controversy, voted overwhelmingly to severely limit closed meetings of committees by requiring that all meetings must be open to the public unless a majority of the committee, by roll call vote with a quorum present, votes to close them. In the past approximately 40 per cent of all meetings were closed, and most that were open were public hearings. Eighty per cent of sessions to discuss, "mark up," and vote on bills were closed. Now at least that percentage or more are open.

We have noted previously such steps as altering the role of the House Rules Committee, revivifying the Steering and Policy committees, creating a congressional budget system, expanding leadership opportunity for the speaker, restructuring the standing committees and their jurisdictions, limiting the power of committee chairmen, restricting multiple committee memberships in order to guarantee more meaningful roles for all members, and providing greater caucus responsibility for committee assignments and committee leadership.

Efficiency in the legislative process is not necessarily a primary goal, since it is designed to represent and give voice to the varied viewpoints present in a large and complex society. Yet it is true that the system in the United States gives a tremendous advantage to those seeking to preserve the status quo. We have observed the vast number of hurdles that proponents of legislation must overcome to achieve passage. How much easier is the task of the opponents! They need only succeed in blocking the bill at any *one* of the numerous stages in either of the two houses or in shunting it aside by a procedural maneuver. It is not really necessary for opponents to persuade a majority of 435 members of Congress or even of a quorum in either of the two houses: a majority of one in some subcommittee with perhaps five members present may suffice, even though there are ways for supporters to carry on the battle.

A number of needs remain untouched, in part because there is no complete agreement that they are in fact needs. Inertia is hard to overcome in a large body that has been operated by established customs and controlled by those who have worked with the system the longest. Some of the reform possibilities are structural or technical, such as ending the possibility of filibuster, eliminating the demands that administrative agencies clear their actions in advance with a committee, and more adequately controlling investigative committees. Others, however, arise out of attitudes and habit patterns, such as unethical behavior (misuse of committee funds or abuse of congressional immunity), overemphasis on minor issues at the expense of crisis questions like environmental protection, an excessively parochial viewpoint, and an unwillingness to give to the leadership still more effective ways of carrying out a party program. In time these and still other improvements may be achieved, at least if there continues to be organized public pressure to aid reform-minded members. But recent change has been striking, and whatever its faults, Congress has generally been a successful instrument of popular government and a microcosm of the nation it serves.

BASIC CONCEPTS AND TERMS

gerrymander
loaded district
one man–one vote doctrine
reapportionment
congressional staff role
congressional immunity
disciplining members
ethics codes and committees
party caucuses
speaker of the House
president pro tempore of the
 Senate
floor leaders
party whips
standing committees
seniority system

powers of committee chairmen
Steering and Policy committees
unofficial organizations in
 Congress
House Rules Committee
Appropriations Committee
Ways and Means Committee
Budget Committee
Committee of the Whole
filibuster
cloture
conference committee
lobbying
congressional investigations
congressional reform

THE
JUDICIARY
IN THE
POLITICAL
PROCESS

10

Everyone knows that judicial decisions are not brought by constitutional storks. They are the products of people who have been given special status and independence to perform a special role. In few other countries do the courts exercise such political power as they do in the United States. "Sooner or later," a foreign observer once commented, "every major political issue in the United States is resolved into a judicial question." Whether or not the statement is totally true, it merits serious consideration.

The judiciary, Alexander Hamilton contended, is the weakest of the three branches, because it controls neither the sword nor the purse.* Later political leaders referred to the American doctrine of judicial supremacy. Paradoxically, both observations are accurate. The courts have the power to determine the validity of the acts of the other branches of government, protect citizens against abuse of

---

The Federalist, number 78. The argument continues: "It may truly be said to have neither *force* nor *will,* but merely judgment; and must ultimately depend upon the aid of the executive arm even for the efficacy of its judgments."

government power, and decide disputes concerning national versus state powers. The United States Supreme Court has often been in the center of national controversy, which, though it has varied in intensity, is indicative of the crucial role played by that body. At times the Court has functioned as a brake on social change; at other times it moves ahead of and stimulates public opinion.

THE DUAL SYSTEM OF NATIONAL AND STATE COURTS

Alone among the federal systems, the United States has two (or, more accurately, fifty-one) separate and complete court systems. The national courts and the state courts have separate jurisdictions, though there are a few areas in which they have concurrent authority, and they operate independently except for the possible ultimate review of decisions by the United States Supreme Court (see Figure 10.1).

ORGANIZATION

In the national judicial structure the district courts, the "trial courts," have original jurisdiction. This is where national cases normally begin and where most end, since only a fraction are appealed. There are at present approximately ninety district courts, at least one in each state; states with the larger populations have correspondingly more trial courts. Such courts may consist of a number of judges, each of whom conducts proceedings independently. Decisions are rendered by a single presiding judge and, depending on the nature of the case, by a jury.

A litigant dissatisfied with a trial-court decision may appeal to the appropriate United States Court of Appeals (still commonly termed the circuit court). One of these exists for each of ten regions of the country, and there is one for the District of Columbia. These courts have virtually no original jurisdiction, but they review the actions and judgments of the district courts and certain administrative boards and commissions. Cases are usually heard by a panel of three judges. An appellate court has three options in disposing of a case: it may affirm the lower-court decision, it may reverse that decision, or it may, on discovering a procedural error, remand the case to the district court for a retrial. For example, a person convicted on criminal charges in a district court may claim on appeal that the trial judge instructed the jury improperly. If the court of appeals agrees, it holds that the individual has not in the full sense had a fair trial but sees no reason simply to turn the defendant free. Instead, it orders the case

FIGURE 10.1　Structure of the National and State Court Systems

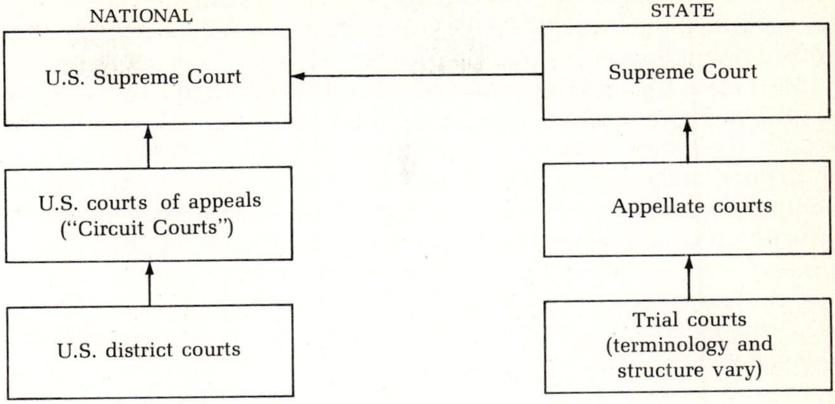

NATIONAL	STATE
U.S. Supreme Court	Supreme Court
U.S. courts of appeals ("Circuit Courts")	Appellate courts
U.S. district courts	Trial courts (terminology and structure vary)

tried again, this time with the proper instructions to a different jury to insure that justice will be done.

Under certain circumstances it is possible to request review of an appellate-court decision by the United States Supreme Court. But because the Supreme Court is the court of final appeal for a nation of approximately 220 million people, it must severely limit the number and types of cases it will hear. It is primarily concerned with constitutional interpretation and with conflicting lower-court decisions that have made uniform interpretation of a law necessary for the entire country. Since this court has for the most part power to choose the cases it will handle, one can appeal to it only under very limited conditions. Usually one asks the Court to issue a writ of certiorari (an order from a higher court to a lower one directing it to certify the record of a case being considered for review). At least four of the nine justices must agree that the case merits consideration before the writ will be issued. Like the courts of appeals, the Supreme Court can affirm or reverse a decision or remand a case to a trial court. Requests for review cover a wide spectrum: desegregation, legislative districting, tax deductions, state laws on obscenity, and so on.

The Constitution specifies that the Supreme Court has original jurisdiction in cases involving a state as one of the litigants and in those involving diplomatic personnel. Because it does not have time to sit as a trial court, the Supreme Court usually appoints for these cases a "special master" (commonly a retired judge of eminence) to hear the evidence and arguments, develop a record, and submit recommendations to the Court. After study of these materials, the decision is then rendered by the Supreme Court.

Supplementing these national courts are a few specialized courts such as the Court of Claims, the Customs Court, and the Court of Customs and Patent Appeals. Because they deal with a great amount of technical litigation, these courts relieve the regular courts of a considerable burden.

Most state court systems follow the national system's three-tiered arrangement of trial, appellate, and supreme courts, though the names given the courts vary widely. They function in fashion similar to the national courts, but state supreme courts ordinarily have little control over which cases they will hear. In certain types of case, usually involving national constitutional issues (individual liberties, for example), it is possible to ask the United States Supreme Court to review the decisions of state supreme courts. In that sense the Supreme Court is the court of final appeal for both the national and the state court systems.

JURISDICTION

In distinguishing between national and state court jurisdiction, the simplest approach is to note what constitutes national jurisdiction and to recognize that jurisdiction over all other matters lies with the states. There are two basic grounds for national court jurisdiction. The first is the existence in a case of a federal question, such as alleged violations of national laws, rights under the United States Constitution, actions of national government agencies or officials, and relations with foreign nations. The second is diversity of citizenship, referring to cases involving suits between persons who are citizens of different states or in which a state is one of the litigants. Concurrent jurisdiction with the state courts involves suits that could be filed in either the state or the national court system, but the largest body of litigation is handled by state courts. Once a case has been tried in one system, it stays within that system for appeal, except for the few state court decisions ultimately reviewed by the United States Supreme Court.

The national courts do not render advisory opinions (that is, they do not answer hypothetical questions) even for Congress or the president: they act only in connection with genuinely adversary cases or controversies.* This means in practice that many issues of the gravest import may be dealt with only if and when some private individual or organization initiates legal action on proper grounds. It is true, however, that a legislative body can on occasion deliberately set the stage for a test case. An unusual but dramatic example was the Massachusetts act forbidding the sending of any resident of the state to fight abroad except when war has been declared by Congress, an

---

*Some state supreme courts render on request advisory opinions to the governor or the legislature.

unsuccessful attempt to have the military action in Vietnam, and similar situations, declared unconstitutional. Relatively quick court action (including by-passing one appellate level) can be secured when the public interest demands it, as in the case of determining the constitutionality of the congressional act lowering the voting age to eighteen or the question of whether the president could refuse to surrender White House tapes subpoenaed as evidence in a criminal trial.

In addition to deciding the more familiar suits involving interpretation and application of a law, courts may act to afford an individual protection against injury or damage when no law sufficiently covers the particular situation. The most common device is the injunction: a court order directing someone not to take or to cease a particular action. Suppose, for example, that your next-door neighbor, despite your remonstrances, continually uses the front yard as a staging area for demonstrations and that the resultant noise and traffic hazard make living in the area extremely unpleasant, if not dangerous, for you and your family. If there is no law specifically covering such a nuisance and you are unable to secure help from other officials, you may ask a judge to enjoin such activity in the future. Should the judge agree to do so, the order is enforced through the power of the judiciary to punish people for contempt of court. The injunctive power has great potential scope, and it is therefore exercised only after certain conditions have been met. The applicant seeking an injunction is expected to show that she or he is being (or is about to be) subjected to irreparable damage and has exhausted the other possible sources of relief and that no other remedy at law is available. At times injunctions are sought to protect the public or public property, as when an assembly is thought likely to result in a riot, but this practice ordinarily raises a serious constitutional problem.

WHO ARE THE JUDGES?

All judges of the national courts are appointed by the president, with Senate confirmation, and serve indefinite terms ("during good behavior" is the constitutional phrase). While provision is made for retirement at certain ages, with a generous pension, retirement is not compulsory, and a number of judges serve until they reach very advanced years. In order to preserve judicial independence, the Constitution provided that judges can be removed from office only by conviction in impeachment proceedings and that a judge's salary cannot be reduced during office. Impeachment is rarely undertaken (only nine instances involving judges of national courts in the history of the country), a fact that emphasizes judicial independence, and convictions (there have been only four) are even rarer. Occasionally, political pressure and the weight of public opinion have forced resignations. Although most unusual in connection with the Supreme Court, such an event did occur in 1969 when Justice Fortas stepped down after widespread furor in Congress and from the press concerning his acceptance of a fee for legal services from a foundation established by a man who was later convicted of violating a law on the sale of securities. Although no conclusive evidence of impropriety came to light, critics stressed that a judge must avoid "even the appearance of impropriety." Fortas resigned so that the court could proceed without a cloud of controversy. One by-product of this episode was the establishment of a detailed code of ethical behavior for national court judges (applicable to the Supreme Court only by voluntary acceptance), which restricts types of association and sources of income not connected with judicial responsibilities.

Presidential appointments to the district courts and the courts of appeals are controlled by the practice of senatorial courtesy, so in reality the president's choices are extremely limited. A district-court vacancy in a given state is filled on the recommendation of a senator of the president's party from that state. Because the courts of appeals serve regions rather than states, it might appear that the president would be unfettered in choosing these judges, but by tradition a

The Justices of the United States Supreme Court. (Left to right, front row: Associate Justices Byron R. White; William J. Brennan, Jr.; Chief Justice Warren R. Burger; Associate Justices Potter Stewart; and Thurgood Marshall. Left to right, back row: Associate Justices William H. Rehnquist; Harry A. Blackmun; Lewis F. Powell; and John P. Stevens.)

system of rotation of appointments among the states within the region has evolved. If the appropriate senators do not make the selection, they possess at least an effective veto over possible appointees. A president may thus have to take the blame for an undesirable appointment without having made that choice or may be put in an almost impossible situation by conflicting pressures.*

APPOINTMENT OF SUPREME COURT JUSTICES

In Supreme Court appointments the practice of senatorial courtesy does not apply, since no senator or state has more right than any other to be heard on these appointments. A president is presumed to give the deepest consideration to possible nominees for this court, which possesses vast power to shape the future of the nation, and prospective appointees are ordinarily carefully screened by the Department of Justice. A president is expected to seek a person of outstanding ability and integrity who is trained in the law, although the latter is not a constitutional requirement. Previous judicial experience has not been given great weight by most presidents—Eisenhower and perhaps Nixon are exceptions. Previous legislative and executive experience has been more highly valued, for this court, unlike a trial court, is fundamentally concerned less with the technical aspects of law than with broad issues of public policy in a legal context. The need is for a genuine breadth of vision and understanding. A number of other factors must also be taken into consideration.

A president understandably chooses someone who shares in large measure the administration's views on social policy and on the role of the Court in the political system. Usually the individual will be of the president's party, though a president who has the opportunity to make several appointments may in time provide balance by making a selection from the other party. Even so, only persons who subscribe to his own preferences in public policy will be considered. Once on the bench, a judge is expected to put aside all partisanship, but his or her basic sociopolitical orientation remains extremely important. A selection may also be the result of a campaign pledge to change the direction of the Court. President Nixon redeemed such a pledge in the appointments of Chief Justice Burger and Justices Harry Blackmun, Lewis Powell, and William Rehnquist, thought to be strict constructionists† and likely to place less emphasis than their predecessors on protecting the rights of persons accused of crime.

---

*For example, see the case study on President Johnson's appointment of Judge Coleman, discussed in Chapter 7.

†Usually defined as those who would limit rather narrowly the permissible scope of national government action. A judge may be strict on one matter but not on another, and what is considered strict changes over time. The concept of strict construction is thus somewhat empty and is as much a slogan as a definition or doctrine.

Sometimes a president, by only one or two appointments, is able drastically to change the orientation of the Court. But history is filled with examples showing that there is no guarantee that judges will fulfill presidential expectations.

Another factor in an appointment is the degree of regional balance on the Court. This does not mean that judges are picked to represent states or regions, but no president would permit the Court to become composed predominantly of persons from only one section of the country. One unwritten understanding is that there should always be at least one southerner on the court. There are other such unwritten understandings, nowhere prescribed as rules but traditionally followed. For example, it has been understood that at least one Jewish and one Catholic judge will be on the Supreme Court. Justice Brandeis was followed by Frankfurter, he in turn by Goldberg and Fortas. President Nixon announced that he did not intend to be bound by these understandings, and he did not appoint a Jewish successor to Fortas. President Johnson's appointment of Justice Marshall, the first black member of the court, may have established a new precedent within this tradition. On occasion one individual may satisfy several requirements. When President Eisenhower decided to name a Democrat to the bench, he needed also a Catholic, and he preferred someone with previous judicial experience. Justice Brennan, then a judge of the New Jersey Supreme Court, met all these requirements and was selected.

CONTROVERSIAL APPOINTMENTS

Reacting to the Fortas controversy and widespread charges of "cronyism" in the previous administration, President Nixon indicated at the time of the appointment of Chief Justice Burger that he had ruled out consideration of his close friends and associates. To many observers this seemed a dubious principle to apply indefinitely, for it can exclude a number of outstanding potential appointees. He also stated that he planned to submit judicial nominations to the American Bar Association for approval, a plan that generated dispute over whether this gave undue influence to the legal profession. This system functioned for a time, but after sharp criticism of some of his nominees from the ABA committee the president terminated the practice. The committee continues on its own to issue evaluative statements on persons considered prospective nominees for judgeships.

The process of selecting a chief justice is no different from that for selecting an associate justice, but the appointment may be more significant. A strong chief justice can exert considerable influence on the orientation of the Court, as did Chief Justice Warren, despite the fact that members of the Supreme Court tend to be independent and that each has only one vote. Chief justices are normally appointed from outside the Court rather than from among the associate justices. Although the latter has been done, it is a delicate matter to select one from among equals for this elevated position.

Confirmation of nominees for the Supreme Court is usually secured with little, if any, contest in the Senate. In times of sharp ideological division and of notable conflicts between Congress and the Court, however, serious challenges have been made. Three of the most significant instances occurred in rapid succession between 1968 and 1970. In 1968 President Johnson nominated Abe Fortas, then a member of the Court, for chief justice. Retiring Chief Justice Warren, a Republican but considered a social liberal, had made his retirement effective upon the appointment of a successor. Republicans, especially, saw this condition as an attempt to fill the position with a liberal at that time as a hedge against the possible election of a less liberal Republican president in November. A coalition of Republicans and southern Democrats was formed to block the nomination. Some hoped that a Republican president would soon be available to make the appointment, and others were motivated primarily by a desire to "punish" the Court for decisions with which they disagreed, especially in civil liberties and desegregation. Extended interrogation of the nominee by the judiciary committee, and in particular the vehement attacks of Senator Thurmond of South Carolina, ultimately raised serious questions about the separation of powers between the legislative and judicial branches. The interrogation had little to do with the personal qualifications of Justice Fortas or, indeed, with his connection to the Wolfson Foundation, which did not come to light until months later. It consisted mainly of questions on whether the nominee agreed with various decisions of the Court and on how he would expect to decide issues likely to come before the Court in the future. Fortas declined to answer these questions on the grounds that to give an opinion in advance was unjudicial and that an attempt to force an advance opinion would tend to destroy the independence of the judiciary. His opponents were able to stall confirmation long enough to make the nomination by an outgoing president no longer feasible, and his name was finally withdrawn.

President Nixon filled the position of chief justice soon after taking office, encountering no significant opposition, and a few months later the resignation of Justice Fortas provided him the opportunity for another appointment. The president's desire for another strict constructionist and his wish to demonstrate to the South his continuing concern for the interests of that section led to his nomination in August 1969 of Clement F. Haynsworth, Jr., of South Carolina, a judge of the United States Court of Appeals for the Fourth Circuit. The Haynsworth nomination stirred a hornet's nest of opposition, in part because many felt his decisions showed a prosegregation bias and in part because he had decided several cases involving companies in which he was a stockholder or had some other personal interest. There was no evidence of corruption, but again there arose the issues of the appearance of impropriety and ethical insensitivity. Supporters of Haynsworth insisted that he was being opposed solely because he was a southerner, but his opponents gained strength as more cases involving personal interest were uncovered. Although widely urged to withdraw the nomination, President Nixon stoutly defended his choice, only to see Haynsworth rejected after three months of intermittent investigation and debate on a 55 to 45 vote, with even the Republican floor leader voting against confirmation.

The blow to the president's prestige and pride was considerable, but of course he had to submit another nomination. The Senate was exhausted by the long and acrimonious Haynsworth battle, and the general feeling was that it would approve any reasonable nomination with a minimum of discussion. In fact, the Senate appeared ready to lean over backward to give the president his next choice, but many members reacted with dismay when President Nixon named G. Harrold Carswell of Florida, a judge of the United States Court of Appeals for the Fifth Circuit. Carswell had an undistinguished judicial record, which included a high rate of reversals of his opinions by higher courts. To many he clearly seemed to lack the stature of a Supreme Court justice. Not long after the nomination, a newspaper reporter dug up an account of a "segregation forever" speech delivered by Carswell in 1948 when campaigning for a legislative seat, and the fat was once again in the fire. Judge Carswell announced that he was embarrassed by the speech and that he certainly no longer subscribed to the views of his youth. But various attorneys and former litigants before the judge came forth to claim that he had often shown prejudice toward blacks in his court. It further developed that he had in recent years been one of a group that had incorporated a public golf club as a private club, presumably to retain its "whites only" character.

Almost reluctantly at first, but then with swiftly gathering momentum, the Senate opposition regrouped. Once again the president stood by his choice, though it appeared that he had made the nomination solely on the recommendation of Attorney General Mitchell, without having talked to Carswell. Frustrated by the situation and irritated at the opposition, the president hurt his own cause by issuing a statement that blasted the opponents and suggested strongly that it was the proper function of the Senate to consent to presidential selections for such offices. Even his supporters in the Senate responded sharply that the role of the Senate was to *advise* and consent. And one conservative Republican senator was no help at all with a public remark that there ought to be room for a mediocre judge on the Court, since there were many mediocre people and even mediocre attorneys in the country who deserved some representation! The result was a second rejection in the middle of April 1970, this time by a 51 to 45 vote, in which thirteen Republicans and four southern Democrats deserted the president. President Nixon's subsequent nomination of another court of appeals judge, Harry A. Blackmun of Minnesota, a jurist of outstanding reputation and apparently impeccable personal qualities, met with widespread approbation, and the Senate responded with an unusual unanimous vote of confirmation. Approval of Powell (a southerner) and Rehnquist was also accomplished with little difficulty, although Rehnquist was opposed because of what many considered to be his rightwing views and actions.

DOES WHO IS APPOINTED MAKE ANY DIFFERENCE?

The essentially political (not partisan) role of the Supreme Court and the influence a president can have with a few appointments are suggested by the first full term of the Court after the seating of the four Nixon appointees. Although three-fourths of the Court's decisions in that term were by divided votes (in fact 20 per cent were 5 to 4 and 26 per cent were 6 to 3) the four new members voted identically on 70 per cent of the cases decided, and the percentage was much higher in cases dealing with certain kinds of topic. The three holdover social liberals, Justices Brennan, Douglas, and Marshall, also voted together in almost the same number of cases. Since Justice White (a Kennedy appointee) voted with the new bloc of four 94 per cent of the time, they constituted a new majority and changed the direction of the Court in some significant ways. Justice Stewart, an Eisenhower appointee, often was a swing vote, not uncommonly joining the liberal group. It could probably be said that the views of the president enjoyed majority support on the Court, though not *because* they were his views, on issues of criminal law, obscenity, business regulation, and tax policy. The reverse was true on the issues of abortion and public aid to church-related schools, while the "new majority" was often divided on issues of alleged race and sex discrimination. Previous history shows similar instances in which the Court's position has shifted in attitude and specifics, when a president has sought change and has had the opportunity to make several appointments. Because the judges serve for a long period of years, a president's appointments to the Supreme Court may constitute one of his most lasting influences on the course of American politics.

The Burger court proved in time to be relatively fragmented and unpredictable, and the chief justice found himself rather frequently outvoted. The Court divided three ways ideologically: Burger and Rehnquist reflected a conservative posture, Brennan and Marshall displayed the liberal, while the other five constituted a moderate bloc less easy to predict. As a whole the Court was not as strongly or consistently doctrinaire as expected, and Ford's appointee, Justice John Paul Stevens, proved a highly independent member of the moderate group.

JUDICIAL ACTIVISM VERSUS JUDICIAL SELF-RESTRAINT

Should a judge in making decisions act within the narrow limits of the constitutional and legal issues of a case before the court or permit personal opinion of the social desirability of a statute to influence judgment on whether it should be upheld? And even if a judge proposes rigid self-limitation, is this realistically possible? Is not everyone influenced by background, training, and sense of social values? Such questions have been for centuries at the core of arguments over the proper role of the courts. In recent years the principal schools of thought on this matter have been judicial activism and judicial self-restraint.

If a sharp delineation of these positions were possible, the activist judge could be described as one who decides questions of statutory validity largely on the basis of whether or not she or he believes the law will promote the social good. The advocate of self-restraint, on the other hand, insists that the question of whether a statute is good or bad is solely a matter for legislative determination and that the role of judge is merely to decide whether the act is constitutional. The question of constitutionality, however, is not simple or clear-cut but involves interpretation and judgment. Few judges would classify themselves as activists in the pure sense; most claim to follow self-restraint, but the manner in which they decide what is constitutional varies. Although the two definitions are useful for analysis, judges obviously do not fit neatly into categories. A court may be activist on one kind of subject and not on others, or its activism may have a conservative bent on some subjects, liberal on others. Some would argue that the latter was true of the Burger court in the criminal law and the abortion decisions, for example.

The self-restraint that most judges accept in principle was stated clearly by Justice Frankfurter in a dissenting opinion in the second flag-salute case (discussed in Chapter 3). The West Virginia statute was in his opinion unwise and unlikely to accomplish its avowed purpose. Had he been a member of the legislative body, he said, he would have voted against it. But, he went on, there is no specific constitutional bar to such legislation, and "I deem it beyond my constitutional power to assert my view of the wisdom of this law

From *The Herblock Gallery* (Simon & Schuster, 1968).

"How are we going to stop lawlessness if you fellows insist on observing the laws?"

against the view of the state of West Virginia." There is little dispute over the principle of self-restraint, but differences come to light in its application. In the second flag-salute case six judges thought that a constitutional bar to the statute did exist.

It should be emphasized that the activism versus self-restraint controversy has nothing to do with the political philosophy of judges, though there is much popular confusion over this matter. There have been liberal activist judges and conservative activist judges; similarly, the self-restraint group includes both conservatives and liberals. It is a question not of liberalism or conservatism but of the function of judging and the way in which the power of the courts is to be used. One other point should be kept in mind:

Americans have a habit of confusing constitutionality with the quality of legislation. The warning voiced by Justice Frankfurter in the case mentioned above deserves pondering:

> The tendency of focusing attention on constitutionality is to make constitutionality synonymous with wisdom, to regard a law as all right if it is constitutional. . . . Particularly in legislation affecting freedom of thought and freedom of speech much which should offend a free-spirited society is constitutional. Reliance for the most precious interests of civilization, therefore, must be found outside of their vindication in courts of law. Only a persistent positive translation of the faith of a free society into the convictions and habits and actions of a community is the ultimate reliance against unabated temptations to fetter the human spirit.*

INSIDE THE SUPREME COURT

The visitor to the Supreme Court is impressed at once with the aura of formality and solemnity that surrounds its actions: the Court opens with the ancient call of the crier, the black-robed justices sit in high-backed chairs on a dais before dark velvet curtains, the attorneys are in morning clothes, a hush pervades the audience, and an awareness of the presence of high authority is everywhere. Yet informality appears in some respects, as justices interrogate an attorney from the bench, for example. Regardless of the nature of the case at hand, the drama is fascinating to watch.

Oral argument is a minor element of the legal process at this level, and it is usually limited to an hour for each side. The justices have before them the complete record of the proceedings in both the trial and the appellate courts, and this is supplemented by extensive briefs submitted by the attorneys for each party to the case. Long hours of study precede the oral hearing, which is the time ordinarily used by the justices to bring into focus the issues on which they believe the case will turn. The attorney's time is not his own. The oral presentation may be just launched when one of the justices leans forward to interrupt, saying, "Mr. Doe, I think we have perhaps heard enough on this particular point. Would you expand a bit on the argument made in your brief on page 223, and how do you rationalize that argument with the evidence appearing at page 482 of the trial-court record?" The attorney may later return to the presentation, probably soon to be interrupted again as the Court presses him to defend his views on the aspects they deem crucial to a decision.

Almost every Friday during a Court term the nine justices meet in conference for discussion of cases before them. The conference con-

West Virginia State Board of Education v. *Barnette* (1943).

siders requests for certiorari and cases that have been heard and are to be decided. A writ of certiorari accepting a case is granted when any four judges believe that review by the Court is merited, but these four votes are hard to acquire. (Of the roughly 5,000 requests considered annually, the Court usually selects between 150 and 170 cases for decision.) Cases come before this conference only after each justice has had time for full study of all relevant materials. Throughout the decision process no work is done by committees and no responsibility is delegated. Every justice participates fully in every decision. As they convene, each in turn shakes hands with all eight colleagues, a tradition established long ago that symbolizes a harmony of goals if not of viewpoints. No one is present but the justices, not even law clerks, secretaries, or pages. The chief justice speaks first regarding each item on the agenda, and discussion proceeds in order of seniority. Voting is in reverse order.

HOW CASES ARE DECIDED

The vote that is taken after the discussion of a case ready for decision constitutes only a tentative decision. The chief justice, if he voted with the majority, assigns the writing of the opinion. When he is not of the majority, the opinion is assigned by the senior justice in the majority group. The dissenters determine among themselves who is to prepare the dissenting opinion, but each member is free to write his own dissent, just as a justice who agrees with the majority for somewhat different reasons than those cited in the opinion may write a separate concurring opinion.

The writer of an opinion may be involved in weeks of painstaking research and writing, for the work must satisfy not only colleagues but an intensely critical audience throughout the country. When the writer is satisfied with a final draft, it is printed and circulated among the other members of the Court, dissenters as well as the majority, and each of the majority at least will reply with a detailed response. It is not unheard of for an opinion to go through as many as eight or ten drafts before everyone reaches full agreement. Moreover, circulation of the majority and dissenting drafts occasionally causes a change in votes, and there are times when what began as a majority opinion must be converted into dissent. A constant interchange of ideas by telephone and memoranda and over the luncheon table occurs, and the decision is not final until a majority of the justices has signed the opinion. At least six members must hear a case, and a majority vote is always required for a formal decision. Should the Court divide either 3 to 3 or 4 to 4, which might happen when there is a vacancy or when some member disqualifies himself from sitting on a particular case, no decision is made and the lower-court decision stands.

TOPPIX

"—And now for the crackpot dissenting opinion."

Unlike members of the legislative or executive branches, members of the Court must provide in published form the complete rationale for their decisions. Although it is freer from the immediate pressures of time and the tactics of interest groups, the Court is not free from public attack. Many of its decisions have stirred major conflict and have had great impact on the political and social development of the nation. One need only mention in illustration a few decisions of the Warren court, such as those on reapportionment, desegregation, police conduct, and prayer and Bible reading in the public schools, or of the Burger court on capital punishment and abortion. "We are very quiet there," remarked Justice Holmes over half a century ago, "but it is the quiet of a storm center."

THE WORKLOAD OF THE COURTS

In terms of the number of cases docketed, the workload of the United States Supreme Court more than quadrupled over the past three decades. While the number of cases actually heard and decided each year has remained about the same for over thirty years, the Court must nevertheless determine which ones it should hear from an increasingly larger pool. There are a variety of views as to how to deal with this problem and even as to whether it constitutes a problem.

At the end of 1972 a special study commission appointed by Chief Justice Burger recommended steps that stirred immediate controversy. Its central proposal was for the creation of a new "national court of appeals" as an adjunct to the Supreme Court, rather than an additional level in the court system, with seven judges to be drawn by rotation from the United States courts of appeals to serve staggered three-year terms. This group would screen all cases that the Supreme Court is asked to consider, referring to the Court the approximately four hundred that it considered most important. From this vastly reduced number, the Court would presumably continue to hear about the same number as at present or perhaps slightly more. The new body would also be free, at its own discretion, to hear and decide cases involving conflicting decisions on the same point of law by courts within two or more different judicial circuits.

The contention of the commission is that the volume of cases going to the Supreme Court will continue to increase and that the Court is already overwhelmed. The proposed arrangement, they say, would permit the Court to concentrate more adequately on the most serious and significant problems. A number of attorneys protest that this would deny last-resort access to the Supreme Court for many persons and would seriously reduce the Court's independence. This view was echoed by Justice Douglas, who argued that the Court is by no means overworked and should not permit itself to lose the power to decide which cases to hear: "Selection of cases across the broad spectrum of issues presented is the very heart of the judicial process."

A more basic question is whether too much is expected of the courts in the United States. It is not only that they are forced to deal with a great volume of cases including many time-consuming minor offenses. Traffic violations and so-called victimless crimes, like gambling or prostitution, might be handled as fairly and more efficiently in administrative hearings. Some might simply be decriminalized. More fundamental is the fact that American society turns to the courts to resolve virtually every kind of social conflict or disagreement, whether or not they are matters on which judges are likely to have any special competence. A complex society will doubtless have more and more laws. But should courts rule on every social issue? Should they decide, as in recent cases, whether to prohibit a Mennonite church from forcing members to ostracize a person expelled from membership, how to resolve a highly technical problem relative to natural gas transmission, or until what stage in the nine-month gestation period an abortion might be permissible?

During a recent five-year period the number of civil cases alone filed annually in the United States district courts jumped 120 per cent and the backlog increased 129 per cent. In the appeals courts the increase was even greater, 282 per cent and 365 per cent, respectively. The number of judges constantly increases but does not keep pace. Lately the Supreme Court on split votes has been limiting access to the courts in several types of cases, a trend bitterly opposed by advocates for the poor and for civil rights and consumer causes. These groups have often been more successful in the courts than in the legislative halls. Is the answer merely to continue to appoint more judges, or can ways be found to reduce the welter of procedural delays without injuring the rights of litigants and to alter the public attitudes that the courts can and should do everything?

JUDICIAL REVIEW

When we speak of the political power of the courts, the term *judicial review* does not refer to the review by higher courts of lower-court decisions. It refers to the power of the judiciary to declare acts of the legislative and executive branches unconstitutional. In effect, a court simply indicates that acts it considers unconstitutional will not be enforced by the judiciary. The United States Supreme Court, as the final arbiter, may exercise this power over the other branches of the national government and the state governments. The number of acts of Congress that have been invalidated is not large, but the significance of the power is, of course, not measurable by the number of times it has been used. Invalidation of state actions has been much more common, partly because there are more of them but also because protection of the nation against encroachments by the states has been a necessary part of preserving the Union.

The Constitution does not specifically grant to the courts this power of judicial review, and its legitimacy has been in dispute almost since the beginning of the republic. The power was assumed by the Supreme Court under Chief Justice Marshall in 1803 in the famous case of *Marbury* v. *Madison,* and despite some continuing argument it has been widely accepted by the American people and by political leaders. The power is defended on the grounds that the justices take an oath to support and defend the Constitution and that when a law is challenged, they are obliged to determine whether the law is in accord with the Constitution. It is contended further that some body must exist to determine the boundaries dividing national and state powers and the powers of the three branches of government and to protect citizens against unwarranted invasions of liberty by the government. It is best, proponents say, that such power be vested in a body that can be independent of outside pressures and that can take the time for thorough consideration.

Critics of judicial review have usually stressed the fact that the Supreme Court is not representative and is not responsible to the public, that its members are appointed for life and may become out of touch with popular sentiment, and that to permit the elected representatives of the people to be overruled by nine men who are not subject to the popular will is essentially undemocratic. They also take a dim view of the fact that acts can be declared unconstitutional by a one-vote majority on the court, even though they are passed by an overwhelming majority of Congress and supported by the president. They point out that legislators and chief executives take the same oath to support and defend the Constitution and view their responsibility with equal seriousness. However, it remains true that someone must make these decisions. While there are alternative methods, as in the Swiss federal union where the determination of constitutionality is made by the parliament (subject to the possibility of a popular referendum), the practice of judicial review has become well established in this country.

Under a system in which the powers of government have been divided among different branches, each branch is, as has been indicated, jealous of its prerogatives. Court decisions that affect the freedom of action of the legislature or the executive are apt to stimulate vehement reactions. Thus, from time to time attempts have been made to change the structure of the Court or to limit its jurisdiction, but they have been motivated most often by strong ideological disagreement with certain decisions, and they have not been successful. The Powell decision in 1969, in which the Court ruled that the House had acted unconstitutionally in refusing to seat Congressman Adam Clayton Powell* and suggested that he might be entitled to back pay and restoration of seniority, caused some House members to react with a paraphrase of a famous remark of President Andrew Jackson: "The Supreme Court has made its decision; now let it enforce it." The decision was accepted, but the pay and seniority questions remained subject to the discretion of the House. The sword and the purse were clearly still in other hands.

*See Chapter 9.

PROPOSALS TO CURB THE COURT

The amount of public support that the Court has enjoyed is far more impressive than the criticism so frequently aimed at it and certain of its decisions. It is enlightening to notice how the basis of criticism shifts from one era to another. Late in the 1930s, after the Court had struck down a series of major acts of the New Deal Congresses, social liberals were attacking the Court as obstructive to progress and reform and guilty of "judicial legislation" designed to protect a conservative economic philosophy. Conservatives organized to defend the Court as "the last bastion of individual liberty." In the 1950s and 1960s the Court, then deeply concerned with the protection of civil liberties, became the darling of the liberals, and conservatives denounced one decision after another. Some archconservatives conducted propaganda campaigns urging impeachment of the justices. Thus many who professed a desire to protect individual freedoms in the face of what they felt were threatened, or actual, government encroachments were in the curious position of attacking the Court when it handed down decisions designed to protect individual freedoms. With the Nixon appointees now often dominant, liberals are again becoming somewhat suspicious of the Court.

From the perennial controversies a variety of proposals have emerged for restricting in some way the power of the Supreme Court. Most would require constitutional amendments. Some are serious suggestions, others little more than political threats. One frequently heard proposal is that seven votes instead of five should be required to declare an act of Congress unconstitutional. Other proposals include permitting the Senate at any time to withdraw its original consent to a justice's appointment, holding popular referenda on judicial decisions, electing the justices by popular vote, requiring a certain number of years of judicial experience prior to appointment, having the Senate periodically reconfirm appointments, and creating a court composed of the chief justices of the fifty states with power to review Supreme Court decisions. None of these proposals has progressed beyond the talking stage, and they seem unlikely to do so.

The Supreme Court is surely not above criticism, especially criticism based on intelligent and fair analysis of what the Court has actually said and done. Legitimate criticism, for example, could be based on the claim that the Court improperly departed from precedent or misinterpreted the intent of Congress or the like, matters over which people can reasonably differ. Unfortunately, a number of highly publicized criticisms of the Court are essentially nonrational and thus produce confusion and misunderstanding.

A few years ago Senator James Eastland provided a fascinating

From *Herblock's State of the Union* (Simon & Schuster, 1972).

Shadowed

exercise in logic by contending on the floor of the Senate that the political orientation and objectives of the Supreme Court could be determined simply on the basis of whom the justices voted for in cases before the Court. He offered his colleagues a twenty-year tally of the votes of the justices on selected cases, presumably dealing with subversive activities, classified in the following fashion: every vote that "favored" a litigant who was a Communist or suspected Communist or "Communist sympathizer" and every vote that "agreed" with the Communist position, as defined by Senator Eastland (including such matters as racial integration), was scored as a "pro-Communist vote"; all other votes were "anti-Communist votes."

No court, of course, is supposed to decide cases by whether it likes or dislikes the litigants or whether it agrees with their personal opinions. In a free-speech case, for example, the question to be decided is whether an individual's freedom of speech has been improperly restricted, regardless of who the individual is. The senator's figures purported to show that one justice had cast 102 "pro-Communist" votes in 102 cases, and that a solid majority of the Court had voted over 80 per cent "pro-Communist." These alleged facts were publicized far and wide by a prominent right-wing organization; a reproduction of the tally as a letterhead was even made for people desiring to "alert" unaware friends and business contacts. By this logic, if the Court acquits a person who happens to be a homosexual, one may conclude that the Court is ruling in favor of homosexuality. Senator Javits suggested in reply to Senator Eastland that a vote in favor of freedom of religion or of protecting individuals against unwarranted search of their homes might reasonably be considered a "pro-American" vote.

THE NATIONAL ROLE IN LAW ENFORCEMENT

In the United States, law enforcement has always been primarily a responsibility of local government, the function of city police and county sheriffs. With limited exceptions, the principal function of state police has been to patrol the highways, although there are frequently also certain special authorities, such as those dealing with violations of narcotics laws. No national police force of general jurisdiction exists, but there are likewise a number of specialized law enforcement bodies.

The best known because of extensive publicity is the Federal Bureau of Investigation, the investigative arm of the Department of Justice, the department that also includes the United States attorneys who are responsible for prosecuting alleged offenses against national law. In addition to its part in enforcing national laws, the FBI aids local law enforcement agencies on request, and it makes available to them such services as specialized training programs, fingerprint files, and technical advice. The FBI has generally enjoyed tremendous prestige, although there have been a growing number of critics and arguments that it has operated almost completely without effective control by the public or even by Congress. It was not helped by politicization during the Watergate era. In the late 1970s the Senate committee looking into intelligence activities developed evidence that the FBI for many years had provided presidents with essentially

Engelhardt in the St. Louis Post-Dispatch

"How else can we protect our democratic ideals if we don't beat the Commies at their own game?"

political intelligence on political opponents, journalists, and critics. J. Edgar Hoover during his long tenure as director maintained separate files of politically useful information and was not above using them for FBI advantage. Files were developed on everyone elected to Congress and were at times used in the FBI's dealings with that body. There were illegal surveillances of private citizens, burglaries to secure evidence, and, in an effort to discredit certain organizations, use of anonymous letters and threats and even the forging of a signature on abusive letters to Mafia-owned businesses in the expectation that reprisals would result. The FBI is now finding it necessary to devote major effort to rehabilitating its reputation and is seeking a specific charter from Congress spelling out the scope and limitations of its authority.

Other national law enforcement agencies and groups include the Secret Service, originally organized in the Treasury Department to deal with such problems as counterfeiting but probably best known for its role in protecting presidents and vice presidents, the Bureau of Narcotics, the postal inspectors, and a number of others.

In several other ways beyond the use of its own personnel, however, the activities of the national government in law enforcement have been expanding. Deep popular concern about crime has resulted in pressures on Congress for national involvement, and Congress has responded with several measures. It has, for example, provided grants to the states for improving technical and research efforts in crime control, prohibited mail-order and out-of-state sales of various kinds of guns and ammunition, required licensing of dealers, manufacturers, and importers of handguns, and loosened restrictions on wire tapping, police interrogation, and other police methods. Proponents of the registration of firearms and the licensing of owners are disappointed at what they consider inadequate controls; others consider some provisions of legislation to be dangerous threats to civil liberties. The 1970 legislation for Washington, D.C., and for drug abuse cases, authorizing "no knock" entry of private homes (with a warrant) when there were grounds for reasonable suspicion, as well as "preventive detention" in some circumstances, generated similar controversy and was repealed in 1973. The Nixon administration continuously proposed "tougher" penalty legislation, including certain mandatory sentences, refusals of parole, and denials of bail in some cases. The assumption was that this would deter crime, an assumption that most criminologists reject, claiming that a higher degree of certainty of punishment is what counts.

Interesting conflicts and inconsistencies have come to light as a result of the expanding national role in law enforcement. Strange bedfellows have appeared: both the ultraconservative "Liberty Lobby" and the Black Panthers opposed gun-control legislation. Moreover, many groups that have advocated diminishing the role of the national government have demanded that it assume responsibility for keeping the streets safe in every community. Many who say they are antagonistic to all government activity are among the staunchest supporters of the police.

Since the last years of the 1960s the law-and-order issue has come to be one of the most crucial in the public mind. People have been alarmed by rising crime rates and by what they have felt to be an increasing instability in their institutions and orderly processes. The courts, inevitably, were deeply involved in the controversy. Some citizens accused them of aiding and abetting these conditions by being too lenient and overprotective of the rights of accused persons. Yet others denounced them as mere tools of an oppressive establishment, and in a few instances some sought to disrupt court proceedings to make normal functioning impossible or to force a court into errors that might result in reversals on appeal.

Although judges may have occasionally lost their "cool," the judicial system in general, from the United States Supreme Court down, has struggled to avoid undue pressure from both extremes and to abide rigorously by its traditions of fair and impartial treatment of all persons and issues. There are surely at times miscarriages of justice, inequities, and even incompetence. Judges, too, are human beings, influenced by their own backgrounds, experiences, and training, but in most cases they are firmly dedicated to the legal tradition. Although clearly imperfect, as are all human institutions, the courts have nevertheless continued to be a vital element and example of stability and order with justice that most people so strongly desire.

BASIC CONCEPTS AND TERMS

doctrine of judicial supremacy
district (or trial) court
original jurisdiction
circuit court (United States Court of Appeals)
appellate jurisdiction
Supreme Court
writ of certiorari
bases of national court jurisdiction
concurrent jurisdiction
injunction

criteria for judicial appointments
strict constructionist
judicial activism
judicial self-restraint
the judicial decision process
reduction of court workloads
power of judicial review
proposals to curb the Supreme Court
judicial legislation
national government's role in law enforcement

THE
NATIONAL
GOVERNMENT
AND
DOMESTIC
POLICY

11

America changed greatly in the 1960s, even more in the 1970s. Those years brought new problems as well as a new awareness of old problems that should long since have been resolved. There is a sharpened sense of urgency about the domestic issues facing the nation but also a greater polarization of groups and hardening of positions. At one and the same time the demands on government for problem solving increase dramatically while a significant segment of the population expresses antagonism to government as the instrument for doing so. There is a feeling that time is running out. Reform sentiment is strong relative to government, business, education, the church, and virtually every other institution. Long quiet racial and ethnic minority groups have discovered new self-pride and more effective political roles; women are more insistently demanding equal status; the "invisible poor" are becoming increasingly visible; energy problems threaten an entire way of life; consumer and environment interests are gaining popular support.

AMERICA'S RESPONSE TO DOMESTIC CRISIS

What will be the long-range response of the political system to these new developments? Can it adapt, as it has in the past, to meet new problems and changing emphases, including the insistence on immediate answers? Is there any justification for millions of people to live in poverty in a nation of unparalleled productivity and affluence? Can the insidious plague of discrimination, destructive for whites as well as for blacks, at last be erased? Is it inevitable that our housing and the cores of our cities will decay unchecked? Can the problem of narcotics addiction be dealt with intelligently and effectively? Must people live in fear of crime? Can we halt and control our ravaging and polluting of the natural environment that sustains us? Can a rational use, conservation, and development of energy be achieved?

To the most casual observer it is evident that none of these problems is isolated from the others. The relationships of racial discrimination to poverty and of poverty and ghetto housing to crime scarcely need elaboration. International and domestic affairs also are intertwined and continually affect one another, although they can be examined separately. Even though one can appreciate the magnitude of these problems, it would be inaccurate to conclude that nothing has been done or is being done about them. The 1930s was a period of social upheaval: government assumed new roles to deal with human problems; sociopolitical experimentation became widely acceptable. The legacy of the New Deal is embodied in most existing social legislation. The 1960s brought further innovations.

It appears, however, that the public is not capable of sustaining a high level of social concern for prolonged periods of time. The early and middle years of the 1970s were one of the occasional eras of negative reaction. Verbal attacks on so-called welfare chiselers and on permissiveness in social relations drew more enthusiastic public response than did efforts to deal with the problems themselves. Just as President Franklin Roosevelt had successfully appealed to a majority that was poor but eager for social experimentation, Presidents Nixon and Ford appealed successfully to a majority that was no longer poor and interested more in government retrenchment and tax reduction than in effective government and improved public services. While retaining many elements of the social programs that had been built up over the preceding forty years, and even fostering several new ones, President Nixon placed great emphasis on dismantling many and shifting the responsibility of others to state and local governments. In practice such shifts often meant program demolition, if for no other reason than that local units lacked the resources (and sometimes the desire) to accomplish a task and neither existing grants nor new revenue sharing made up the shortage.

With the coming of Jimmy Carter to the presidency a modest spirit of innovation in social policy returned, evidenced by such proposals as those for welfare reform, an energy policy, and tax reform, although his approach was a basically cautious one. Public attitudes are never monolithic, and the active debate over what the role of government should be continued undiminished.

GOVERNMENT AND SOCIAL LEGISLATION

It is entirely reasonable to ask whether government is properly the instrument for the resolution of these varied social problems. Surely it is not the only one, but its primary responsibility is dictated by the fact that it alone serves the entire society. Who else, amid the conflict of competing interest groups, can and will speak for the public interest? In a highly populous society facing the stresses of urban concentration, does not the role of government necessarily become greater and more vital? Government traditionally has been and is today the one commonly shared instrument by which we can aim to insure reasonably fair and equitable distribution of the benefits achieved by society, to encourage a healthy economy, to protect the weak against possible abuse by the powerful, to preserve resources for future generations, to sustain and strengthen a cultural heritage, in short to seek the conditions under which life can be most meaningfully humane. But it is quite true that this means a role for government in our increasingly complex society that will almost inevitably show a gradual and steady expansion, despite a certain amount of rhetoric to the contrary.

The process of determining whether government should play a role in each of these contexts, and if so to what extent and in what manner, and how priorities among a multitude of worthy objectives are to be decided is the heart of politics. In the crucible of day-to-day public-policy decision making one sees the constant struggle of competing forces and ideologies, the interplay of all the elements of American politics that we have been examining—the activities of political parties and interest groups, the exercise of presidential power, the uses of the congressional committee system, the influencing of public opinion, the effort to persuade the courts to throw their weight to one side or another, and so on. Rarely are these clear-cut and easy decisions, and rare also is total victory at any given moment. As we have noted before, important issues almost invariably become extremely complicated, and success within a structure based on free debate is likely to be measured in half-loaves. These are nevertheless the steppingstones toward goals not initially agreed on that in time receive broad societal acceptance.

Auth in the Philadelphia Inquirer.

"The problem of the ghettos? The ghettos, my dear, are a solution, not a problem."

Case Study
THE BREEDER REACTOR DECISION

At stake was the very existence of the projected Clinch River, Tennessee, breeder reactor, a plutonium-powered demonstration nuclear plant designed to generate ("breed") more plutonium than it consumed. The goal was the development of a dependable and environmentally clean source of energy for electrical power plants, which were under fire as polluters but faced greater and greater demands for power. Estimated cost of this experimental model: at least $2 billion. The task for the congressional appropriations committees was to decide whether to approve the $150 million tentatively recommended for this purpose for the following year or to terminate the entire program as too great a risk and an unnecessary expense.

The issue had been brought to a head by a recommendation from the president to stop development. There were dangers in the operation of any nuclear plant, he said, and the risks of even greater nuclear proliferation "would be vastly increased by the further spread of sensitive technologies which entail direct access to plutonium . . . or other weapons-usable material." He went beyond a mere recommendation by proposing to the major allies of the United States in Europe, to Japan, and to the Soviet Union that all agree to cease breeder development to avoid magnifying risks, and he indicated that the United States would take the lead and seek to set an example. Opponents to the reactor also argued that adoption of a policy of developing the breeder reactor would legitimize the whole plutonium technology and would be used by every country to justify building the much more dangerous reprocessing facilities. Moreover, they contended, no one knew whether the reactor would be wanted once it was available. Since development would take a number of years, emphasis should be placed on seeking more desirable alternatives, and it would still be possible to turn to the reactor later if all else failed. Finally, there were more crucial needs for available public funds.

Proponents, however, took strong exception to these lines of argument. The need for an energy source, and particularly a clean one, was now, they said, and since the process was a long one, it was foolish to delay further. The president, in their view, was confusing nuclear power plants and bombs: "Power plants do not contain sufficient fissile material to sustain a nuclear explosion," commented the chairman of the House Science Committee. In addition, nuclear plants had an excellent safety record. It was already evident from public statements, spokesmen for the program pointed out, that other countries intended to proceed with development. The United States would not only be left behind if it acted unilaterally but would also be isolated and lose influence in shaping worldwide nuclear policy, thus inviting "nuclear anarchy." Concluding the argument, the leading supporter of the breeder reactor on the House nuclear energy subcommittee insisted that all nuclear power plants, not just the breeder, produced some plutonium and that no nation had ever produced a weapon by extracting fissionable material from a nuclear energy cycle. The way to block proliferation was to develop international controls on reprocessing fuel rather than worrying about power plants or breeder reactors. Policy determinations should be based on reason, he argued, not on unsubstantiated fears.

Possessed now of the arguments of both sides, how were the appropriations committees to arrive at a rational decision and on what criteria should it be based? Where did the public interest lie?

Government affects almost every facet of our lives, but because it is a part of the web of our daily existence, we tend to underestimate its impact. It may aid our social and economic efforts, regulate behavior, stimulate new activity, exert moral pressure, protect against disorder, and provide help in case of disaster. Although aid is an aspect of government that receives little publicity, much more effort and money are devoted to assisting citizens than to regulating their activities. Neither government aid nor government regulation can be ignored in our attempt to understand and evaluate contemporary issues of domestic policy, but there is good reason for emphasizing the areas of controversy, where the decisions of the future will have to be made. Perhaps the most real issue is not whether there is to be big government, but whether that government is to serve primarily the interests of the affluent and powerful or the needs of the less fortunate in the society.

Contrary to popular belief, the national government has no open-ended authority to intervene at will in social and economic problems simply in the name of serving the general welfare. Unrestricted authority in these areas lies with the states; the national government must find constitutional authorization for all its actions. In aid and regulation the principal basis is the commerce power. Other powers, such as those of taxation, expenditure, postal service, and currency regulation, may be invoked in certain circumstances, but the work-horse is the authority "to regulate commerce . . . among the several states." Like many constitutional phrases, this was undefined by the framers, and its meaning has evolved in response to the social and economic imperatives of each stage of the nation's development. The president, Congress, and the Supreme Court have all participated in the process.

The key phrase for this purpose in most legislation is the statement that the law will deal with "all persons in or affecting interstate commerce," and thus it is necessary to determine whose activities affect interstate commerce. How much effect? Since amounts are not constitutionally stipulated, it appears to mean any effect whatsoever, and it is hard to find any kind of economic activity that does not affect interstate commerce. Actually, government has always had the power to regulate, and the only question has been whether that power is to be exercised by the national government or by state and local governments. The economy has long since become national or international in scope, and regulation, if it is to be effective, must have a comparable scope. Congress today can aid or regulate vir-tually any kind of economic activity in any way it thinks desirable. At its discretion certain kinds of organizations may be exempted from the impact of a statute, or the state and local governments may be permitted to share in the regulatory or service activity. Local retailers and educational and charitable institutions, for example, are not affected by the Wages and Hours Act, but this exemption stems from a policy decision by Congress rather than from lack of power to include them.

When the nation was brought face to face with the need for drastic government action at the onset of the Great Depression, few Ameri-can precedents were available to indicate what action was needed and what form it should take. The role of government had tradition-ally been minor and peripheral. The depression followed a decade of inaction, during which Will Rogers could accurately say of one president, "He didn't do nothin', but that's what the people wanted done." But when unemployment reached staggering levels and mil-lions were going hungry and mortgages were being foreclosed and business abuses and stock market manipulation were rampant and the prices of farm products were so low that harvesting crops was not worth the effort, then people demanded that government somehow provide solutions. As state and local governments proved incapable of coping with problems of such magnitude, it was clear that the national government was the only resort.

Social and economic legislation did not begin with the 1930s. Antitrust and utility-regulation laws had been passed before the turn of the century, and there were also requirements for protection of women in industry. Yet the Great Depression was a strong impetus for intervention, and in the 1930s the atmosphere was ripe for widespread public acceptance of government's programs to initiate new social services. National government dominance has been on the ascendant ever since. In time, once controversial measures like old age insurance have come to be viewed as commonplace and have been adapted and refined over the years. Government-initiated social actions have developed into the great body of social legislation that serves the nation today.

AID AND REGULATION OF BUSINESS

The relation between business and government has long been intimate. As a major taxpayer and campaign contributor, business has been influential and has benefited from the strong probusiness environment traditional to America throughout most of its history. American business has grown rapidly to giant proportions and a high degree of concentration, has shown unusual creativity and innovation, and has helped produce in this country a virtually unparalleled standard of living. Under these circumstances, the maintenance of a healthy environment for business has been considered a logical function of government. Assistance takes many forms: market research and information; preservation of the sanctity of contracts; promotion of trade with other countries; protection of patents, trademarks, and copyrights; support of land, air, and water transportation; tariffs; technical advisory services; subsidies for certain activities (in larger measure than for agriculture, which receives most of the publicity and criticism); and establishment of commercial standards.

Despite all its advantages, however, the free enterprise system generates potential abuses. Thus it is natural for government, as the single representative of all the people, to be enlisted in protecting both the honest member of the business community and the general public. Although more personnel and money are devoted to aiding and promoting business than to regulating it, most controversy crops up under the latter aspect.

BREAKING UP MONOPOLIES

The problem of monopolistic practices is chronic to a free enterprise system. In any profit-motivated economy some people are tempted to seek to maximize profits by eliminating their competition. Since it is part of the basic theory of free enterprise that competition is the element that protects the consumer in respect to price and quality of product or service, it is assumed to be a legitimate responsibility of government to aid in preserving and fostering competition. Beginning with the famous Sherman Antitrust Act of 1890 and continuing with the Clayton Act, the Federal Trade Commission Act, and others, the national government has sought to block or break up monopolies or potential monopolies, but with only partial success.

In breaking up an alleged monopoly, responsibility lies primarily with the Antitrust Division of the Department of Justice, which must file suit in a court to get an order requiring the changes the division feels necessary. Unless the company concerned accepts a consent decree, by which it agrees to the changes, consequent trials are likely to be extremely time-consuming and expensive. Since the Antitrust Division has rarely if ever been bountifully financed, it must as a rule pick and choose only the cases it thinks most important to prosecute. A citizen may envision such actions in terms of a contest between the government giant and the lone beleaguered business executive. In fact, it is quite likely to be the other way around. In suits against great corporations, one or two attorneys from the Antitrust Division will probably be pitted against an impressive array of some of the nation's foremost legal talent. Some years ago one company against which an action had been filed spent more money in one month to advertise its position in daily and weekly newspapers across the country than the entire appropriation for the Antitrust Division for the year. The process of using lawsuits as a means of enforcement is unwieldy and fraught with pitfalls.

Many cases are resolved by negotiation, but under certain conditions this kind of settlement may raise serious questions of propriety. In a widely publicized case an attempt to force International Telephone and Telegraph in 1971 to divest itself of certain insurance company holdings was dropped, although other requirements by the Department of Justice were complied with. There were allegations, firmly denied, that the Justice Department's actions were related to ITT's offer of $400,000 (the amount and nature of the offer were also in dispute) to help finance the costs of the Republican national convention. The attorney general denied that he had received any White House pressure on this matter, though the denial proved to turn on rather narrow technical definitions. President Nixon later conceded that he had ordered the attorney general not to appeal a court ruling favorable to ITT but said he subsequently withdrew his opposition when convinced that the Justice Department was not merely operating on an assumption that bigness in and of itself is necessarily bad.

A 1976 act sought to strengthen antimonopoly effort by authorizing state attorneys general to bring triple-damage suits on behalf of state citizens as a group against antitrust violators. The teeth in the law were effectively pulled, however, when the Supreme Court the following year ruled (*Illinois Brick Co.* v. *Illinois*) that such class action suits were not permissible and that only direct purchasers of a product from the manufacturer (the only ones deemed by the Court majority to have been directly injured) had standing to sue.

The Federal Trade Commission was created primarily to deal with "unfair or deceptive" practices that may contribute to monopoly, but it is not required to obtain court orders. After studying a case and reaching a conclusion, if the company does not accept a stipulation (another type of agreed settlement), the commission may issue a cease and desist order enforceable by penalties. Such an order may be appealed to the courts, but there the presumption will be in favor of the commission's action.

Although it has served a useful purpose, the FTC is illustrative of a malady common to the regulatory commissions—the tendency to drift into a path of least resistance. Originally established as an antimonopoly agency, the FTC now devotes most of its effort to combating false and misleading advertising, misbranding, and the like, which may possibly contribute to monopoly situations. Regulatory commissions are usually established on a wave of popular excitement about a particular issue. Once the legislation is enacted, however, the public typically loses interest, feeling the job has been accomplished. The commission is left on its own to act for the public, but public backing is sadly absent. Organizations subject to regulation, however, do not forget the commission. They camp on its doorstep and breathe continuously down the back of its neck. Thus it is easy for a commission to concentrate on the aspects of its task that are least controversial and perhaps helpful to the honest business entrepreneur, especially if the courts or further legislation hamper its activities. Efforts by citizen lobbies in recent years, particularly Ralph Nader's investigating groups, have begun to have some effect in restoring a stronger focus on the public interest.

THE MULTINATIONAL CORPORATIONS

Multinational corporations, those operating in many different countries and often owned by stockholders in a variety of countries as well, are hardly new on the economic scene, but awareness of them has been sharply increasing. Those based in the United States are the most prevalent, but they are by no means purely an American phenomenon, as Shell (Dutch), Unilever (British), Nestlé (Swiss), and Sony (Japanese) illustrate. A quite natural development in today's highly interrelated world, these corporations pose a variety of complex problems for national governments.

As the magnitude and power of the multinationals have become more widely recognized, the volume of criticism has grown correspondingly. Organized labor, for example, charges that as they move capital and jobs abroad, they create severe unemployment in the United States. It challenges the tax advantages given to companies operating overseas, claiming that this serves to encourage movement abroad. In turn the corporations argue that foreign taxes are usually higher than in this country and that they are bringing profits back to the United States from the nations in which they are located. There remains a strong feeling among the public that the fair share of United States taxes is being avoided and that by playing one country off against another the corporations are not in reality subject to adequate regulation anywhere.

Some of the most serious criticisms, in fact, relate to efforts of the multinationals to protect their favored status through extensive intervention in the internal politics of other countries. Widespread evidence of huge fees or bribes paid to intermediaries or government officials abroad, as a means of assuring sales or protecting their investments, has not helped the image. Unfavorable publicity has resulted in company policy changes, and legislation now exists making illegal such uses of corporate funds, but there is as yet little agreement on comprehensive ways to control effectively these massive concentrations of economic power. There are embryonic steps toward the international control that is obviously necessary, notably in the European Economic Community, but for the most part responsibility continues to lie with individual countries. In most of them the multinational corporations wield tremendous influence; in some they may be more powerful than the governments themselves.

REGULATING SECURITIES MARKETS

Because dubious speculative practices on the stock exchanges were widely believed to have contributed in a major way to the great crash at the onset of the depression, regulation in this area was a priority item of the first New Deal Congress. The role of the Securities and Exchange Commission, created at that time, is unusual because, although it prescribes some rules, one of its important functions is to see that the exchanges do a satisfactory job of policing themselves. The major exchanges elect officers, write their own rules, and have the power to enforce them; the SEC acts as a sort of "gun behind the door." The other principal task of the commission in regulating the stock market is to insure that the potential buyer of corporate securities is given honest, accurate, and complete information about a stock issue. The SEC naturally makes no guarantee of the quality of a possible investment. It does require the issuing corporation to file a registration statement certifying under oath that the information provided is full and accurate.

PUBLIC UTILITIES

In a special category are the public utilities, often termed natural monopolies because they provide services in which it is assumed that competition is not feasible or desirable. Transportation, power, and communications are deemed essential to the entire population. Few people would argue that it is practical to have several competing electric power companies crisscrossing their lines over a city, for example, and thus it is customary to grant a franchise to one company to serve a given region. But this procedure eliminates the competition that helps guarantee to the consumer good service at reasonable rates, so a substitute must be found. The substitute ordinarily takes the form of a commission representing the public, empowered to regulate the quality, availability, and price of service.

Agencies of the state and national governments regulate utilities, the former dealing with intrastate businesses and the latter with interstate ones. At the national level the most common pattern is that of the independent regulatory commission, specialized to deal only with one type of enterprise, such as power or communications. These commissions are peculiar hybrids in the world of administrative organization, combining in one agency executive, legislative, and judicial roles. While relatively independent of executive control, they are obviously administrative in nature, but they also are quasi-legislative and quasi-judicial bodies; that is, they engage in rule making within a framework established by Congress, and they adjudicate disputes within their area of specialization, subject to appeal to the courts from their decisions. Commission members are appointed by the president, usually for fairly long and overlapping terms, and the composition of the group is ordinarily required to be bipartisan.

In many other nations utilities are almost all publicly owned, but public *regulation* has been the common practice in the United States. The utility management and the public authority in a sense share in making the important decisions. An airline, for instance, cannot institute a new service or issue a new rate schedule at its own discretion. If it can convince the Civil Aeronautics Board that new fares are needed, the board will establish them. Interstate electric power companies and distributors of natural gas are the responsibility of the Federal Power Commission. In establishing rates for these utilities, a regulatory agency has the difficult task of attempting to guarantee simultaneously reasonable rates to consumers and a fair rate of return on investment to stockholders of the utility. The public, when granting a monopoly privilege to a company, not only expects the lowest possible rates and high-quality service but also assumes that everyone within the franchise area will be served at a reasonably equivalent level. In some instances in which it appears that regulation has become more a protection than a control for the industry, there are movements toward deregulation: allowing more unrestrained competition among the airlines, for example. This is admittedly an uncertain prospect. If done, will the public simply benefit from lower prices, or will one or two giants come to monopolize the industry with ability to set prices wherever they want?

Transportation Despite considerable interest in developing an integrated system of control, national regulation of transportation is not yet in the hands of a single agency. Railroads and truck carriers are regulated by the Interstate Commerce Commission, the oldest independent regulatory agency. The Civil Aeronautics Board controls all commercial air carriers. Control of the water carriers depends on whether an inland, coastal, intercoastal, or foreign carrier is involved. The Maritime Commission is the principal agency for water carriers, but its jurisdiction is more limited than that of agencies dealing with other forms of transportation. Pipeline carriers are also regulated, in much the same fashion as the others. The creation of the Department of Transportation in 1966 finally consolidated many, but not all, administrative functions related to transportation;

Air traffic controllers at work.

Raytheon Company Photograph

most regulation, however, remains separate. Those who have been advocating the development of a coordinated national transportation policy are still advocating.

After years of complaints by most railroads that they continually lost money on passenger service, coupled with passengers' complaints about quality of service, and following the bankruptcy through mismanagement of the nation's largest rail system, Congress created a semipublic corporation to take responsibility for long-distance passenger service. This new National Railroad Passenger Corporation, known operationally as Amtrak, was provided public funds and loan guarantees to help improve equipment and services and was empowered to plan a single nationwide network of passenger trains linking the major cities (not including commuter service). Actual operation of trains remains generally in the hands of the railroad companies, under contract with Amtrak. The corporation inherited a run-down system afflicted by a quarter-century of neglect, and despite improvements passenger use continues far below the point at which it would be possible to break even financially. Subsidies run in the neighborhood of $300 million per year. More recently the national government has found it necessary, in order to maintain needed rail freight service, to create Conrail (Consolidated Rail Corporation) to take over and operate seven bankrupt lines in the Northeast and Midwest.

One of the crucial problems of mass population is the expeditious movement of people within great urban areas. Streets and freeways continue to be improved yet remain clogged with the ever increasing numbers of automobiles. Movement is slow and uncomfortable, and parking is at a premium, even though more and more parking lots replace still usable downtown buildings. Air pollution has steadily worsened. The need for more adequate urban mass transit systems, convenient, comfortable, and reasonable in cost to users, has been obvious for years, but progress, with a few exceptions, has been meager. The American's attachment to the automobile is legendary, and the cost of building transit systems is high. It seems, oddly, to have been generally accepted that it is proper to spend vast sums of tax money on building and maintaining roads but that there is something totally wrong with supporting alternative transportation systems in the same way. Only recently has this attitude begun significantly to change, and new experiments are developing. In 1973 for the first time, despite the continued opposition of the automobile, road construction, and oil company lobbies, Congress opened the door for the cities to use a portion of national gas-tax revenues for mass transit. Before this time the vast Highway Trust Fund, fed handsomely by revenues from gasoline and other motor-vehicle user taxes, could be utilized for no purpose other than highways. Spurred by the energy crisis, Congress in the following year authorized subsidies for the operating expenses of ailing urban mass transit systems, supplementing previous capital grants for building or rehabilitating systems, but amounts available made little more than a dent in the problem.

Television and radio   Control of television and radio broadcasting has distinctive features of special importance. Nature imposes limits on the number of stations that can broadcast in a given area, and the grant of a license to broadcast is considered a privilege subject to public control, a situation quite different from that prevailing for newspapers. Broadcasting control is also a good example of regulation that came into existence largely at the request of those who were to be regulated. In the early days of radio anyone could broadcast at any wavelength and with any amount of power, but this resulted in attempts simply to blast out competitors. The consequent chaos led broadcasters to seek government intervention after attempts at self-regulation proved inadequate.

The Communications Act of 1934, a comprehensive revision of earlier legislation, created the Federal Communications Commission and gave it the power to license and assign wavelengths, power, and hours of operation. Commercial licenses are subject to periodic renewal, and in order to retain a license the holder is required to show that he or she is operating "in the public interest, convenience, or necessity." This somewhat vague statement is interpreted to mean that no individual or group has the right to use a commercial broadcasting facility solely to support its own beliefs or exclusively for its own benefit. A reasonable amount of public service broadcasting and some variety of viewpoint must be presented, and standards of good taste must be maintained. The FCC is specifically prohibited from exercising censorship, and it thus does not seek to tell any station what it may or may not broadcast. But when a license comes up for renewal, the station is held responsible for its broadcast policies over the preceding period.

Denial of licenses has been rare and words of warning have ordinarily brought about the rather minimal corrections usually demanded by the FCC, but a few broadcasters have not had their licenses renewed. Some years ago a station owned by an independent church group devoted most of its time to advocacy of the group's religious position and vehement denunciation of other religious bodies, and it was refused renewal after numerous warnings. Likewise the commission ultimately denied renewal for a midwestern station owner whose sole activity was prescribing his "goat gland medicine" for listeners who wrote in describing their ills. In practice, license renewals have been nearly automatic, and the broadcasters have clearly had great influence on the commission.

The law requires stations that make time available to a candidate for public office to make equal time available at the same rates to other candidates for the same office. Since costs are high, this practice may be meaningless on a large scale for any but candidates who have large campaign funds. The existence of the equal-time requirement is the reason for Congress having to pass a special act of exemption to authorize the networks to make free time available for debates between *major* presidential candidates; otherwise the candidates of the Vegetarian and Constitution parties and others could demand free time equivalent to that granted the Democrats and Republicans. The alternative, followed in 1976, is to let the debates be covered simply as a news event, which is clearly something of a subterfuge. Broadcasters would like to see the equal-time requirement abolished, claiming its removal would make possible greater freedom of political debate. But such a change would place the power to determine who should be heard and to what extent in the hands of the stations and networks, which are already involved in heated verbal exchanges and lawsuits when the two major parties demand time to respond to each other and are sometimes refused.

Much more significant than the equal-time requirement is the FCC's so-called fairness doctrine. This requires a station to provide time for rebuttal to any person or organization attacked on a broadcast and specifies that the person attacked must be contacted within one week after the initial airing and provided a transcript or tape of the program on which the attack occurred. The FCC views this requirement not as an attempt to prevent the expression of ideas but as a means to prevent the suppression of viewpoints contrasting to those already aired. Some stations contend that the rule involves more paperwork than they can assume and that they must therefore keep certain provocative speakers off the air.

Because of their free-swinging attacks on people with different views, extensive broadcasts by certain well-financed fundamentalist religious groups and right-wing political organizations seem to generate the most friction. One of the more interesting cases, fought in the courts and before the FCC late in the 1960s, was that between writer Fred J. Cook and the Red Lion Broadcasting Company, owner of WQCB in Red Lion, Pennsylvania. After Cook had been publicly castigated over that station by Billy James Hargis of the "Christian Crusade," he complained that he had not been notified and he demanded free time to reply to Hargis's statements. WQCB agreed to make time available but specified that it would be free time only if Cook were unable to pay. Cook asked why he should have to pay to defend himself against false statements in an unprovoked attack and took the matter to the FCC, which directed that free time be provided. The ruling was subsequently upheld by the Supreme Court (*Red Lion Broadcasting Co.* v. *FCC*, 1969). Although it is still controversial, the fairness doctrine as a matter of principle appears to have wide support.

Limited efforts to provide public funds in support of more extensive public service broadcasting, although assumed to be a necessity in many countries, has remained somewhat controversial in the United States. The Corporation for Public Broadcasting was established in 1967 to allocate appropriations and grants from private organizations to noncommercial television and radio stations. Two years later it created a Public Broadcasting Service, which furnished technical services to these broadcasters and for about four years selected and promoted a variety of television programs. Since total agreement on such matters is never possible, there were inevitably arguments over the degree of objectivity or fairness in programs in which controversial issues were discussed, although almost 50 per cent of the funds went into a series of highly regarded children's programs. Opponents contended that PBS had become a fourth national network, and it continued to have funding problems.

In 1975 the FCC adopted a rule prohibiting in the future single ownership of broadcast media and newspapers in the same city, but it made no move against the approximately eighty combined ownerships then existing. Public-interest-group challenges to the latter are working their way through the courts.

Public service projects   In utilities there are also related but different government activities. Probably most familiar are the huge water and power developments, usually built by the Army Corps of Engineers or by the Bureau of Reclamation in the Department of the Interior. The Grand Coulee and Bonneville projects in the state of Washington, Hoover Dam on the lower Colorado River, and projects in the Arkansas and Missouri valleys are well-known examples. Power from these projects is wholesaled, and distribution to consumers is handled by public, cooperative, or privately owned utilities. Even better known is the famous Tennessee Valley Authority, a government corporation with broad authority to develop the water resources of the entire region surrounding the Tennessee River valley. TVA administers a coordinated program of flood control, power supply, navigational improvement, land reclamation, and development of recreational facilities. Its success in helping to transform the middle South has made the government project immensely popular in that region, but intense conservative and private utilities opposition and high costs have so far blocked similar developments proposed for other parts of the country.

One of President Carter's first economy moves once in office was a proposal to delete funding for a large number of water projects across the country that he deemed to be largely pork-barrel enterprises. Predictably this produced a confrontation with Congress. In some degree this involved disagreement on the facts, but it was also true that many members had worked long and hard to "bring home" such a project to their districts. In the end the president prevailed insofar as the total number of dams was sharply scaled down, yet the bulk of the projects remained intact.

The development and control of atomic energy, although vitally important, has been the subject of rather limited public information for obvious reasons. In 1946 Congress created the Atomic Energy Commission (now called the Nuclear Regulatory Commission), an independent bipartisan body, and gave it a monopoly of research, development, and production for both peaceful and military uses. A joint committee of the two houses of Congress was also established to keep track of these activities. In 1954, and again in 1964, the government monopoly was modified and somewhat limited. Since then, private developments have greatly expanded, subject to rather careful public control.

When the United States Post Office Department was transformed in 1971 into a public corporation known as the United States Postal Service, there was great fanfare to the effect that the new business orientation would soon make the Post Office a model of efficiency. Instead, within less than two years it was being subjected to an unprecedented volume of complaints from the general public and especially from businesses about slow, erratic, and undependable service. Meanwhile much of the most profitable part of its service was being siphoned off by electronic transmission systems. To cap its problems, Congress directed it to become self-sustaining by 1985. The situation was another chapter in a running controversy nearly as old as the country: Is the primary goal of a postal service to operate as a successful business on at least a break-even basis, or is it to provide a rapid and low-cost national communications system even if doing so requires some tax support as other public services do?

LABOR-MANAGEMENT RELATIONS

Until recently the great political problems for labor were the basic ones of gaining and protecting the right to bargain collectively, of making that bargaining effective, and of securing protective legislation regarding matters such as wages and hours, health and safety. Now added to these is that of unemployment persisting even during general prosperity—unemployment resulting from increasingly advanced technology, strong foreign competition, and a massive influx of women into the labor market—and this has become the dominant concern.

As organized labor has grown large and powerful, the public has become increasingly concerned about holding labor responsible for its actions, even as in an earlier period there was an effort to protect against business abuses. Moreover, although it is important that the rights of both labor and management be guarded, is collusion not possible between them at the expense of the general populace?

Labor came on the scene as an organized force relatively recently, and not until the mid-1930s did the rights to organize and bargain collectively achieve lasting, formal recognition in the famous National Labor Relations Act (1935), commonly known as the Wagner Act. This act created the National Labor Relations Board, whose primary responsibility is supervising elections to determine whether employees of a plant or industry desire to be represented by a union and, if so, by which one. If the vote is for representation, the NLRB certifies the bargaining agent with whom the employer is expected to deal and seeks to insure that both sides bargain in good faith. The law also restricts the ability of employers to interfere with labor organizing.

Labor embraced the Wagner Act as "labor's Magna Charta," but many employers took a dimmer view and were especially critical of the restrictions placed on them in the absence of comparable restraints on the unions. The Taft-Hartley Act, passed when the Republicans gained control of Congress immediately after World War II and officially called the Labor Management Act of 1947, at once established restrictions on unions and eased those on employers. Although it outlawed the closed shop (one in which only union members may be hired), it did not tamper with the right to bargain collectively as a principle. Bitterly unhappy with the law, labor has not been able to muster the strength to alter it. Supplementary legislation twelve years later, the Landrum-Griffin Act, incorporated still more restraints on unions and attempted to insure democratic practices within the unions. Because the stakes are high and affect the whole economy, the seesaw legislative attempts to protect and balance the rights of both workers and management are unlikely to produce universal satisfaction.

Most industrial negotiations result in peaceful settlements, but when disputes lead to threatened or actual strikes or lockouts, the Federal Mediation and Conciliation Service is available to help resolve the conflicts. It has no enforcement powers but can act as an effective go-between and as a mechanism for keeping the disputants around the bargaining table. The Taft-Hartley Act further provides for devices such as presidential fact-finding boards whose investigations are made public, eighty-day cooling-off periods, and temporary injunctions against work stoppages when a national emergency would result. It is frequently ineffective, as when President Carter invoked the act in the 1978 coal strike but union miners did not obey. Clearly, the general public, as well as labor and management, has a considerable stake in an orderly process of resolving disputes.

Assorted pieces of protective legislation have been passed over the years, some dealing with safety regulations, others with conditions of work for women and children. Establishing the legitimacy of such laws paved the way for the more comprehensive stipulation of minimum wages and maximum hours of employment outlined in the Fair

TOPPIX

2·24

"I go all the way back to when the acceptable unemployment was only 3 or 4 per cent."

Labor Standards Act of 1938. The minimum wage rates have been raised periodically, and the categories of workers covered by the law have been expanded, although farm workers are still granted a lower standard than others. Since 1971 the Occupational Safety and Health Administration (OSHA) has existed to establish and enforce health and safety standards in employment. The national government has also provided for public employment offices to match workers with jobs, unemployment compensation for those unable to secure work, and assistance for training or retraining workers who need new or additional skills, especially those who have suffered discrimination or have lost jobs because of automation. Unemployment is not only an overwhelming problem to the individual affected; it also raises welfare costs, and the large reduction of purchasing power resulting from a high rate of unemployment may contribute to a general recession.

With the unemployment problem remaining critical, the national government in the late 1970s moved into a variety of job-creating programs, most involving grants to state and local governments, which handle the actual administration. These include a countercyclical aid program that helps the local units avoid layoffs without increasing local taxes, an emergency public works program to encourage construction of public facilities, a youth program providing employment on conservation and recreation facility projects, and a program of supplemental jobs in state and local government, also particularly for youth, coupled with support for job-related training efforts. There has been little careful analysis of just how well these work. How much help is it to stimulate jobs requiring skills when a great deal of unemployment is among the unskilled? In a crash program is it possible to provide meaningful work for all those employed? Do the state and local governments merely use the funds for things they would otherwise fund themselves? In any case they claim that considerable need exists: When the 1976 public works program was enacted, state-local applications totaling more than $20 billion were submitted for the $2 billion available.

HOW AGRICULTURE SURVIVES

For many years the United States was predominantly an agricultural country. As the society rapidly grew more urban and industrial in the post–Civil War period, the strains on farmers and farm organizations were substantial. Today farmers constitute only about 5 per cent of the population, yet the rest of the population depends on them for food and many raw materials used by industry. Recently the character of farming has been undergoing tremendous change, with the growth of extremely large-scale enterprises and extensive mechanization.

Traditionally farmers have been rather isolated and not very effectively organized for economic influence. They have had an inadequate share of the social benefits that others have taken for granted, such as medical services and electric power. Their average income has lagged far behind that of others. They have often been victimized by moneylenders, railroads, and buyers' agents. Inevitably their personal circumstances have been severely affected by conditions over which they have had no immediate control, like insects and the weather. Most important of all is the fact that farmers have for the most part both bought and sold on a market that someone else has controlled. When in need of seed and fertilizer, the farmers ask the dealers the price and pay it; but when they sell their crops no one asks them, "How much is a bushel of wheat?" Instead, they normally put their crops on the auction market and in effect say, "How much will you offer for it?" Buyers, on the other hand, are organized.

Moreover, although a manufacturer can ordinarily adjust supply to anticipated demand, the individual farm operator is too small a unit of production to have a significant effect in such planning, even if conditions permitted it.

An impressive variety of specialized services to aid agriculture has been developed over the years—programs of farmer education, research on crop improvement and the control of plant and animal diseases, aid in soil conservation, rural electrification, credit assistance, market forecasting, establishment of standards and grades, assistance in selling commodities abroad, crop insurance against natural hazards, regulation of commodity exchanges, and disaster relief. The Department of Agriculture, however, is not solely concerned with assisting farmers. A major part of its activity is in consumer protection, such as meat inspection, and in the resource-management work of the Forest Service. The department is also involved in aiding school-lunch programs and making milk available to undernourished children.

The principal controversies about agricultural policy lie not with the foregoing activities but rather have related to the program of parity price maintenance designed to help stabilize the agricultural economy and assist farmers in securing a reasonable return on their investment and labor. The concept of parity means simply that the prices farmers receive for products ought to keep pace with the prices of the things they must buy. For several decades the national government has used a number of devices to bolster the prices of farm commodities—purchase and storage of surplus commodities, which raise prices by increasing demand in the market; loans at the parity guarantee level on anticipated crops, the crops being forfeit to the government in satisfaction of the loans if market prices fall below the guarantee figure (always something less than 100 per cent parity) at time of harvest; payments for removing land from production, since the individual farmer cannot be expected to bear the resultant loss of income; assistance to farmers for temporarily storing their crops, so that prices will not be unduly depressed by the need to market an entire crop at time of harvest; and a system of production and marketing controls, limiting the amount of certain commodities each farmer may produce or may market within a given period, such controls being imposed only when requested in a referendum vote by two-thirds of the farmers raising that commodity. The most serious defect of the price maintenance program has been that it channeled most of the aid to those who needed it least, the big farmers, and benefited but little the struggling, small producer.

By 1973, when increasing demands at home coupled with critical food shortages in many other countries had pushed prices well beyond previous guarantee levels, some modifications of the old system became possible. While most of the programs just mentioned were retained as protection in case of a future slump, the central change was to substitute for the purchasing and storage programs a system of direct subsidy payments to farmers when market prices fall below "target price" levels. Target prices, "fair" unit prices fixed by Congress on certain basic commodities, are intended to be flexible and move with changing economic conditions. The principle has fairly broad support, but there are prospects of frequent lengthy congressional battles over these fair prices, featuring intensive bargaining and trade-offs. Nor has the program, of course, been tested in years of severe agricultural adversity. An economic squeeze on farmers did, however, touch off an agricultural strike in late 1977 and early 1978, designed to press demands for full parity guarantees.

Although consumer food prices have steadily increased, average farm incomes compared with the earnings of other workers have, as a general rule, remained static or declined. Contrary to popular belief, farmers normally receive for their products only a very small fraction of the ultimate cost of food to the consumer, the rest going to processing, packaging, advertising, wholesaler and retailer profits and costs, and transportation.* A House Agriculture Committee study has claimed that despite high prices the average American family spends less of its income on food than was the case twenty years earlier, the lowest percentage of any country in the world. The migration of people away from the farms continues, as does the trend away from the family farm and toward the large-scale corporation farm.

During the Johnson administration, the Food for Peace program was introduced, authorizing expanded distribution of surplus foods abroad through gifts and by sale for nonconvertible local currencies. In addition, the food stamp program was inaugurated to make foods available at discount prices to the poor within this country, and some direct distribution of surplus commodities was authorized.

The old battles over agricultural policy were based largely on how to deal with surpluses, but the Department of Agriculture now finds itself actively encouraging vastly increased production. The term *surplus*, when applied to food, has always been a misnomer. From a world perspective, the problem in agriculture has never been overproduction but maldistribution. It is fatuous to speak of food surpluses in a world in which a third of the population goes hungry every day and starvation is an imminent threat for great multitudes of people. Nor is the United States, the most affluent nation the world has ever known, immune from hunger. The real challenge is how to insure that those who need food, wherever they live, are able to obtain it. There is tremendous need for a world food policy and

---

*The difference between what the farmer receives and what the consumer pays ranges as high as 1,500 per cent on certain breakfast cereals.

system of reserves, rather than purely national ones. As population continues to multiply at a staggering rate and food production increases only gradually, the threat on the not-too-distant horizon is famine. Limitation of population growth is clearly vital, but so is a better system of food distribution. Former Secretary of Agriculture Orville Freeman put it succinctly on his return from a trip to India: "future generations should not have to say that our civilization was able to put satellites in the sky but was not able to put bread into the hands of hungry children."

SOCIAL SERVICES

Despite the high average level of affluence that has characterized the United States, an all too large percentage of the population lives in poverty. Most of the poor have an extremely limited background of education and training. The problems created by these limitations have been particularly acute among minority groups, who typically in the past received the poorest education and faced discrimination in employment. Large numbers of elderly people find themselves

There are over a million migrant workers in the country today, and they are probably America's most disadvantaged group.

Steve Schapiro/Black Star

without adequate resources to live decently in the years after their retirement, a condition growing more serious as the average life span increases. Respectable housing for the poor and the old is commonly unavailable or priced far beyond their ability to pay. Even temporary unemployment takes a harsh toll on families unless there are ways to tide them over bleak periods and to help them find and train for new jobs. For a surprisingly large part of the population, extending far beyond the ranks of the poor, the financing of medical services, especially during an emergency or disaster, is a nearly insuperable problem. Most government programs designed to cope with such problems originated in the era of the Great Depression, although major alterations have been made since the 1960s.

SOCIAL SECURITY

In every civilized society there is a keenly felt obligation to prevent hardship on the aged, disabled, and otherwise disadvantaged. In the broadest sense there are about four possible approaches to dealing with these problems: such people can simply be allowed to starve (not a humanely conceivable option); welfare payments to the needy may be made from general tax resources; systems of social insurance may be instituted, allowing people during their employable years to contribute to an insurance fund that will provide needed benefits; some generally applicable program of income maintenance could be created. The last three are not mutually exclusive.

For years the traditional pattern was direct relief, and we still have extensive programs providing financial grants to the needy aged, the blind, deaf, and disabled, and the children whose parents are incapable of supporting them. In addition, there are specialized services such as assisting in the production of braille reading materials for the blind. The vocational rehabilitation program makes it possible for disabled persons to receive medical treatment, artificial limbs, and retraining so that they may become self-sufficient and contributing members of society. Some direct-assistance programs are administered by the states but heavily supported (in a few cases 100 per cent) by financial grants from the national government, while other aid has recently come to be provided directly by national agencies.

The social insurance programs are among those operated by the national government itself. The basic element of the Social Security program, which includes some of the aid programs just described, is Old Age and Survivors Insurance, which now covers the bulk of the nation's employed workers and many self-employed. Workers and employers both contribute into the OASI trust fund, from which individual workers or eligible survivors draw monthly benefits after retirement.

Compulsory coverage of most employed persons spreads the risk widely and assures that people who most need the coverage actually have it. OASI benefits mean that many who would otherwise need direct relief find it unnecessary, and there is a definite psychological advantage to drawing from insurance to which one has contributed rather than from "charity." The question is sometimes raised as to whether some people benefit more than others from such a system. The answer, of course, is yes. That is the nature of insurance. Someone may die at sixty, leaving no survivors, while another lives to be ninety-eight, drawing benefits continuously after retirement. Insurance spreads risk. It is not known who will die in a given year, but life insurance specialists can forecast accurately how many will die. Unquestionably the way to gain the greatest benefit from one's life insurance policy is to die shortly after having paid the first premium, though the idea may be otherwise unattractive. In this sense some are always benefiting more than others, but we are all simply hedging against an uncertain future.

Considerable publicity has been given lately to the fact that social security benefit payments have been exceeding income earned by the system, resulting in repeated increases in the rate of the payroll tax required of employers and employees. Actually, the most serious criticism relates to the extremely regressive nature of the system. The tax falls upon all earnings, however small, at the same rate; moreover, there is a maximum amount of income annually subject to tax. A person with an income of $20,000, let us say, pays social security tax on the entire income (the precise amount of the ceiling changes from time to time), while someone with a $300,000 income also pays on only $20,000. Finally, only income from wages and salaries is taxed; that from dividends, interest, and rents is immune. In effect, therefore, the burden of supporting the entire system is borne primarily by those least able to pay. There are proposals to amend the law by establishing exemptions for the lowest incomes, raising or eliminating the ceilings, and financing a significant percentage of the benefit payments from general treasury revenues (which come from more progressive taxes), but these have not yet been given the serious attention they deserve.

Unemployment compensation is also run like insurance, the cost in most states borne entirely by employers. It has simply become a part of the cost of doing business, and the avoidance of fluctuating employment is encouraged by providing that the fewer layoffs an employer has, the lower payroll taxes for unemployment compensation will be. The program is operated primarily by the states, but participation by all the states is guaranteed by the interesting device of the tax offset. Employers of four or more persons are subject to a national payroll tax but are excused from most of that tax if they are in a state operating an unemployment compensation system under laws that meet national standards. The states also administer workmen's compensation insurance programs, providing benefits to workers injured on the job.

HOUSING

Interest by the national government in the difficult problems of housing has grown substantially in the last three of four decades. The relation between poor housing and problems of health, crime and delinquency, family life, school attendance, and narcotics scarcely needs elaboration. Slum areas constitute a tremendous social cost to any community, and they are also a direct economic drain. They cost the city the most in terms of police and fire protection, health services, and welfare, while returning the least in taxes. Cities depend heavily on the property tax, and the amount of the tax is based on the assessed valuation of the property. Most substandard housing is rental property and is likely to be quite profitable to the owners because the costs of both upkeep and taxes are minimal. It is evident that in numerous ways slum clearance and the provision of adequate housing are highly advantageous to a community as well as to the people immediately affected.

The loan guarantee programs of the Federal Housing Administration and the Veterans' Administration have had little if any effect on these problems, though in the years following World War II they unquestionably built suburbia. Individuals secured home loans from banks and other private lending agencies, but the loans were guaranteed against default by the FHA or VA. Since the banks took no risk, lower rates of interest and smaller down payments were possible. Thus private construction of housing was stimulated enormously, but little of it was in a price range that low-income people could consider. When much higher interest rates could be secured elsewhere, lending institutions ceased such loans, or their purpose was circumvented by a system of "points," requiring payments in advance in addition to interest for the "privilege" of getting a loan.

The development of low-cost public housing for low-income groups was intended to meet the needs of the poorest members of society and made significant headway within the restrictions imposed by very limited appropriations. Even though the public housing program is primarily a loan program whose cost to the taxpayer is quite modest, it has proved difficult to persuade comfortable people of the need for more money, and little more than a dent has been made on a problem of such magnitude. The role of the national government has been to make available to local governments small planning grants and long-term low-interest loans, while the local units determine needs, select locations, and let contracts for construction. They also administer the housing, subject to certain mimimal rules established by the national government, including the requirement that one slum unit be eliminated for each new unit constructed.

Much popular misunderstanding prevails concerning public housing. It is often argued that it constitutes unfair competition with private housing. Such criticism overlooks the fact that public housing competes only with substandard private housing that is already in violation of local building codes. The income ceilings for eligibility insure that public housing is available only to people unable to rent or purchase standard-quality private housing. Another criticism is that public housing is undesirable because it does not pay taxes, an argument that is technically true but actually false. As long as there is a national loan on the property, the rule of intergovernmental tax immunity applies and local governments may not tax it. But the truth is that public housing projects make regular payments in lieu of taxes to all local governments in whose jurisdiction they lie. A city will get more from almost any "in lieu" payment than it got from the property tax on the slum housing replaced, while at the same time the city's service costs are likely to be reduced. President Nixon brought virtually the entire public housing program to a halt by early 1973, but it was revived by Congress in 1976.

If imaginatively conceived and properly managed, public housing can be considerably more than merely putting a roof over people's heads, however valuable that may be. For many families it may mean gaining for the first time a sense of self-respect and responsibility, a recognition that others care, and a feeling of having some stake in the community. Yet there has been growing criticism that the construction of "housing projects," although improving living conditions, continues to concentrate the poor in certain areas, with concomitant undesirable social effects. Building scattered single-family units is vastly more expensive. An interesting experiment in some communities involves the purchase and rehabilitation of old homes here and there throughout the city, which are then rented to low-income families. The creation of a new Department of Housing and Urban Development in 1965 did not in itself bring about new programs, but it collected under one organization a number of previously scattered related programs and clearly symbolized the concern of the national government at that time for the crisis of the cities. Congress did, however, at the same time accept President Johnson's recommendation for an innovative rent-subsidy program. Rather than involving government in building and managing housing, it encouraged such action by private developers or nonprofit organizations like churches, through agreement by the national government to make up the difference between rental costs and the amounts poor families

Although the national government has frequently concerned itself during the last fifty years with the problem of substandard housing, much remains to be done, as can be seen from this picture of an urban slum.

could pay. The program has met with significant success but again has not been anywhere near the magnitude necessary to succeed in eliminating slums. It is conceivable, though the day of acceptance seems now remote, that at some time in the future the provision of adequate housing for all in need will be viewed, as it is in many countries, as simply another normal everyday service of government.

URBAN RENEWAL

The Urban Renewal Program was not primarily directed toward housing, although there is much popular confusion on the matter. It was designed to aid cities in clearing blighted areas, often the old central sections that have existed long enough to deteriorate badly, and to redevelop those areas in ways that are useful and attractive. Sometimes new housing may be a by-product, but most renewal projects have been devoted to modern commercial uses, new civic and convention centers, and cultural and recreational facilities. The Model Cities Program, another product of the Johnson administration, offered aid to communities that developed and implemented comprehensive plans for attacking the whole complex of urban problems (housing, center-city rehabilitation, transportation, poverty, and crime, to name but a few), instead of approaching them in a piecemeal fashion. For this and several other grant programs directed toward solution of urban problems, the Nixon administration persuaded Congress to substitute "special revenue sharing" under his Better Communities Act, leaving specific plans to the localities.

HEALTH CARE

The establishment of the Medicare program has meant that health care has also been absorbed at least partially into the realm of social insurance. Government involvement in health services is not new, but publicly operated health insurance in any form was bitterly contested for decades. The national government has not only provided extensive medical care facilities for veterans, members of the armed services, Indians, and others but also has been actively engaged in health inspection at ports, control of drug manufacture and sale, health education, and medical research. In addition it has furnished substantial financial aid to the states for construction of hospitals and other medical service facilities, for maternal and child health programs, and for research.

In 1965, after decades of controversy, Congress created the Medicare program of hospital and health care insurance for people over sixty-five, financed by an increase in the required employee and employer contributions under the social security system. There is also assistance to the states for medical services to the needy aged, a

FIGURE 11.1   Outlays for Health for Fiscal Years 1969–1980

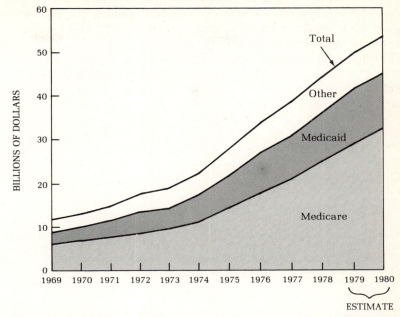

Source: Office of Management and Budget, *The Budget in Brief, Fiscal Year 1979*, Government Printing Office, Washington, D.C., 1978, p. 53.

program known as Medicaid. The cost of these and other health care plans has risen dramatically in the past decade (see Figure 11.1). Such programs have unquestionably been a great boon to millions of older Americans, and in practice the principal problems have arisen from abuses of the system by a few doctors, necessitating the establishment of somewhat tighter controls.

EDUCATION

Public education has been essentially a responsibility of state and local governments, although the national government has always played a gradually expanding role. Since the days of the original land grants for the support of education, most national action has been for specific purposes rather than aid to general educational programs. Veterans, farmers, libraries, school-lunch services, and vocational education have received support from the national government. Especially in the years since World War II there has been a growth of new specialized activities, including aid for strengthened science education, language training, fellowships and loans for students in colleges and universities, construction grants and loans for higher education facilities, and improved teacher training. The national government has become a principal support for scientific research, especially through the National Science Foundation. The comparable but much younger National Foundation on the Arts and Humanities has so far received only modest funding.

Bills to authorize financial aid from the national government to the general program of elementary and secondary education have been before every session of Congress for fifty years, but not until 1965 was such a program instituted. In the beginning the primary emphasis was on helping schools in poor areas, allocations being based on the number in each school of school-age children from families with incomes below a poverty level. The problems of whether aid could be given to church-related schools, one rock on which many previous proposals had foundered, was resolved technically by providing

Project Headstart concentrates on eliminating some of the handicaps of social and economic deprivation that children from rural and urban slums often have when they enter kindergarten or first grade. It has been one of the most successful and better known programs of the Office of Economic Opportunity.

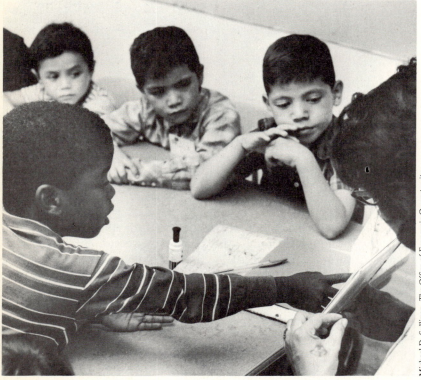

Michael D. Sullivan, The Office of Economic Opportunity.

assistance in such cases to the children or families rather than to the school. In light of the severe financial crisis afflicting most school districts across the country, continued and expanded national aid is a virtual certainty.

The shortcomings in achieving our professed goal of equal educational opportunity for all are acutely evident relative to poor and minority-group children. A recent Senate committee study indicated a multitude of examples of this inequality, including statistics such as these: two-thirds of all American Indians have never gone beyond elementary school; there are less than one-fourth as many Mexican-Americans enrolled in universities in certain states than would be anticipated on the basis of their percentage of the population; 43.8 per cent of black adults have less than nine years of schooling, compared to 26.6 per cent of white adults. The reasons are many and complex and doubtless will not be solved by dollars alone, but a clear commitment to rectify these imbalances is long overdue.

MATCHING SOCIAL PROGRAMS TO FUTURE NEEDS

Most social legislation we have been examining has served necessary purposes, and many programs will continue to be valuable. Still others are inadequate to meet rapidly changing conditions. New approaches and bold experimentation will be required. How are we to meet the new aspects of crisis in poverty, urban decay, energy, racial conflict, employment insecurity, and environmental pollution?

ELIMINATION OF POVERTY

Census data indicate that more than one-tenth of the nation still lives at income levels below what is officially defined as poverty, but without government assistance programs the figure would be a staggering 25 per cent. Although there are disputes over the definition and over whether certain classifications of people (students, for example) should properly be included, few would deny the genuine seriousness of the problem. As a new public consciousness of the plight of these formerly "invisible" Americans developed, new social efforts to change their conditions were initiated. For some special problems progress is embryonic. Such is the plight of migratory agricultural workers, who have commonly suffered below-minimum standard wages and the sorriest of working and living conditions while being denied elementary social benefits and protections afforded other workers. On a broader scale, responding to President Johnson's call for a "war on poverty," Congress passed in 1964 the Economic Opportunity Act, creating and funding a new agency to coordinate a great variety of programs designed to attack this problem. Some of the better-known programs were directed at youth, like Project Headstart, to bring preschool children from disadvantaged backgrounds up to a competitive starting point with other children, and Upward Bound, a program for high school students from similar backgrounds helping them improve their educational performance and view the prospect of further education as a realistic possibility. Under the umbrella of a war on poverty were diverse programs for assistance in developing businesses and farms, for help in job finding, for establishment of child-care centers to enable mothers to take remunerative employment, and for introduction of basic adult education.

The legislation specified that in planning local community programs there should be maximum participation by the poor themselves, and although that has often been difficult to achieve, it has contributed strikingly to the development of indigenous leadership among the poor. In its initial years the poverty war suffered from the use of inexperienced people in positions of responsibility, conspicuous infighting, and conflicts with the established social agencies and community leaders, but some of these obstacles eventually disappeared. The central problem was that the volume of money appropriated, although appearing substantial in a block, was more appropriate to a skirmish than to a war. The Vietnam War drained resources, but above all Congress, the president, and the general public have seemed unwilling to make an all-out commitment to eliminate poverty.

In 1973 President Nixon moved to demolish the Office of Economic Opportunity, which administered the poverty program, but this was stalled by court action. In 1975 the agency was officially abolished, with the bulk of its community action programs transferred to a new Community Services Administration in the Department of Health, Education, and Welfare. Certain programs were scattered to other agencies, and an independent corporation was created to handle the always controversial provision of legal services for the poor.

We do not intend to let the poor starve. Thus the only real question is what form the redistribution of income should take. Traditional welfare has proved increasingly unsatisfactory. The existing system has been sharply criticized for perpetuating poverty in families and militating against efforts to improve, for example, by reducing grants whenever one succeeds in earning a bit of additional income. Furthermore, its operation requires a vast bureaucracy.

Recently interest in experimenting with some type of income maintenance plan as an alternative has been growing. This could assume the form of a guaranteed annual income, a plan by which the government makes up the difference in a cash payment to families whose income drops below a poverty line; a family allowance paid to families with children below a certain age; a "salary" paid to mothers, on the theory that motherhood has forced them out of the labor market, but they are performing a societal function in child rearing; the use of government as an "employer of last resort," guaranteeing jobs in public services to all who are able but unemployed; or what is called the negative income tax, a convenient device for income redistribution whereby everyone files an income tax return, but people above a certain level would pay graduated taxes as now, while others below that level would receive graduated payments instead. Incentives would be written in to encourage people to move out of the recipient category.

Some sort of income maintenance plan has been receiving support from an unlikely combination of social theorists and big-business leaders. Proponents argue that it would provide help where needed and in the most useful form (cash), that the economy would be stabilized by maintaining high purchasing power, and that the current high costs of welfare administration would be essentially eliminated. Although problems are clearly evident, not least the need for reassessing our national "puritan ethic," such plans are likely to receive increasingly serious consideration. President Nixon's "workfare" proposal of 1969, embodying the concept of a guaranteed minimum income for all people working or willing to work as well as for those incapable of working, was the first major step in the direction of a comprehensive system of income maintenance. The president did not, however, actively push the proposal in Congress during the next three years, and he quietly collaborated in its death.

President Carter's proposal also stressed the work theme and embodied elements from several different plans. It too was a guaranteed annual minimum income program, which emphasized correction of the worst features of the existing system and offered much simplified administration. The two basic elements were (1) an attempt to assure access to a job for every employable person having family responsibilities, with the emphasis on private sector employment but with government's serving as employer of last resort and (2) cash assistance to all others in a single consolidated program replacing the existing miscellany of separate classes of aids. Incentives to work if able were built in, both by keeping welfare benefits considerably below standard work-income levels and by changing the old provisions that resulted in reducing benefits by the amount earned when someone secured a low-paying or part-time job, for example. There were likewise incentives to keep families together and the establishment of an essentially uniform level of benefits throughout the nation. In addition, increased national funding was to relieve partially the overwhelming burden on city and county governments, although there was no move to transfer the total program to national administration, as local officials had hoped.

The myths about welfare remain a powerful force. Welfare runs counter to the American dream and the Horatio Alger tradition; antagonism to the welfare recipient is pervasive and often virulent. The comfortable majority tends eagerly to lap up demagogic themes that the welfare rolls are packed with able-bodied loafers, that most children on welfare are illegitimate, that most people on welfare are chiselers, that most welfare families are black, that additional money for welfare recipients would be spent on liquor and big cars, and the like. It is easy to demonstrate that none of these notions is true, but they are widely believed. The overwhelming majority of people on welfare are children (72 per cent), the elderly, the disabled, and mothers with children to care for; probably only about 10 per cent are employable on a full-time basis. Suspected fraud occurs in slightly less than 0.4 per cent of the nation's total welfare case load. Yet it *is* true that the present system is demoralizing and corrosive, lacking adequate assistance in breaking the cycle of poverty that people inherit, just as others inherit wealth. The need for different and creative approaches is urgent.

INCREASED EFFORTS AT COMBATING DISCRIMINATION

With the problems of poverty and racial discrimination so closely intertwined, it is evident that effective change of economic circumstances would have a major impact on some aspects of race relations. But not all elements of racial discrimination lie in the purely economic realm. Since the battles to end de jure segregation have been largely won, the scene has shifted to the more difficult and sensitive problems of de facto segregation: "understandings" that prevent an open housing market, school imbalances resulting from discriminatory housing patterns, inferior educational programs ill-suited to the needs of children from disadvantaged backgrounds, informal barriers to employment, and lack of capital to establish businesses for people from minority groups.

For some years the most controversial aspect of protective labor legislation has been the fair employment practices laws (usually called FEPC laws because of the habit of including in the title the commission such laws establish). About half the states and a number of municipalities have such statutes, but comparable national legislation has been slow to appear because such proposals were subjected to filibuster in the Senate. FEP laws are actually very simple: they specify that no employer may discriminate in policies on hiring and conditions of work and that no labor union may discriminate in its membership policies on race, color, religion, or national origin. In essence they say to an employer: "If you have two or more applicants for a job, hire the best qualified one—paying no attention to irrelevant considerations like color." FEP laws usually contain sufficient enforcement clauses, but commissions have as a rule emphasized persuasion and education in order to change people's attitudes, viewing this course to be more significant than merely forcing the employment of a particular individual.

A comprehensive national FEP law has been passed several times by the House, only to falter when filibustered in the Senate, although fair employment rules are applied by executive order to employers holding national government contracts. The Civil Rights Act of 1964 outlawed certain discriminatory employment practices by the larger employers. The act carried no enforcement power, but that was provided by the Equal Employment Opportunities Act of 1972.

The latter law brought a rapid expansion of the national government's role in fighting employment discrimination. It forbade discrimination against women and older persons, as well as against racial, national origin, or religious minorities, and required rigid application of the principle of equal pay for equal work. Significantly, the newly created Equal Employment Opportunities Commission was given authority to initiate actions as well as to handle complaints. Although it can issue orders to cease discriminatory practices, it is dependent on the courts for enforcement. A fairly high percentage of its investigations, however, result in negotiated settlements and have sometimes involved agreements for sizable amounts of back pay.

Antidiscrimination rules per se result in little if any argument, since they represent elemental fairness, but continual controversy swirls around the pressures for "compensatory" hiring, designed to make up for past injustices (though to others than those now seeking to be hired, and very likely on the part of other employers) and to demonstrate affirmative action. The implication of the latter term is that it is not sufficient merely to avoid obviously discriminatory practices; an employer should go further by making a continuous positive effort to locate and hire qualified persons from groups subject to discrimination in the past. Again, such a goal would appear to be beyond reproach, but the problems, if any, most likely to occur lie in interpretation and enforcement. Many employers complain that in actual practice they are virtually forced to hire quotas from certain groups, almost regardless of qualifications, in order to prove that they have been practicing affirmative action, and that they are too easily subjected to expensive and time-consuming harassment through challenges and prolonged investigations.

The national government has for a time placed emphasis on aiding "black capitalism" (and comparable efforts of other minority groups), although it has often seemed that the amount of rhetoric has dwarfed the amount of funds made available. Special education and vocational training programs for the disadvantaged have been instituted, and public employment itself has been used in a compensatory fashion. Publicly aided housing is open to all eligible people on the same terms, but meaningful pressure against restrictive real-estate market practices is still embryonic. Some issues are less amenable to government solutions than others, but even when the problem is essentially one of attitudes, government can do a great deal in establishing a climate conducive to fair and harmonious relations. The nation's top political figures can if they choose provide a tone of moral leadership that can be vastly influential. Probably the most significant progress will be achieved in the long run as minority groups move increasingly into the mainstream of politics, exploiting their very real weight as voters and accelerating the already notable movement into elective offices.

NEW PLANS IN HEALTH CARE

With Medicare an accomplished fact, the fundamental controversy continues over whether medical care is a right of all human beings or merely a privilege. There has been very little backing in the United States for a system of socialized medicine, wherein medical personnel become in essence public employees, but support for a health insurance program covering all citizens has grown steadily. Proponents call attention to the large numbers of people who even in an era of prosperity are unable to finance adequate medical care. They contend that it is far more desirable to put such care on a prepaid insurance basis than to prolong a system in which people unable to pay the full costs either postpone treatment or are forced to prevail upon the charity of the doctor or a city or county hospital. Opponents express fears of restricting the freedom of choice of doctor and patient, of possible excessive red tape, and of the dangers of "mixing politics and medicine."

In every session of Congress there are a number of bills to create one type or another of national health insurance. They range from broad-gauge programs of essentially universal coverage financed by payroll deductions and employer contributions, with perhaps some allocations from general revenue particularly to cover the poor and unemployed, to those that are only for catastrophic medical expense or those that would extend the Medicare principle only to maternal and child health services. Others have suggested requiring employers to make available shared-cost programs for their employees or granting sliding-scale income tax credits for the purchase of private health insurance—both with government subsidies for low-income persons.

"The question," said a recent president of the American Medical Association, in a sharp departure from the organization's previous

positions, "is not whether we shall have national health insurance in this country. It is, rather, what kind of national health insurance we shall have." AMA has seemingly, however, continued to drag its feet, for example, by helping to water down legislation to encourage the development of health maintenance organizations (HMOs), organizations offering comprehensive prepaid medical care on a contract basis, a system that would place stress on preventive medicine because of the financial advantage to the provider of services if participants are kept healthy. Such legislation with modest funding was passed late in 1973, but development of HMOs has been extremely slow.

Medical costs have continued to skyrocket much more rapidly than the general rate of inflation, fueled by huge malpractice insurance costs, widespread use of extremely expensive equipment, the practice of "defensive medicine" (requiring all manner of tests to avoid possible malpractice charges), overuse of hospitals, and a monopoly situation in which there are no incentives for economy. As a stopgap measure the Carter administration sought legislation to place a ceiling on the annual rate of increase in hospital costs, the largest single component, in the hope of forcing economies of operation, but found the proposal difficult to sell.

Whatever the precise outcome of current debates, there appears to be steadily growing concern inside and outside the medical profession over the inadequacy and unequal availability of medical services and a recognition that some progressive steps are necessary. The utter inadequacy or total absence of health services in the city ghettos and poverty-stricken rural areas has only recently come to the awareness of the majority of Americans. Even if vast sums of money were immediately available, these problems would not be quickly solved. That the nation is producing far too few doctors is a critical situation, and many more paramedical personnel are needed to enable doctors to use their time more efficiently.

Hunger and malnutrition, serious health problems, were until lately almost ignored in the United States. The average citizen's initial reaction was one of disbelief of reports of families, especially in depressed rural areas, living barely above starvation levels and of children whose diets leave them stunted in physical and mental development. Many people find it hard to accept the fact that such conditions could exist in the most prosperous of nations.

Welfare benefits in some states are pegged so low as to be insufficient even for food, let alone other needs (sometimes deliberately, in the hope of forcing recipients to move to other states). The school-lunch and milk-distribution programs conducted by the Department of Agriculture are immensely valuable, yet do not reach children too ill or poorly clothed to go to school and did not until rather recently exist where local authorities chose not to administer such programs. The food stamp program was originally designed to supplement inadequate diets and help dispose of surplus agricultural commodities, but it rather quickly became a general welfare program supplementing the income of the poor. Unfortunately there was also a rather high potential for abuse, and President Carter advocated its merger into his reformed welfare program.

TOWARD GUARANTEEING EMPLOYMENT SECURITY

Argument over some of the perennial issues of labor relations has lately been relegated to the background as attention has focused on the critical problem of maintaining full employment in a rapidly changing economy. A unique feature of the 1970s was a high level of unemployment even *during* a period of war and of general prosperity. It has remained critical, especially for minority groups and youth. Unfortunately, most of the approaches to solutions have been of the band-aid variety, and the realities of contemporary economic circumstances have not as a rule been squarely faced. Automation does, of course, create new jobs as well as displace workers but not in comparable numbers or by making use of the same skills. Despite the obvious justice of equal employment opportunities for women, the fact can hardly be ignored that the vast increase in the numbers of working women in recent years has mushroomed the labor force without increasing the number of consumers (and thus the demand upon productive capacity). Many more people are employed than ever before in the history of the country, but the rate of unemployment continues high. It is not uncommon for families to have two full-time income-producing jobs, either of which would be adequate to live on, while other families lack any job at all. It would be both unfair and pointless to argue for turning the clock back; the point is that such crucial factors are seemingly not being taken into account in the nation's social planning. Yet another comparable factor is the increasing rate of "moonlighting" (holding a second job), the number of two job workers having reached a peak of 4.6 million by 1977.

Dealing with the problem of adequate employment opportunity is a jointly private and public responsibility, and much planning is required to accomplish significant results. Most efforts, however useful in themselves, have been largely palliatives. They include slow pacing of the introduction of automation so that a company's present employees are not displaced, retraining assistance, and proposals for prolonging compulsory education. Most observers concede that the economy does not need the number of workers potentially available, at least on current work schedules. There is nothing sacrosanct about the eight-hour day, just as there was not about the earlier ten- and twelve-hour days, but at the present level further reductions would produce complicated results by encouraging even more moonlighting, which could mean little improvement in overall employment. Thus there is under way more alteration of the work week than the work day, and thought is being given to altering the work year more than the work week, through such devices as more holidays and three-day weekends, longer vacations, and even leaves of absence.

Other more precedent-shattering approaches usually relate to one of the various income maintenance proposals, discussed previously, perhaps ultimately breaking the long-hallowed compulsory link between employment in a traditional type of job and access to the benefits of the society.

The most far-reaching proposal to take specific form was introduced in Congress in 1976, universally referred to as the Humphrey-Hawkins bill. This bill would declare it the right of all employable adult Americans to receive employment at fair compensation and, toward achievement of that objective, would have the nation embark upon two related courses of action: (1) a major effort to stimulate private job creation, with government providing jobs to satisfy unmet public needs, insofar as the private sector fails to accomplish full employment and (2) the establishment of machinery for continuing national economic planning, involving the setting of goals for production, purchasing power, and employment and the recommending of legislative policies to achieve such goals. Although others disagreed, the principal sponsors contended that costs of the program would be fully offset by taxes from previously unemployed people and the reduction in unemployment compensation and welfare benefits. The legislation was subsequently modified to avoid a firm commitment for enough public jobs to eliminate unemployment.

There has finally developed a more general awareness of the circular relation between full employment, or at least maintenance of purchasing power, and a healthy total economy. This truth is nowhere more succinctly put than in the classic response of the late United Auto Workers president Walter Reuther when a Ford vice president, who was showing him through a new, highly automated plant, asked jokingly: "How are you going to get these machines to pay union dues?" After a moment's pause, Reuther rejoined: "I haven't got that figured out. But how are you going to get these machines to buy Fords?"

THE ENERGY CRISIS

In the midst of trying to cope with broad problems of economic stability, the nation suddenly found itself face to face with a critical shortage of energy resources, and an entire populace was startled into an awareness of how utterly dependent it was on oil and electricity. Less heat in winter and less cooling in summer, plus at least doubled prices for gasoline and other fuels, became an immediate reality. More serious were economic dislocations as shortages

Signs of the energy crisis.

Tim Carlson/Stock Boston

resulted in temporary plant closures and large numbers of people being thrown out of work. The threat of economic depression loomed. Forecasts for the future were dire. The immediate onset of the oil crisis was linked in the popular mind with the embargo imposed by the Arab nations of the Middle East as they sought to use their vast oil resources as a weapon to diminish support for Israel, but the crisis would doubtless have occurred soon, regardless of this element. As far back as the time of the Truman administration, official studies had forecast critical shortages in about twenty-five years, but apparently industry, government, and the general public failed to take this and subsequent reports seriously.

As the crisis grew, a number of states took limited steps to restrict panic buying, for example, but the energy problem was nationwide and demanded national government action. The president, with congressional authorization and support, established a Federal Energy Administration, whose director was promptly labeled the "energy czar." While standby plans were developed for rationing if needed, the principal emphasis was on allocations and controls, designed to spread supplies with reasonable equity, to preserve balances such as between the production of motor-vehicle fuel and heating oils, and to see that the most crucial needs received priority. Such decisions are inherently difficult and fraught with controversy. People who believe themselves unjustly disadvantaged can easily turn to violence, as the truckers' strikes and blockades evidenced. Yet farmers must be able to maintain or increase food production, foodstuffs and raw materials must continue to move in the channels of transportation, unemployment must be minimized to prevent the entire economy from sliding downhill, and the list of priorities to be balanced has only begun. Still another emphasis was on notably increased government support for research and development of expanded and alternative energy sources.

One of the threatened victims of the crisis was the still new effort at environmental improvement: energy needs and pollution control came into frequent conflict. The long-stalled Alaskan pipeline was authorized by Congress and constructed, some communities relaxed air-pollution standards, and a few new electric-generating plants received approvals that had previously been delayed or denied. Yet despite some actions of this type, surprisingly strong public and official support for environmental protection remained intact, even in the face of crisis, and the ground lost was probably not as great as some people had originally feared. In one sense the need for conservation had become sharply clearer.

As his predecessor had also sought to do, President Carter devoted considerable effort to an attempt to persuade the public that the energy crisis was real and could only get worse if inaction prevailed. It was a difficult task, as most people were understandably reluctant

"We all have to make some sacrifices"

to give up even a portion of a comfortable and easygoing way of life; the lights still came on when one flipped a switch, and people did not feel personally any economic effects when massive imports of high-cost oil could turn what otherwise would have been a favorable balance of foreign trade into severe annual deficits. But as government warnings were joined by those of the utilities and the media, public and congressional opinion gradually swung behind more stringent conservation practices. At the president's request Congress created a new Cabinet-rank Department of Energy, which would consolidate energy-related programs scattered among many agencies and assume some powers of price and rate fixing, allocations of supply, public information, and the like.

Congress subsequently acted to accept the bulk of the administration's recommendations for conservation programs and reduction of dependence on external sources, although the inevitably strong differences of opinion as to the most desirable methods resulted in defeat for some elements of the proposal. Included were such steps as trying to discourage use by making energy cost more, providing incentives for exploration and development of new domestic sources, requiring new business buildings to be energy efficient, encouraging home insulation, requiring improved automobile gas mileage and increased taxes on new "gas guzzler" cars, and applying strong pressures and offering assistance for utility and industrial conversion to coal, of which the United States has extensive reserves (together utilities and industry burn 25 per cent of the oil and 60 per cent of the natural gas used in the country). The fundamental target was waste, as the amount of fuel used unnecessarily in the United States was staggering. This act, over 500 pages in length, touched almost every facet of energy problems and represented a major departure from the past, although it would of necessity require continuous adaptation as the nation learned by experience.

CONSUMER PROTECTION

The old maxim "let the buyer beware" is more hallowed by antiquity than by common sense. In practice, few people can be sufficiently expert on technical matters—the ingredients of a new medicine or the feasible safety devices for automobiles, for example—to make competent judgments on many products. Nor can they know until it is too late whether a canned food is contaminated. Beyond these questions are the fundamental ones of whether the buyer is receiving a reasonable approximation of a dollar's value for a dollar spent and whether the advertising and the labels are accurate or misleading. We all depend on the integrity of manufacturers and processors, on laws specifying sanitation requirements and standards of quality, and on government agencies created to guard the public interest in this respect.

American standards have been generally high, but there are always some individuals whose greed for a fast buck easily overcomes scruples. Moreover, there are inevitable differences of opinion on some matters as to what standards are really necessary or precisely what the public is willing to pay for. Sound information to consumers has been spotty, although a few privately supported research organizations have helped fill the need. Public interest itself fluctuates, being fanned by an occasional sensational case or by the efforts of a well-publicized crusader like Ralph Nader. Aroused public sentiment can bring results, however, as the Nader campaign on automobile safety demonstrated.

As stated earlier, much of the work of the Federal Trade Commission constitutes, at least potentially, significant consumer protection. The Food and Drug Administration in the Department of Health, Education, and Welfare as well as the food inspection services of the Department of Agriculture also contribute to such protection. The FTC, for example, has waged for decades a battle with the cigarette manufacturers over questions of false and misleading advertising. During this period the range of advertising has been great: from the days of testimonials to the benefits of smoking through an interim of manufacturers' claims of "less throat irritants" to the era of lung-cancer research, package warnings, anticigarette advertising, and finally a ban altogether on cigarette advertising over television. The possibilities for fraud are endless in advertising for such familiar items as toothpaste, reducing pills, and far-out offerings like a $6.98 "mind-power machine" that was promised to "strengthen all eleven

vital functions of your mind," thus helping the purchaser to "develop radar-like concentration, overcome worry and fear, develop X-ray powers of observation, and make problems half-solve themselves."

A new approach to truth-in-advertising efforts began in 1971 when the FTC instituted an advertising substantiation campaign, which required manufacturers to document with reliable research data the claims made in their advertising. The agency began with the makers of automobiles, television receivers, cold and cough remedies, electric shavers, dentifrices, and air conditioners, periodically adding new products to the list. Analysis of the data indicated that approximately 30 per cent of the claims were unconvincingly documented, and in addition some companies agreed without submitting data to cease certain claims. The practice of making the findings public is assumed to have a salutary effect on future advertising. Since 1974 the commission has been authorized to seek penalties against any company doing something previously outlawed in another cease and desist order, as long as it has knowledge that the action is illegal. Thus the FTC need not repeat long investigations and orders for each separate but identical case, as it formerly was required to do.

The responsibility of the Food and Drug Administration is to protect against impure, adulterated, and dangerous food and drugs in the channels of interstate commerce. The FDA is a small agency with only limited power to inspect manufacturing and processing plants, and it must operate largely by spot checks and in response to complaints. A random selection of FDA confiscation orders may illustrate the kinds of situation in which the agency acts: (1) a shipment of cream-style sweet corn containing worms and worm fragments; (2) packaged bread contaminated with "insects, insect fragments, and rodent hair fragments"; (3) a shipment of sherry, port, and muscatel wines containing "fruit flies, fruit fly pupae, mites, and aphids"; and (4) a "reducing cream" that claimed to produce results merely by rubbing it on the unduly fleshy portions of the body but that produced severe burns on a number of people before it could be removed from the market. Since the 1962 uproar over thalidomide and its capacity to deform unborn babies, controls on the testing and sale of new drugs have been considerably strengthened. The FDA has recently moved to require accurate labeling of packaged foods—for example, the actual percentage of orange juice in "orange drink" or the fact that meat must be added separately to the "roast beef casserole."

Laws requiring accurate labeling have been in existence for many years, but one of the newer consumer protection laws is the so-called Truth-in-Lending Act. Its most significant requirement is that consumers borrowing money or making purchases on installment plans must be informed not only of monthly charges but also of the interest rates on an annual basis calculated by a prescribed formula. Consumers can thus know precisely what they are paying and are in a position to compare alternative possibilities. The Truth-in-Packaging Act requires information about package contents to help consumers compare prices per unit, although industry opposition defeated a proposal for standard package sizes. One of the newest regulatory agencies, the Consumer Product Safety Commission, investigates and can order corrections in everyday consumer products from toys to power tools that kill or injure thousands of people each year.

Recent presidents have had as part of their staff a "consumer counsel," but the office has had no power other than what exhortation and publicity can do. Through several successive sessions of Congress there have been efforts by public-interest and consumer groups to have established an independent Agency for Consumer Protection, with power to represent consumer interests before other national government agencies and courts. Massive opposition from business groups has blocked enactment. Some major departments, such as the Department of Transportation, have created new agencies with power to prescribe safety and quality standards for consumer protection within their area of responsibility. Possibilities of government regulation in several other areas remain untapped, and in each case there is the familiar problem of preventing undue influence over these agencies by the parties they are supposed to be regulating.

NATURAL ENVIRONMENT PROTECTION

Tides affect political issues, as they do other affairs of people, and as the decade of the 1960s changed to the 1970s the environment issue reached full tide. Long a concern of conservationists, the problems of pollution and destruction of natural resources at last penetrated the public consciousness. Veteran fighters for the cause were astonished at the rush with which environment suddenly became everyone's issue: presidents, governors, legislators, interest groups, the news media—including some surprising and unlikely converts. Competing proposals for protection and restoration vied for attention in legislative halls, campaigns for office were developed around this theme, popular demonstrations arose, industries launched advertising campaigns to demonstrate their commitment to the goal, pollution problems became newsworthy, and dramatic features in newspapers and on television besieged citizens from all sides. There was perhaps still more rhetoric than effective action, but long years of relative neglect were succeeded by a new crusade.

At this point in history no city dweller needs a scientific analysis to be persuaded of the existence of health-damaging air pollution; no camper or hiker is unaware of the disaster that has befallen once beautiful lakes and streams. Sewage and industrial waste pouring into rivers and lakes have reached a saturation point and have turned many waterways into virtual cesspools of filth. Human litter has defaced much of the landscape. Much wildlife has been destroyed. Pesticides to save crops from destruction have introduced a hazard of poison in foods, and as pesticides wash off the land, marine life dies. Oil leakage from offshore wells has wreaked havoc on lovely beaches. Vast quantities of refuse discarded by a large and affluent society have raised the specter of a populace gradually being buried in its own trash.

In part problems of pollution go with vast population growth. Too many people could in time destroy the earth's capacity for supporting life, and birth control, once an almost taboo subject, has come to be recognized as a vital necessity and a practice worthy of government as well as private support. Population growth and concentration have magnified a multitude of social problems and, indeed, have provoked new problems. Moreover, as growth and continuing urbanization march inexorably forward, human need for access to nature has become more sharply evident.

Some of the most wanton destruction of forests and soil had been arrested by the conservation battles of an earlier generation, but the contest between exploiters and protectors is perennial. At its founding, the United States was endowed with natural resources in such fabulous abundance that it seemed unnecessary to give thought to their protection, and throughout much of its history they have been used with abandon. Under the pressure of the enlightened few who saw the dangers early, we began years ago to move gradually in the other direction with scientific logging and reforestation, wildlife protection, and efforts in soil conservation, but the progress has been insufficient and the pace often agonizingly slow. Conservation has been one of those good words toward which almost everyone made deferential little bows, but at putting conservation into practice we have a notably less-than-sensational record.

Can owners of private land be effectively regulated in matters of

In recent years pollution and consequent efforts to protect our environment have gained much attention, and the problem of pollution is one that transcends partisan party politics.

conservation? To what extent is public ownership necessary and desirable to accomplish the purpose? Is public ownership necessary for some things and not for others? These are perplexing questions to which firm answers are not available, although the need for additional public lands for recreational purposes, for example, is scarcely debatable. There are, however, many divergent views as to how best to make use of recreational lands. Should the aim be primarily to preserve wilderness areas, or would it be better to develop more national parks that can be used by far greater numbers of people? A mixture will doubtless continue, but the proper balance is in dispute.

Conservation and environmental protection efforts are shared

The National Park System is made up of 214 units in the United States with a total area of more than 29,000,000 acres. The parks are administered by the National Park Service, a bureau of the Department of the Interior. Most areas, such as Canyon de Chelly in Arizona pictured here, are set aside to be preserved as unparalleled examples of national scenery.

United States Department of the Interior, National Park Service Photo by Fred E. Mang, Jr.

among national, state, and local governments, but a great many
aspects of the problem do not follow state and local boundaries.
Neither can they be realistically confined to national boundaries. Air
over the United States may be polluted by a bomb test in China, and
the supply and purity of water in the United States are often jointly a
concern with Canada and Mexico. Conservation activities and programs are scattered throughout the agencies of the national government, but they are concentrated primarily in the departments of
Interior and Agriculture. A new Environmental Protection Agency
came into being late in 1970, consolidating a number of programs
and exercising some enforcement powers. Major programs in water
supply and conservation, irrigation, and flood control have been
under way for years but effective control of water pollution is only
just beginning. The same is true of air pollution. New government
programs of research and the application of stringent controls, operating at all three levels of government, have been introduced into the
struggle to reverse the disastrous trends of past years, although
energy problems as well as uncertainties of technological development have produced some delays, as, for example, in the determination of a feasible rate of reduction in auto emissions. Much intergovernmental cooperation exists, but unfortunately there is also a certain
amount of intergovernmental buck-passing.

It is certainly true that it is now possible to pass environmental
protection legislation that would have been virtually inconceivable
only a few years ago. Cases in point are laws banning unregulated
dumping of wastes in oceans and coastal waters, establishing pesticide controls, protecting endangered species of animals and plants,
creating noise-emission standards, cracking down on industrial pollution of streams, authorizing enforcement of severe air-pollution
standards, and establishing rules for coastline management. After
having the legislation vetoed twice by President Ford, Congress with
the encouragement of President Carter again passed an act to control
strip mining and provide for rehabilitation of previously stripped
areas. Funds for building a supersonic transport plane were denied,
despite massive lobbying by the president and the Department of
Transportation as well as industry groups, largely though not exclusively on environmental grounds. The National Environmental
Quality Act directs all national government agencies to include the
environment in their decision making and requires that all agency
recommendations and reports on proposed legislation and other
major national government actions affecting the environment
include an "environmental impact statement" and an indication of
possible alternative actions. It may reasonably be argued that legislation accomplished so far is only a small beginning, but it has established highly significant precedents. Public support continues to

"Could you hurry and find a cure for cancer? That would be so much easier than prevention"

grow, as legislators are well aware and as passage of environmental initiative measures in a number of states and localities has demonstrated.

This public support is relatively easy to obtain when someone else must pay the price, directly or indirectly, but becomes far more difficult when people find that the price is personal, such as the imposition of higher costs for or restrictions on the use of automobiles, or when they find themselves in favor of two conflicting objectives. The Alaska pipeline controversy is a clear-cut illustration: unquestioned damage to the environment (though the degree is in dispute) versus a greatly improved supply of oil and reduced dependence on foreign sources. The Environmental Protection Agency provided major shock therapy in the middle of 1973 when it proposed to deal with air pollution by severe traffic controls in a dozen metropolitan areas including New York, Los Angeles, Dallas, Boston, and Minneapolis–St. Paul. Although details varied in the different regions, typically proposed steps included gasoline rationing, sharp reduction of downtown parking space, ceilings on motorcycle registrations, restriction of deliveries to hours outside the normal work day, required antipollution devices and strict vehicle inspection, special bus and car-pool lanes on roads, improved mass transit systems, staggered working hours, limitations on taxi-cruising, and the like. Though not given effect, these proposals did stimulate some related local actions and they perhaps offer a view of future possibilities.

The United States, like all the other developed countries, must face revision of treasured assumptions such as the "gospel of progress," defined in terms of steadily increasing material comforts. The solution to problems of environmental pollution and destruction of vital ecological balance cannot be found solely in controls on industry but also requires radically changed patterns of attitude and behavior on the part of individual citizens. Who demands the unfettered use of increasing numbers of automobiles, with high-powered engines and high-performance (and highly polluting) fuels? The freedom to dispose of trash in any handy forest or stream? The continued expansion of air travel, with jet engines producing both air pollution and noise pollution? The use of vast numbers of electrical appliances, despite the fact that many power plants producing electricity are major polluters and that energy resources have become critical? The opportunity for weekend off-road vehicle events that leave miles of desert or seashore in ruin? The use of products that eat up forests at excessive rates? May the price of failure to act not be worse?

Some benefits, like those that come from easy travel and electricity, we are not likely to abandon. One valid approach is to seek alternatives to the worst pollution and waste offenders—internal combustion engines, fossil-fuel electrical power plants, and bottles and other containers that do not decompose into natural elements. Perhaps the energy crisis or the occasional drought will contribute by forcing some changes. But the costs of any real solution to the critical problems of the environment are greater than money and will require some changes in our way of life. Is the public ready to pay this kind of personal price?

As the following case study indicates, feelings are strong and both sides have persuasive arguments. Which needs are most important? How much effort is enough? How much money can be used efficiently within a given time period? What level of taxation is feasible? Who should have the final decision? In the matter of the amendments to the Water Pollution Control Act, both houses overwhelmingly overrode President Nixon's veto.

Case Study
VETO OF THE 1972 WATER POLLUTION CONTROL ACT AMENDMENTS

The Speaker laid before the House the following veto message (dated October 17, 1972) from the President of the United States:

. . . I am compelled to withhold my approval from S. 1770, the Federal Water Pollution Control Act Amendments of 1972—a bill whose laudable intent is outweighed by its unconscionable $24 billion price tag. My proposed legislation, as reflected in my budget, provided sufficient funds to fulfill that same intent in a fiscally responsible manner. Unfortunately the Congress ignored our other vital national concerns and broke the budget with this legislation.

Environmental protection has been one of my highest priorities as President. . . .the water pollution control bill which I originally sent to the Congress last year was fully consistent with the concept of a balanced, full-employment budget. It would have committed $6 billion in federal funds over a three-year period, enough to continue and accelerate the momentum toward that high standard of cleanliness which all of us want in America's waters

If this veto is not sustained, let the issue be clearly drawn . . . a vote to sustain the veto is a vote against a tax increase. A vote to override the veto is a vote to increase the likelihood of higher taxes. . . .

THE SPEAKER: The objections of the President will be spread at large upon the Journal.

The question is, Will the House, on reconsideration, pass the bill, the objections of the President to the contrary notwithstanding?

MR. JONES OF ALABAMA: Mr. Speaker, for ten days and nights I have prayed that this issue would not be brought before the House; indeed, I had become convinced by the President's own words and those of his closest environmental advisers that he could not, in good conscience and with due regard for the national interest, allow himself to veto this bill.

The President of the United States has told us time and time again that we must come forward with a strong and effective water pollution control law if we are to save our environment. And we have done so.

The President's own environmental protection administrator has warned that the entire pollution control program "probably will be destroyed" if this act is permitted to die under the knife blade of a presidential veto.

The President's own Council on Environmental Quality warned him most solemnly in its third annual report, just two short months ago, that the life-or-death need to save our environment must not be subordinated to short-run, temporary economic considerations.

From U.S. Congress, House, *Congressional Record*, 92d Cong., 2d sess., October 18, 1972, pp. H10266–70.

Now, Mr. Speaker, we are told in the President's veto message that the cost which Congress has placed on the survival of our environment—a cost arrived at after fifteen months of the most soul-searching deliberation—is "unconscionable," that America is not prepared to pay the price.

Mr. Speaker, this is a decisive hour in our nation's history. We have known for a long, long time, and the President has known for a long, long time, that this is a costly undertaking. But we know also that the people who are this greatest nation on earth are prepared to pay the price of this undertaking, provided they are given a program that will restore and preserve the waters upon which our future depends.

We have produced such a program. We have set deadlines for our industries, and for our cities and towns, to clean up their waters, to make them fit for our children to swim in by 1983. We have set as a national goal the complete elimination of all pollution from our rivers, lakes, and streams by 1985. And we have authorized the President of the United States to use the money and the enforcement measures that are needed to get the job done. . . .

We cannot postpone action on our environmental crisis. The pollution that is fast destroying our waters will not go away of itself, nor can it be eliminated by halfway, bargain basement measures.

To those who say that we cannot afford to start now on the restoration of our waters, on the scale that Congress believes is essential, I say that we dare not postpone this undertaking. Every day of inaction most certainly will add to this ultimate cost; another year of inaction may well destroy all hope of saving our environment. . . .

MR. DELLUMS: Mr. Speaker, I support the override of this veto.

Yet, I am glad the President attempted this veto. It shows clearly how phony is the Nixon commitment to the environment. . . .

At least the President has not said he is against clean water.

But, for him, the need for clean water is less important than billion-dollar handouts to Lockheed and Penn Central, less important than the SST, less important than give-aways to foreign dictatorships and represssive regimes, less important than the highway program which strangles our central cities, and less important than the myriad of costly, unneeded defense boondoggles.

I urge overturn of this absurd veto.

SOLVING DOMESTIC PROBLEMS THROUGH POLITICS

Domestic problems and even crises are nothing new, yet their nature and urgency clearly vary from one period to another. Some problems may be relatively novel, such as the side-effects of a new pesticide, but the bulk are enduring issues like labor-management relations, within which new aspects and developments frequently appear. Problem solving in the public arena is likely to be a complicated enterprise, even if completely good will prevails. The American public is uncertain and mercurial in its attitude toward the use of government. These ambiguous and ambivalent feelings are frustrating to government officials and others who devote time to political and social action; the public one day demands action on a particular problem and the next day denounces government intervention or complains about the taxes needed to do the job (unfortunately some political leaders are not above encouraging such attitudes). And the government official is acutely aware that most of the people are never actually heard from at all. The willingness to accept government action and experiments is great in times of crisis, such as a depression, but rapidly diminishes at other times.

The processes of democracy, based on negotiation and debate rather than on authoritarian decisions, are often slow, though the long-term results may be desirable. Yet it is also true that many features of American governmental practice contribute unnecessarily to delay or stalemate, weighting the system in favor of the status quo. The checks and balances, the various procedural complexities in Congress, and the divisions inherent in federalism all impede certain kinds of progress. It is too easy, however, to assume that quick solutions to problems are not found simply because the system is unresponsive or because some institution is preventing action. Although such obstacles appear, it must be remembered that acceptable solutions to all problems do not necessarily lie ready at hand. Reasonable people may disagree over the great issues of the day, and it is the task of political leadership to seek all possible alternatives, to be open to new and different viewpoints, to attempt to smooth out the conflicts, and above all to find ways to develop the popular support necessity to implement and nurture needed and progressive programs. There is ample evidence that the political system can work—if there is a genuine willingness to work at using it.

BASIC CONCEPTS AND TERMS

the commerce power
antimonopoly legislation
consent decree
Federal Trade Commission
stipulation
cease and desist order
control of multinational
   corporations
Securities and Exchange
   Commission

natural monopolies
regulatory commissions
public regulation versus public
   ownership
Civil Aeronautics Board
Federal Power Commission
Interstate Commerce
   Commission
Department of Transportation
Amtrak

Federal Communications
  Commission
Tennessee Valley Authority
United States Postal Service
collective bargaining rights
employment security programs
National Labor Relations Act
Taft-Hartley Act
Fair Labor Standards Act
parity price maintenance in
  agriculture
Food for Peace program
food stamp program
social security (insurance)
  program
unemployment compensation
public housing rationale
Department of Housing and
  Urban Development
rent-subsidy program

Medicare and Medicaid
war on poverty
income maintenance plans
negative income tax
welfare reform
fair employment practices laws
Equal Employment
  Opportunities Act
national health insurance
full employment planning
energy sufficiency programs
Department of Energy
consumer protection programs
Food and Drug Administration
Truth-in-Lending Act
Truth-in-Packaging Act
environmental protection
  legislation
Environmental Protection
  Agency

THE
NATIONAL
GOVERNMENT
AND
INTERNATIONAL
POLICY

12

"We travel together, passengers on a little spaceship, dependent on its vulnerable reserves of air and soil, all committed for our safety to its security and peace; preserved from annihilation only by the care, the work and I will say the love we give our fragile craft," said Adlai Stevenson in his last formal speech as United States ambassador to the United Nations. "We cannot maintain it half fortunate, half miserable, half confident, half despairing; half slave to the ancient enemies of man, half free in liberation of resources undreamed of until this day. No craft, no crew can travel safely with such vast contradictions. On their resolution depends the survival of us all."*

Our lives are dominated today by issues that are international in scope and that continually influence domestic affairs. Unless resolved in the not-distant future, these problems that preoccupy every major nation and its leaders may make all other issues inconsequential. The various ways in which people seek to live in peace with one another, and particularly the role of the United States in this quest, are the focus of this chapter.

*Adlai E. Stevenson, address before the United Nations Economic and Social Council, Geneva, July 9, 1965.

HOW MUCH AMERICAN INVOLVEMENT ABROAD?

Probably no single factor contributed more to the divisions, fears, and antagonisms besetting America late in the 1960s and early in the 1970s than the war in Vietnam. Although a majority of the people appeared to continue to support American involvement virtually to the end, opposition and criticism reached almost staggering proportions. What was seen at the beginning during the Eisenhower and Kennedy years as aid to a free people seeking to preserve their independence in the face of Communist aggression became far less clearly so. Most Americans became uncertain about the validity of the goals and dismayed by the tactics. The costs were all but incomprehensible. More than forty-six thousand Americans lost their lives along with two hundred fifty thousand South Vietnamese and an unknown number (probably several hundred thousand) North Vietnamese soldiers. Of civilian deaths there is no record. The tonnage of bombs dropped was five times the total for World War II. The direct financial costs to the American taxpayer are reported by the Defense Department to have been approximately $141 billion, but this takes no account of such things as veterans' costs far into the future or economic aid. The twelve-day renewal of heavy bombing at Christmas in 1972 by itself cost $500 million, about the same as the total appropriation for operation of the State Department and the conduct of foreign relations throughout the world during an entire year. There is no way to put a price tag on human disability and misery, property loss, and environmental damage. Over six million people were made refugees, at least temporarily, in Vietnam alone.

Inability to achieve a satisfactory settlement of the war forced the retirement of a president whose accomplishments in domestic legislation were virtually unparalleled. His successor, equally unsuccessful through most of his first term, espoused a program of gradual withdrawal and "Vietnamization" that led finally to American extrication, although neither side could claim a victory. A few months later it was disclosed that the United States was then and had been for four years carrying on aerial warfare in Cambodia, where North Vietnamese troops were allegedly involved, while falsifying reports and publicly claiming to be respecting the neutrality of Cambodia. An end to this was forced ultimately by Congress.

For a number of years before it became evident that involvement in Vietnam was a dead-end street, the United States had generally been quite sure of its proper role in world affairs. As one of the superpowers, it was aware of its obligations to maintain stability, to help feed the hungry, to share the advantages of modern technology, to aid and protect people threatened by totalitarian forces, and to promote cooperative international action toward these ends. In those terms it would be hard to dispute such laudable objectives, but events spread across the world from the jungles of Southeast Asia to the Arab deserts conspired to raise doubts about the desirable scope and nature of United States commitments. Could this country in fact operate as a kind of policeman for the entire world? How much foreign aid should be provided, how much if any of it should be related to the military, and should certain types of government be excluded from receiving it? Could covert intervention in the politics of other nations be justified? Did regional associations contribute to peace or increase tensions?

In 1969 President Nixon signaled a policy shift in Asia with a statement subsequently labeled the Nixon doctrine. In essence it indicated that the intention of the United States, while continuing to honor its obligations, was to withdraw from an automatic assumption of the burdens mentioned above, to stress economic aid and avoid war involvements, and to provide assistance primarily to nations demonstrating a willingness to defend and help themselves. The attitude undoubtedly struck a responsive chord in many Americans and was in certain senses clearly defensible. But many others worried about the implications (although this was certainly not the intention of the administration), if the effect were to add impetus to a gathering wave of new isolationism.

Both the nation and its leaders found the situation in Southeast Asia utterly frustrating. How was the line to be drawn between responsibly helping people in other parts of the world to protect their freedom and appearing to be a sort of international busybody? Could the United States insure democratic institutions and responsible governments in countries it sought to protect and aid? Would withdrawal from a commitment mean that the nation's word would not be trusted in the future? What of small nations like Thailand that felt themselves threatened and had entrusted their security to cooperative relations with the United States? Was it necessary to hide from the American people the truth about what was being done in their name?

In the aftermath of withdrawal from Vietnam, other troubling and awkward questions were asked. Why should the defense budget be larger than ever if the war was over, the world safer, and America approaching, as the administration announced, "a generation of peace"? Why should vast sums of money be proposed for the reconstruction of war-ravaged countries, however justifiable that might be in itself, while the president was severely cutting the funds for reconstruction of slums in American cities? Were our national priorities in order if we assumed that money spent to control water pollution or to rescue poor children from the lasting damage of malnutrition was dangerously inflationary but that money spent for more missiles was not? If the latter were essential, did it really have to be an either-or choice?

" . . . *And this little item is guaranteed to make your neighboring Third World country a fourth world country!*"

Thoughtful persons are also deeply concerned that the United States has continued to be the world's largest arms merchant, not uncommonly supplying both sides in a conflict situation in the name of maintaining equitable balance. Although varying from year to year, such sales have lately been in the neighborhood of $10 billion annually. The impact on jobs, corporate profits, tax revenues, and the balance of foreign trade scarcely needs elaboration, and any proposed restriction generates mammoth lobbying efforts.

The complexities of the situation are manifold, as President Carter discovered in seeking to cut back on the nation's arms-supplier role. It is by no means solely a matter of impact on the domestic economy. New and developing nations see their own defense as a prime responsibility and military strength as a symbol of independence. Some have adventurist rulers. When one country secures a new fighter plane, a chain reaction is begun, as its neighbors feel they must be at least equally equipped. A movement in the United States to restrict sales, viewed here as having a high moral purpose, is likely to be seen in those countries as abandoning them to their enemies. The immediate response is that if the United States will not provide them, the arms will be purchased from the Soviet Union, France, or others. A special problem exists in areas where two countries have a tradition of mutual hostility, one depending on the Soviet Union for supply and the other having a pattern of dependence upon the United States. Restraint by one country alone is thus relatively meaningless, and the clear need is for limitation agreements on the part of arms manufacturing nations or for international instruments of control.

Nevertheless, a beginning must be made somewhere. Not only is the peace of the entire world threatened by continuous arms build-ups, but the price in human suffering is almost beyond comprehension. In the developing countries nearly 500 million people are suffering from severe malnutrition, and approximately half the deaths of children under five years are attributable to food deficiencies. Most spend a pittance on health services or literacy training, but their arms expenditures are huge, proportionately much greater than those of developed nations. Carter did begin to limit both the amount of sales and the active sales promotion of arms abroad, stating also that the United States would not introduce new sophisticated weapons systems first into areas where they have not existed. Serious steps toward international agreements are being initiated and pursued. In addition, Congress has established its own power to exercise a broad veto over arms sales beyond a certain magnitude.

For comparative purposes the Institute for World Order has prepared a global social budget:

Proposed goal	*Cost in billions*
End illiteracy in five years	$1.5
Provide universal family planning	2.0
Double spending for medical research	4.0
Feed 200 million undernourished children	4.0
Treble food production in poor nations	3.5
Create peace-keeping forces of 100,000	1.5

This totals $16.5 billion—less than 7 percent of global military spending in one year.

CONTROL OF THE
MILITARY-INDUSTRIAL COMPLEX

One haunting question for many years has been whether any meaningful public control can be exercised over the political power of the military-industrial complex, as President Eisenhower labeled it— that intimate amalgam of defense contractors, the Pentagon, and its allies in the congressional armed services committees. Defense policy and access to vast sums of public money are dominated by this complex; moreover, defense contracts are a major element of the total economy and the source of many thousands of jobs.

It is not necessary to imagine conspiracy in order to realize the vast influence this complex exerts on public policy decision making. Understandably, the professional military tends to think in terms of military answers to international problems, and its policy recommendations receive strong support from the powerful industrial interests whose future is bound up with the ability of this viewpoint to prevail. Boards of directors and high administrative positions in many of these corporations are well stocked with retired generals and admirals. Presidents have needed, of course, to depend on the recommendations of their military advisers, but many individuals have questioned whether this influence has been disproportionate or adequately balanced by nonmilitary counsel. Congress has traditionally found itself unable to cope with either the magnitude of problems and costs in this area or the barrage of specialists and highly technical language with which it is inundated when decisions are to be made. Nor can it be forgotten that many a legislator's re-election often hinges to a significant extent on the defense contracts or installations acquired for a district. Those rare occasions when the military-industrial complex is defeated on a major policy issue become spectacularly newsworthy, as when President Carter decided to drop the $100-million-per-plane B-1 bomber program or when he subsequently postponed indefinitely the production of the neutron bomb. Both decisions stimulated vehement reactions in Congress.

The framers of the Constitution sought to guarantee control over the defense establishment partly by establishing the principle of civilian supremacy. The president was made commander in chief of the armed forces, and even when a general has been elected president, he has upon his inauguration technically become a civilian. By tradition the secretary of defense and the subordinate secretaries of the Army, Navy, and Air Force are civilians, aided by professional military staff. Never in history has the military's accession to political power shown this to be an attractive alternative.

The power to declare war is vested exclusively in Congress, although a president could exercise a veto. Normally Congress acts on the basis of recommendations or requests from the president, but declarations of war hark back to the days when opposing armies were drawn up on a battlefield and the bugles sounded. Actually, a declaration is likely to confirm the existence of a state of war. Its principal function is to authorize government actions that are not normally permissible in times of peace. In the past the courts have agreed that the president may use troops and weapons anywhere in the world when he believes he must, and wars have been fought, from the Barbary Pirates to Vietnam, without formal declarations. In such situations presidents have sometimes had support from Congress, as President Johnson did in the Gulf of Tonkin Resolution, which backed expanded effort in Vietnam. Of course, the provision of funds is a kind of tacit congressional approval.

In its very nature war tends to concentrate power in the hands of the national government, especially within the executive branch. Yet Congress retains great power and can constitute an impressive check when it chooses. Sessions from 1970 on, for example, saw monumental struggles over such issues as denying funds to fight the war beyond a fixed date, directing the president to withdraw troops by a specified time, and demanding consultation with the Senate before troops or financial resources could be committed abroad. Although proponents of these measures originally had only very limited success, the pressure significantly influenced the course of national policy. Presidents, of course, are not eager to feel their hands tied in a crisis, and they strive to retain the greatest possible latitude for decision making.

By 1973 both houses were willing to risk a showdown over legislative-executive relations, and in the face of a threat of presidential veto they passed legislation, the War Powers Act, providing that any presidential commitment of armed forces abroad automatically terminates in sixty days unless Congress declares war or otherwise specifically approves the action. The time period can be extended thirty days to permit the safe withdrawal of troops. Moreover, Congress can halt an unauthorized action at any time before the end of the sixty-day limit by a concurrent resolution, a procedure not subject to presidential veto. As expected, President Nixon did veto this act, terming it both unconstitutional and dangerous, but both the House and Senate shortly overrode his veto. Some observers are doubtful that this act constitutes a meaningful restraint and suggest that it may be unfortunate to concede formally a right of presidents to use the armed forces at their sole discretion, a power previously only assumed. At least, by this legislation, a principle of congressional responsibility has been established.

However important they might be, these mechanisms of control remain within the traditional channels of international relations. Still ignored is the potentially most effective means of resolving international conflicts and lessening the dangers of mutual annihilation— namely, a genuine willingness to use international instruments in place of unilateral actions to deal with international problems.

CONTEMPORARY APPROACHES TO DEFENSE AND NATIONAL SECURITY

Traditionally the principle of national sovereignty and the spirit of nationalism have impelled most nations to place primary emphasis on maintaining their security through military strength. Occasionally that strength is reinforced by treaties with friendly nations or participation in associations of nations. Ultimate reliance has remained on individual physical prowess, however, a principle discarded centuries ago as the means for controlling the relationships among people *within* a nation. Internally all nations have turned to some form of rule of law and judicial process. Earlier, we remarked on the huge percentage of resources that the United States spends annually on national defense. The picture is similar for all major nations, each protecting itself against immediate or potential threat from other nations.

The Constitution outlined extensive and fairly specific war powers for the national government. The states were authorized to maintain their own militias, but in practice these have now been all but completely nationalized into the National Guard. There is no single war power, like the interstate commerce power. In interpreting the authority of the president and Congress in foreign affairs, the courts have always referred collectively to war powers, embracing a number of separate constitutional authorizations. It appears that in time of war there are few limitations on the national government's actions in prosecuting the war. The government has been able, for example, to draft men for military service, fix prices and wages, ration food, clothing, and fuel, and prevent workers from leaving or changing jobs. The courts have held that war powers may be extended to periods of preparation for or recovery from war but more restrictively than during the war.

THE DEFENSE ESTABLISHMENT

The Department of Defense was created in 1947, bringing together the Departments of War and Navy, each of which had its own air force. Although unification has been accomplished on paper, and to a considerable extent in reality, it is far from total. Interservice rivalries and overlapping still constitute problems. The military commands—Army, Navy, Air Force, and the semi-independent Marine Corps—are headed by top career military men known as chiefs of staff (the Navy term is chief of naval operations), who are at the same time principal military advisers to the civilian secretaries. Under the chairmanship of the chief of staff to the secretary of defense, they constitute the highest-level professional policy body in the Defense Department, the Joint Chiefs of Staff. The department is one of the most huge and complex administrative organizations on earth, and many people have questioned whether one administrator can effectively keep the reins in hand.

Also created in 1947 was the National Security Council, designed to serve the president as a top-level advisory and consultative body on security matters. Its membership in addition to the president and vice president includes the secretaries of state and defense and the White House national security adviser; other top officials can be appointed with Senate confirmation. Different presidents have used the NSC variously, some relying on it as a major advisory body, others virtually ignoring it. The Central Intelligence Agency operates under the council's general jurisdiction. Final decisions are the president's, and in practice the president may consult with the council to the extent he wishes. Most of the NSC's activities, understandably, are cloaked in secrecy.

THE DRAFT

A perennial and highly emotional issue related to war powers and the defense organization has been that of conscription. First used during the Civil War, the draft operated in peacetime as well as in wartime almost continuously from 1940 to 1973. In the operation of a draft, the principal questions that arise are fairness and how least to disrupt people's lives. The lottery system begun in 1969 was designed to make all young men eligible during one year at age nineteen unless they sought educational deferment. Those not drafted during the year were then free to follow their normal plans without the cloud of possible service hanging over them. The basic question, however, was whether the draft was really essential, at least in peacetime. Could the armed forces be kept at sufficient strength with volunteers, if service were made more rewarding financially? Would the cost then be prohibitive or less than present repetitive training costs? Does the public really want a large professional military organization in its midst?

Exemption from military service because of conscientious objection to the taking of another human life has long been a recognized practice in the United States but is always difficult to administer. Some view it only as sophisticated draft-dodging, but the true conscientious objector has been willing to pay the price society exacts and to serve in other ways. Some entered the armed services as noncombatants, ordinarily as medical corpsmen, while others who refused any military affiliation were supposed to be assigned to civilian service projects without pay. The few who refused even to register normally wound up in prison. It was long the accepted rule that CO status could be claimed only by people possessing religious convictions against war, that this conviction should be one not suddenly acquired, and that it must be an opposition to all war. The religious limitation was upset in 1970 when the Supreme Court ruled that CO status could be claimed by someone who based opposition to war on ethical and philosophic grounds unrelated to religious belief (*Welsh* v. *U.S.*). Some trial-court decisions suggested that it might even be possible to have a conscientious objection to a particular war.

President Nixon, desirous of moving to an all-volunteer army if possible, ended the draft early in 1973 simply by ceasing draft calls and not asking for further extension of the draft authority that was soon to expire. The Selective Service machinery and the power to continue to register eligibles was maintained, and a limited authority to draft doctors and dentists if necessary was continued. Improved pay, benefits, and enlistment bonuses were offered, and the services undertook to reduce some types of duty and petty regulations that servicemen had found most irksome.

Despite these inducements the services had serious trouble keeping up to authorized strength except in periods of economic recession. Reserve organization strength also slipped in the absence of a draft threat, and the existence of ready reserves is presumably vital to the volunteer army concept. Costs proved extremely high. Many were also concerned that the armed forces were becoming too heavily composed of the poor, blacks, and those of limited education. Critics claim that the military does not use its personnel efficiently, retains unnecessary fringe benefits like retirement after twenty years, and rejects almost one-third of the applicants as physically unqualified (although the most common cause is being overweight, which is in most cases correctable). In the light of recruitment problems some voices urge a reinstituting of the draft, but it is clearly not a politically attractive prospect.

Opinion: Art Buchwald
A PLAN TO END ALL WARS

Great minds are at work in this country trying to figure out a way we can avoid getting ourselves into . . . [a war] again.

Many solutions have been offered. My favorite is the Haak Plan, suggested by Leo Haak, of East Lansing, Michigan.

Mr. Haak told me, "The reason the war lasted so long was that only the young people in this country were truly involved in Vietnam. While the rest of the country grew rich and fat, this small minority of the population, with no political clout, were shipped off to Indochina to hold back Communist aggression. This made it rather easy for the rest of the Americans to show no urgency to end the war."

"That's true," I said. "But what do you propose?"

"The Haak plan provides that if you draft young men to fight a future war, then you must also draft the money of the men too old to go, to pay for it."

"How would it work?"

"When a man became 40 years old, he would register for a wealth draft. His peak earning years are from 40 to 53, just as the peak physical years of a young man are 18 to 26. A lottery would be held and the man would be assigned a number according to his birthday. Those with low numbers would have to turn over all their money to the government to finance the war.

"Those with high numbers could go about their lives just as young men with high draft numbers go about their business without fear of being called up."

"Would you have draft boards?" I asked.

"Yes," Haak replied. "They would be composed of young men under the age of 26."

"Why young men?" I asked.

"Well, you have older men sending off young men to die in a war, so you should have young men deciding who must give their money to pay for it. The draft board could give exemptions in hardship cases and deal with conscientious objectors."

"By conscientious objectors you mean those who refuse to give money to a war because it's against their religion?"

"Yes, exactly. If a man can prove he is a serious conscientious objector, we would let him donate his wealth to a hospital or an educational institution."

"What about men over 40 who would flee to Canada to avoid having their money drafted?"

"The Haak plan does not provide for amnesty. We think it's the patriotic duty of every American to proudly serve his country, if not with his body, then with his fortune."

"How much of his fortune?"

"Everything," Haak said. "When we draft young men we ask them to give up everything, don't we?"

"It sounds like a crazy plan," I said.

"No crazier than what we've been doing for ten years. Had the Haak plan been in effect when we first got into Vietnam, the howls of the money draftees would have been heard from Maine to California. Picture, if you will, millions of well-dressed men in their forties descending on Washington demanding the President and Congress end the war. How long do you think any politician could survive if the country were drafting the entire wealth of its middle-aged citizens?"

"Not very long," I admitted.

Haak said, "Sending young people off to an undeclared war is a thing people don't like, but will put up with. But drafting the fortunes of the men who stay at home is something nobody in this country will tolerate for very long."

THE IMPACT OF NUCLEAR WEAPONS

The development of nuclear weapons and incredibly fast and sophisticated delivery systems has radically changed not only the character

ROOFTOP O'TOOLE   by Fearing and Farmer

of modern warfare but also the conditions for the entire conduct of international relations (see Table 12.1). In the past it was usually assumed, for example, that major nations could do as they pleased while the smaller ones had to accept the actions of their more powerful neighbors, short of the most extreme. In the nuclear age small countries often act with relative impunity, while the major powers, possessing destructive capacity so vast that its use cannot be considered except in an ultimate crisis, are forced to exercise great restraint. One result of this situation has been the development of the strategy known as limited war, where a war is fought, as in Korea and Vietnam, only with conventional weapons.* One can no longer seriously contemplate the possibility of a nation operating in isolation from other nations. The leaders of nations must constantly recognize the realities of nuclear power and the capacity to strike almost instantly.

When the first atomic bombs were exploded toward the end of World War II, this nation and the entire world reacted with tremendous shock. There was wide agreement that international means of controlling the atom had to be found, quickly. But as testing continued and pictures of the mushroom cloud became commonplace, we rapidly became immunized and pushed this unpleasantness from our concern. Yet to be able to evaluate international policy, we must resharpen that awareness periodically. World War II blockbuster bombs consisted of a few tons of TNT; an ordinary H-bomb is equivalent to 20 million tons of TNT. One of these twenty-megaton bombs releases more destructive energy than did all the bombs dropped on Germany and Japan during the entire course of World War II. With scientific dispassion Harrison Brown and James Real describe the results of the explosion of a ten-megaton bomb, about one-fifth the size of the largest so far detonated:

The bomb material and surrounding air are heated to extremely high temperatures, and the resultant fireball grows quickly to a diameter of

---

*The concept that certain lethal weapons are humane while others are inhumane is curious to ponder.

TABLE 12.1   Weapon System Evolution

Weapon	Number of parts	Strike range	Use	Source
Rock	1	100 feet	Civilian and military	Man
Bow and arrow	6	200 feet	Civilian and military	Man
Rifle	30	0.5 mile	Civilian and military	Arsenal
Tank	5,000	1 mile	Military	Arsenal and industry
Military aircraft	100,000	2,000 miles (4 hours)	Military	Industry
ICBM system	1,000,000	5,000 miles (20 minutes)	Military	Industry
ABM system	10,000,000	300 miles	Military	Industry

Source: Aerospace Corporation. Reprinted by permission.

about three and one-half miles. The heat flash persists for about twenty seconds and on a clear day can produce third-degree burns out to about twenty miles and second-degree burns out to a distance of twenty-five miles from the explosion. A ten-megaton burst in the atmosphere thirty miles above the earth could set fire to combustibles over 5,000 square miles on a clear day.

A surface burst of a ten-megaton bomb would produce a crater about 250 feet deep and a half mile wide. The zone of complete demolition would be about three miles in diameter. Severe blast damage would extend to about nine miles from the center of the explosion, and moderate to major damage would extend out to twelve miles, or over an area of 450 square miles.

It is likely that firestorms will result from a thermonuclear burst over a large city. A firestorm is a huge fire in which cooler air is drawn to the center of the burning area, elevating the temperature and perpetuating the conflagration. Winds reach hurricane velocities. The holocaust consumes the available oxygen with the result that persons not burned to death may die of suffocation or of carbon monoxide poisoning.

The explosion results in the instantaneous emission of nuclear radiation in quantities that can be lethal at distances up to two miles, but since persons in that area would be killed anyway by the blast and thermal effects, this is not an important factor. Far more dangerous is the radiation from radioactive products which are produced in the explosion and which are scattered over the countryside as "fall-out."

. . . The heavier particles of debris fall back to earth within the first hour or so. The lighter particles are carried downward and, depending upon the wind conditions, will be deposited over an area fifteen to thirty miles wide and 100 to 500 miles long. A thermonuclear bomb exploded at low altitude deposits about 80 per cent of its fallout locally in this manner. The balance is injected into the stratosphere and is distributed globally . . . in the event of a large-scale thermonuclear attack and in the absence of radiation protection, far more deaths would result from radiation effects than from heat or blast.*

It is also the age of overkill. The size of stockpiles is classified information, but as far back as 1956 a congressional advocate of still greater build-up claimed that the United States had enough twenty-megaton bombs to destroy the world ten times over. In contrast, the Soviet Union had only enough to destroy it six times! Most effort now goes into perfecting weapons and improving the speed, accuracy, and protection of delivery systems. Since the end of World War II delivery time for a bomb flown between Moscow and Washington has been cut from sixteen hours to less than twenty minutes.

CONTEMPORARY APPROACHES TO WORLD PEACE

THE STRATEGY OF DETERRENCE

The search for world peace involves several possible, though not necessarily mutually exclusive, approaches. Discarding, as has the United States, the theoretical possibility of imposing peace by conquest or annihilation of all potential opponents (an odd use of the term *peace*), what are the alternatives? This nation's policy, like those of the other major powers, has long been based on the strategy of deterrence. This assumes that peace will be best maintained by possessing such overwhelming military power and capacity to retaliate that no would-be aggressor would dare a first strike. The official language for military strategists is "mutual assured destruction," sometimes referred to by critics as the MAD doctrine.

Awareness of the potentialities of modern war unquestionably generates restraint in many nations, though perhaps not all, but only to the point at which national interest is felt to be vitally threatened. No nation will concede that it is committing aggression; rather, it says it is defending itself against aggression, actual or potential, while insisting on the purity of its own motives. What is aggression? Is it only the moving of troops or firing of explosives into the territory of another country? Or might it include infiltration, sabotage, subversion, or training of revolutionaries? Since proof is usually impossible, it is easy to claim aggressive intent on the other's part, and such suspicions give rise to real fears.

*Harrison Brown and James Real, *Community of Fear*, Center for the Study of Democratic Institutions, Santa Barbara, 1960, pp. 13–14.

History does not afford much confidence that deterrence will succeed in preventing wars. It may provide stand-offs of varying duration, particularly in regard to all-out wars, but no permanent solution. A policy of deterrence assures a continuous arms race. In one sense it actually constitutes incentive more than deterrent. When China announces the development of a terrible new weapon, does the United States throw up its hands in despair or does it redouble its efforts to find still more potent counterdevices? If the United States displays some new technological achievement, does that not spur the Soviet Union or China? Annual expenditures for armaments throughout the world approximate $300 billion, more than the total annual income of Central and South America, and this sum does not include the cost of depleted natural resources.

Deterrence also assumes that the greatest, if not the only, risk is from aggression. Yet under present conditions there is possibly a greater danger of accidental war. A state of readiness for instant retaliation intensifies this danger. The pyramiding of military strength magnifies suspicions and fears. All that is necessary for disaster is some event like the erroneous radar signals a few years ago from the early-warning station in Greenland, an accidental nuclear explosion, faulty intelligence, a mentally unstable bomber pilot or missile commander, or a technical control failure. Every precaution is taken to avoid such accidents, but perfection is impossible. The risk of miscalculation or technical malfunction is the basic reason for the hot line between Washington and Moscow. As more nations achieve nuclear competence, the dangers multiply.

"SUFFICIENCY" AND DÉTENTE

Given the uncertainties of a deterrence policy and the staggering cost of trying to preserve a position of military superiority, the Nixon administration began in the 1970s an effort at developing a spirit of détente, or improved understandings on peaceful coexistence and cooperation, with the major powers that had long been viewed as the principal antagonists of the United States—the Soviet Union and

China. The policy met with some initial successes, as the other two powers likewise considered it in their own best interests (in part because they feared each other), but conflicts of goals and decades of mutual suspicion are not erased overnight. As one aspect of the effort to build reciprocal confidence, international negotiations on arms limitations were undertaken and the United States indicated that it would cease the attempt to maintain superiority, being content with an undefined "sufficiency" or balance of military power. Potentially valuable as at least a step away from continuous confrontations and toward normalized relationships, the policy of sufficiency and détente remained little more than a modification of the policy of deterrence.

MAINTAINING COLLECTIVE SECURITY

A second approach to the search for peace lies in placing heavy emphasis on instruments of collective security. These range from alliances and regional defense associations to cooperation with world organizations like the United Nations. Useful as such steps often are, they may simply align larger blocs against each other unless their scope is worldwide. The effectiveness of the worldwide body is severely limited as long as the member states are able to decide when they will cooperate and when they will act independently in their own self-interest.

DISARMAMENT OR A WORLD RULE OF LAW

Still another effort has been to seek agreements on mutual disarmament, for which responsibility the United States created in 1961 the Arms Control and Disarmament Agency, an organization that has rarely been provided much authority or budget. Disarmament negotiations among nations have gone on for decades spasmodically and for a number of years on a continuing basis under United Nations auspices. The most notable result in modern times has been the achievement in 1963 of the Limited Nuclear Test-ban Treaty, based mainly on agreement between the United States and the Soviet Union and signed by more than one hundred countries. The treaty provided for indefinite suspension of all except underground nuclear testing, in order to eliminate pollution of the world's atmosphere by fallout. A nondissemination treaty, pledging the signatory nuclear powers not to make nuclear devices available to others and the nonnuclear powers not to seek them, was approved by many nations in 1968, but France and China, both nuclear powers, refused to sign. A modest further step occurred with the conclusion of the United States–Soviet Union Arms Control Agreement in 1972, limiting the number of long-range offensive missiles and antiballistic missile

From *The Herblock Gallery* (Simon & Schuster, 1968).

"As nearly as we can translate, it says: 'We are agreed in principle on preventing the spread of nuclear weapons; however . . .'"

systems to be deployed by the two countries. There was cautious hope but hardly optimism for long-term progress from the multination Strategic Arms Limitation talks (SALT) and Mutual Balanced Force Reduction (MBFR) negotiations.

Some reduction of armaments was accomplished in the period between the two world wars. Obviously, however, it did not prevent the onset of history's greatest war. Although dealing with different weapons, essentially the arguments that were advanced in the negotiations of the 1920s and 1930s are repeated today, and it is hard to avoid the feeling of having heard it all before. Accomplishments may occur from time to time, but mere armament reduction or even elimination of certain types of weapon will not bring peace. Either would simply reduce the technical sophistication of the next war's opening battles. As long as the traditions of unfettered national sovereignty exist, the political or military leaders of each country will feel compelled to keep a few potent weapons, even secretly, to guard against treachery by others. If they could trust one another, there would be no worry over armaments.

In an article published several years ago throughout Western Europe, Emery Reves argues that if we are seriously interested in peace, we will have to end our twin delusions—that we can secure peace by armament and that we can secure it by disarmament:

> Endless historical evidence proves the incontrovertible fact that peace is not a technical problem, not a military problem, but an essentially political and social problem.
>
> Within a certain political structure, no weapon, not even the hydrogen bomb or the long-range rocket, represents any danger. The people of the State of New York are not afraid of the nuclear weapons manufactured in the State of New Mexico or the rockets launched in Florida. But the people of the Ukraine are frightened of them. The people of the Ukraine are not afraid of the hydrogen bombs and rockets manufactured and launched in Central Sibera, but the people of New York and Chicago are.
>
> Peace between conflicting groups of men was never possible and wars succeeded one another until some sovereign power and source of law was set up over and above the clashing social units, integrating them into a higher sovereignty.
>
> If human society were organized according to present-day scientific, technical and industrial realities, so that relations between groups and units in contact were regulated by democratically-controlled law and legal institutions, then modern technology could go ahead in devising and producing the most devasting weapons, yet there would be no war. But if we allow sovereign rights to reside in the separate units and groups without regulating their relations by law, then we can prohibit every weapon, even penknives, and people will beat out each other's brains with clubs.
>
> Most practical politicians will smile and say that any integration of the sovereign nation-states in a higher legal order is Utopia. This is a debatable assertion. But there can be no question that the ideal of disarmament between the highly industrialized sovereign nation-states of the twentieth century, with or without controls, is the Utopia of Utopias.*

Many, indeed, will smile, and no one of right mind would discount the difficulties of achieving a world rule of law. Yet every responsible individual must ask whether Reves's analysis is correct. If not, either the status quo must be defended or some other alternative more likely to bring lasting peace must be offered. It is easy to raise problems. But does anyone assume that the present system of peace keeping is problem free? We are inclined to compare many

---

*Emery Reves, "To Arm or Disarm: The Great Double Fallacy," *London Sunday Times*, November 27, 1960. Reves is also the author of the well-known book *The Anatomy of Peace*, Harper & Row, New York, 1946, which discusses the question of a world rule of law more thoroughly. The quotation is reprinted by permission of Mr. Reves.

proposals for change to Utopia, but to do so is unreal. Since we do not live in Utopia, we must compare proposals to realistic alternatives by weighing and balancing problems and possible solutions. The quest for peace is one of humanity's oldest dreams and goals. In an age when the prospect of instantaneous annihilation threatens the world it has become an urgency that surpasses all other public issues.

THE CONDUCT OF DIPLOMACY

The preceding discussion covers certain aspects of relations among nations, but likewise important is the peacetime conduct of international affairs. The foreign policy of a nation consists of both the broad general principles it tries to maintain in its relations with other countries and the specific current attitudes toward nations, groups of nations, and problem situations. Many citizens speak as if they expect foreign policy to be a set of immutable rules engraved on tablets of bronze, but a moment's reflection will make it clear that a successful foreign policy must be dynamic and adaptable to constantly changing conditions. Much depends, after all, on the actions of other nations.

Americans are inclined to believe that solutions are available for every problem, if enough research and money can be applied. They find it hard to accept the fact that some problems may have no answers, at least immediately at hand, and that it may be necessary to learn to live with more or less permanent conditions of crisis. They also see many public policy decisions as clear choices between good and bad alternatives, though such simplicity rarely exists. The really tough decisions frequently involve a bad and a somewhat less bad option, and reasonable people commonly disagree on which is which. Yet the decisions must be made. Nor is the dilemma solved by avoidance, for in reality that cannot be done. Agreeing not to act or allowing a situation to continue is actually a decision and carries its own consequences.

AMERICAN FOREIGN POLICY GOALS

It is not difficult to state broad principles to which a nation may be dedicated; the difficulty lies in whether they provide clear guidelines for day-to-day decisions and actions. We might readily agree, for example, that United States foreign policy includes a desire for peace, opposition to colonialism, support for independence, and belief in the principle of self-determination. Does our national commitment to peace tell us whether we should support the Arab or the Israeli cause in the Middle East, or perhaps keep hands off, even if others intervene? Does it indicate whether we should avoid commitments to Thailand or whether we should help it protect itself against Communist takeover or possible Chinese expansionism? If independence is a good thing, to whom does it extend—to Tibet, Hong Kong, Puerto Rico? Should support for self-determination require us to have backed the Ian Smith regime in Rhodesia or that of Fidel Castro in Cuba? Given these underlying principles, decisions in specific situations must be made on the basis of careful judgment about the best interests of the United States and the other countries involved. We thus contribute to the broader goals if our judgment is correct.

The complications of generalized policy statements were well illustrated by the experience of President Carter when, at the very beginning of his administration, he stressed that in its relations with other countries the United States would put the greatest of emphasis on the protection and furtherance of human rights in every country. Surely this was a commendable goal in keeping with the best traditions of America, and most fellow citizens applauded the spirit of the pronouncement. There followed strongly worded criticisms of practices in the Soviet Union and its satellites, plus verbal encouragement of dissidents within those countries. Strong pressures were applied to a number of nations, including several developing Third World countries (with whose aspirations the United States was presumably in sympathy), and there was a withdrawal of aid programs from some regimes in Africa, Asia, and Latin America. In a few cases pressure appeared to result in some relaxation of repressive tactics, but in most it produced strong hostility. The United States was accused of interfering in the domestic affairs of other nations, arms limitation talks were bogged down, the dissidents in some countries were harassed even more ruthlessly, and the still embryonic spirit of détente was at least temporarily threatened. Opponents in Congress seized on the human rights theme as a handle to embarrass the administration, hanging "human rights amendments" on all manner of legislation where such restrictions could be expected to produce flarebacks from other countries or international organizations. Without abandoning its goals, the administration learned to use more careful language, to weigh probable outcomes of actions, and to choose tactics most likely to accomplish realistic steps toward the goals.

There is a sense in which democracies face greater difficulties than do totalitarian states in the conduct of foreign relations. Democracies must be more open in their activities and must seek to carry the public in support of policy. They find it harder to make shifts when conditions suddenly change. Totalitarian governments may not be more efficient; they may simply be better able to cover up their inefficiencies, but at any rate their public difficulties are fewer. If devoted to the maintenance of peace and harmony, the democracies are likely to find themselves continually on the defensive, just because it is easier to set fire to haystacks than to put the fires out. There is, moreover, a serious risk that in striving for peace a nation may find itself merely trying to keep things as they are and thus be labeled a defender of the status quo. The status quo is hardly attractive to large segments—indeed, the majority—of the world's population.

WHO MAKES FOREIGN POLICY?

As the only official spokesman for the United States in foreign affairs, the president holds basic responsibility for making foreign policy. Others, such as a member of the Senate Foreign Relations Committee, may speak on foreign affairs and perhaps receive a great deal of attention, but their statements are not the policy of the government. The secretary of state does enunciate policy but is the agent of the president on these matters and speaks with his knowledge and approval. Otherwise, the president will need to find a new secretary of state without delay. Many people and groups, indeed, contribute to the making of foreign policy, particularly the professionals in the State Department, White House staff advisers, the members of Congress, and even some with special expertness outside of government. The Senate Foreign Relations Committee and the House International Relations Committee are especially influential, though the Senate has special responsibilities and prerogatives in foreign affairs and is more important in this area.

On occasion Senate ratification of a treaty (requiring a two-thirds favorable vote) becomes the focal point of both an international crisis and a highly emotional domestic controversy, as was the case with the Panama Canal treaties that were narrowly approved in 1978. Senators were subjected to tremendous political pressures, particularly from well-financed opposition groups, and the White House found it necessary to go all out—marshaling compelling arguments to sway senators and shift public opinion, and engaging in a vast amount of high stakes bargaining with key members.

Influences on the making of foreign policy are exerted by many interest groups, just as is true of domestic policy, but the variety of groups involved is naturally smaller. Yet the range is considerable. There are groups solely devoted to the study of foreign policy questions such as the Council on Foreign Relations, those lobbying for a particular style of foreign policy like New Directions, or those whose interests focus on some specific area of the world. There are groups with worldwide humanitarian concerns, typified by many church organizations. And it is understandable that virtually every economic interest—business, agriculture, or labor—has a stake in policies that affect international commerce. The modern-day growth to positions of immense economic power by the huge multinational corporations, whose operations extend to every corner of the globe, has raised for some a fear that they may constitute a threat to peace, especially when they have been involved in efforts to manipulate friendly governments or subvert unfriendly ones. Others contend that economic self-interest may make the multinationals a potent force for peace, since as entities transcending national boundaries they have a vital concern with the maintenance of harmonious relations.

Although there is elaborate formal machinery for the planning of foreign policy, all decisions ultimately are made by people, and the final responsibility belongs to the president, who nevertheless is by no means a totally free agent. Many actions require congressional approval or the appropriation of funds. The appointment of top diplomatic representatives must have Senate confirmation. One reason for the general constancy of policy from one administration to the next is that commitments and courses of action set by predecessors can be changed only gradually. Freedom of action is limited by several factors. First, there is the existence of treaties with other countries. Then there are associations with international organizations, historical friendships, severe time pressures, inflexibility of the foreign affairs bureaucracy, financial restrictions, and possible conflict between humanitarian motives and national self-interest. Finally, intelligence may be inadequate or full of misinformation. The fact remains though, that the leadership is the president's, and so is the burden of responsibility. Day or night the president can never escape the awareness that on his decisions rest the safety and well-being of 220 million fellow citizens, if not all the peoples of the world.

Virtually the only power in this area of diplomacy that rests exclusively with the president is the recognition of new foreign governments, though even on this matter appropriate congressional leaders may be consulted informally. When the president decides to accept the credentials of an ambassador, recognition has been accorded. This may occur very quickly after a change of government; sometimes it has been delayed for many years. Recognition indicates not necessarily approval of another government but only that we plan to carry on normal relations with it. Again, there are few specific guiding rules (would the United States be in a defensible position to announce, for instance, that it will not recognize any government that comes into power by revolution?), but a separate judgment of best interest must be made in each individual case.

In conducting foreign relations, the president leans heavily on several forces that interlock closely in day-to-day operations. These include the Department of Defense, the National Security Council, the Central Intelligence Agency, White House foreign affairs advisers, and of course, the Department of State. In practical terms, despite the president's ultimate responsibility, it is inevitable that much foreign policy is developed within these bureaucracies. The president and top advisers are likely to perform essentially a judging function, choosing among possible policy options and providing broadly gauged direction. But when the staff experts are fairly well agreed, or when the spokesman for one agency has achieved a stature of dominant influence, as Henry Kissinger did in the Nixon and Ford administrations, their views are overwhelmingly likely to be accepted. Alternatives can also be painted in such a way as to make them appear to be dubious choices, and there have even been situations in which a president (and perhaps everyone else) did not know until after decision and action the complete and accurate circumstances on which the action was based. Under other than unforeseen emergency conditions, however, it is expected that policy options and their implications will be thoroughly researched by teams of experts and blueprints for possible actions in virtually every conceivable situation kept in readiness.

Case Study
WHAT RESPONSE TO INTERNATIONAL BOYCOTT?

As a part of their effort to put an effective squeeze on Israel, which they believe to have been created illegally from Arab territories and to be oppressing the Arabs who were dispossessed, the Arab nations sought to bring pressure upon Israel's principal supporter, the United States. Separate from the temporary oil embargo was an elaborate economic sanction: (1) as a condition of doing business with Arab countries, United States companies were required to stop any trade with Israel or Israeli companies and (2) as a further condition, they were required to cease dealings with other United States companies that either traded with Israel or had Jewish owners or employees. A company might be required to furnish information on the names, race, and religion of its officers and employees.

Indignation at these tactics ran high in Congress, but a solution was not simple. United States exports to the Arab world were running at an impressive $7 billion a year, and a cutoff might contribute to economic recession and would certainly cause a loss of many jobs. Extensive exports were particularly vital because the United States was heavily dependent upon importing oil from the Middle East. Other countries were willing and eager to sell to the Arab states, which would thus not really be hurt by a cessation of American exports, and markets once lost to competitors might never be regained. The executive branch preferred the route of diplomatic contacts to ease the Arab terms, rather than legislation. Moreover, the administration was involved in delicate negotiations in an effort to find a broad-scale resolution of the whole Middle East conflict situation. It wanted negotiating room—to avoid any action that would encourage the Arab nations to take unyielding positions and to be able to "lean" on Israel at least a bit if necessary to help bring the two sides together.

Congress, nevertheless, feeling an important principle to be at stake, was firm in preserving the nation's long-time commitment to Israel and was sensitive to the strong pressure from American Jewish organizations. It began work on legislation. The resultant internal negotiations were also delicate and lasted no less than the life of two Congresses; involved in addition to numerous members of Congress were representatives of the White House and State Department, spokesmen for the Jewish organizations, and leaders of the Business Roundtable, who are top executives of major United States corporations.

The outcome was an antiboycott act that dealt with all the major issues, making it illegal for an American company to (1) refrain from doing business with Israel when asked to do so by an Arab state; (2) furnish information as to whether a business or person has traded with Israel or done business with a blacklisted firm; (3) refrain from doing business with any country, company, or individual for reasons of the boycott; (4) refuse to employ (or otherwise discriminate against) persons on a basis of national origin, race, or religion; and (5) furnish information concerning an individual's national origin, race, or religion, when requested by an Arab state. In addition, all requests for trade information and the responses were to be made public. Necessarily, however, most of these stipulations were hedged with many exceptions and qualifications (for example, that the mere absence of a business relationship with Israel or some particular company did not by itself constitute a violation), and it was these that required much bargaining.

Delay had its usefulness. During the years that passed while the act was taking shape, attitudes began to shift in some leading Arab countries toward greater accommodation, and diplomatic negotiations also had some degree of success. How much effect the impending legislation may have had is impossible to measure. At any rate, in a number of Arab nations the boycott rules, while not abolished, gradually came to be ignored, and trade with the United States continued.

THE STATE DEPARTMENT

The State Department has traditionally been the president's arm for the actual conduct of foreign relations (although during the Nixon administration, as a culmination to a gradual trend, important functions were transferred to a special national security adviser on the White House staff, and the practice was continued with the appointment of Zbigniew Brzezinski by President Carter). It handles the varied aspects of international political and economic communications and negotiations and is concerned with the development of treaties and executive agreements. It fosters and controls international trade and travel, promotes better understanding of the United States abroad (a primary responsibility of the United States Information Agency), and operates programs of cultural exchange. The Department's Foreign Service represents the United States in other countries. It is divided into the diplomatic service and the consular service, though these wings are parts of one body and their personnel may be assigned interchangeably. The diplomatic service represents this government to other governments, and its personnel are located in foreign capitals. The consular service, scattered among foreign port cities and other commercial centers, is concerned primarily with the relations between United States citizens and another nation or its citizens. Consular offices aid Americans traveling abroad, handle visas and immigration requests for foreign nationals, carry on economic research, promote trade, and the like.

PERSONAL DIPLOMACY IN THE ELECTRONIC AGE

Modern transportation and communication have made possible rather frequent personal meetings between heads of state. These meetings at the summit may lessen somewhat complete reliance on the diplomatic service as a channel of communication. "Summitry" has certain obvious advantages but carries its own risks. As a rule there needs to be careful advance preparation by the professionals; the president must be exceptionally well informed, and there must be efforts to see that the public does not expect too much in immediate results. Personal diplomacy achieved perhaps its most striking accomplishment when President Carter brought Egypt's President Sadat and Israel's Prime Minister Begin together at Camp David, Maryland, in September 1978 in an attempt to find a basis for a Mideast peace treaty. Facing tough negotiators with seemingly irreconcilable positions, Carter for thirteen consecutive days played the go-between, cajoling, pushing, suggesting one alternative linguistic formula after another. In the end, with failure appearing inevitable, the two leaders made concessions they had sworn never to do, and a weary but jubilant president could announce that a framework for peace negotiations had been achieved. Continuing opposition flamed in several countries, but the logjam between these long-time enemy neighbors was broken, and both Begin and Sadat acknowledged that this would never have occurred except for the political effectiveness of President Carter.

The realities of international negotiation are rarely well understood by outsiders. In the best of all possible worlds most of us would probably feel that negotiations should always be open and in public view. But meaningful negotiations are unlikely to occur under those circumstances. Domestic political pressures or attitudes of other nations may make public concessions impossible. The mediating role of some country not party to the negotiations might need to be protected. In open sessions some official representatives feel compelled to make statements for popular consumption at home or for propaganda purposes elsewhere, as the long months of Vietnam peace talks in Paris amply illustrated. Significant discussions are more likely to take place during the coffee breaks. The negotiations that finally brought a formal end to the Vietnam War were not the official talks at all but a series of secret meetings between two special emissaries of the United States and North Vietnam.

Negotiation is by definition a process of give-and-take and of mutual exploration of positions. Suppose that in the presence of the press the American negotiator says to a Russian counterpart, "What if the United States were to end all its assistance to Abracadabra? How would your country respond?" Within minutes the wire services would be transmitting headlines proclaiming "U.S. Proposes to Stop Aid to Abracadabra." But the United States did not propose any such thing. This was an exploratory question to test reaction, a trial balloon to provide a basis for further exploration. Because the negotiator knows the headlines will result, the question cannot be asked at all. If negotiations between opponents are to have any meaningful substance, they will almost always take place in private talks, although it is not usually necessary that the results remain secret.

THE UNITED STATES AND INTERNATIONAL COOPERATION

Since the final years of the 1930s the United States has discarded its old but no longer realistic dream of isolating itself from the problems of others. Instead it has turned to active participation and leadership in programs of collective security. There are always voices demanding a return to some form of isolationism, but they are far from dominant either in the councils of government or among the public—although some observers fear a new isolationism arising from disillusion with the Southeast Asia involvement. Without abandoning traditional national defense efforts, major emphasis has been placed on international organizations for protection and the attainment of world peace. As one of the world's most powerful nations, the role of the United States in these organizations is usually crucial.

REGIONAL SECURITY PACTS

There exist several regional security associations, of which the oldest is the Organization of American States (OAS), an outgrowth of the Pan American Union. The periodic meetings of the member states, including all the independent nations of the Western Hemisphere except Canada and Cuba (the latter having been expelled, although steps toward readmission have begun), provide opportunity for developing economic and social programs of common interest and for thrashing out problems that arise among members. OAS has helped on occasion to mediate disputes, even when they have deteriorated into armed conflict. In terms of common defense against possible external threat, the language of the Rio Pact, which formed the OAS, states that an armed attack against any American state will be considered an attack against all and that each one "undertakes to assist in meeting the attack." This is a general commitment, but something less than a specific military alliance, since each member retains discretion as to how it will meet the attack.

The North Atlantic Treaty Organization (NATO) is based on similar language. NATO has served as a key element of United States defense policy and of the joint defense of Western Europe. Recently it has become a notable instrument for political consultation and for cooperative educational and scientific projects as well. With changes in the nature of warfare, with decreasing fear of the Soviet Union, and particularly with a rather uncooperative French attitude, NATO has declined somewhat in military significance but still plays an important role.

THE UNITED NATIONS

The one body that comes close to the proportions of a truly world-wide organization is the United Nations. In contrast to its retreat from participation in the League of Nations, the United States was not only one of the founders of the United Nations but also has continued its role of active leadership. Throughout the early existence of the UN the United States could count on a sufficient number of supporters almost to guarantee victory on any issue before the body, but with the more recent extensive growth of membership that situation has changed. When its own interests are clearly at stake, the United States like most other nations has usually been unwilling to allow the UN freedom to work at resolving the problems or, as in Vietnam, even to accept it as a mediator.

Oddly enough, the United Nations has always been subject to criticism from two diametrically opposite sources: those who attack it by claiming it is a world government destructive of national sovereignty and those who complain that it is *not* a world government. The United Nations is an instrument of world cooperation, but member nations have been unwilling to modify their national sovereignty sufficiently to provide the UN with the attributes necessary to a government: the ability to make and enforce law, the power to tax, and the power to affect its own citizens directly rather than to deal only with governments.

The principal organs of the United Nations include the General Assembly, the Security Council, the Economic and Social Council, the Secretariat, the Trusteeship Council, and the International Court of Justice. In addition, there are a number of specialized agencies and commissions, like the Universal Postal Union, the Food and Agriculture Organization, the International Civil Aviation Organization, and the Educational, Scientific, and Cultural Organization (UNESCO).

The General Assembly, in which each member nation is represented, is fundamentally an international forum in which any topic embraced by the charter may be discussed and recommendations formulated. It has general powers of supervision over the activities of the other organs, elects many of their members, and approves budgets and assessments. The Security Council is charged with no less than preserving international peace. The fifteen-member council (originally eleven) includes as permanent members the five major powers at the end of World War II—the United States, the Soviet Union, Great Britain, France, and China. The nonpermanent members are elected for two-year terms by the General Assembly: normally they represent some variety of geographic and ideological blocs. Any substantive question (anything other than procedure) requires nine affirmative votes, which must include those of the five permanent members. This ability of any one of the major powers to kill a proposal by casting a negative vote constitutes the much-criticized veto power, but the permanent members have shown no desire to limit their power by abolishing this prerogative. As a result the Security Council is sometimes by-passed by actions of the General Assembly or its executive committee.

The Economic and Social Council seeks to help alleviate some of the critical economic and social problems that are often the underlying causes of wars. Agencies under its general direction aid in the improvement of education, in population control, in nutrition and health services, and in industrial and agricultural development, in a variety of areas where such problems are severe. The International Court of Justice has compulsory jurisdiction only where nations have agreed thereto, confined largely to the interpretation of treaties and other international obligations. Its role has therefore understandably been minor. It has no authority to consider "domestic questions," and a number of nations, including the United States, reserve to themselves the determination of what is domestic.

With all its shortcomings, there is no question that the United Nations has been a most valuable organization. The very existence of an international forum where conflicting viewpoints can be aired and world opinion mobilized is in itself worthwhile. There have been notable successes in dealing with disputes that in another era might have resulted in war and in settling conflicts involving minor powers. Much work in social and economic fields and the services of

From The Herblock Gallery (Simon & Schuster, 1968).

"Those emerging nations may end up submerging us all"

the specialized agencies like the World Health Organization or the International Meteorological Organization have been outstanding. Significant contributions to international law have been developed.

Yet peace has not been achieved. Nations still depend more on their own strength than on international cooperation, and the immensity of human need dwarfs the efforts to alleviate misery. Although notable progress has been made, bigger steps remain to be taken. Numerous proposals have been made for strengthening the United Nations, many of them involving amendment of the charter, which is a cumbersome procedure.

Most center on a modification of the veto power in the Security Council and a more equitable basis of representation and vote in the General Assembly. The situation in the assembly, where tiny nations with populations of a few thousand, less than one small city, have the same voting strength as the Soviet Union or the United States, cannot prevail indefinitely. Although a one person—one vote formula appears unrealistic, some system of weighted voting is certainly feasible. In the long run, many observers would argue, the essential need is to grant the power to make and enforce world law relating to matters on which peace depends. Rather than being destructive of national sovereignty, this power would lift much of the weight of fear and the burden of defense expenditures that now keep nations from being truly sovereign and able to use their powers to serve the needs of their citizens.

AMERICAN AID AROUND THE WORLD

Since the end of World War II the United States has provided large amounts of economic assistance, as well as military material, to a host of countries around the world. The Marshall Plan was a vital element in rebuilding the shattered economies of Western Europe in the immediate postwar years, economic development has been aided in Africa and Latin America, and wheat shipments have helped avert the worst horrors of famine in India. Foreign aid, as it is commonly termed, has been a major instrument of United States foreign policy, frequently showing both humanitarianism and the intent to build friendship and support in the world. Though sometimes criticized as having conflicting motives, there is nothing inherently wrong with the accomplishment of two objectives in the same action.

Undoubtedly support for American policy is least likely to be won when aid is granted with strings attached. Certainly no nation should be expected automatically to support positions of the United States. Aid is best provided simply to meet human need; if there are valuable by-products, no objection is likely to be voiced. Too often, perhaps, economic aid has played second fiddle to military aid, and though it has not always been wisely administered, economic aid retains a great potential for good. A central problem is always that of insuring that aid actually reaches and provides direct benefits to the poorest elements of the population. In recent years the emphasis has shifted from large-scale projects such as industrial development and transportation to improving nutrition, education, and population control. Aid programs on the part of other major powers have notably expanded: in 1965 the United States provided about 60 per cent of all aid contributed by the world's nations, but the figure is now approximately 25 per cent. In the long run there are advantages to placing less emphasis on unilateral aid programs and greater reliance on distribution through international organizations.

Unquestionably, one of the principal reasons for the early wide acceptance and success of the Peace Corps is that it was seen not as a tool of cold-war policy but as a genuine program of people-to-people assistance in dealing with basic social problems at the grassroots. Where initial success has lessened, the cause has often been that a host country (or occasionally some Peace Corps volunteers) has believed these attitudes to have ceased to exist. The Technical Assistance (Point IV) Program, a means for sharing technological know-how with underdeveloped nations to enable them more effectively to help themselves, has likewise been highly attractive. Even if it chose to try, the United States could not long fill all the empty rice bowls in the world. But these "government missionaries," experts in agricultural production, water supply and irrigation, industrial planning, and health and sanitation, have helped many countries solve their own problems, a far more satisfying process.

In evaluating United States aid programs, Americans might well ponder the questions put poignantly by a diplomat from a developing nation, long a close friend of the United States: "We are deeply appreciative of all that you have done, and we know you do not have to do it. But it is also impossible to escape the nagging questions: Are we being helped, or bribed? Are we being aided because we are loved—or because we are needed?"

Here a Peace Corps volunteer teaches proper nutrition in an Ivory Coast village. The Peace Corps was established by President Kennedy in 1961; it was intended to be "a pool of trained American men and women sent overseas by the United States Government to help foreign countries meet their urgent needs for skilled manpower," but it has served many purposes, both idealistic and materially constructive.

Peace Corps

MEETING THE LONG-RANGE CRISES

If we are ever to achieve lasting peace, or even if we are merely to avert disaster, much depends on our coping meaningfully with the crises that dominate people's lives. The threat of totalitarianism is perennial, whether from the right or the left, and the thoughtful person can only be perturbed at how much the two extremes have in common. The desire to reject the sometimes slow processes of democracy in order that a group convinced of its rightness might ram its policies through rapidly is not a characteristic confined to Nazi Germany or the Soviet Union.

No one with common sense can deny that communism and fascism pose a great challenge to democracy, but it is not a challenge that can be met by hysteria and a search under the bed for bogeymen. The threat or reality of the use of force may at times have to be combated, but in the longer run ideas will be defeated only by better ideas. Communism is at least as much an effect as a cause. The common tendency has been to blame all the troubles in the world on the machinations of communism, and the Communists have indeed often masterfully capitalized upon unrest and misery wherever it has existed. Yet many of the world's most severe problems are the result of that human misery and would have occurred even if communism did not exist.

The United States has a revolutionary tradition, and the ideals that its people take for granted are still revolutionary—and tremendously attractive—in much of the world. That tradition has been too easily forgotten. The need is to identify once again with the revolutionary hopes of fellow human beings, not in the sense of blood running in the streets but of radical change in the conditions of life. For a person who is starving, social philosophy ranks far down on the list of concerns. If a choice is merely between the promise of bread or no bread, no one will hesitate. But the democracies can offer hopes that the Communist nations do not: the prospect of bread and human freedom, too—if they do not delay too long.

People are also in the process of dangerously polluting and poisoning the environment and of overpopulating the earth to the point of catastrophe. Everyone is aware of the social problems caused by increasing numbers and crowding, but few fully comprehend the staggering *rate* of increase, which is the crucial factor. It took from the dawn of human history until the year 1830 for the population of the world to reach 1 billion. It took only another one hundred years to increase to 2 billion, thirty-one years to add the third billion, and it is requiring but fifteen years to add the fourth. No miracles of science or of American generosity can change the limited amount of earth available or make it support an unlimited number of people.

From *Straight Herblock* (Simon & Schuster, 1964).

World-wide non-missile gap

The growth is by far the greatest in the areas of the world least able to support more population, and these are the masses who will follow any leader who promises hope. They can turn to violent revolution or explode out of national boundaries—not because they are evil or vicious but because they are hungry. Techniques for population limitation are available; what is lacking is understanding and social will.

What has occurred to intensify the urgency of problems has been aptly labeled the revolution of rising expectations. A major segment of the world's people, living under conditions incomprehensible to the average American, has always been aware of its absolute poverty but has only recently become aware of its relative poverty. Lately it has discovered that not everyone in the world lives under these conditions, that it is not *necessary* to exist in perpetual sickness, illiteracy, and hunger. Once that discovery has been made, these people will do anything in their power to bring about change, just as the more fortunate would do under similar circumstances. Americans and citizens of other wealthy nations cannot judge the actions and motivations of the world's impoverished masses in their own terms; the bases are radically different. It is terribly difficult to walk in someone else's shoes, but the attempt must be made. For those who are convinced that they could not possibly be any worse off, it is perfectly logical to assume that *anything* is worth trying.

How will the new expectations of the suddenly awakened masses be met? Just as no person is an island, no nation now stands alone. The present world is interrelated and interdependent. Its citizens who are hungry outnumber the well fed; those who suffer outnumber the comfortable; those who demand change outnumber those who are content with things as they are. The West cannot long remain an affluent island in a world of poverty. It must use its wealth, its ideals, and its politics of democracy for the betterment of all. It must thus sway the direction of the future or be overwhelmed by it. "The only kind of war we seek," said President Harry S Truman, "is the good old fight against man's ancient enemies . . . poverty, disease, hunger and illiteracy."

In the aftermath of the Vietnam War, poet and playwright Archibald MacLeish wrote of America's need to recover its sense of its own identity:

They had known who they were for almost two hundred years: a nation of free men who believed in men and in freedom—and not only here at home on their own continent but everywhere else throughout the earth.

Their compassion was famous—so famous indeed that European novelists, and even some of their own, made fun of their notorious proclivity for saving the world, converting the heathen, feeding the victims of Indian famines, rebuilding the earthquake-shattered cities of Italy, fighting wars to make the world safe for democracy.

That was the way they were: friends of man, a nation held together, as Lincoln himself had testified, by that promise made to the whole world in 1776 that "the weights should some day be lifted from the shoulders of all men."

But what had been so certain for almost 200 years . . . was certain no longer and we knew it. . . .

If the American people are a Great Power, then . . . freedom means nothing: it is enough to be a citizen of Number One. And in the world of Great Powers humanity is an irrelevance: wars are justified not by their decency but by their success. But if . . . we are still the Great Republic—great republic first and power in the world afterward—then nothing matters as *much* as our passion for liberty, our belief in man, our love of humanity. For without them we will have no power. And will lose ourselves.*

BASIC CONCEPTS AND TERMS

spaceship earth

arms merchant policy

the military-industrial complex

civilian supremacy

declaration of war

national war powers

War Powers Act

Department of Defense

National Security Council

Central Intelligence Agency

conscription

conscientious objection

limited war

strategy of deterrence

détente policy

collective security

Limited Nuclear Test-ban Treaty

world rule of law

foreign-policy making

State Department

treaties and executive
  agreements

recognition power

diplomatic service

consular service

summitry

isolationism

Organization of American States

North Atlantic Treaty
  Organization

strengths and shortcomings of
  United Nations

economic aid programs

Peace Corps

Technical Assistance (Point IV)
  Program

population explosion

revolution of rising expectations

STATE
AND
LOCAL
GOVERNMENT

13

"Local self-government is considered in many countries to be a useful tool; in the United States one bows before it as a divinely inspired political principle," a European observer once remarked. As a federation, spread across a vast region of the earth and embracing strongly independent areas of differing backgrounds, America has traditionally placed a high premium on vigorous state and local government. At times this high regard has been abused, used as a cloak for practices that would not be tolerated by most of the nation or as a shield for special-interest dominance, but at its best the tradition of local self-government is a noble one. Even if they are not always so, state and local units *can* be close and responsive to the people they serve while providing a laboratory for new ideas and techniques in government, a training ground in the political process, a counterbalance to excessive conformity and centralization, and a foundation for developing the true sense of community that is the cement holding together a heterogeneous society.

In this day and age when the dominant public problems are

usually national or international, there is an understandable tendency to depreciate the significance of regional and local governments, yet these affect intimately almost every aspect of our daily lives. They record our births and deaths, educate us, provide us with a supply of safe drinking water, maintain our streets and highways and other modes of transportation, furnish police and fire protection, offer recreational and cultural opportunities, protect our health—and the list goes on. Such services are so much a part of the web of daily life that it is easy to take them for granted. We become conscious of them only when they fail to work properly. But as we become more and more an urban nation, the complex problems of our living together in huge metropolitan clusters are forcing questions of local government policy to the forefront of our consciousness.

STATE-LOCAL RELATIONS

It would be unrealistic to look upon national, state, and local governments as totally separate political entities. They secure revenue from much the same sources, cooperate in the administration of numerous services, from welfare to transportation, and serve the same people, in different capacities. They are inextricably intertwined and interdependent, yet they retain their own special spheres of responsibility.

The states are component parts of a larger union and thus lack the quality of sovereignty. Nevertheless they have an assured and protected position in our federal system. They possess a high degree of discretion in the performance of a great variety of functions, their boundaries may not be changed without their consent, and they can in fact take any action that is not prohibited to them by the national Constitution or their own state constitutions.

Local governments, in contrast, are creatures of the state. Legally, the states give them their existence, can abolish them, can alter their powers or boundaries, and can direct them to serve in many ways as agents of the state. In practice, of course, the exercise of such extraordinary power is limited by political considerations, and occasionally by state constitutional provisions, and the states normally grant to local governments a wide range of freedom to determine their activities and the means of carrying them out.

City or county charters are a sort of local constitution, but they are granted or authorized by the state, and the governments of local units must operate in general conformity to state law. Most but not all states grant to cities home rule (the power to draft a charter and operate under it with considerable local discretion), while a much lesser number make home rule available to counties as well. Some states achieve the same goal by providing very flexible state laws under which nonchartered cities operate.

HOW STATE GOVERNMENT DIFFERS
FROM NATIONAL GOVERNMENT

There is a great similarity between the general structure and function of state governments and the national government. Questions of civil liberties are universal, as our earlier discussion in Chapter 3 noted. The role of political parties and pressure groups is similar as well, and many of them are organized along national-state-local lines. Many policy issues are substantially the same or closely interrelated.

Yet there are also notable differences between national and state governments. Thus it is logical for us to focus attention on these differences while assuming in all other aspects general similarity to the national government.

STATE CONSTITUTIONS

State constitutions differ from the national constitution primarily in that they are a limitation on power, whereas that of the nation is a delegation of power. States as the possessors of residual power in the American federal system can do anything not prohibited to them.

State constitutions tend to be much more lengthy and detailed than the national Constitution, and as a result most have been subject to numerous amendments. Some states have already adopted new and modernized constitutions, ordinarily after prolonged battles, and movements toward such a goal are currently under way in a number of other states.

STATE LEGISLATURES

One of the bitterest controversies surrounding the state legislatures for many years, that of reapportionment, has been essentially resolved, though not completely ended, as a result of the Supreme Court's one man–one vote decisions. Before the beginning of this series of court decisions in the 1960s, some states had not reapportioned their legislatures for sixty or seventy years. Many others had requirements guaranteeing representation to every county or town, no matter how tiny, and it was common for representation to be based in one house of a state legislature on population and in the other on geographic area. Such arrangements frequently resulted in gross inequities in voting strength, for they continued rural political dominance in most states at a time when the population of the nation had long since shifted to the cities. Thus Stratton, Vermont, with 38 residents, had the same representation in the state's lower house as Burlington, with 35,300. Los Angeles County, California, with more than 6 million people comprising about 38 percent of the population of the state, had the same representation in the state senate as did the three mountain and desert counties of Alpine, Inyo, and Mono, with a combined total population of 14,200. The state senator from Los

Angeles County had fifteen national congressional districts within his state legislative district. All state legislatures have now been reapportioned, although disputes continue in some states about acceptable redistricting formulas. As noted earlier, mathematical equality alone is not a guarantee of fairness.

Other questions remain, however. Can adequately responsible legislatures be maintained on a part-time basis, with low pay and little if any staff assistance? Are two-chamber legislatures really needed at the state level? Do short terms of office and brief sessions make sense in the present day?

Two-year terms in the lower house of state legislatures and four-year terms in the upper are the most common pattern, although there are some variations. All state legislatures are bicameral bodies except that of Nebraska, which since the 1930s has operated a unicameral legislature very successfully. Until recently most legislatures met for only one session in two years, and the sessions were normally of a mere two or three months' duration. Even in the smallest states this was rarely adequate, and special sessions became common. The trend lately has been toward annual sessions, now the rule in thirty-seven states (although in six of those the off-year session is almost exclusively devoted to budget), often with no constitutionally established time limit.

As the legislative task becomes of vastly greater magnitude, the tradition of the citizen-legislator who left his plow for a couple of months every other year to handle the legislative business of the state is very slowly being superseded by that of the full-time legislator. Even when a legislature is not in session there are extensive demands on legislators' time. They must frequently work on special committees, keep in close contact with constituents, and perform other responsibilities associated with their job.

Legislative pay has shown extreme variation, although in many states it has remained at a level dictated by the citizen-legislator concept (see Table 13.1). In recent years the average has improved fairly rapidly, but there are still only fourteen states that pay their legislators more than $10,000 per year. Salaries are augmented appreciably in many states, however, by per diem allocations for expenses. Legislative salaries are often written into state constitutions, and amendments to change these have not been easy to get passed.

One result of low salaries has been to make the legislator depend on the generosity of lobbyists, clearly an unhealthy situation. Another has been legislative moonlighting. Since it is usually necessary for a state legislator to have a source of income in addition to legislative pay, legislators tend to come predominantly from occupations that permit periodic absences. The great majority are lawyers, businessmen (particularly in real estate or insurance), and farmers. It is hardly a comfortable thought that in one state capital legislators have worked part-time as ushers at a nearby race track in order to make ends meet. If truly responsible and effective legislatures are really desired, the need for adequate compensation hardly needs further elaboration.

The legislative process in the states is not as a rule radically different from that in Congress, but most state legislatures operate not only under greater pressures of time but with much less in the way of facilities and technical assistance. Almost half the states do not even provide office space for legislators, and for most a private secretary, let alone research staff services, is unheard of. Only a handful of states provide their legislators with administrative assistants, and very few furnish permanent staffs for committees. Without such help the legislator, struggling to deal with complex problems, is at the mercy of lobbyists and administrative agencies. There is a gradual trend toward establishing at least a limited professional staff serving the entire legislature, and a number of states have instituted legislative councils, groups consisting of a few members of each house and a professional staff whose function is to study between sessions forthcoming issues and to recommend adequately drafted and researched bills on key subjects when the legislature convenes.

The legislative process is further complicated in twenty-one states where the initiative is authorized. There the law permits legislation (and in seventeen of the states constitutional amendments also) to be placed on the ballot by petition and enacted by popular vote. Twenty-four states authorize the referendum, whereby petitions can force a popular vote on whether to sustain an act already passed by the legislature. A lesser number (thirteen) permit the recall of public officers by a similar process of petition and vote. A number of worthwhile accomplishments can be claimed for the initiative, but today initiative campaigns are likely to be essentially contests between competing professional public-relations firms.

STATE EXECUTIVES

In one respect at least, most governors are in weaker positions as chief executives than is the president. In many states the heads of several major departments are not appointed by the governor but are instead elected. Commonly in this category are positions such as attorney general, treasurer, controller, secretary of state, and superintendent of public instruction. The heads of the other state departments are normally appointees of the governor, and in some states his patronage power for lesser positions is very extensive. In many states the existence of a number of independent or semi-independent boards and commissions, such as highway commissions, further dilutes executive power.

TABLE 13.1   Annual Compensation Received by State Legislators, 1977

State	Salary (in dollars)	Per diem payments while in session (in dollars)
Alabama	3,600	50 (maximum 30 days)
Alaska	14,720	48
Arizona	6,000	
Arkansas	7,500	45
California	23,232	30
Colorado	7,600	35 (for nonsession meetings)
Connecticut	6,500 (incls. 1,000 expenses)	
Delaware	9,000	
Florida	12,000	
Georgia	4,200	25
Hawaii	12,000	
Idaho	3,000	25
Illinois	20,000	
Indiana	6,000	25 (+ 100 per mo. when not in session)
Iowa	8,000	20
Kansas		69 (+ 200 per mo. when not in session)
Kentucky		100 (+ 550 per mo. expenses)
Louisiana		50 (+ 1,000 per mo. expenses)
Maine	4,500 (+ 2,500 for special session)	
Maryland	12,500	
Massachusetts	14,400	
Michigan	24,000 (+ 4,600 expenses)	
Minnesota	8,400 (+ expenses)	
Mississippi	8,100	(+ 210 per mo. when not in session)

Sources: *World Almanac 1978*, Newspaper Enterprise Assn., New York, 1978, pp. 249–252 and *Book of the States, 1976–1977*, Council of State Governments, Lexington, Ky., 1976, pp. 49–53.

Note: In most states additional expenses may be claimed for travel, special sessions, hearings, and the like.

In broad terms, however, the two chief executives are comparable. The typical governor, like the president, recommends a policy program to the legislature, has the power to veto legislation, prepares and recommends a budget, provides general direction to the state's administrative agencies, calls special sessions of the legislature, exercises the clemency power in connection with state offenses, and is the political leader of the party's state organization. Finally, the news-making potential of the office can be used to build popular support for programs, although the office does not command the level of attention that automatically attaches to the presidency.

Despite the slightly weaker comparable position, some governors have certain powers that the president lacks. Most significant is the

State	Salary (in dollars)	Per diem payments while in session (in dollars)
Missouri	8,400	
Montana		31.62 + 40 expenses
Nebraska	4,800	
Nevada		60 + 40 expenses (for 60 days, + 20 days special session)
New Hampshire	200	
New Jersey	10,000	
New Mexico		24 (maximum 60 days)
New York	23,500	
North Carolina	6,000 (incls. 1,200 expenses)	(+ subsistence)
North Dakota		65 (+ 75 per mo. expenses)
Ohio	17,500	
Oklahoma	12,948	
Oregon	5,808	39 (+ 175 per mo. when not in session)
Pennsylvania	18,720 (+ 10,000 expenses)	
Rhode Island		5 (maximum 60 days)
South Carolina	7,000	25
South Dakota	2,500	25
Tennessee	7,800	58.99
Texas	7,200 (+ expenses)	
Utah		35
Vermont	4,500	30 (for special sessions only)
Virginia	5,475	
Washington	7,200	40
West Virginia	9,600	
Wisconsin	15,678	25
Wyoming		30 + 36 expenses

governor's ability in forty-three states to veto particular sections of a bill while accepting the rest. The president, of course, must take all or nothing and does not have this item veto power. In most instances the item veto applies only to budgets and appropriations, but these of course are of key importance for preserving executive influence or policy control. By virtue of this power a governor may be placed in a strong bargaining position in dealings with the legislature. In several states the governor also has the power to determine the agenda for special, though not regular, sessions of the legislature, whereas the president may only make recommendations to a Congress called into special session. Such a prerogative likewise strengthens a governor's bargaining hand.

Nevertheless, governors often find themselves in exposed and politically difficult situations, and the turnover tends to be high. The rate of defeat for incumbent governors is considerably higher than that for United States senators, although both have the same state-wide constituencies. A governor, as the single visible symbol of state government, is held responsible by the voters for running the state well yet often lacks the constitutional or legal authority to deal with many state problems. Moreoever, while people tend to demand a great variety and high level of state services, they resent being taxed to pay for them. An easy way of expressing their resentment at high taxes is to throw out the governor, whether or not at fault. He or she becomes a sort of voodoo doll into which the voters may stick pins.

In an earlier period of American history, a governorship was the best steppingstone to the presidency. In modern times, given this vulnerability to political attack and the increased importance of international affairs, this is no longer necessarily so. The experience of having governed a state may no longer be looked upon as the best criterion for national leadership. United States senators, whose work keeps them more closely in touch with national issues and whose office can secure them much greater nationwide publicity (by their championing particular causes and traveling around the country), are now generally assumed to have replaced governors as prime presidential candidates, although governors are obviously not out of the picture. Ex-Governor Jimmy Carter, in fact, capitalized on an "anti-Washington" theme in his presidential campaign with notable success, and ex-Governor Ronald Reagan came close to being his 1976 opponent. Carter was aided by the fact that a multiplicity of candidates from the Senate and one from the House tended to divide the same potential vote.

STATE JUDICIARY

Many commonly heard public complaints are directed at the administration of justice. Problems such as long delays in cases coming to trial and the slowness of the trials themselves, unequal access to justice by the poor, rich, and middle class, the seeming impropriety of judges campaigning for election, and the apparent shortcomings of the jury system are at the root of contemporary judicial reform movements. On the state level in particular, the judicial system has been the subject of much public concern.

Most states use the familiar three-tiered pattern of trial courts, appellate courts, and a state supreme court, although the actual names vary from state to state. In addition, there are ordinarily several types of court attached to counties and cities, which technically are part of the state court system. Some of the local courts have general jurisdiction over minor state offenses and local ordinances;

others, such as juvenile courts, courts of domestic relations, and probate courts, are specialized. In the rural areas and small towns of some parts of the country, the office of justice of the peace still exists. An elected judge dealing with minor cases, a justice of the peace has not necessarily been trained in the law and often receives as compensation a share of the fines levied, plus fees received for the performing of marriage ceremonies.

All judges of the national courts are appointed, but this is not always the case for state judges. In some states judges are elected on the same partisan ballot with other candidates, and in others they are elected on a separate nonpartisan ballot, while in still others they are appointed by the governor. There are many combinations or modifications of these arrangements. The selection of trial and appellate court judges is sometimes handled differently, the former being elected and the latter appointed. Even when judges are initially appointed, provision is sometimes made for approval by the voters every few years. A judge under this practice is said to "run against the record," since no other names are on the ballot; the voter is merely asked, "Shall Judge ——— be retained on the court of appeals for another term?" Such "elections" are virtually meaningless, inasmuch as the voters rarely possess much if any information about the record of judges, especially at the appellate level.

In states where judges are elected, the electoral process may not involve much contest. There often exists an "understanding" that judges planning to retire should do so a few months before the expiration of their term to enable the governor to fill the vacancies. The new appointees will then be able to run as incumbents. Since most voters feel that they lack any basis for decisions about judicial contests, they tend either to re-elect incumbents or to follow the recommendations of local bar associations, which normally also support incumbents.

Where there are contests there are also campaigns, and the necessities of campaigning and fund raising can have their effects on the independence of judges. Thus there has been a slow but steady trend toward systems of merit appointment, known originally as the Missouri Plan. The usual pattern requires a governor to appoint judges from a brief list submitted for each vacancy by a bipartisan nominating commission composed of lawyers and members of the public, with the lawyers ordinarily predominating. A recent related development is the creation in a few states of commissions on judicial qualifications. Established to deal with problems of judicial incapacity, incompetence, or unethical practices, they have the power to discipline or to recommend the removal of offending judges, although the number of cases is happily not large. Under the latter circumstances, however, most judges choose to resign.

Spurred by a growing awareness of the need to correct the most serious deficiencies in our system of justice, progress is also being made in a variety of other ways. The use of public defenders to help insure equal justice to the poor in criminal cases is increasing, though slowly. Central administrative agencies are being created to enable courts to operate more efficiently. Backlogs of cases going back two to three years are being sharply reduced through the use of conciliation courts and pretrial conferences. More extensive and sophisticated social work assistance has become available. Other aspects of the operation of the courts are less easily remedied. For instance, numerous controversies continue over the composition and functioning of juries, whether they are fair cross sections of the populace and whether they decide cases on emotional grounds. Plea bargaining generates a good deal of public controversy. Some states have taken giant strides in judicial reform. But despite signs of progress, the system changes slowly; unfortunately in many states significant reform seems a long way off.

LOCAL GOVERNMENT

More than any other country in the world, the United States has an almost bewildering variety of local governments, including counties, cities, towns, townships, school districts, and a host of other types of special district. At the time of the last census of governments in 1972, there were no less than 78,218 separate units of local government in the United States, distributed by type as indicated in Table 13.2. Nine states, each containing more than 3,000 governments, accounted for almost half of the government units in the nation, with Illinois, Pennsylvania, California, and Kansas, in that order, leading the other states (see Figure 13.1). The average number per state was 1,565, but Illinois had 6,386 while Hawaii had only 20. Some local units served less than a dozen persons, while others served as many as 8 million.

TABLE 13.2   Units of Local Government

Type of government	1972	1967	1962
Counties	3,044	3,049	3,043
Municipalities	18,517	18,048	18,000
Townships	16,991	17,105	17,142
School districts	15,781	21,782	34,678
Special districts	23,885	21,264	18,323
Total	78,218	81,248	91,186

Source: Bureau of the Census, Census of Governments, 1972, *Governmental Organization,* Government Printing Office, Washington, D.C., 1973, p. 1.

FIGURE 13.1   Units of Local Government in the States, 1972

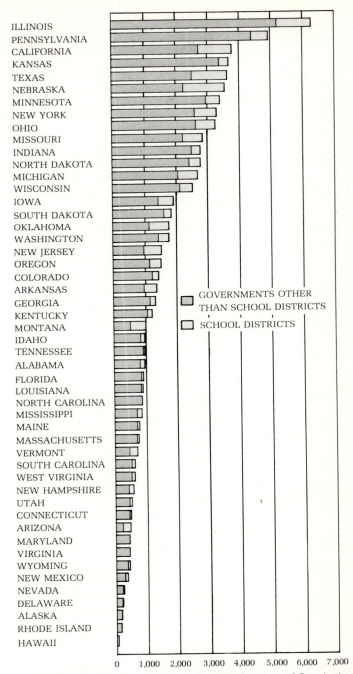

Source: Bureau of the Census, Census of Governments, 1972, *Governmental Organization*, Government Printing Office, Washington, D.C., 1973, p. 17.

COUNTIES

County governments are the only local units that cover almost the entire nation. There are some exceptions. Counties were abolished in Rhode Island and Connecticut; several counties in different parts of the nation have been consolidated with major cities; cities in Virginia are separate and independent from counties; and there are a few other minor exceptions. Otherwise almost everyone in the United States lives under the jurisdiction of a county government.* Originally created by the states to serve primarily as administrative subdivisions for state purposes, counties today still possess considerably less discretion than do cities. Nevertheless, they have long since become units of local *self*-government in addition to their responsibilities for carrying out functions dictated by the states. Aside from New England, where their role has always been minor, the range of county functions today is broad.

Although all counties generally perform similar functions, including health and welfare services, road maintenance, law enforcement, probation services, maintenance of correctional institutions, provision of parks and other recreational facilities, preservation of vital statistics and property records, and planning and zoning, the scope and quality of the services vary widely. Certain types of service are performed for all county residents, whereas other services are performed almost exclusively for people living outside the cities (the counties being viewed as principally concerned with the unincorporated areas.)

In other respects, such as size, population, and wealth, counties exhibit vast differences (see Figure 13.2). They range in size from the 20,119 square miles of San Bernardino County, California (almost twice the size of the Netherlands and larger than the combined areas of Maryland, Delaware, and New Jersey), to the 24 square miles of Arlington County, Virginia. At one population extreme is Los Angeles County, California, whose more than 7 million inhabitants surpass the individual populations of forty-three of the fifty states, while at the other extreme stands Loving County, Texas, with its 112 persons.

The organizational structure of the average county government can be described only as incoherent and as more representative of the rural past than of contemporary America. Governing authority is usually scattered among a county board, several independently elected administrative officers such as the county auditor, sheriff, assessor, and coroner, and a miscellaneous group of independent boards and commissions with responsibilities for parks, hospitals,

---

*The term *parish* is used in Louisiana and *borough* in Alaska.

FIGURE 13.2   County Governments and Their Population by Population Size, 1972

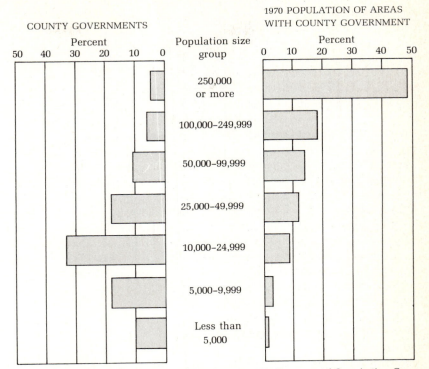

Source: Bureau of the Census, Census of Governments, 1972, *Governmental Organization,* Government Printing Office, Washington, D.C., 1973, p. 17.

libraries, and the like (see Figure 13.3). There is as a rule no single body with overall legislative and coordinating authority. The county board, as the central governing body, is assumed by most people to have such broad authority, but it must legislate within the very real limits imposed by both the state and the spheres of independence of the administrative officers and boards. In itself the county board ordinarily possesses a mixture of legislative and administrative powers, since most counties have no chief executive.

The uncoordinated and frequently irresponsible nature of county government has been a chronic problem in American history, but as long as a county's functions were minor, the public was largely unconcerned. With increasing responsibilities and a greater degree of discretion have come the beginnings of reform movements. Most efforts to improve county government have centered on the establishment of some type of county executive, and a few states have

FIGURE 13.3 Typical County Organization

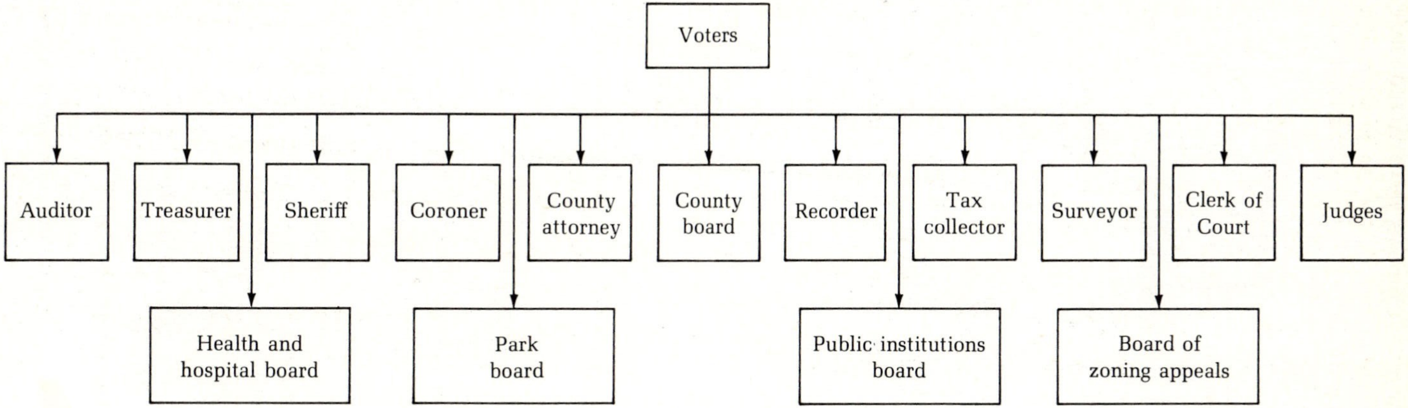

permitted counties to develop charters and thus adapt organization to local needs. Experience with elected county executives has been extremely limited in the past, but a scattering of such positions has appeared in recent years.

More common, though still involving a small percentage of all counties, has been the use of county managers or chief administrative officers (CAOs), management specialists employed by county boards to supervise and coordinate the entire spectrum of day-to-day administration. This practice requires either county home rule or permissive state legislation, and to be truly effective a reduction in the number of independently elected administrative officers and boards is necessary. The manager plan is the same as the council-manager plan of city government, and the CAO arrangement differs mainly in that such an official usually possesses a somewhat more limited range of powers than does a manager, especially in relation to the appointment of department heads.

Some counties have become purveyors of extensive urban services to vast populations, and in a few instances smaller and newer cities simply have hired the county to provide certain services (in occasional cases almost all) within their boundaries. Under this scheme small cities can thus secure the advantages of large-scale operation and professionalization while still being able to determine the precise nature and level of services they desire.

Decades ago the counties were termed "the dark continent of American politics" because of their relative backwardness and the low level of public awareness and understanding of their role. The label has stuck, but county government today has begun to move out of the darkness and to establish itself as an increasingly important segment of local government. As the need for a more broadly based approach to the solution of local problems continues to grow, their potential may be even greater.

TOWNS, TOWNSHIPS, AND SPECIAL DISTRICTS

The New England town is the general-purpose unit of local government in that region. Counties in New England, if they exist at all, have few functions, and the schools are normally operated by the towns rather than by separate school districts. Town governments commonly embrace both urban and rural territory. Virtually all local services are thus town responsibilities, though the largest cities are now often separate incorporations.

The most distinctive feature of New England town government is the use of the town meeting, one of the few remaining examples of direct democracy in the entire world. This annual assemblage of all the town's eligible voters debates and enacts local ordinances and the town's budget, sets the tax levy, approves reports of officials, and elects a list of administrative officers. A board of selectmen is chosen to provide overall supervision, but unlike a city council the board is not a legislative body. Its function is to see that the will of the town meeting is carried out, although within that framework it necessarily must exercise a fair amount of discretion. The town meeting form of government can work very well in small and relatively homogeneous communities, but when communities become larger and more complex, it is generally unsatisfactory. The biggest cities adopt one of the standard patterns of representative city government (discussed later in this chapter), and the smaller ones sometimes make use of a representative town meeting, composed of a sizable group of people whom the voters have elected to function as a town meeting.

During the time of the Continental Congress a comprehensive survey of what was then the Northwest Territory was authorized. When settlers began to migrate from New England into the trans-Appalachian West, they naturally carried with them the government forms to which they were accustomed, and the town was thus transplanted to the Midwest. But on the land maps the settlers found six-mile-on-a-side squares known as survey "townships," and it seemed logical to utilize these areas as the basic unit of local government. The land areas were called "congressional townships," and within them "civil townships" were gradually created.

Although the town meeting form of government was used, the Midwest township was never quite the same as the New England town. Structurally they were comparable, but counties in the Midwest assumed many of the local functions, and the states tended to limit the township role narrowly. With such artificial boundaries whatever sense of community arose was only by chance. Moreover, in this region it became customary for community centers as they developed to incorporate separately as villages, operating as small cities with representative government. Likewise the schools were operated by separate governmental entities.

Little by little, in modern times, most township functions have been transferred to the counties, and many of the townships have atrophied. The total number slowly diminishes, although most townships continue to exist, performing whatever minimal services they can.

In contrast to the gradually disappearing townships, special districts (or ad hoc districts) seem to increase in number each year, with the exception of school districts. A special district is a government unit distinct from general purpose governments (and thus "special"), created to provide an area with one or more needed services that are not being provided by any other existing government unit (see Figure 13.4). Special districts may commonly overlap the boundaries of counties and cities and are most often established when the

problems to be met do not conform to existing government boundaries. Either the problem may affect a wide region, so that no one
existing unit is adequate, or it may affect only a small part of a larger
unit, necessitating a service that the larger unit does not normally
supply to all its residents. Examples of the former might be flood
control and mosquito abatement; of the latter, perhaps street lighting
and fire protection.

Special districts are usually very simple in organizational structure, consisting perhaps of a small board of directors that hires such
other personnel as may be necessary. Some special districts have no
regular employees, while others, like port districts or metropolitan
transit districts, have thousands. Their budgets likewise range from
tiny sums to many millions of dollars annually. Most perform a
single service, but multifunctional districts are becoming more common, especially in metropolitan areas. Because they are separate
governments, each has in almost all cases its own tax and debt limits.
Thus special districts may at times be used as a means of expanding
these revenue sources for cities or counties that have reached their
state-imposed limits.

The most familiar of the special districts are the independent
school districts, the predominant mechanism used for the administration of public education in most of the states (see Figure 13.5). In
five states and the District of Columbia all public schools are administered by agencies of city or county governments (Alaska, Maryland,
North Carolina, and Virginia) or of the state (Hawaii), and in fifteen

A New England town meeting.

FIGURE 13.4   Special Districts by Function, 1972

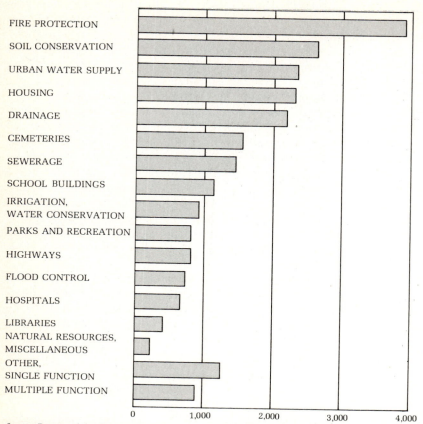

Source: Bureau of the Census, Census of Governments, 1972, *Governmental Organization*, Government Printing Office, Washington, D.C., 1973, p. 18.

other states there is a mixture of independent districts and "dependent" school systems. As a result of concerted efforts in almost every state since the end of World War II, there has been a drastic reduction in the total number of school districts, many of which served only a few pupils in one-room schools. Between 1942 and 1972 the number of districts dropped from 108,579 to 15,781, and some further reductions are likely.

Although school districts are frequently in the center of public controversy, most special districts are rarely in the limelight, and there is little awareness of them by the general public. Election of their governing boards is often by a mere handful of voters, and frequently the seats go uncontested. Thus special districts can hardly be said to be democratically responsible. They are created under

FIGURE 13.5 Public School Systems by State, 1972

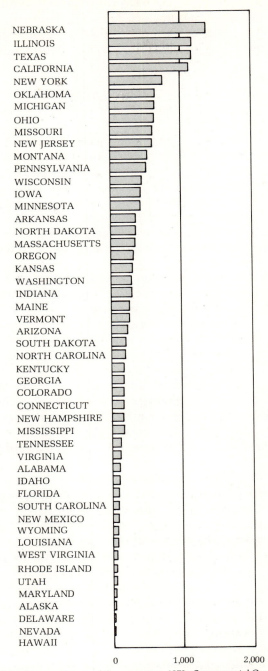

Source: Bureau of the Census, Census of Governments, 1972, *Governmental Organization,* Government Printing Office, Washington, D.C., 1973, p. 19.

permissive state legislation that has been enacted to meet specific local demands, and there has been little or no coordination at the state level, even as to the types of districts authorized. Many could probably be absorbed by general purpose governments, but under present circumstances a sizable number will continue.

MEETING THE CHALLENGES
OF URBAN AMERICA

The United States late in the 1960s was suddenly and belatedly plunged into an awareness of the crisis of great cities. The country had become dominantly urban some decades earlier, so it was a crisis that had been building for many years but that had been largely ignored amid the other preoccupations of a generally affluent society. The problems comprising America's urban crisis are not new, but their existence seems strangely incongruous in a nation possessing the greatest wealth and the most advanced technology the world has ever known.

Why should millions of American citizens live in grinding poverty? Why should some people receive a grossly less adequate education or diet than others simply because of the state or locality in which they happen to reside? Why should vast numbers of people be living in substandard and overcrowded housing? Why should racial ghettos continue to exist? Why should movement about our cities be progressively slower and more uncomfortable? Why should crime statistics rise while efforts at law enforcement are viewed with resentment by sizable segments of the populace? Why should the core of our cities continue to decay? Why should our air and water be horribly polluted? Why should we seem incapable of adequately financing even existing services, let alone meeting the new problems?

Although these crucial problems are by no means exclusively urban (rural poverty, for example, is at least as grinding and debilitating as that in the cities), many are distinctively an aspect of today's urban culture. Certainly they have surfaced and reached a critical stage more rapidly in the areas of great population concentration. Nor are these matters that can be dealt with by local governments alone; they affect an entire society, and the resources of state and national governments must be joined in the attack.

Technological advances throughout the twentieth century stimulated the growth of cities both by reducing employment opportunities on the farms and in small towns and by expanding industrial and related employment, as well as by radically altering the nation's transportation and communication systems. The staggering increase

Vicious circle

in urban population that resulted from these changes meant over-crowded housing and educational facilities and, in time, a dangerous pollution of our environment. It also brought a greater impersonality and anonymity and thus a diminishing of the sense of community and mutual responsibility that bolsters social stability.

In the years during and following World War II a large portion of the suddenly more mobile minority groups migrated to the major cities. There poverty and restrictive practices in the sale and rental of housing jammed them into slowly expanding ghettos. The more affluent whites, including many whose ethnic groups had immi-grated to America only decades before, felt themselves threatened and dug in their heels. There was a separation rather than a mixture

From *The Herblock Gallery* (Simon & Schuster, 1968).

"You want business in this town or don't you?"

of groups and classes, and misunderstanding, ill will, and fears pyramided. Many a metropolitan area came to be a predominantly black central city ringed by white sections and suburbs.

Today the central city still serves the growing economic, cultural, and recreational demands of the entire metropolitan area, but now at the very time of its greatest need for funds, its principal source of money—the middle-class taxpayer—has been migrating to communities outside the central city. Caught in this vicious circle, urban governments must seek to attract middle-class residents by making cities truly livable again. To accomplish this task, the most effective and responsive forms of government organization are required, but even more necessary are the freeing of cities from state-imposed restraints, the large-scale providing of financial assistance by the national and state governments, and the drawing of people into

FIGURE 13.6   Standard Metropolitan Statistical Areas, 1972

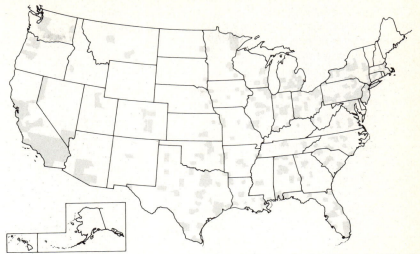

Source: Bureau of the Census, Census of Governments, 1972, *Governmental Organization*, Government Printing Office, Washington, D.C., 1973, p. 21.

urban government who can provide vigorous and high-quality political leadership.

GOVERNING METROPOLITAN AREAS

The steady influx of population into the nation's metropolitan areas has created problems considerably more vast than mere crowding alone, yet we are still trying to deal with problems that are regional in scope through government machinery that is almost hopelessly scattered. In an economic and social sense the metropolitan area is to a large degree a single unit, but in government organization quite the opposite is true. Figure 13.6 shows the location of standard metropolitan statistical areas in the United States.*

As many as three or four hundred separate units of government within a single metropolitan area (a good percentage being special districts) is not an uncommon situation. This splintering of government services results in a chronic lack of coordinated planning as

---

*A standard metropolitan statistical area (SMSA), defined by the Bureau of the Census, is an integrated social and economic area having a large population nucleus—at least one city with at least fifty thousand inhabitants. The SMSA includes the county of such a city and adjacent counties "found to be metropolitan in character and economically and socially integrated with the county of the central city."

well as in duplication, overlap, and uneven quality. Friction between a central city and its suburbs is a familiar sight. In one extreme case, a suburb of Chicago refused a civil defense agreement to pool its fire-fighting equipment in the event of an air attack on the Chicago area. Vast numbers of suburbanites earn their incomes in the central city, use its commercial facilities, enjoy its recreational and cultural opportunities, but pay taxes in their "bedroom communities."

To deal with the developing complex of problems facing urban America, there have been experiments aimed at achieving a more effective metropolitan integration. At first glance it may appear that the most logical step is to establish one local government to serve an entire metropolitan area, but selling such an idea to the public is probably a political impossibility, and so large a unit might be unwieldy and remote from its citizens. Duplication between county and city units has been eliminated in some places by county-city consolidation, but such consolidation has usually had little or no effect on other local governments. Various interesting versions of consolidation, adding to a number of earlier experiments, have developed in fairly recent times in Indianapolis and Marion County, Indiana, in Nashville and Davidson County, Tennessee, and in the Twin Cities region of Minneapolis and St. Paul, Minnesota. In Virginia, in contrast, cities have been made independent of counties and are permitted to add, by means of court suits, adjoining territory as it becomes urbanized, thereby reducing the number of suburban governments.

Other steps are also possible—granting to central cities the ability to exercise limited power outside their boundaries, making easier the political task of territorial annexations, developing cooperative agreements among local units for rendering certain services. But however useful these may be, they clearly constitute no thorough-going solution.

Three different and more comprehensive approaches to metropoli-tan integration have had fairly extensive trial: the multipurpose special district, the metropolitan county, and metropolitan federa-tion. The multipurpose special district, such as that existing in the Seattle–King County region of Washington, involves creation of a special district including all or most of the metropolitan area, to which can be assigned any number of functions serving the whole region, such as mass transit, sanitation, and water supply. The pre-existing local units continue to operate as before, except for the functions granted to the district. The Seattle experience has been quite successful with a very limited range of functions, but Seattle suburbs particularly have been wary of granting more functions to the special district.

Metropolitan Dade County, Florida (the Miami Metro), now well established and reasonably successful, is an example of the metropolitan county. Dade County government provides an extensive variety of areawide services and is further empowered to fix minimum standards for services performed by its twenty-seven municipalities. Should a municipality fail to meet those standards for a particular service, the county may take over the function. A limitation on the use of the metropolitan county as a solution is that a good many of the country's metropolitan areas extend beyond the boundaries of a single county; indeed twenty-three of them embrace parts of two or more states, and a few, like Detroit or El Paso, are international.

Metropolitan federation, sometimes called the borough plan, is merely the application of the principle of federalism at the local level. A metropolitan government is created from the union of all local governments in the area. The local governments continue to perform most services while delegating certain areawide functions to the metropolitan government. Although the system has been frequently discussed in the United States, the only significant examples close at hand are certain Canadian cities, for example, Toronto, with over two decades of experience, and Winnipeg. In both instances metropolitan federation did not come into being by action of local citizenry but was established by the provincial government.

The Toronto Metro has been successful in many respects but has struggled with the problems peculiar to all federations. What is the proper division of powers between the central and subordinate governments? Will the latter ultimately be submerged? How can equitable taxation be realized? Should the governing body of the metropolitan government represent people or constituent governments or some combination of both? These are not, certainly, insurmountable problems, and the system has a good deal to commend it for people experienced in the practice of federalism.

FORMS OF CITY GOVERNMENT

The transition of the United States from an almost entirely agrarian nation to an overwhelmingly urban one has been one of the most rapid and significant shifts in human history. More than 80 percent of America's population is now urban, with about two-thirds of the people living in what the Census Bureau classifies as metropolitan areas. In recent years, the complex and volatile problems of these great population concentrations have moved to the center of the national stage, yet cities still have a vast and attractive potential, culturally as well as economically, for desirable living. The achievement of a responsible politics to help the metropolis solve its problems and fulfill its potential is one of the most important domestic challenges before us.

Revitalization of a run-down urban area. Before and after pictures of the Quincy Market, one of Boston's oldest landmarks, which was reopened in 1976.

FIGURE 13.7   Weak-Mayor-and-Council City Government

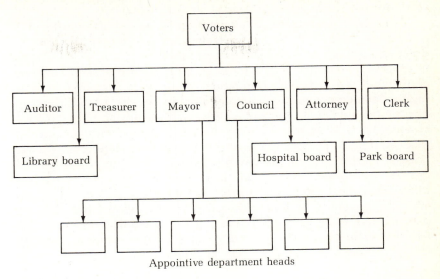

Appointive department heads

City governments are organized along varying lines, but five basic patterns stand out. While it would be foolish to assert that any particular form guarantees either good government or bad government, it would be equally foolish to claim that the type of government a city has is unrelated to the quality of its services or democratic responsiveness. Even more important than administrative efficiency is the ability of a community to determine its social priorities democratically and to encourage the leadership necessary to achieve its goals. City government is not just a matter of running a business or household efficiently; good government in its true sense must go beyond this limited definition to mean an effective way of visualizing and accomplishing meaningful social aspirations.

WEAK MAYOR AND COUNCIL

Mayor-council government, in somewhat differing forms, is the oldest and still most prevalent type of city government. The earliest version, which exists in a number of cities but is gradually being replaced, is commonly termed the weak-mayor plan because the mayor is primarily a ceremonial head of the city and lacks extensive powers as a chief administrator. The voters elect not only the mayor and council but also the administrative heads of many city departments and several independent boards and commissions (see Figure 13.7). The mayor usually presides at council meetings but as a rule lacks a veto power or has only a very limited one. The power of appointment is modest, and the mayor's power to coordinate the work of the various city agencies is almost nonexistent.

The lack of an integrated city operation, wherein different parts of what is supposed to be the same team are often pulling in opposite directions and are in a chronic state of ignorance about the activities of other departments, is the most striking feature of weak-mayor-and-council government. Defenders often insist that this form is highly democratic because so many officials are elected and thus are directly responsible to the voters. Yet it is basically an unresponsive system. There is no focus of responsibility, no individual or group that can be held accountable to the voters. When numerous officials must be elected, the voters have no adequate basis for judgment and exercise very little if any control. If displeased, they may unseat one individual, most likely the mayor, but such action has almost no effect on the total government. Bossism has often flourished, in large part because of the difficulty of placing responsibility. Policy formulation is diffused among various groups, with no central planning for the whole city. Effective central budgetary control is virtually impossible.

STRONG MAYOR AND COUNCIL

In order to eliminate the shortcomings of the weak-mayor plan, one approach has been to strengthen the powers of the mayor and to delineate responsibility more clearly. Under the strong-mayor plan the voters elect only the council and the mayor, holding them accountable for the satisfactory operation of the entire city (see Figure 13.8). The mayor is the actual as well as titular executive of the city, appointing all department heads, supervising the city's administration, and having a veto power over legislation as well as the prerogative of recommending policy. Although the mayor and council naturally share similar concerns, their primary responsibilities are separate. This plan is obviously analogous to the structure of the national government in that the roles of the chief executives and their relationships to the legislative branches are comparable.

The strong-mayor-and-council setup makes possible a unified and coordinated administration, but even more important it offers firm and responsible policy leadership. The mayor is at the focal point of the public's attention on policy and can run on a platform with some hope of carrying it out. The task of the voter is made fairly simple and intelligible. Opponents of the idea commonly argue that it concentrates too much power in one person, but experience has clearly indicated that it is far less dangerous to concentrate power that is held accountable than it is to scatter it so that effective control is impossible. It is not power that is dangerous but irresponsible power. Power is essential to the accomplishment of goals.

FIGURE 13.8   Strong-Mayor-and-Council City Government

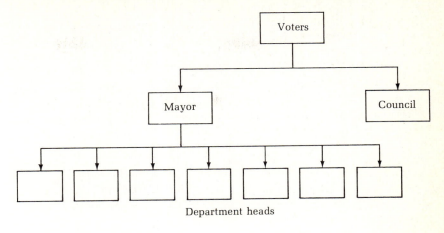

Department heads

Most of the nation's big cities, and many smaller ones, today utilize the strong-mayor-and-council plan. For the sake of clarity, two extremely different kinds of mayor-council government have been described. In practice one is likely to find many city governments falling somewhere between these extremes, but the trend is definitely in the direction of the strong-mayor-and-council type.

COMMISSION

The commission plan of city government rose to prominence early in the 1900s, also as a means of focusing responsibility where the weak-mayor-and-council plan had resulted in serious inadequacies. Under this sytem the voters elect a small commission (council), composed ordinarily of five or seven members in whom full responsibility for the city's operation is vested (see Figure 13.9). Individually each commissioner is head of a major segment of city administration, such as public works or public safety, while collectively the commissioners constitute the legislative body. The commission elects one of its members as mayor, but this is merely a formal position without notably greater powers than those possessed by the other members. The mayor may assign commissioners to departments when they are not elected to specific slots. Since commissioners cannot be expected to have time for more than broad supervision of their departments, it is assumed that professional department heads also will be appointed.

The practice of placing both legislative and executive authority in one body does provide a kind of integration and makes the voter's job somewhat easier. Deadlocks between a mayor and council are

FIGURE 13.9   Commission City Government

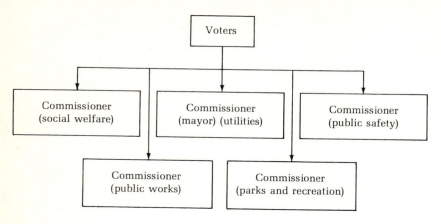

impossible. Problems have arisen, however. No one person is responsible for coordinating the administrative functions of the city, and buck-passing is the norm. The natural tendency is to follow a principle of "You keep your nose out of my business, and I'll keep mine out of yours." Budget requests are submitted to a legislative body whose only members are those making the requests, and reciprocal back-scratching is the inevitable result. The important function of internal criticism within the government is virtually eliminated. Commission government has rarely been creative, and its responsiveness to public control has been spotty. In recent years the number of commission-governed cities has been steadily declining, and today the system is found mainly in some smaller cities.

COUNCIL-MANAGER

The first experiments with council-manager government began about 1912. Since that time use of the plan has grown steadily to the point at which it is numerically the most popular form of city government if one counts weak-mayor-and-council and strong-mayor-and-council governments separately. It exists primarily in the small and medium-size cities, and its geographic spread is extremely irregular. In some states, like Maine and California, it is by far the most common system; others, such as Indiana, have no council-manager cities at all.

The council-manager plan is another effort to create a government pattern that is both unified and highly responsible. Its essential features are a concentration of powers in the hands of a council, a short ballot to make popular control effective, and highly professionalized administration. The voters elect a council only and hold it fully responsible. In turn the council selects a professional administrator

FIGURE 13.10   Council-Manager City Government

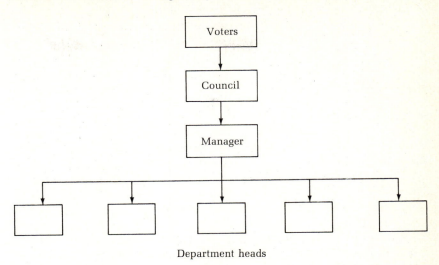

Department heads

as city manager with power to supervise all city services, held completely to account for administrative performance. The manager appoints the department heads, prepares the budget, and acts as the agent of the council in both policy research and execution. Service as manager continues for as long as the work remains satisfactory to a majority of the council. The lines of responsibility from department heads to city manager to council to the voters are clear and easily understood (see Figure 13.10).

Council-manager government is not based on the principle of separation of powers. All powers of legislation and of control over administration, as distinct from the day-to-day conduct of administration, are in the hands of the council. The council selects one of its members as mayor to preside at meetings, sign official documents, and represent the city formally.* The vote of the mayor is equal to those of his or her colleagues. The council may choose as manager the best person it can find in the country at a salary it is willing to pay, and it can dismiss that person at any time. It passes all the ordinances and resolutions within which the administration must operate and approves all budgets and appropriations. It may investigate the quality of administration at any time, and it is the duty of the manager to be present at all meetings of the council to answer questions and provide information.

Some persons have argued that in fact many councils rely too

---

*In some council-manager cities, the mayor is independently elected but is nevertheless principally a formal head of the city.

heavily on their managers, who may come to dominate the councils. In its actions a council unquestionably places heavy weight on the professional expertness and fact-gathering abilities of its manager, but that behavior does not in itself make it a rubber stamp. The manager is the agent of the council, not only in the sense of carrying out its directives but also in studying policy questions and bringing recommendations before the council. The manager may recommend one course of action or present alternatives, but final decision rests with the council.

Another common criticism is that this system, with its bias toward professionalism, may easily become too antiseptic and removed from the real needs of the public. Certainly, council-manager government does not always provide adequate community political leadership. The council is a multiple body, from which it is often difficult for clear leadership to arise, and the manager is theoretically expected to avoid a role of public leadership. As a practical necessity managers more and more have come to perform this function to some degree, but it is clearly more limited and different from what can be undertaken by an elected chief executive. This reason has kept council-manager government out of most of the major cities and has given the strong-mayor-and-council plan dominance there. The heartland of council-manager government, though by no means its exclusive locale, has been the suburban residential city where the "business-like" nature of the system is appreciated and where social problems are thought to be at a relatively uncritical stage. Council-manager government has had great overall success, and it and the strong-mayor plan appear likely to be the most widely used forms for some time to come.

MAYOR-ADMINISTRATOR

In recent years a few large cities have sought to combine the advantages of the strong-mayor and council-manager forms. The resulting pattern has so far had no formal name but is commonly called the mayor-administrator plan. It is simply the strong-mayor-and-council arrangement with the addition of a professional administrator to supervise and coordinate the work of administrative agencies, appointed by and serving at the pleasure of the mayor. The mayor retains basic responsibility but can devote much time to the vital role of community leadership (see Figure 13.11).

THE POLITICS OF LOCAL DECISION MAKING

The degree of representativeness of local public officials is affected by many factors. It makes a difference whether they are elected on partisan or nonpartisan ballots, the former tending to give more

FIGURE 13.11   Mayor-Administrator City Government

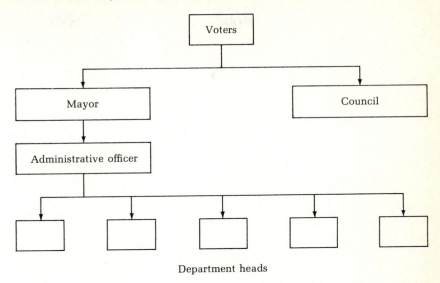

Department heads

emphasis to issues and party positions and the latter to personalities and interest groups. (Elections without national party labels may, however, help separate local issues from national party positions.) It makes a further difference whether councils or boards are elected by wards, at large, or by proportional representation. Looking at municipalities as an example, election by wards or districts guarantees representation to each section of a city but tends to make council members act as errand runners for their particular districts. Election at large theoretically should result in the interests of the whole city being placed ahead of purely sectional interests, but one group may win all the seats, thus denying minority representation, and the council may or may not show much geographical spread. Combinations of these systems have proved satisfactory in some communities, electing part of the council from wards and part at large or, better, nominating candidates by wards with voters of the entire city then electing one from each ward. Proportional representation, not widely used in the United States, assures that the council will be a quite accurate mirror of the various groups participating in the election, but it does tend to emphasize specialized interests and perhaps fragment the council.*

Campaigning for office at the local level is commonly a rather informal affair except in the largest cities, where a mayoralty race

---

*On the basis of recent court decisions it is conceivable, though not at all certain, that some of these various election systems might be ruled unconstitutional on the grounds that they deny equality of representation.

may take on the proportions of a campaign for a governorship or the United States Senate. Elsewhere it is often heavily a matter of building name recognition and mobilizing the support of organized groups in the community, especially where the party role is minimized. Excepting the largest cities, most council positions are either unpaid or only nominally paid, a matter that restricts membership to business and professional persons who can arrange their own time to suit the demands of the office or to retired persons. The position of mayor in the medium-size or large city is usually full-time and is today attracting many very competent people. The big cities of the United States have in recent years had as their mayors some of the truly outstanding political leaders that the country has produced, and clearly the critical problems of the cities pose a good test of political leadership.

The internal politics of local legislative bodies, the majority of which contain from five to nine members, is of a somewhat different nature from that in large bodies like Congress or a state legislature. Procedures are much less formal, and neutrality is difficult on any issue when each vote is as crucial as it obviously is on a five- or seven-person council. The local legislator lives in the intimate communion with constituents that is much valued by theorists but frequently less attractive to the person who must face and respond to this political heat 365 days a year. One is never remote from fellow citizens, who can visit at home or phone with ease, and the council meetings, although rarely well attended on a continuing basis, are readily accessible to any organized group. Although many matters coming before a local council may seem petty and inconsequential to an outside observer, the citizen who is personally affected by a zoning change, a building code, or a dog-control ordinance is likely to have strong feelings about them. In the modern city, moreover, council members have to make many major policy decisions of far-reaching significance, often involving sharp cleavages of social philosophy.

In a small council, which meets on a regular basis rather than for time-limited sessions, differences on specific issues are normally hammered out through long weeks and months of informal discussions and negotiation involving not only council members and administrators but also the individuals and groups to be affected by the legislation. The differences are frequently over the best methods of accomplishing a goal, and these are matters readily subject to modification and compromise. As a consequence, it is commonly true that the final passage of an originally controversial ordinance may be without fanfare and accompanied by little if any debate; such passage is a ratification of the treaties already arrived at. On some matters, of course, differences cannot be fully resolved, and the finale is one of heated debate and a tense vote.

The basic question for the representative, to insure the responsiveness of the political system, is how to be certain of fairness and thoroughness in hearing the viewpoints of all elements of the community. There are always those who make themselves heard, and there is the great silent mass whose interests are also to be protected. Not all those who wield political power in a community hold public office. In each community there are the "influentials," who through willingness to work, personal contacts, and organizational leadership are the ones who get things done. They are the backbone of the community, but they are not the whole of the community. Where is the public interest, and how can it best be given effect?

BASIC CONCEPTS AND TERMS

charter (city or county)
home rule
state legislative reform
legislative council
initiative
referendum
recall
powers of governors
state judicial reform
county board
county chief administrative
  officer (manager)
town meeting
board of selectmen
representative town meeting
township
special district

problems of the urban crisis
multipurpose special district
metropolitan county
metropolitan federation
weak-mayor-and-council
  government
strong-mayor-and-council
  government
commission government
council-manager government
mayor-administrator
  government
election by wards
election at large
proportional representation
nature of local decision making

EPILOGUE

As the entire world watched with rapt fascination the first landing of men on the moon in the summer of 1969, there was probably no sensitive person who did not ask: "If we can marshal the abilities and resources to accomplish such a fantastically complex task, why can't we solve the problems of human misery and conflict?" So often was this question posed that it became trite, but that in itself was public recognition that social challenges too must be met. Such challenges are problems not likely to be solved by technology (though in some cases it can help), for they are primarily problems of human relationships. Nor will they be solved by money alone.

What might be done with the problem of poverty in our society, for example, if we directed to its elimination in the next few years the $24 billion originally allocated to achieving a lunar landing, let alone subsequent missions? Like space exploration, might not the expunging of poverty produce a host of currently unknown benefits to society? In 1961 our national leaders set the goal of a moon landing by 1970, and the nation willingly paid the cost in money, skill, and effort. What if we were to set a goal of the elimination of poverty in

America in eight years, agreeing to devote whatever talents and treasure are necessary to its achievement? This is not to argue that space exploration should not be undertaken; people will always pursue the unknown, and the scientific and economic feedback to the society is significant. But we are capable of both, and we need to reflect on our priorities.

Are we ready to make a genuinely serious national effort to meet the intensely human political problems that demand solution? We know how to build houses, how to eliminate the pollution of our streams and lakes, how to provide sufficient food for our entire population, how to limit excessive population growth, how to provide efficient systems of urban mass transportation, how to equalize educational opportunity, and how to organize a system for the rule of law in international relations. What is lacking is the social will and commitment as well as broad public understanding of these tremendously complicated problems. Human beings and their motivations are infinitely more complex than engineering problems, but social problems too can be solved. There are new frontiers in space to be conquered; there are even greater challenges, demanding the dedication of our best minds, to be faced and conquered closer to home. Is this no more than a romantic dream— as travel to the moon was but a decade or two ago?

We are a people and a generation long on analysis and criticism, short on willingness to devote time and effort to solutions. We are fed up with organizations and seek simpler relationships in our frustration with complex problems. Yet most of us realize that in a large heterogeneous society accomplishment depends on the organization of people and resources. Democracy is not self-executing. People are needed to make it work, and in this enterprise every individual counts, either in making a contribution to progress or as adding dead weight for preservation of the status quo. It is not enough that people be capable of governing themselves; they must be willing to bear the responsibilities of governing themselves.

It is not realistic to assume that all people necessarily desire democracy. Its critics have always been many and vocal, and indeed criticisms are easily made. But the realist must compare any system with the possible alternatives and recognize that there is a price to be paid for each. Some people, because they are unhappy with a particular outcome, cry that democracy has not worked. Perhaps they simply lost. There is no guarantee that one who plays the game will always win, any more than we assume that a basketball team that plays hard is entitled to win. But the freedom to try again if one loses may be terribly important, and such freedom is not offered by all political systems. The self-righteous in any society—those who are convinced of the absolute rightness of their own positions and the absolute wrongness of all others—invariably despise the processes

of democracy that permit equal expression to those who think differently. Those who would preserve freedom for themselves must be
willing to insure it for others. Such freedom is not really divisible.

Politics is the alternative to violence in human and international
affairs, the method of seeking the ways in which people can live
together and move forward together in reasonable harmony. Both
war and domestic violence are in fact the rejection of politics. The
political system in a democracy, in contrast to totalitarianism, is by
no means rigid and static; for those with the will to work at it, that
system has repeatedly shown itself remarkably adaptive to change.

Certainly no system is perfect, and every system should always be
subject to scrutiny and criticism in the interest of improvement. But
history affords little hope for improvement by means of destruction;
the problem is to motivate people genuinely to use the system of
democracy, constantly adjusting it to make it more responsive and
effective in serving human needs. The long-run goal is a kind of
practical idealism. Life without ideals for which to strive is sterile;
without practical use of the political system to bring about their
accomplishment, ideals remain nothing but visions. Often in human
affairs the crucial question is whether one is interested in a fireworks
display, which is fascinating but of no lasting effect, or in real
accomplishment. A huge population, vast natural resources,
advanced scientific achievement, a vigorous and efficient economy—
all these may make a nation strong, but only its ideals can make it
great.

THE
CONSTITUTION
OF THE
UNITED STATES

We the People of the United States, in Order to form a more perfect Union, establish Justice, insure domestic Tranquility, provide for the common defence, promote the general Welfare, and secure the Blessings of Liberty to ourselves and our Posterity, do ordain and establish this Constitution for the United States of America.

ARTICLE 1

Section 1   All legislative Powers herein granted shall be vested in a Congress of the United States, which shall consist of a Senate and House of Representatives.

Section 2   The House of Representatives shall be composed of Members chosen every second Year by the People of the several States, and the Electors in each State shall have the Qualifications requisite for Electors of the most numerous Branch of the State Legislature.

No Person shall be a Representative who shall not have attained to the Age of twenty five Years, and been seven Years a Citizen of the United States, and who shall not, when elected, be an Inhabitant of that State in which he shall be chosen.

Representatives and direct Taxes shall be apportioned among the several States which may be included within this Union, according to their respective Numbers, which shall be determined by adding to the whole Number of free Persons, including those bound to Service for a Term of Years, and excluding Indians not taxed, three fifths of all other Persons. The actual Enumeration shall be made within three Years after the first Meeting of the Congress of the United States, and within every subsequent Term of ten Years, in such Manner as they shall by Law direct. The Number of

Representatives shall not exceed one for every thirty Thousand, but each State shall have at Least one Representative; and until such enumeration shall be made, the State of New Hampshire shall be entitled to chuse three, Massachusetts eight, Rhode-Island and Providence Plantations one, Connecticut five, New-York six, New Jersey four, Pennsylvania eight, Delaware one, Maryland six, Virginia ten, North Carolina five, South Carolina five, and Georgia three.

When vacancies happen in the Representation from any State, the Executive Authority thereof shall issue Writs of Election to fill such Vacancies.

The House of Representatives shall chuse their speaker and other Officers; and shall have the sole Power of Impeachment.

Section 3   The Senate of the United States shall be composed of two Senators from each State, chosen by the Legislature thereof, for six Years; and each Senator shall have one Vote.

Immediately after they shall be assembled in Consequence of the first Election, they shall be divided as equally as may be into three Classes. The Seats of the Senators of the first Class shall be vacated at the Expiration of the second Year, of the second Class at the Expiration of the fourth Year, and of the third Class at the Expiration of the sixth Year, so that one third may be chosen every second Year; and if Vacancies happen by Resignation, or otherwise, during the Recess of the Legislature of any State, the Executive thereof may make temporary Appointments until the next Meeting of the Legislature, which shall then fill such Vacancies.

No Person shall be a Senator who shall not have attained to the Age of thirty Years, and been nine Years a Citizen of the United States, and who shall not, when elected, be an Inhabitant of that State for which he shall be chosen.

The Vice President of the United States shall be President of the Senate, but shall have no Vote, unless they be equally divided.

The Senate shall chuse their other Officers, and also a President pro tempore, in the Absence of the Vice President, or when he shall exercise the Office of President of the United States.

The Senate shall have the sole Power to try all Impeachments. When sitting for that Purpose, they shall be on Oath or Affirmation. When the President of the United States is tried, the Chief Justice shall preside: And no Person shall be convicted without the Concurrence of two thirds of the Members present.

Judgment in Cases of Impeachment shall not extend further than to removal from Office, and disqualification to hold and enjoy any Office of honor, Trust or Profit under the United States: but the Party convicted shall nevertheless be liable and subject to Indictment, Trial, Judgment and Punishment, according to law.

Section 4   The Times, Places and Manner of holding Elections for Senators and Representatives, shall be prescribed in each State by the Legislature thereof; but the Congress may at any time by Law make or alter such Regulations, except as to the Places of chusing Senators.

The Congress shall assemble at least once in every Year, and such Meeting shall be on the first Monday in December, unless they shall by Law appoint a different Day.

Section 5   Each House shall be the Judge of the Elections, Returns and Qualifications of its own Members, and a Majority of each shall constitute a Quorum to do Business; but a smaller Number may adjourn from day to day, and may be authorized to compel the Attendance of absent Members, in such Manner, and under such Penalties as each House may provide.

Each House may determine the Rules of its Proceedings, punish its Members for disorderly Behaviour, and, with the Concurrence of two thirds, expel a Member.

Each House shall keep a Journal of its Proceedings, and from time to time publish the same, excepting such Parts as may in their Judgment require Secrecy; and the Yeas and Nays of the Members of either House on any question shall, at the Desire of one fifth of those Present, be entered on the Journal.

Neither House, during the Session of Congress, shall, without the Consent of the other, adjourn for more than three days, nor to any other Place than that in which the two Houses shall be sitting.

Section 6   The Senators and Representatives shall receive a Compensation for their Services, to be ascertained by Law, and paid out of the Treasury of the United States. They shall in all Cases, except Treason, Felony and Breach of the Peace, be privileged from Arrest during their Attendance at the Session of their respective Houses, and in going to and returning from the same; and for any Speech or Debate in either House, they shall not be questioned in any other Place.

No Senator or Representative shall, during the Time for which he was elected, be appointed to any civil Office under the Authority of the United States, which shall have been created, or the Emoluments whereof shall have been encreased during such time; and no Person holding any Office under the United States, shall be a Member of either House during his Continuance in Office.

Section 7   All Bills for raising Revenue shall originate in the House of Representatives; but the Senate may propose or concur with Amendments as on other Bills.

Every Bill which shall have passed the House of Representatives and the Senate, shall, before it become a Law, be presented to the President of the United States; If he approve he shall sign it, but if not he shall return it, with his Objections to that House in which it shall have originated, who shall enter the Objections at large on their Journal, and proceed to reconsider it. If after such Reconsideration two thirds of that House shall agree to pass the Bill, it shall be sent, together with the Objections, to the other House, by which it shall likewise be reconsidered, and if approved by two thirds of that House, it shall become a Law. But in all such Cases the Votes of both Houses shall be determined by Yeas and Nays, and the Names of the Persons voting for and against the Bill shall be entered on the Journal of each House respectively. If any Bill shall not be returned by the President within ten Days (Sundays excepted) after it shall have been presented to him, the Same shall be a Law, in like Manner as if he had signed it, unless the Congress by their Adjournment prevent its Return, in which Case it shall not be a Law.

Every Order, Resolution, or Vote to which the Concurrence of the Senate and House of Representatives may be necessary (except on a question of Adjournment) shall be presented to the President of the United States; and before the Same shall take Effect, shall be approved by him, or being disapproved by him, shall be repassed by two thirds of the Senate and House of Representatives, according to the Rules and Limitations prescribed in the Case of a Bill.

Section 8   The Congress shall have Power To lay and collect Taxes, Duties, Imposts and Excises, to pay the Debts and provide for the common Defence and general Welfare of the United States; but all Duties, Imposts and Excises shall be uniform throughout the United States.

To borrow Money on the Credit of the United States;

To regulate Commerce with foreign Nations, and among the several States, and with the Indian Tribes;

To establish an uniform Rule of Naturalization, and uniform Laws on the subject of Bankruptcies throughout the United States;

To coin Money, regulate the Value thereof, and of foreign Coin, and fix the Standard of Weights and Measures;

To provide for the Punishment of counterfeiting the Securities and current Coin of the United States;

To establish Post Offices and post Roads;

To promote the Progress of Science and useful Arts, by securing for limited Times to Authors and Inventors the exclusive Right to their respective Writings and Discoveries;

To constitute Tribunals inferior to the supreme Court;

To define and punish Piracies and Felonies committed on the high Seas, and Offences against the Law of Nations;

To declare War, grant Letters of Marque and Reprisal, and make Rules concerning Captures on Land and Water;

To raise and support Armies, but no Appropriation of Money to that Use shall be for a longer Term than two Years;

To provide and maintain a Navy;

To make Rules for the Government and Regulation of the land and naval Forces;

To provide for calling forth the Militia to execute the Laws of the Union, suppress Insurrections and repel Invasions;

To provide for organizing, arming, and disciplining, the Militia, and for governing such Part of them as may be employed in the Service of the United States, reserving to the States respectively, the Appointment of the Officers, and the Authority of training the Militia according to the discipline prescribed by Congress;

To exercise exclusive Legislation in all Cases whatsoever, over such District (not exceeding ten Miles square) as may, by Cession of particular States, and the Acceptance of Congress, become the Seat of the Government of the United States, and to exercise like Authority over all Places purchased by the Consent of the Legislature of the State in which the Same shall be for the Erection of Forts, Magazines, Arsenals, dock-Yards, and other needful Buildings;—And

To make all Laws which shall be necessary and proper for carrying into Execution the foregoing Powers, and all other Powers vested by this Constitution in the Government of the United States, or in any Department or Officer thereof.

Section 9 The Migration or Importation of such Persons as any of the States now existing shall think proper to admit, shall not be prohibited by the Congress prior to the Year one thousand eight hundred and eight, but a Tax or duty may be imposed on such Importation, not exceeding ten dollars for each Person.

The Privilege of the Writ of Habeas Corpus shall not be suspended, unless when in Cases of Rebellion or Invasion the public Safety may require it.

No Bill of Attainder or ex post facto Law shall be passed.

No Capitation, or other direct, Tax shall be laid, unless in Proportion to the Census or Enumeration herein before directed to be taken.

No Tax or Duty shall be laid on Articles exported from any State.

No Preference shall be given by any Regulation of Commerce or Revenue to the Ports of one State over those of another: nor shall Vessels bound to, or from, one State, be obliged to enter, clear, or pay Duties in another.

No Money shall be drawn from the Treasury, but in Consequence of Appropriations made by Law; and a regular Statement and Account of the Receipts and Expenditures of all public Money shall be published from time to time.

No Title of Nobility shall be granted by the United States: And no Person holding any Office of Profit or Trust under them, shall, without the Consent of the Congress, accept of any present, Emolument, Office, or Title, of any kind whatever, from any King, Prince, or foreign State.

Section 10 No State shall enter into any Treaty, Alliance, or Confederation; grant Letters of Marque and Reprisal; coin Money, emit Bills of Credit; make any Thing but gold and silver Coin a Tender in Payment of Debts; pass any Bill of Attainder, ex post facto Law, or Law impairing the Obligation of Contracts, or grant any Title of Nobility.

No State shall, without the Consent of the Congress, lay any Imposts or Duties on Imports or Exports, except what may be absolutely necessary for executing its inspection Laws: and the net Produce of all Duties and Imposts, laid by any State on Imports or Exports, shall be for the Use of the Treasury of the United States; and all such Laws shall be subject to the Revision and Controul of the Congress.

No State shall, without the Consent of Congress, lay any Duty of Tonnage, keep Troops, or Ships of War in time of Peace, enter into any Agreement or Compact with another State, or with a foreign Power, or engage in War, unless actually invaded, or in such imminent Danger as will not admit of delay.

ARTICLE II

Section 1   The executive Power shall be vested in a President of the United States of America. He shall hold his Office during the Term of four Years, and, together with the Vice President, chosen for the same term, be elected, as follows

Each State shall appoint, in such Manner as the Legislature thereof may direct, a Number of Electors, equal to the whole Number of Senators and Representatives to which the State may be entitled in the Congress: but no Senator or Representative, or Person holding an Office of Trust or Profit under the United States, shall be appointed an Elector.

The Electors shall meet in their respective States, and vote by Ballot for two Persons, of whom one at least shall not be an Inhabitant of the same State with themselves. And they shall make a List of all the Persons voted for, and of the Number of Votes for each; which List they shall sign and certify, and transmit sealed to the Seat of the Government of the United States, directed to the President of the Senate. The President of the Senate shall, in the Presence of the Senate and House of Representatives, open all the Certificates, and the Votes shall then be counted. The Person having the greatest Number of Votes shall be the President, if such Number be a Majority of the whole Number of Electors appointed; and if there be more than one who have such Majority, and have an equal Number of Votes, then the House of Representatives shall immediately chuse by Ballot one of them for President: and if no Person have a Majority, then from the five highest on the List the said House shall in like Manner chuse the President. But in chusing the President, the Votes shall be taken by States, the Representation from each State having one Vote; A quorum for this Purpose shall consist of a Member or Members from two thirds of the states, and a Majority of all the states shall be necessary to a Choice. In every Case, after the Choice of the President, the Person having the greatest Number of Votes of the Electors shall be the Vice President. But if there should remain two or more who have equal Votes, the Senate shall chuse from them by Ballot the Vice President.

The Congress may determine the Time of chusing the Electors, and the Day on which they shall give their Votes; which Day shall be the same throughout the United States.

No Person except a natural born Citizen, or a Citizen of the United States, at the time of the Adoption of this Constitution, shall be eligible to the Office of President; neither shall any Person be eligible to that Office who shall not have attained to the Age of thirty five Years, and been fourteen Years a Resident within the United States.

In Case of the Removal of the President from Office, or of his Death, Resignation, or Inability to discharge the Powers and Duties of the said Office, the Same shall devolve on the Vice President, and the Congress may by Law provide for the Case of Removal, Death, Resignation or Inability, both of the President and Vice President, declaring what Officer shall then act as President, and such Officer shall act accordingly, until the Disability be removed, or a President shall be elected.

The President shall, at stated Times, receive for his Services a Compensation, which shall neither be encreased nor diminished during the Period for which he shall have been elected, and he shall not receive within that Period any other Emolument from the United States, or any of them.

Before he enter on the Execution of his Office, he shall take the following Oath or Affirmation:—"I do solemnly swear (or affirm) that I will faithfully execute the Office of President of the United States, and will to the best of my Ability, preserve, protect and defend the Constitution of the United States."

Section 2   The President shall be Commander in Chief of the Army and Navy of the United States, and of the Militia of the several States, when called into the actual Service of the United States; he may require the Opinion, in writing, of the principal Officer in each of the executive Departments, upon any Subject relating to the Duties of their respective Offices, and he shall have Power to grant Reprieves and Pardons for Offences against the United States, except in Cases of Impeachment.

He shall have Power, by and with the Advice and Consent of the Senate, to make Treaties, provided two thirds of the Senators present concur; and he shall nominate, and by and with the Advice and Consent of the Senate, shall appoint Ambassadors, other public Ministers and Consuls, Judges of the supreme Court, and all other Officers of the United States, whose Appointments are not herein otherwise provided for, and which shall be established by Law; but the Congress may by Law vest the Appointment of such inferior Officers, as they think proper, in the President alone, in the Courts of Law, or in the Heads of Departments.

The President shall have Power to fill up all Vacancies that may happen during the Recess of the Senate, by granting Commissions which shall expire at the End of their next Session.

Section 3   He shall from time to time give to the Congress Information of the State of the Union, and recommend to their Consideration such Measures as he shall judge necessary and expedient; he may, on extraordinary Occasions, convene both Houses, or either of them, and in Case of Disagreement between them, with Respect to the Time of Adjournment, he may adjourn them to such Time as he shall think proper; he shall receive Ambassadors and other public Ministers; he shall take Care that the Laws be faithfully executed, and shall Commission all the Officers of the United States.

Section 4   The President, Vice President and all civil Officers of the United States, shall be removed from Office on Impeachment for, and Conviction of, Treason, Bribery, or other High Crimes and Misdemeanors.

ARTICLE III

Section 1   The judicial Power of the United States, shall be vested in one supreme Court, and in such inferior Courts as the Congress may from time to time ordain and establish. The Judges, both of the supreme and inferior Courts, shall hold their Offices during good Behaviour, and shall, at stated Times, receive for their Services, a Compensation, which shall not be diminished during their Continuance in Office.

Section 2   The judicial Power shall extend to all Cases, in Law and Equity, arising under this Constitution, the Laws of the United States, and Treaties made, or which shall be made, under their Authority;—to all Cases affecting Ambassadors, other public Ministers and Consuls;—to all Cases of admiralty and maritime Jurisdiction;—to Controversies to which the United States shall be a Party;—to Controversies between two or more States;—between a State and Citizens of another State;—between Citizens of different States;—between Citizens of the same State claiming Lands under Grants of different States, and between a State, or the Citizens thereof, and foreign States, Citizens or Subjects.

In all Cases affecting Ambassadors, other public Ministers and Consuls, and those in which a State shall be Party, the supreme Court shall have original Jurisdiction. In all the other Cases before mentioned, the supreme Court shall have appellate Jurisdiction, both as to Law and Fact, with such Exceptions, and under such Regulations as the Congress shall make.

The Trial of all Crimes, except in Cases of Impeachment, shall be by Jury; and such Trial shall be held in the State where the said Crimes shall have been committed; but when not committed within any State, the Trial shall be at such Place or Places as the Congress may by Law have directed.

Section 3   Treason against the United States, shall consist only in levying War against them, or in adhering to their Enemies, giving them Aid and Comfort. No Person shall be convicted of Treason unless on the Testimony of two Witnesses to the same overt Act, or on Confession in open Court.

The Congress shall have Power to declare the Punishment of Treason, but no Attainder of Treason shall work Corruption of Blood, or Forfeiture except during the Life of the Person attainted.

ARTICLE IV

Section 1   Full Faith and Credit shall be given in each State to the public Acts, Records, and judicial Proceedings of every other State. And the Congress may by general Laws prescribe the Manner in which such Acts, Records and Proceedings shall be proved, and the Effect thereof.

Section 2   The Citizens of each State shall be entitled to all Privileges and Immunities of Citizens in the several States.

A Person charged in any State with Treason, Felony, or other Crime, who shall flee from Justice, and be found in another State, shall on Demand of the executive Authority of the State from which he fled, be delivered up, to be removed to the State having Jurisdiction of the Crime.

No Person held to Service or Labour in one State, under the Laws thereof, escaping into another, shall, in Consequence of any Law or Regulation therein, be discharged from such Service or Labour, but shall be delivered up on Claim of the Party to whom such Service or Labour may be due.

Section 3   New States may be admitted by the Congress into this Union; but no new State shall be formed or erected within the Jurisdiction of any other State; nor any State be formed by the Junction of two or more States, or Parts of States, without the Consent of the Legislatures of the States concerned as well as of the Congress.

The Congress shall have Power to dispose of and make all needful Rules and Regulations respecting the Territory or other Property belonging to the United States; and nothing in this Constitution shall be so construed as to Prejudice any Claims of the United States, or of any particular State.

Section 4   The United States shall guarantee to every State in this Union a Republican Form of Government, and shall protect each of them against Invasion; and on Application of the Legislature, or of the Executive (when the Legislature cannot be convened) against domestic Violence.

ARTICLE V

The Congress, whenever two thirds of both Houses shall deem it necessary, shall propose Amendments to this Constitution, or, on the Application of the Legislatures of two thirds of the several States, shall call a Convention for proposing Amendments, which, in either Case, shall be valid to all Intents and Purposes, as Part of this Constitution, when ratified by the Legislatures of three fourths of the several States, or by Conventions in three fourths thereof, as the one or the other Mode of Ratification may be proposed by the Congress; Provided that no Amendment which may be made prior to the Year One thousand eight hundred and eight shall in any Manner affect the first and fourth Clauses in the Ninth Section of the first Article; and that no State, without its Consent, shall be deprived of its equal Suffrage in the Senate.

ARTICLE VI

All Debts contracted and Engagements entered into, before the Adoption of this Constitution, shall be as valid against the United States under this Constitution, as under the Confederation.

This Constitution, and the Laws of the United States which shall be made in Pursuance thereof; and all Treaties made, or which shall be made, under the Authority of the United States, shall be the supreme Law of the Land; and the Judges in every State shall be bound thereby, any Thing in the Constitution or Laws of any State to the Contrary notwithstanding.

The Senators and Representatives before mentioned, and the Members of the several State Legislatures, and all executive and judicial Officers, both of the United States and of the several States, shall be bound by Oath or Affirmation, to support this Constitution; but no religious Test shall ever be required as a Qualification to any Office or public Trust under the United States.

ARTICLE VII

The Ratification of the Conventions of nine States, shall be sufficient for the Establishment of this Constitution between the States so ratifying the Same.

Done in Convention by the Unanimous Consent of the States present the Seventeenth Day of September in the Year of our Lord one thousand seven hundred and eighty seven and of the Independence of the United States of America the twelfth. In witness whereof We have hereunto subscribed our Names.

(The first ten amendments were ratified on December 15, 1791, and form what is known as the Bill of Rights.)

AMENDMENT 1

Congress shall make no law respecting an establishment of religion, or prohibiting the free exercise thereof; or abridging the freedom of speech, or of the press; or the right of the people peaceably to assemble, and to petition the Government for a redress of grievances.

AMENDMENT 2

A well regulated Militia, being necessary to the security of a free State, the right of the people to keep and bear Arms, shall not be infringed.

AMENDMENT 3

No Soldier shall, in time of peace be quartered in any house, without the consent of the Owner, nor in time of war, but in a manner to be prescribed by law.

AMENDMENT 4

The right of the people to be secure in their persons, houses, papers, and effects, against unreasonable searches and seizures, shall not be violated, and no Warrants shall issue, but upon probable cause, supported by Oath or affirmation, and particularly describing the place to be searched, and the persons or things to be seized.

AMENDMENT 5

No person shall be held to answer for a capital, or otherwise infamous crime, unless on a presentment or indictment of a Grand Jury, except in cases arising in the land or naval forces, or in the Militia, when in actual service in time of War or public danger; nor shall any person be subject for the same offense to be twice put in jeopardy of life or limb; nor shall be compelled in any criminal case to be a witness against himself, nor be deprived of life, liberty, or property, without due process of law; nor shall private property be taken for public use, without just compensation.

AMENDMENT 6

In all criminal prosecutions, the accused shall enjoy the right to a speedy and public trial, by an impartial jury of the State and district wherein the crime shall have been committed, which district shall have been previously ascertained by law, and to be informed of the nature and cause of the accusation; to be confronted with the witnesses against him; to have compulsory process for obtaining witnesses in his favor, and to have the Assistance of Counsel for his defence.

AMENDMENT 7

In Suits at common law, where the value in controversy shall exceed twenty dollars, the right of trial by jury shall be preserved, and no fact tried by jury, shall be otherwise reexamined in any Court of the United States, than according to the rules of the common law.

AMENDMENT 8

Excessive bail shall not be required, nor excessive fines imposed, nor cruel and unusual punishments inflicted.

AMENDMENT 9

The enumeration in the Constitution, of certain rights, shall not be construed to deny or disparage others retained by the people.

AMENDMENT 10

The powers not delegated to the United States by the Constitution, nor prohibited by it to the States, are reserved to the States respectively, or to the people.

AMENDMENT 11

The Judicial power of the United States shall not be construed to extend to any suit in law or equity, commenced or prosecuted against one of the United States by Citizens of another State, or by Citizens or Subjects of any Foreign State. (Ratified February 7, 1795)

AMENDMENT 12

The Electors shall meet in their respective states and vote by ballot for President and Vice-President, one of whom, at least, shall not be an inhabitant of the same state with themselves; they shall name in their ballots the person voted for as President, and in distinct ballots the person voted for as Vice-President, and they shall make distinct lists of all persons voted for as President, and of all persons voted for as Vice-President, and of the number of votes for each, which lists they shall sign and certify, and transmit sealed to the seat of the government of the United States, directed to the President of the Senate;—The President of the Senate shall, in the presence of the Senate and House of Representatives, open all the certificates and the votes shall then be counted;—The person having the greatest number of votes for President, shall be the President, if such number be a majority of the whole number of Electors appointed; and if no person have such majority then from the persons having the highest numbers not exceeding three on the list of those voted for as President, the House of Representatives shall choose immediately, by ballot, the President. But in choosing the President, the votes shall be taken by states, the representation from each state having one vote; a quorum for this purpose shall consist of a member or members from two-thirds of the states, and a majority of all the states shall be necessary to a choice. And if the House of Representatives shall not choose a President whenever the right of choice shall devolve upon them, before the fourth day of March next following, then the Vice-President shall act as President, as in the case of the death or other constitutional disability of the President.—The person having the greatest number of votes as Vice-President, shall be the Vice-President, if such number be a majority of the whole number of Electors appointed, and if no person have a majority, then from the two highest numbers on the list, the Senate shall choose the Vice-President; a quorum for the purpose shall consist of two-thirds of the whole number of Senators, and a majority of the whole number shall be necessary to a choice. But no person constitutionally ineligible to the office of President shall be eligible to that of Vice-President of the United States. (Ratified July 27, 1804)

AMENDMENT 13

Section 1   Neither slavery nor involuntary servitude, except as a punishment for crime whereof the party shall have been duly convicted, shall exist within the United States, or any place subject to their jurisdiction.

Section 2   Congress shall have power to enforce this article by appropriate legislation. (Ratified December 6, 1865)

AMENDMENT 14

Section 1   All persons born or naturalized in the United States, and subject to the jurisdiction thereof, are citizens of the United States and of the State wherein they reside. No State shall make or enforce any law which shall abridge the privileges or immunities of citizens of the United States; nor shall any State deprive any person of life, liberty, or property, without due process of law; nor deny to any person within its jurisdiction the equal protection of the laws.

Section 2   Representatives shall be apportioned among the several States according to their respective numbers, counting the whole number of persons in each State, excluding Indians not taxed. But when the right to vote at any election for the choice of electors for President and Vice President of the United States, Representatives in Congress, the Executive and Judicial officers of a State, or the members of the Legislature thereof, is denied to any of the male inhabitants of such State, being twenty-one years of age, and citizens of the United States, or in any way abridged, except for participation in rebellion, or other crime, the basis of representation therein shall be reduced in the proportion which the number of such male citizens shall bear to the whole number of male citizens twenty-one years of age in such State.

Section 3   No person shall be a Senator or Representative in Congress, or elector of President and Vice President, or hold any office, civil or military, under the United States, or under any State, who, having previously taken an oath, as a member of Congress, or as an officer of the United States, or as a member of any State legislature, or as an executive or judicial officer of any State, to support the Constitution of the United States, shall have engaged in insurrection or rebellion against the same, or given aid or comfort to the enemies thereof. But Congress may by a vote of two-thirds of each House, remove such disability.

Section 4   The validity of the public debt of the United States, authorized by law, including debts incurred for payment of pensions and bounties for services in suppressing insurrection or rebellion, shall not be questioned. But neither the United States nor any State shall assume or pay any debt or obligation incurred in aid of insurrection or rebellion against the United States, or any claim for the loss or emancipation of any slave; but all such debts, obligations and claims shall be held illegal and void.

Section 5   The Congress shall have power to enforce, by appropriate legislation, the provisions of this article. *(Ratified July 9, 1868)*

AMENDMENT 15

Section 1   The right of citizens of the United States to vote shall not be denied or abridged by the United States or by any State on account of race, color, or previous condition of servitude.

Section 2   The Congress shall have power to enforce this article by appropriate legislation. *(Ratified February 3, 1870)*

AMENDMENT 16

The Congress shall have power to lay and collect taxes on incomes, from whatever source derived, without apportionment among the several States, and without regard to any census or enumeration. *(Ratified February 3, 1913)*

AMENDMENT 17

The Senate of the United States shall be composed of two Senators from each State, elected by the people thereof for six years; and each Senator shall have one vote. The electors in each State shall have the qualifications requisite for electors of the most numerous branch of the State legislatures.

When vacancies happen in the representation of any State in the Senate, the executive authority of such State shall issue writs of election to fill such vacancies: Provided, That the legislature of any State may empower the executive thereof to make temporary appointments until the people fill the vacancies by election as the legislature may direct.

This amendment shall not be so construed as to affect the election or term of any Senator chosen before it becomes valid as part of the Constitution. *(Ratified April 8, 1913)*

AMENDMENT 18

Section 1   After one year from the ratification of this article the manufacture, sale, or transportation of intoxicating liquors within, the importation thereof into, or the exportation thereof from the United States and all territory subject to the jurisdiction thereof for beverage purposes is hereby prohibited.

Section 2   The Congress and the several States shall have concurrent power to enforce this article by appropriate legislation.

Section 3   This article shall be inoperative unless it shall have been ratified as an amendment to the Constitution by the legislatures of the several States, as provided in the Constitution, within seven years from the date of the submission hereof to the States by the Congress. *(Ratified January 16, 1919)*

AMENDMENT 19

The right of citizens of the United States to vote shall not be denied or abridged by the United States or by any State on account of sex.

Congress shall have power to enforce this article by appropriate legislation. *(Ratified August 18, 1920)*

AMENDMENT 20

Section 1   The terms of the President and Vice President shall end at noon on the 20th day of January, and the terms of Senators and Representatives at noon on the 3d day of January, of the years in which such terms would have ended if this article had not been ratified; and the terms of their successors shall then begin.

Section 2   The Congress shall assemble at least once in every year, and such meeting shall begin at noon on the 3d day of January, unless they shall by law appoint a different day.

Section 3   If, at the time fixed for the beginning of the term of the President, the President elect shall have died, the Vice President elect shall become President. If a President shall not have been chosen before the time fixed for the beginning of his term, or if the President elect shall have failed to qualify, then the Vice President elect shall act as President until a President shall have qualified; and the Congress may by law provide for the case wherein neither a President elect nor a Vice President elect shall have qualified, declaring who shall then act as President, or the manner in which one who is to act shall be selected, and such person shall act accordingly until a President or Vice President shall have qualified.

Section 4   The Congress may by law provide for the case of the death of any of the persons from whom the House of Representatives may choose a President whenever the right of choice shall have devolved upon them, and for the case of the death of any of the persons from whom the Senate may choose a Vice President whenever the right of choice shall have devolved upon them.

Section 5   Sections 1 and 2 shall take effect on the 15th day of October following the ratification of this article.

Section 6   This article shall be inoperative unless it shall have been ratified as an amendment to the Constitution by the legislatures of three-fourths of the several States within seven years from the date of its submission. *(Ratified January 23, 1933)*

AMENDMENT 21

Section 1   The Eighteenth article of amendment to the Constitution of the United States is hereby repealed.

Section 2   The transportation or importation into any State, Territory, or possession of the United States for delivery or use therein of intoxicating liquors, in violation of the laws thereof, is hereby prohibited.

Section 3   This article shall be inoperative unless it shall have been ratified as an amendment to the Constitution by conventions in the several States, as provided in the Constitution, within seven years from the date of the submission hereof to the States by the Congress. *(Ratified December 5, 1933)*

AMENDMENT 22

Section 1   No person shall be elected to the office of the President more than twice, and no person who has held the office of President, or acted as President, for more than two years of a term to which some other person was elected President shall be elected to the office of the President more than once. But this Article shall not apply to any person holding the office of President when this Article was proposed by the Congress, and shall not prevent any person who may be holding the office of President, or acting as President, during the term within which this Article becomes operative from holding the office of President or acting as President during the remainder of such term.

Section 2   This article shall be inoperative unless it shall have been ratified as an amendment to the Constitution by the legislatures of three-fourths of the several States within seven years from the date of its submission to the States by the Congress. *(Ratified February 27, 1951)*

AMENDMENT 23

Section 1   The District constituting the seat of Government of the United States shall appoint in such manner as the Congress may direct:

A number of electors of President and Vice President equal to the whole number of Senators and Representatives in Congress to which the District would be entitled if it were a State, but in no event more than the least populous State; they shall be in addition to those appointed by the States, but they shall be considered, for the purposes of the election of President and Vice President, to be electors appointed by a State; and they shall meet in the District and perform such duties as provided by the twelfth article of amendment.

Section 2   The Congress shall have power to enforce this article by appropriate legislation. *(Ratified March 29, 1961)*

AMENDMENT 24

Section 1   The right of citizens of the United States to vote in any primary or other election for President or Vice President, for electors for President or Vice President, or for Senator or Representative in Congress, shall not be denied or abridged by the United States or any State by reason of failure to pay any poll tax or other tax.

Section 2   The Congress shall have power to enforce this article by appropriate legislation. *(Ratified January 23, 1964)*

AMENDMENT 25

Section 1   In case of the removal of the President from office or of his death or resignation, the Vice President shall become President.

Section 2   Whenever there is a vacancy in the office of the Vice President, the President shall nominate a Vice President who shall take office upon confirmation by a majority vote of both Houses of Congress.

Section 3   Whenever the President transmits to the President pro tempore of the Senate and the Speaker of the House of Representatives his written declaration that he is unable to discharge the powers and duties of his office, and until he transmits to them a written declaration to the contrary, such powers and duties shall be discharged by the Vice President as Acting President.

Section 4   Whenever the Vice President and a majority of either the principal officers of the executive departments or of such other body as Congress may by law provide, transmit to the President pro tempore of the Senate and the Speaker of the House of Representatives their written declaration that the President is unable to discharge the powers and duties of his office, the Vice President shall immediately assume the powers and duties of the office as Acting President.

Thereafter, when the President transmits to the President pro tempore of the Senate and the Speaker of the House of Representatives his written declaration that no inability exists, he shall resume the powers and duties of his office unless the Vice President and a majority of either the principal officers of the executive department or of such other body as Congress may by law provide, transmit within four days to the President pro tempore of the Senate and the Speaker of the House of Representatives their written declaration that the President is unable to discharge the powers and duties of his office. Thereupon Congress shall decide the issue, assembling within forty-eight hours for that purpose if not in session. If the Congress, within twenty-one days after receipt of the latter written declaration, or, if Congress is not in session, within twenty-one days after Congress is required to assemble, determines by two-thirds vote of both Houses that the President is unable to discharge the powers and duties of his office, the Vice President shall continue to discharge the same as Acting President; otherwise, the President shall resume the powers and duties of his office. *(Ratified February 10, 1967)*

AMENDMENT 26

Section 1   The right of citizens of the United States, who are eighteen years of age or older, to vote shall not be denied or abridged by the United States or by any State on account of age.

Section 2   The Congress shall have power to enforce this article by appropriate legislation. *(Ratified July 5, 1971)*

GLOSSARY

The following list of selected political terms is intended to cover terms useful to the well-informed citizen. Terms are defined according to common usage and not necessarily in as technical and elaborate a fashion as may be found in unabridged and specialized dictionaries.

Amnesty   A mass forgiveness granted to a group or class of offenders by a chief executive.

Bicameral   Consisting of two chambers or houses.

Bill of attainder   An act of a legislative body judging a person guilty of some offense and leveling punishment upon him or her without a judicial trial. (Such an act is prohibited by the United States Constitution.)

Bill of Rights   The first ten amendments to the United States Constitution.

Blanket primary   A direct primary system in which voters may not only vote in the primary of any political party without public indication of which primary they have participated in, but may vote in the primaries of more than one party if they vote for candidates for different offices. They may not vote among the candidates of different parties for the same office.

Block grant   A financial grant from one level of government to another that allows complete or at least fairly wide discretion as to use by the receiving government.

Bureaucracy   Any organization having a formal structure of responsibilities and relationships and some system of special qualifications for entering into the various positions of the organization; a term commonly used to refer to governmental administrations in general.

Cabinet   The heads of the major executive departments and such other high executive officials as the president wishes to designate, serving as an advisory body to the president.

Capital punishment   The death penalty.

Categorical grant   A financial grant from one level of government to another with a requirement that the money be spent exclusively for a particular category of public service.

Caucus, party (congressional)   The members of a political party within either house meeting regularly to transact party business or to establish a party position on issues or questions to come before that house.

Censure   A formal act of either house of Congress that disciplines a member by a public statement indicating the belief of that house that the member has been guilty of conduct unbecoming to a member and stating the reasons for this judgment.

Certiorari, writ of   An order from a higher court to a lower court directing that the record of proceedings in the lower court be certified up for review.

Challenge primary   A nominating system involving selection of party nominees in a delegate convention, but with provision that any losing candidate who secures a specified percentage of the vote in that convention may challenge the outcome and force the holding of a primary to choose the nominee for that office.

Charter (city or county)   A document setting forth the structure and powers of a city or county government and the limitations upon its ability to act; a local constitution.

Checks and balances   The practice of providing that relatively independent legislative, executive, and judicial branches of a government have some power to restrain one another.

Civilian supremacy doctrine   The theory, embodied in constitutional provisions, that the military ought always to be subject to ultimate civilian control.

Clear-and-present-danger doctrine   The doctrine that freedom of speech may be restricted at the point at which the speech in question brings about a clear and present danger of some substantive evil that the government has a right to protect itself against.

Clemency power   The ability of chief executives to grant pardons, commutations of sentence, reprieves, and amnesty for offenses against the laws of their particular jurisdiction.

Closed primary   A direct primary in which only party members are permitted to vote, their membership usually being demonstrated by advance registration.

Cloture (closure)   The process of terminating debate, especially in the Senate when some group is conducting a filibuster. Senate cloture requires a three-fifths vote.

Commission government   A system of local government in which the voters elect a small commission whose members serve collectively as the legislative body and individually as heads of the major administrative departments.

Committee of the Whole   The whole House sitting as a committee, for the purpose of expediting business under the somewhat simpler rules of a committee.

Commutation of sentence   A clemency action by a chief executive that simply terminates the serving of a sentence at a given point without granting a pardon.

Concurrent powers   Powers possessed by both the national government and the states simultaneously.

Conference committee   A committee consisting of representatives from the two houses, appointed to iron out differences between the House and Senate versions of a particular bill and to recommend a single version back to the two houses.

Congressional immunity   The protection afforded members of Congress guaranteeing that they not be subject to suit in connection with statements made on the floor of Congress or in committee.

Congressional veto   Invalidation by congressional resolution of an administrative regulation issued under authority of an act of Congress, when the law itself provides for such invalidating action.

Consent decree   A court judgment based on agreement between the prosecutors and the defendant, in which the defendant agrees to cease or correct the activity or situations complained of; widely used in connection with antitrust suits.

Consular service   That branch of the foreign service of the State Department concerned primarily with the relationships between citizens of the United States and citizens and governments of other countries, particularly in matters of trade and travel.

Corporation, government   A governmental agency organized in the manner of a corporation, with a board of directors which hires a general manager; often used for organizations involved in services similar to business activity.

Council-manager government   A system of local government in which the voters elect only a council, which serves as the legislative body and appoints a professional manager to supervise the administration of local affairs subject to the council's ultimate authority.

County central committee   The governing body chosen by the county convention of a political party to carry out the work of that party within the county in the years between conventions.

Creative federalism   A cooperative effort on the part of national, state, and local governments to find the best ways to serve the public effectively, often with all three levels participating, in contrast to jurisdictional disputes among various levels.

Credentials committee   A convention committee responsible for investigating contested delegations to the convention and recommending in the case of contest which delegation is entitled to be seated.

Cross-filing primary   A direct primary system in which a candidate who has filed to seek the nomination of a political party in that party's primary may also file to seek the nomination of one or more other political parties at the same time.

Dark-horse candidate   A candidate for the nomination of a political convention who has only limited support but who might be a compromise candidate if the convention deadlocked between the major contenders.

De facto segregation   Segregation that exists in fact or in reality even though not required by law.

De jure segregation   Segregation required by law.

Delegated powers   Those powers specifically enumerated in a constitution as belonging to a particular government.

Democracy   A political system in which rule is based on majority will, normally with protection of the free exchange of information and ideas and of freedom of action.

Détente   A spirit of improved cooperation and relaxation of tensions, primarily with reference to international relations.

Deterrence strategy   The assumption that peace can be best achieved by a national policy of maintaining such overwhelming military strength and retaliatory capacity that no aggressor would attack.

Diplomatic service   That branch of the foreign service of the State Department that is primarily concerned with representing the interests of the United States government to foreign governments and providing a channel of communication between those governments.

Direct primary   A nominating process in which the members of a political party choose their candidates by voting among those seeking the party nomination for each office.

Double jeopardy protection   A protection against being tried twice or punished twice for the same offense.

Elastic clause   The necessary-and-proper clause, which has permitted the development of the concept of implied powers.

Electoral college   The body of electors chosen in the fifty states whose votes actually elect the president of the United States.

Equal protection of the laws   The requirement that government treat all its citizens alike, that there be no second-class citizenship.

Equal Rights Amendment   A proposed constitutional amendment prohibiting any type of discrimination based on sex.

Equal-time requirement   The requirement that broadcasting stations make available equal time to all candidates for the same political office.

Executive privilege   The claim by presidents that conversations with or communications to the president from his advisers are privileged and may not be disclosed to the other branches of government, in the name of protecting the independence of the executive branch.

Ex post facto law   A law that makes an action committed at an earlier time illegal and/or punishable, even though it was not illegal at the time committed. (Such a law is prohibited by the United States Constitution.)

Extradition   *See* Rendition. (*Extradition* properly applies to international return of fugitives from justice, but the two terms have become interchangeable in common usage.)

Fair employment practices law   A law prohibiting discrimination on the basis of race, sex, religion, or national origin in the policies of employers on hiring and work conditions and in the membership policies of labor unions.

Fairness doctrine   A requirement by the Federal Communications Commission that broadcasting stations notify individuals who have been verbally attacked in any broadcast over that station, provide them with a tape or transcript of the broadcast, and make available to them time for a response or rebuttal.

Favorite-son candidate   A candidate seeking nomination by a convention who has the support of the delegates from his or her own state but is not considered a serious contender. Such a candidacy is often used to achieve bargaining power, to obtain personal publicity, or to discourage other candidates from entering a state preferential primary.

Federalism (federal system of government)   A system of government in which power is divided between a central government and a group of regional governments, with each side having some degree of independent discretionary authority.

Filibuster   The practice of talking indefinitely on a bill, under the rules of the Senate that permit unlimited debate, in order to block action on the bill by the entire Senate.

Floor leader   The chief spokesman and chief tactician for a political party in a legislative house, elected by the party caucus.

Full-faith-and-credit requirement   The requirement that each member state of the federation must accept the validity of the legal acts and judgments of another state involving persons over whom it has jurisdiction.

Gag order   A court order barring attorneys, court officers, or law enforcement officers from disclosing information concerning a defendant or evidence in a case prior to trial.

Gerrymander   The drawing of election district boundaries in such a way as to favor in subsequent elections the party or individuals in power. The term is especially used when odd-shaped districts are created.

Good character test   A requirement that an individual provide evidence of good character in order to be eligible to vote. Such requirements have often been enforced in a discriminatory fashion as a means of preventing certain groups from voting.

Grand jury   A jury whose function is to hear the evidence concerning a person who has been arrested and to determine whether it is sufficient to warrant holding that individual for trial. Such a jury may also engage in certain investigative functions.

Habeas corpus, writ of   An order requiring law enforcement officials having custody of a prisoner to bring that prisoner before a court to determine whether there are sufficient grounds for him or her to be held. A person who has been arrested has a constitutional right to such a writ.

Home rule   An authority granted by either state constitution or state statute to local governments, allowing them to draft their own charters, which establish the structure and powers of the local government.

Hoover Commission   A special commission that studied and made recommendations for reorganizing and improving the effectiveness of the executive branch of the national government.

Impeachment   Formal charges voted by the House of Representatives against an executive or judicial officer accusing that person of "high crimes and misdemeanors" and setting in motion a trial before the Senate to determine whether the officer should be removed from office.

Implied powers   Those powers necessary to the carrying out of delegated powers, even though not in themselves specifically granted (in the United States Constitution, implied from the "necessary and proper" clause).

Impoundment   Refusal by a president to allow the expenditure of certain funds despite their appropriation for that specific purpose by Congress.

Incumbent   The person currently holding a particular office.

Informal organization   The real lines of influence and power within an organization, which may not conform fully to the official organization chart.

Inherent powers   Those powers that belong to the government of any nation simply because it is a nation, without the necessity of any specific grant (principally the power to conduct foreign relations).

Initiative   A process of direct legislation whereby a law or constitutional amendment may be enacted by popular vote, the matter having been placed on the ballot by a petition signed by a specified number of registered voters.

Injunction   A court order prohibiting or ordering the cessation of a particular action, presumably available only when persons claim they are being subjected to irreparable damage and no other remedy is available at law. Violation of such an order may be punished as contempt of court.

Interest group   Any association that seeks to influence the actions of government.

Interstate compact   A formal agreement between two or more states, requiring congressional approval.

Item veto   The ability of a chief executive to veto items or sections of a legislative enactment while allowing the rest of the act to become law. Such a power is possessed in some form by many state governors, but not by the president of the United States.

Judicial activism   That theory of the role of judging that accepts the possibility that judges may invalidate as unconstitutional laws they believe to endanger the social good.

Judicial review power   The power of the courts to rule on the constitutionality or unconstitutionality of acts of the legislative or executive branches.

Judicial self-restraint   That theory of the role of judging that holds that judges ought not to permit their own view of the desirability of a particular piece of legislation to influence their determination of its constitutionality.

Judicial supremacy doctrine   The theory that although the three branches of government are presumed to be equal, the judicial branch is actually more powerful than the others because it can invalidate their actions.

Legislative council   A body composed of members chosen from each house of a legislature, with professional staff, having responsibility to study between sessions of the legislature the major issues expected to arise during the next session and to recommend appropriate legislation.

Libel   False and malicious defamation of character that occurs in writing.

Literacy test   A test designed to prove that a person can read and write, as a requirement for being eligible to vote. Such tests have often been enforced in a discriminatory fashion to prevent certain groups of people from voting.

Loaded district   In redistricting, the practice of concentrating as many voters of the opposition party as possible in a particular district in order to make it more likely for the party in power to elect its own candidates in the surrounding districts.

Lobbyist   A person who represents the views of an interest group before a legislative body, seeking to build support or opposition to measures before that body in accord with the objectives of the organization represented; a legislative advocate.

Logrolling   The practice in legislative bodies of trading votes in order to achieve individual legislative objectives ("You vote for my bill and I'll vote for yours").

Matching grant   A grant from one level of government to another that requires the receiving government to match all or part of the grant with expenditures of its own funds for the same purpose, as a condition of receiving the grant.

Mayor-and-council government   A system of local government in which the voters elect a council to serve as the legislative body and an independent mayor to serve as chief executive. The scope of the mayor's powers to appoint department heads, to prepare and recommend a budget, and so forth determines whether the system is termed a weak-mayor or a strong-mayor form.

Medicare   A system of medical assistance for the elderly financed by payroll taxes on employers and employees.

Merit system   A system of public employment in which personnel are selected and promoted on a basis of demonstrated qualifications and merit rather than political preferment.

Metropolitan federation   A system of metropolitan governance in which an areawide government with limited powers is superimposed on existing local governments, which continue to perform purely local services.

National supremacy doctrine   The assumption that in cases of conflict between the national government and a state or states the national government is supreme as long as it is acting within the scope of its authority. That scope is determined ultimately by elements of the national government.

Negative income tax   A proposal for income maintenance and redistribution whereby those with very limited incomes would receive cash payments instead of having to pay taxes after filing their income tax returns.

Newsmen's privilege   The claim that freedom of the press entitles journalists to withhold, even from law enforcement officers and courts, information or sources that they have pledged to keep confidential. The claim remains in dispute and has not been sustained by the Supreme Court.

Nominating convention   A nominating process in which the candidates of a political party are selected by a convention of delegates representing the party members.

One man—one vote doctrine   The holding by the Supreme Court that legislative districts must be equal in population so that each person's vote will be equal in weight to individual votes cast in other districts.

Open primary   A direct primary system in which registered voters may vote in the primary of any one party without public indication of which party primary they have participated in.

Pardon   A grant of forgiveness to an individual by a chief executive in connection with a criminal offense, intended as a means of mitigating possible undue harshness of the law.

Parity price   A price goal established for specific agricultural commodities, designed to insure that farmers' income keeps pace with the cost of the things they must buy. Governmental price support programs have been designed to try to achieve some reasonable approximation of parity.

Petit jury   A trial jury.

Pocket veto   Refusal by a chief executive to give assent to a legislative enactment, when his refusal occurs after the adjournment of the legislative body. In such a circumstance there is no legislature to consider overriding the veto, and the bill is therefore dead.

Point IV Program　　A program of technical assistance to other nations, particularly underdeveloped ones, and the sharing of technological know-how to help such nations help themselves more successfully.

Police power　　The broad, general power of state and local governments to regulate and promote the health, safety, welfare, and morals of their citizens.

Political party　　Any association that seeks to elect persons to public office and thus to control and direct the machinery of government toward goals favored by the organization.

"Pork-barreling"　　Efforts by a legislator to secure public action and expenditures that will be valuable to the district, or to the residents of the district, that he or she represents.

Precinct　　The basic subdivision of any community for purposes of electoral administration, expected to be small enough in size to make it easy for all residents of the area to vote in one polling place during a given day.

Precinct captain　　A local party official with the principal responsibility for carrying on the activities of a political party within a particular precinct.

Precinct caucus　　A meeting of all the party voters within a precinct who wish to attend, for the purpose of electing party precinct officers and delegates to higher-level conventions.

Preferred position doctrine　　The judicial concept that the First Amendment liberties are so vital to the very existence of democracy that they have a higher status than other elements of the Constitution and should be interpreted as being virtually absolute.

Pre-primary convention　　A political party convention held prior to a primary for the purpose of endorsing candidates in the primary who are preferred by the party activists attending the convention. Such a convention may perhaps also draft a platform.

Presidential preference primary　　A primary in which the voters of a political party in a particular state select the delegates to the party's national nominating convention, usually also instructing those delegates as to the candidate the voters wish the delegates to support at the convention.

Pressure group　　*See* Interest group.

Privacy, right of　　A general protection against the intervention of government in many kinds of personal actions or decisions. No such right is specifically stated in the Constitution, but it has been constructed by the courts out of a number of other guaranteed rights.

Privileges-and-immunities clause　　A requirement that each state in the federation give to citizens of the nation or all other states the basic privileges and immunities accorded its own citizens.

Procedural due process of law　　A requirement that persons may not be deprived of life, liberty, or property except through the careful following of all processes prescribed by law for their protection.

Progressive tax   A tax in which the rate increases with increasing ability to pay.

Proportional representation   A system of election designed to produce through some form of preference voting a legislative body that is an approximate mirror of the strength of the various groups that make up the electorate.

Reapportionment   The periodic reallocation of seats in a legislative body to reflect the changed patterns of population distribution.

Recall   A process by which elected officials, usually at the local level, may be removed from office through a popular vote instigated by petition.

Reciprocal laws   Laws in one state that are conditional upon the existence of similar laws in certain other states, usually conferring certain privileges upon persons from those other states.

Redistricting   The redrawing of legislative district boundaries to achieve more up-to-date and presumably equitable representation of population.

Referendum   A process by which the voters of some states or local governments are enabled to vote on whether to sustain or reject an act previously passed by the legislative body of that government. A petition signed by a specified number of voters, if filed within a certain time after passage of the act, will temporarily suspend the act until the popular vote and will place the matter on the ballot.

Regressive tax   A tax that has the greatest relative impact upon those persons with the least ability to pay.

Rendition   The process of returning a fugitive from justice in one state by a state that has apprehended the fugitive, pursuant to a proper formal request.

Reprieve   A delay in the execution of a sentence, granted by a chief executive.

Republic   A representative democracy, in contrast to a direct democracy.

Residual powers   Powers possessed by that level of government in a federal system to which powers were not delegated; that is, all powers remaining after certain ones have been delegated to one level.

Revenue sharing   Automatic allocation of a percentage of the revenues of one level of government to another level, with no strings (or very few) attached.

Rider   An irrelevant item attached to a bill desired by a chief executive, in the hope that the item will thus become law because the executive does not wish to veto the entire bill.

Rules Committee   In the House of Representatives, the committee that controls the agenda, determining which bills will be considered by the House and in what order, and recommends time limits on debate and possible limitations on the submission of amendments. In a national convention, the committee that recommends rules of procedure under which the convention will operate.

Selectmen, board of   A board chosen by a New England town meeting to oversee the administration of town functions until the next town meeting.

Senatorial courtesy   The practice by which the Senate refuses to confirm a presidential appointment made in one of the states unless the appointee has been recommended by a senator of the president's party from that state.

Seniority system   A system in which positions of leadership and power are allocated primarily on the basis of length of service, especially with reference to the power structure of congressional committees in which chairmanships, for example, ordinarily go to the senior member of the majority party of each committee.

Separate-but-equal doctrine   The now invalidated rule that segregation of the races is permissible as long as the facilities provided are equal.

Separation of powers   The practice of guaranteeing that the legislative, executive, and judicial branches of a government be in some degree independent of one another.

Slander   False and malicious defamation of character that occurs in speech.

Speaker of the House   The presiding officer of the House of Representatives, elected by the membership. In practice the speakership is always determined by the majority party in the House, and the speaker is considered the leader of that party in the House.

Special district   A unit of local government apart from the general purpose units, established to perform one or more particular functions in a specific area. School districts are familiar examples.

State central committee   A committee chosen by a state convention of a political party with responsibility for the conduct of party activity in that state in the years between state conventions.

Steering and Policy Committee   A committee of party leaders in either house of Congress that serves as an executive committee of the party caucus by bringing recommendations to the caucus and by seeking to push the party program to successful completion in legislation.

Stipulation   A statement by a regulatory commission setting forth the actions required to be taken by an industry or other organization subject to its jurisdiction, if that organization is not to be subjected to penalty. Agreement to the stipulation resolves the case without resorting to a trial.

Substantive due process of law   A requirement that no person may be deprived of life, liberty, or property by arbitrary or unreasonable actions of government.

Summitry   The conduct of international negotiations, at least in large degree, through occasional meetings of heads of state.

Sunset law   A statute providing for the automatic termination of administrative agencies at the end of a fixed period of time unless the legislative body acts specifically to continue their existence for another period.

Third party   Any political party other than the two major parties in the United States.

Town meeting   The direct democracy type of government of most towns and townships, consisting of the eligible voters gathered together to pass local ordinances, establish a budget, fix tax rates, and so on.

Understanding test   A test designed to determine whether an individual understands various sections of the Constitution, as a requirement for voting eligibility. Such tests have often been enforced in a discriminatory fashion as a means of preventing certain groups from voting.

Unicameral   Consisting of one chamber or house.

Unitary government   A governmental system in which a single central government has full authority in a country, in contrast to a federal system.

Unit rule   A practice in convention voting whereby a majority vote within a single state delegation controls the casting of the state's vote as a block. This long familiar practice is no longer used in national conventions of either party.

Veterans' preference   The practice of granting to veterans special additions to scores on examinations and advantages in appointment and/or promotion in the civil service.

Veto power   The power of a chief executive to refuse to give assent to a legislative enactment, which then does not become law unless the executive's negation of the act is overridden by an extraordinary vote of the legislative body.

Ward caucus   A local-level convention of delegates selected by precinct caucuses within the ward for the purpose of selecting ward officers and delegates to higher-level conventions.

Ways and Means Committee   That committee of the House of Representatives that has responsibility for recommending all revenue producing legislation, primarily tax bills.

Whip   In a legislative house, a party official who is elected by the caucus and whose functions are to serve as a channel of communication between party leaders and members in that house, to keep track of party members' attitudes on issues, and to be able to locate members when needed for a vote.

Zero-base budgeting   A system of budget formulation in which agencies are required to justify every item requested rather than justifying only the new or increased items.

INDEX